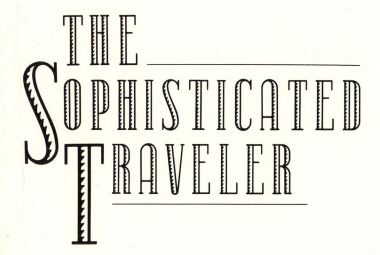

THE SOPHISTICATED TRAVELER

Also in *The Sophisticated Traveler* Series

Beloved Cities: Europe

Winter: Love It or Leave It

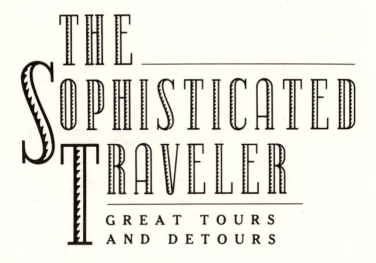

THE SOPHISTICATED TRAVELER

GREAT TOURS AND DETOURS

Edited by
A. M. Rosenthal and Arthur Gelb
in association with Michael J. Leahy,
Nora Kerr and the Travel staff of
The New York Times

 VILLARD BOOKS
New York   1985

When prices are given, they should be taken as a general guide, since inflation and changes in the exchange rates can have a significant effect on costs.

The editors wish to thank Sam Summerlin, who suggested the idea for *The Sophisticated Traveler* book series.

Copyright © 1984, 1985 by The New York Times Syndication Sales Corp. "Chongqing: The Industrial Revolution Comes to Town" copyright © 1984 by Theodore H. White.

Library of Congress Cataloging in Publication Data
Main entry under title:
The Sophisticated traveler.
    Includes index.
    1. Voyages and travels—1951–   —Guide-books.
I. Rosenthal, A. M. (Abraham Michael), 1922–   .
II. Gelb, Arthur, 1924–   . III. New York times.
G153.4.S672 1985   910.4   84-40574
ISBN 0-394-54474-9

Manufactured in the United States of America

9 8 7 6 5 4 3 2

First Edition

Book design by Michaelis/Carpelis Design Assoc.
Illustrations by Tom Lulevitch

Contents

CONTENTS

THE MIDDLE EAST AND AFRICA

CONTENTS

Introduction

The young men from Oxford and Cambridge rode to the Channel, made the crossings, and then, in carriages stuffed with trunks, tutors and servants, drove off to Holland. They toured Europe clockwise—Holland, Germany, France, Italy, always winding up in Florence.

Everywhere they went, they met with learned men and talked gravely of art and history and the learning of Europe, the very center of the earth, beyond which was nothing worth studying. It all took at least six months, often a year, sometimes two. Time was of no account and neither was money, for these were the landed young men who would inherit England and its empire, noblemen almost all of them.

That was the Grand Tour, and it started in the mid-eighteenth century and for about seventy-five years no young man of title was considered quite educated until he had taken it, tutors, trunks, servants and all.

Toward the middle of the nineteenth century and on to World War I, another kind of Grand Tour developed—the leisurely, heavy-laden trips around Europe from spa to spa, from great hotel to great hotel, of rich Europeans and Americans. They had no titles but they had something almost as good: letters of credit from the great banks of London, Paris, New York. The carriages became private railroad coaches and those open touring cars that always seemed to come equipped with goggles.

In this book, drawn from *The Sophisticated Traveler* magazine of *The New York Times* and from its weekly travel section, writers of wit and journalists of experience have set down their own Grand Tour, each writing about a country, a region or city particularly dear to the author's heart and memory.

Muriel Spark travels with the reader in Tuscany, John Russell recalls a beloved Brittany, Anthony Burgess goes back to Vienna. The only difference, of course, is that you don't need a title, the tutors have been replaced by writers of knowledge and taste, and instead of a title or a letter of credit, all you need is a little piece of plastic with your name on it.

But in this book, too, are tours that the most aristocratic and richest of not so very long ago could never have dreamed of.

Here is the Jerusalem of Malachi Martin and Elie Wiesel, the Greece of Nick Gage, who fled the Communists to become a best-selling author in America but carries his home village always in his soul.

Here is Bahrain and the Congo, and China with Theodore White. There is India in this book, and the South Pacific and Indonesia and so many other places that now are part of the Great Tours of the world, the twentieth-century expansion of the Grand Tour. The far countries and special byways are available to millions now. But in this book, the company in the carriage is very, very special.

—A.M.R. & A.G.

EUROPE

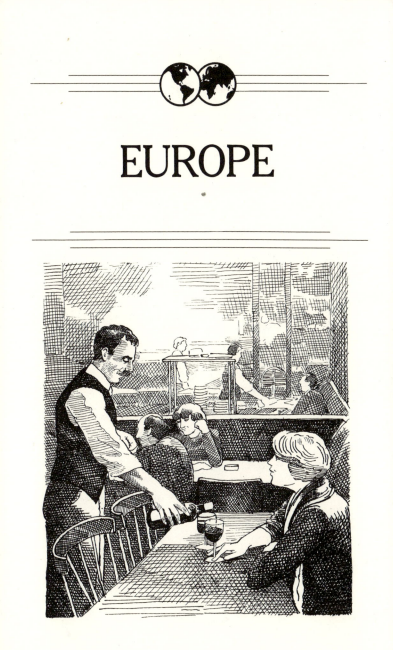

Side Roads of Tuscany

MURIEL SPARK

I T WAS BY CHANCE, NOT choice, that I came to Tuscany more than five years ago, to spend several months at the house of a friend in the olive groves between Arezzo and Siena. So that I have never been properly "on tour" in Tuscany. It is a place where I work and live, visit friends or go for day trips for a special reason—to hear a concert, look at a picture or a building or a square, or to eat at a newly discovered trattoria, coming upon a small hill town or an old parish church on the way. Although Florence is not far away it is another world from rural Tuscany. Florence is Florentine. The same with Siena and all its glories. It is Sienese.

It isn't necessarily the great and famous beauty spots we fall in love with. As with people, so with places: Love is unforeseen, and we can all find ourselves affectionately attached to the minor and the less obvious. I do

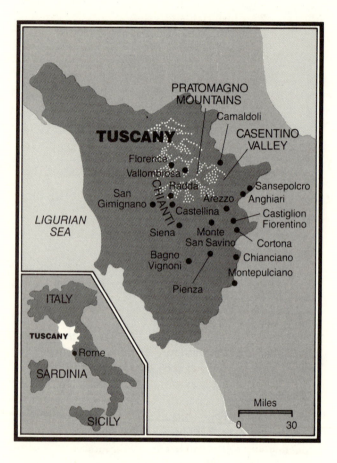

not have an art historian's response to places. I can discern and admire a late-Renaissance gate, a medieval street, a Romanesque church or an Etruscan wall, but my first thoughts are for the warmth of the stone or for the clouds, when they look like a fifteenth-century painting with a chariot or a saint zooming up into them. I notice the light and shade on buildings grouped on a hilltop, the rich skin colors and the shapes of the people around me. I love to watch people, to sit in a trattoria listening in to their talk, imagining the rest.

Nearly every evening I go somewhere in the countryside. One of my shortest drives is to the castle-hamlet of Gargonza, past the medieval market town of Monte San Savino. Dante Alighieri stopped at the castle of Gargonza for the first few days of his exile from Florence. It is an intimate fortification, well restored, with an ancient tower and an airy forest view. In this castle-village, well-equipped cottages are offered for holiday accommodation, moderately priced for families or groups. There are no shops there. The attractions are the woodland walks and the easy access by car to both Florence and Siena and their surrounding fiefdoms.

For people too busy to cook, as I am, it is easy to eat out in this region every evening; the price of a two-course meal with wine is less than $10. I often eat at the Gargonza restaurant, which has a large outdoor terrace and the advantage, always to be looked for in Italy, of being a family concern. The approach to the Gargonza is thickly wooded, and once, at sunset, I saw a wild boar—*cinghiale,* in Italian—sauntering down one of the asphalt roads nearby. It was a beautiful rippling beast. It looked around as it walked like a tourist taking the air. The restaurant itself serves a good preparation of wild boar, as well as *cinghiale* sauce with the pasta. (Another of the specialties is a *rotolo* of spinach and ricotta done in butter. There is a fine wine cellar, but the house wine, white or red, is good and less expensive.)

I went to the wedding of the proprietor's daughter; she was married in the small and lovely Romanesque church. The owner of the Gargonza estate, Count Guicciardini of historic family, was in attendance, languidly standing at the back among the peasants and artisans, friends of the family, foreigners like myself, and the local doctors and lawyers. At the wedding feast, twelve courses were served—on such occasions in Italy, one has to learn to take tiny portions of each dish. A one-man band, who also sang, enlivened the celebration.

I return again and again to Pienza, originally a medieval town that was replanned by Pius II in the fifteenth century. Its central square is small, enclosed by a church and three palaces, all of appropriate and elegant proportions—an attractive example of urban planning. Walking around the square of Pienza, I often have the illusion of being in a roofless temple, as in the Parthenon.

Near Pienza is Montepulciano, grandly endowed with architecture. Long ago someone gave me a relic of the cardinal-saint Robert Bellarmine, and I was delighted to discover that this was his birthplace. It is a tourist spot, and therefore comparatively expensive.

Near Pienza, too, are several *terme,* or sulfur-bath resorts. Chianciano is one of the best known. For me, these towns have too much of an air of people caring greatly for their own health, and really quite healthy people at that; there are smart shops and hairdressers and luxury imports unobtainable in the rest of the region. At Bagno Vignoni, another hot-springs place near Pienza, a fountain in the piazza takes the form of an ancient bath filled with the hot curative waters.

Side Roads of Tuscany

When people come to visit me, I usually take them to see the majestic *Madonna del Parto* of Piero della Francesca. This fresco is to be found entirely on its own, in a small cemetery chapel at Monterchi. The surrounding countryside with its broad sweep of cultivated, undulating fields seems to be out of a painting of the fifteenth century. The picture is planned to represent a stage, the Virgin herself both dramatic protagonist and actual theater, as she undoes her dress to prepare for the historic curtain-rise of the Incarnation. In parallel action, two angels on either side hold back the curtains of the canopy beneath which she stands. Throughout this part of the Tuscan countryside, one can still see indigenous faces that resemble Piero della Francesca's famous model; there is something, too, in the setting of the head on the sturdy neck that is characteristic of many Tuscans today.

From Monterchi, it is only three miles to Sansepolcro, where Piero della Francesca was born. His stupendous fresco of the Resurrection is in the museum.

The streets of the old city are typically medieval to Renaissance. There are good hotel restaurants in Sansepolcro and, between Monterchi and Anghiari at Castello di Sorci, there is an old, capacious farmhouse where a good fixed menu of six courses, with local wine, is served at an all-inclusive price of less than $5. Here again, as in so many hidden places of Tuscany, there is a feeling of timelessness. In the ground-floor kitchens, cooks can be seen skillfully making the pasta, by hand, in different designs.

The city of Cortona is too well known, too crowded, for my comfort. For some reason, when in Tuscany, I find an abundance of English and American voices around me an irritant (this is not so in Rome, which has been cosmopolitan from its foundation). But to be in the midst of an English-speaking fraternity in this wild and natural Italy depresses me greatly. I wonder: What am I doing here? I could just as well have stayed at home. Did I come all this way to hear things like, "Why do they close the museums at the lunch hour?"—an innocent question that opens a huge cultural gulf, since the long midday meal and repose are sacred to the Italians. (Only catering establishments are absolved from the near-religious duty of going home to eat at *il tocco,* one o'clock.) And I remember an English visitor asking me, "Are you stationed out here?" Recalling this, I look out of the window and see Gino the horse farmer riding by proudly with his beasts; nobody has told him he lives "out here," and as for me, there's nothing in my life that corresponds to being stationed.

Cortona, then, is one of the places I avoid, despite its art treasures and antiquities. Even—perhaps especial-ly—in winter, when the flocks of visitors have gone home and the streets are all the more deserted, all the more gloomy, like Edinburgh after the Festival. Better the places that never have this swarming influx.

But to me there is a fascination about Cortona: the road to it that leads south from Arezzo. This indeed is one of the classic Tuscan drives, through the rolling ba-sin of the Valdichiana. From where I live, one comes first to Castiglion Fiorentino, a small town mainly composed of one street that rises up to the very fine mun-icipal arcade, designed by Vasari. There is an old mar-ketplace, from which there is an impressive view, framed by the arches.

In the picture gallery, modestly displayed, is a strange, hypnotic painting of St. Francis receiving the stigmata, beloved of Kenneth Clark, by a little-known mid-fifteenth-century artist, Bartolomeo della Gatta. St. Francis and his companions are unusually represented in green habits in an almost cubistic formation of rocks.

Also on the way to Cortona it is worth stopping to see Montecchio, the recently restored stronghold of Sir John Hawkwood, a fourteenth-century English *condottiere.*

Cortona on its hillside is splendid in the evening light. Just outside the gate, I go to an amusing restaurant, Tonino, where a continuous dish called *antipastissimo* is offered. This consists of a relay of ingenious delicacies, hot and cold, no more than a mouthful of each, but perhaps as many as forty, swiftly served by several waiters. It is amazing how the nibbles mount up into a full meal—I have never been able to finish this awesome and very carefully planned feast. I appreciate good food, but it is seldom that a meal also makes me laugh: This one is positively witty. To complete the picture, Tonino's brochure is translated into joyful English, assuring you, for example, that their "fresch, comfortable cellar is a place for rediscover the old things' taste."

Up the valley of the Casentino, a grand mountain view is to be seen on the way to Camaldoli, where there is a hermitage and monastery, with a few souvenir shops and two unexceptional restaurants. The church has been much restored since its foundation in the thirteenth century; it is now predominantly eighteenth-century baroque and contains some minor Tuscan paintings and frescoes. The main attraction for me is the old monastic pharmacy. There you can purchase such potions as *amaro tonico,* which is described as a neurotonic and digestive and is recommended for nervous exhaustion, for disturbances of the liver and for physical and intellectual stress. It is prepared from roots and aromatic herbs. Try it if you like; I haven't. The pure air and stillness of this great forest are enough balm for my physical and mental stress. Like so many of the vast valley and mountain scenes of Tuscany, the prospect from the heights of Camaldoli makes for a generous heart; it is one where mean thoughts are out of place, where the human spirit responds easily to the expansive benevolence of nature and its silence.

The long, shady forest road to Vallombrosa, glorious in the leafy autumn, is another place I sally forth to. This is on the Pratomagno, a mountain ridge, and leads up to the seventeenth-century Benedictine abbey of Vallombrosa, quite modern for these parts (the original foundation was eleventh century). Here, too, is a scene of wooded hills, canyons, crags and rivers that belongs to no century at all. A short way above Vallombrosa, on the site of a thirteenth-century hermitage, is a modern edifice, the Paradisino, which bears a plaque commemorating the sojourn of the supreme English poet Giovanni Milton in 1638. The inscription goes on to say that he was enamored of this forest and these skies, and one can well believe it. The view from the Paradisino has a feeling of "Paradise Lost," perhaps set to music (Wagner).

Across the highway bridge is Chianti, the vineyard country with its noble farmhouses in the midst of acre upon acre of cultivated plenty. Castellina in Chianti, Radda in Chianti are typical of many wine towns surrounded by vineyards, olive groves and thick woods. Wine merchants offer their tastings. Castellina has a good restaurant, the Antica Trattoria la Torre. It is comparatively high-priced, since in Chianti there is a more prosperous, upper-crust society than one finds near my own central zone of Arezzo. Farther west, San Gimignano, the little town with numerous towers, is a place beloved of the Grand Tourists of the last century, and the

Side Roads of Tuscany

manifold tourists of this; like Cortona, it is a place where I don't go often, lest I be jostled.

Arezzo is the nearest big town to the spot where I spend part of my life. The remains of the original walls are Etruscan, it has a number of notable medieval and Renaissance churches and *palazzi,* but much of the town is modern. The overwhelming attractions of the city are the abundant frescoes of Piero della Francesca. In the cathedral is his fresco of Mary Magdalen, while the church of San Francesco holds his depiction of the Legend of the Holy Cross. Paintings made churchgoing a wonderful picture show for the faithful. I often think, as I look at them, how fortunate it is for us that so few people could read in those days, and were obligingly informed by these wonderful stories in pictures. The Tuscan face of the Madonna del Parto is here in other roles.

Even closer to my second home are the two hill towns I visit most for such practical purposes as shopping or eating out: Monte San Savino and Lucignano. I have grown fond of them.

Serene Lucignano has a simple main street circling the summit of a hill with a dominant collegiate church of the thirteenth century. It is good to approach Lucignano on a winter day, for the winter light in Tuscany is extraordinary. There are two excellent restaurants where I go on alternate days during my Tuscan visits: La Rocca and La Tavernetta, both of which are run by families rightly proud of their fine and inventive cooking.

At Monte San Savino, there is no place to eat of any account, but until recently I used to be invited to lunch every Thursday at the home of an elderly *signora* of that place. She was in her eighties and had wonderful and terrible stories to tell as we made our leisurely way through a meal of Tuscan rarities, cunningly prepared with the herbs and flavorings she knew were the right ones.

Thrilling and terrible were her stories. The Germans had taken her villa during the war—it still stands high on a hillside, but her house at the time I knew her was in the piazza. The Germans had shot her nineteen-year-old son; a street bears his name. She herself, with her daughter, had been put on a truck bound for a train connection to dreaded Germany, but one of the officers on guard, noted for his rigid toughness, nevertheless put them off in the countryside because of a mutual love and knowledge of music.

Love stories, escape stories, stories of the wars and occupations, of her youth, of provincial balls, of visits to the opera: Those Thursday lunches were unforgettable. After lunch, she would play the piano and sing romantic songs from the turn of the century. My favorite was called "Tormento," which she rendered with her whole heart. When she returned the visit, she would bring with her those things befitting a day in the country: her embroidery, her sketchbook and a book of poems by Leopardi.

Carolina died on her ninetieth birthday. She seemed to sum up my Tuscan experience. A whole people, the product of civilized time past, the product of the dramatic landscape, the Tuscans are also the progenitors of what one finds there. It is their spirit of endurance and rejoicing in the goodness of life that inspired the architecture, the paintings, the churches and those ancient cultures of olive groves and vineyards which are the essence of Tuscany.

SETTLING DOWN IN TUSCANY
ARRANGING A STAY

A number of agencies rent properties in rural Tuscany for stays of a week to several months. Accommodations range from studio apartments to castles, and prices vary with the size of the house and the time of year. All rates quoted are for high season, generally July and August; off-season rates are sometimes substantially less.

Rentals usually include furnishings, linens and kitchen equipment; domestic help may be separately negotiated. High-season rentals should be booked as early as January or February.

A sampler of agencies and their offerings:

At Home Abroad, 405 East 56th Street, New York, NY 10022 (telephone: 212-421-9165). A two-bedroom house at the shore is about $850 to $900 a week; a restored farmhouse, with a cook, maid, houseman and pool, accommodating eight, is about $14,500 for two weeks, which is the minimum rental.

Chapter Travel, 102 St. John's Wood Terrace, London NW8 (01-586-9451), is the British agent for Cuendet, a Swiss organization that lists 1,400 properties in Tuscany and Umbria. Prices range from about $150 to $1,500 a week; a color catalogue is available. Credit cards preferred.

Rent a Vacation Everywhere Inc., 500 Triangle Building, Rochester, NY 14604 (716-454-6440). Rates range from about $1,100 for a one-bedroom apartment to about $7,000 to $8,000 per week for a large house with pool and garden, accommodating up to ten people.

Rent Abroad Inc., Post Office Box 5183, Westport, CT 06881 (203-227-9376). A two- or three-bedroom apartment is about $1,500 a month; a fully staffed house, with six or more bedrooms and a pool, is about $25,000 a month.

Resort Villas International, 30 Spring Street, Stamford, CT 06901 (203-965-0261). All rentals are in the coastal resort community of Marina di Pietrasanta; about $910 a week for a two-bedroom house, about $1,150 to $1,400 a week for four bedrooms. Maid service six days a week.

Vacanze in Italia, 153 West 13th Street, New York, NY 10011 (212-242-2145). A small apartment (one of four created from a large Tuscan house) is about $200 a week; a three- or four-bedroom converted farmhouse, usually with a swimming pool, is about $700 to $1,500 a week. Weekly maid service.

Villas International Ltd., 213 East 38th Street, New York, NY 10016 (212-685-4340). About $300 a week for a small apartment sleeping three or four, and up to $5,000 a week for a four- or five-bedroom villa with a pool, on or near the Tuscan coast. A color catalogue of more than 1,000 Tuscan properties is available.

In Milan, La Scala Is Just an Overture

WILLIAM WEAVER

FOR THE MILANESE, AND
for most visitors to the city, Milan begins in Piazza della
Scala. Since its inauguration over two centuries ago, the
legendary opera house has been, beyond dispute, the heart,
emblem, pride of the Lombard capital. When the theater
was nearly destroyed by bombs on the night of August 13,
1943, the citizens were in despair; and within a few days
of the liberation, in April 1945, the rebuilding of the house
began, at popular insistence: the first major reconstruction
in the city. Within a year, La Scala was ready; and on May
11, 1946, Arturo Toscanini, who had returned from self-
imposed exile in America only two weeks before, conducted
a historic reopening concert of works by Rossini, Verdi,
Boito, and Toscanini's own friend, Puccini.

In Milan, La Scala Is Just an Overture

Getting into a performance at La Scala nowadays is not easy: Tickets are expensive and, as a rule, hard to come by. But to get at least an idea of the house and its significance one solution is a visit to the Museo Teatrale in the little wing of the building to the left of the portico. On an upper floor, in a well-arranged suite of rooms— once a gambling casino patronized by the less music-loving Milanese gentlemen while their ladies stayed in their boxes—an array of memorabilia includes old paintings and engravings of La Scala, portraits of the illustrious singers who have graced its stages, from Malibran to Callas, and, in the final rooms, several of Verdi's pianos (and the snaggletoothed spinet on which he played his first notes), manuscripts, drawings, and his death mask, with a few wisps of gray beard caught in the plaster. Unless a rehearsal is in progress on the stage, your admission to the museum also entitles you to peek into the house from a box.

Though Verdi was not born in Milan, he is the city's god. The street named for him runs along La Scala's left flank (Puccini, for many years, kept an apartment at No. 4, near the corner). Stretching northward, more or less, from the theater is the Via Manzoni; and half-way along it is the Grand Hotel et De Milan, where Verdi spent long periods in the latter part of his life, where he decided to write *Otello*, and where, in 1901, he died.

Opposite La Scala, across the square and behind the statue of Leonardo da Vinci (another prized guest of the city), is the Palazzo Marino, the city hall, dating from the sixteenth century but restored several times. To the left of the square, in a big nineteenth-century palazzo, is the Banca Commerciale; and in the corner of the opposite side is the high-arched opening of the Galleria, the cruci-

form arcades of shops and cafés. Thus, in this one space, you have a synopsis of the city: art, business, government, commerce, fun.

In 1868, visiting Milan after a long absence, Verdi wrote to a French friend: "The new Galleria is truly a beautiful thing. A true artistic, monumental thing. In our country still there is the sense of the Great united to the Beautiful."

By "Great" Verdi also meant physically big, and the Galleria is that, though to twentieth-century eyes it may not seem beautiful. But, despite its reputation as a city of go-getting, materialistic businessmen, Milan does not think only of grandeur and show. On the contrary, it is a reticent, even understated city. A walk along the Via Manzoni, the Via Brera, or any of the narrow streets that make up the old part of the city, will be a revelation.

You will pass palaces, great urban residences built, many of them, in the eighteenth or early nineteenth centuries. The façade on the street, however elegant, is likely to be simple, plain. Through the large doorway, if the heavy doors are open, you will see a sober, harmonious paved court (now there may be shops on the ground floor, furnishing a good excuse to enter). But at the back of this court there is likely to be an open arch, another passage, leading to a vast garden with flowering magnolias, broad-branched cedars of Lebanon, leafy oaks. These almost-secret gardens, these hidden explosions of green, are for me a metaphor of Milan's reserved nature.

Of course, there are also public gardens, and in good weather they are a balm. One lies just beyond the Porta Nuova, the gate at the end of Via Manzoni. Within its confines are the Zoo, the Museum of Natural History, the Planetarium, and, along the Via Manin, the Palazzo Dugnani. This charming, dilapidated eighteenth-century building now houses municipal offices, but during the afternoon visitors are allowed to walk past the bulletin boards and posters (one illustrating the fish of Lombardy made me linger the other day) to the high-ceilinged, echoing ballroom, decorated with an airy ceiling fresco by Tiepolo. It is a strange experience, to stand in the dim room and admire the faded allegorical figures, while the clatter of municipal typewriters comes from the surrounding rooms.

A longish walk or short taxi ride will take you from Palazzo Dugnani, scene of private rococo charm, to the vast Castello Sforzesco, reminder of Milan's Renaissance grandeur, residence and stronghold of the Sforza lords of the city. Inside, the collection is vast and heterogeneous (and the jazzy, self-important installation at times irksome), but worth a visit, at least to see the *Rondanini Pietà,* Michelangelo's haunting last work, bought in 1952 by the city from the Rondanini heirs. The painting gallery includes works by Mantegna, Lippi, and—most interesting in this context—many less familiar Lombard artists. Most of all, the castle's collection, which ranges from ceramics to harpsichords and tapestries to wrought iron, gives a sense of richness, artistic as well as material richness, that is peculiarly Milanese.

Outside, another park stretches across flat lawn to Porta Sempione, where an imposing Arco della Pace dates from Napoleonic times and resembles the Arc de Triomphe.

Though Milan had many periods of splendor, from ancient Roman times through the Middle Ages and the Renaissance to the present, it must have been particularly exciting during the nineteenth century. After the Napoleonic period (from which several valuable monuments remain), the time of Rossini and the adopted Milanese Stendhal, there were the great, turbulent years of the Risorgimento, when Verdi was firing the still-disunited nation with his patriotic operas and Alessandro Manzoni was creating the definitive edition of his *I promessi sposi,* giving the Italians a national literary masterpiece (with some vivid descriptions of seventeenth-century Milan). Then, once Italy was united, the city—always prosperous—began its rapid rise to becoming the country's leader in business, industry, and often in taste and the arts, Italy's "moral capital," as the Milanese are fond of calling it, as opposed to the political capital, Rome, considered a mire of pettifogging bureaucracy and windbag debate.

Manzoni, in his later years, lived in a fairly small house in Via Moroni. Now open to the public, it is an obligatory and moving place of pilgrimage for lovers of Italian literature, but it is affecting also for the less specialized tourist. Though most of Manzoni's original furniture is long gone, the very dimensions of the house

suggest how a moderately well-off Milanese lived a century or more ago; and his bedroom—where the furniture
survives—is cell-like, indicating the Spartan austerity
that characterized Manzoni's life.

For an idea of how the richer Milanese lived at that
time, go to the Museo Poldi Pezzoli, in Via Manzoni. In
1853, Gian Giacomo Poldi Pezzoli, a wealthy, aristocratic collector, built the palazzo that still contains his
collection. He had the house decorated (to the hilt) by
leading artists, but the war damaged most of the rooms,
so now only old photographs (to be seen in the museum)
tell of the magnificent nineteenth-century clutter that
Poldi Pezzoli created, then bequeathed to the city.

The collection itself, subsequently enriched by other
bequests, is a wonderful mixture of Oriental rugs, armor, sculpture, glass, scientific instruments and paintings (including some bewitching, tiny Guardis and a
great Pollaiuolo). But the collection is still far from
large: a pleasant, not tiring browse.

For that matter, Milan's most famous art museum, the
Accademia di Brera, is gripping without being exhaust-
ing. The building itself (from La Scala follow the Via
Verdi, which becomes Via Brera), constructed between
1651 and 1780, is striking; the huge doorway is by
Giuseppe Piermarini, the architect of La Scala, the
Royal Palace and other major Milanese buildings.

In the great courtyard you immediately encounter the
over-life-size bronze nude of an idealized Napoleon by
Canova, a further reminder of the period when the city
was the capital of Bonaparte's Cisalpine Republic. The
Brera collection comprises favorite masterpieces by
Mantegna (the grim, foreshortened *Dead Christ*),
Carpaccio (the delicate *Presentation of the Virgin in the
Temple*), Veronese, Titian, and—again—many Lom-

bard painters. There are also some canvases by the Venetian-born Francesco Hayez, contemporary of Manzoni and Verdi, and for many years teacher, then director, at the Brera. His portraits of nineteenth-century notables (Cavour, among them) give a vivid idea of the people of the time, and his historical pageant scenes—*The Sicilian Vespers, The Death of the Doge Marin Faliero*—reflect the period's narrative taste, also reflected in the operas of Verdi and Donizetti.

The Brera quarter has long been Milan's bohemia (and, for a while, in the 1970s, it degenerated into Milan's Needle Park), and you still find there several cheap restaurants (and some less cheap), cafés where painters and students gather, galleries and excellent bookshops (especially for books on the arts). But it is only a few steps from Via Brera to Via San Marco and the little church of that name. Not Milan's most distinguished church architecturally, San Marco has a special meaning for music lovers because there, on May 22, 1874, Verdi conducted the first performance of his *Requiem*, in honor of Manzoni, who had died exactly a year before.

On any visitor's list the first church in Milan to see is Santa Maria delle Grazie (the other side of the Castello from San Marco). In the former refectory of the adjacent convent is Leonardo's *Last Supper*, arguably the most famous work of art in the city. At this writing, the notoriously damaged fresco—it began to show signs of decay in the sixteenth century—is undergoing yet another restoration (generously underwritten by Olivetti), so only a part of it is visible at any given time. When I went to see it recently, the center third was covered by scaffolding and screens, but the rest could be seen, and even in its inevitably damaged state the work still moves. The right-hand third, now restored, is more vital, though, of course, the hand of time is still evident. It's hard to say—and it really doesn't matter—whether the emotion comes from the work's legend or from the painting itself. In any case, the emotion is real.

But don't neglect the church itself. Santa Maria delle Grazie is part Gothic, part Renaissance (Bramante added the harmonious apse and the little silent cloister). There are also the other great Milanese churches to explore, headed by Sant'Ambrogio, dedicated to the city's patron. This is an outstanding example of Lombard Romanesque, solid, almost unassuming.

The Duomo is a chapter to itself. In Italy, if someone wants to say a thing had taken a long time to complete, he says, "like the Duomo of Milan." The cathedral was begun in 1386, at the command of Gian Galeazzo Visconti, and construction continued, at intervals, until 1887, when the last pinnacles were completed. The history of the Duomo reflects the history of the city, of Italy. Its archbishops have been saints, like Ambrose and like the beloved Carlo Borromeo (who also appears in Manzoni's novel), and Popes (the latest was Paul VI Montini). Its artists range from the anonymous carvers of the Middle Ages to the contemporary sculptor Luciano Minguzzi, creator of one of the bronze doors, which appropriately depicts episodes in the building of the Duomo.

The building's history becomes more comprehensible when you visit the nearby Museo del Duomo. Here many works of art have been taken for safekeeping, removed from the lash of the elements (the Milan climate is fierce) and replaced by sturdier modern copies. There are graphic presentations of the cathedral's growth and—in one room—a large wooden model, an ecclesiastical doll's house, of the Duomo as it almost is.

The guidebooks all say the best view of the Duomo is from the square in front of the Royal Palace (the cathedral's left flank). They are right, but the white marble forest of pinnacles and statues, the jungle of spires and gutterspouts, must be enjoyed from within. Take the elevator (outside, in the Duomo's right flank) to the terraces. There the great fabric simply engulfs you.

"Nobody comes to this city to see this city," an American resident in Milan once said to me; and I suppose it's true that many visitors come here purely for business (the annual Trade Fair is one of the most important in the world). And, in a sense, my own first trips to Milan were on business: As a music critic, I was going to La Scala. I discovered Milan's charms only gradually, accidentally. Perhaps this is the best way to become acquainted with any city; but for those who have only a few days, even a hasty inspection is rewarding. Just remember to look beyond the façades.

FROM THE OPERA TO RISOTTO
TOURIST OFFICES

Milan is the gateway to northern Italy, with direct air service from New York and major European cities. The city's byword is efficiency, and this truly applies to the **Ente Provinciale per il Turismo.** The Tourist Office headquarters is at Via Marconi 1 (at the corner of Piazza del Duomo), where a large, ground-floor counter is staffed by informed employees. The E.P.T. has other offices at the Central Railroad Station and, during the tourist season (April–September), on the main highway approaches to the city.

At any of these offices, you should ask for the free

booklet *Tutta Milana* (available in English), which contains telephone numbers (consulates, banks, shops, restaurants), a schematic history of the city and information about the main sights. The E.P.T. also publishes a schedule of museum opening and closing times, a list of hotels with prices and amenities, and other free publications.

The Comune di Milano, the city government, also has an office for the public in the Galleria, at the Scala end (around the corner from Algani's newsstand, which has the best selection of foreign newspapers). This office is chiefly for the Milanese, who have to grapple with the city's bureaucracy; but for the foreign visitor it provides information about what's going on in the theaters.

THEATERS

La Scala opens in early December and the opera season continues until at least late May (there are concerts and ballet evenings during the off-season). The price of tickets varies according to the smartness of the performance. The top prices run from about $65 for a gala to about $25 for nonsubscription (and nonopening) nights. A gallery seat is about $5 and gallery standing room, about $1.50 (but if it is a big occasion you have to wait in line for hours).

There is no easy way to procure tickets. Some suggestions: If you know far in advance the dates of your Milan stay, write directly to the *botteghino* (box office) of La Scala, enclosing a check, with instructions to hold tickets for performances on the nights you name. Then, the minute you arrive in the city, go to the box office and see if you're lucky. Otherwise, if you are staying in a hotel, you can ask the *portiere* (concierge), after tipping him, to do his best to get you seats. His tip should be 10,000 to 20,000 lire (about $5 to $10), depending on the grandeur of the hotel.

Failing all else, look for scalpers lurking outside the entrance to the box office. As a rule, the markup is not excessive, and the scalpers are less dishonest than they sometimes look.

It is difficult to get a calendar of Scala events outside of Milan, and even if you manage to find one, the events are sometimes shifted around (the English magazine *Opera* usually prints a Scala schedule toward the beginning of the season).

Italy's generally finest legitimate theater is the **Piccolo Teatro della Citta di Milano,** founded just after the war (and still directed) by Giorgio Strehler. If you understand Italian or can enjoy theater in a language you don't understand, the Piccolo is not to be missed, especially if Strehler is presenting Goldoni, the eighteenth-century Venetian playwright. Other theaters offer everything from brassy revues to dank avant-garde. There are also English-language movies at the **Angelicum** and, occasionally, at the **Cinemas d'essai** or **Cinema Clubs** (you can join the club at the door, usually for a reasonable sum).

HOTELS

Milan has many visitors and not that many hotels, so it is wise to reserve as far in advance as possible (and unless you are going to the Trade Fair, held in mid-April, avoid its dates).

If I decide to splurge, I choose the **Grand Hotel et De Milan** (telephone: 870757)—the Milan, to its friends—at Via Manzoni 29. It is old, traditional, centrally located. Some American friends complain that it is old-fashioned and could stand refurbishing. Perhaps. If you ask at the desk, and if they're not rushed, they will show you Verdi's sitting room (no longer given to guests), which contains a portrait of the composer, in that same room, painted in 1887. The average price of a double room with bath is about $100.

Also in the deluxe category are the **Principe e Savoia** (less central, marginally less noisy) at Piazzale della Repubblica 17 (6230); and the **Milano Hilton,**

Via Galvani 12 (6983). Both charge about $150 for a double room. The **Carlton Senato,** Via Senato 5 (798583), is set back a bit from the street, giving an impression of quiet (the façade is charming). Its rate is about $75. The **Manin,** Via Manin 7 (6596511), and the **Cavour,** Via Fatebenefratelli 21 (650983), have some quiet inside rooms (ask for them firmly when making your reservation), while the Manin's front rooms have a view of the park. Both are within walking distance of the city center and both charge about $75.

In my student days I used to stay at the **Ambasciatori,** Galleria del Corso 3 (790241), then a favorite place with young theater folk, and efficient if not elegant. About $50. The **Manzoni,** Via Santo Spirito 20 (705700), seems to attract music critics because of its proximity to La Scala and its reasonable rates—$45. There are cheaper hotels and *pensioni,* but they are a matter of taste and luck.

RESTAURANTS

Though Bologna has the reputation of being Italy's culinary capital, Milanese restaurants surely offer wider variety and greater choice. For the grander places it's wise to telephone ahead and reserve a table.

These days, the most fashionable, the most interesting—and probably the most expensive—is **Gualtiero Marchesi,** after its chef-owner. Authorities consider it one of the dozen best restaurants in Europe. The chef himself supervises every meal and usually makes an appearance at the end to shake the departing guest's hand. This is Italian nouvelle cuisine, simply but incomparably prepared. (I once ate a meal consisting of ragout of boned frog's legs, cold; lobster claw meat and boned pigeon breasts steamed with little ravioli stuffed with pureed green peas; cheese from a varied board; and a dessert that it would be inadequate to describe as lemon pie.) The wine selection is discriminating (I drank a delicious Italian Chardonnay). Allow about $60 a person. The restaurant, in the outlying Via Bonvesin de la Riva 9 (741246 or 7386677), has only a dozen tables, so reservations are essential.

On a more quotidian level, I would suggest **Il Ciovassino,** on the little street of the same name (just off Via Brera; 8053868). The menu is imaginative: I once ate gnocchi of carrots and macaroons (yes, macaroons, which added an almondy tang), a salad of gransevola (a kind of Adriatic crab) on a bed of raw spinach, and some cheese. Along with a friend, I consumed a bottle of white Chianti. About $20 each. As at Gualtiero Marchesi's, portions are small.

If you want to gorge, go to Bologna. Or start your meal with a filling, saffron-flavored risotto. They make excellent risottos at **Don Lisander,** in Via Manzoni 12A (790130), and the menu offers traditional northern Italian cooking, including game in season. In warm weather, you can eat in the garden, cool and quiet, under the windows of the Poldi Pezzoli Museum. Again, calculate about $20.

Eating after the theater is sometimes a problem: Italian cities are not great for night life anyway. You can resolve the problem, rather expensively, by reserving a table at **Biffi Scala** (876332), or just drop by on your way into the opera. It is in the Scala building, and they don't mind your staying late. They also make a fine risotto (sometimes, at night, they offer the crunchy risotto al salto, a fried rice-cake). You can order their Chiaretto from Lake Garda, a light, almost rosé wine, in carafes. A meal with wine costs about $25 or $30.

Milan abounds in good cheap restaurants, if you are willing to look for them. There is a whole series in **Corso Garibaldi** (prices are displayed in the window) and in **Corso di Porta Ticinese,** a working-class district not far from the Duomo.

The current food bargain in Milan is the **Sunrise**

Bar (Piazzale Lagosta, corner of Via Trau), where a full meal with wine can cost as little as $5. Crowds are attracted by the good food, too. It is worth the wait.

Inevitably, fast food has also reached Milan, but it has taken on an Italian flavor. Before going to La Scala, for example, if the opera looks to be long, you can stave off hunger pangs with a sandwich at the apparently nameless café on the corner of Via Filodrammatici and Via Santa Margherita (in the building of the Hotel Marino alla Scala). Ask for the *piadina*, a pitalike flat bread, with ham and cheese, toasted. Other bars and cafés have also taken to providing sandwiches and snacks. A sandwich and wine costs about $3 to $4.

TRANSPORT

Though Milan has a bus stop called Passione and a subway stop called Gioia, the city's public transport does not feature passion and joy (they are named, more prosaically, after the church of Santa Maria della Passione and the nineteenth-century humanist Melchiorre Gioia). The system works, however, on a sober level; and the clear signs everywhere allow you to get the hang fairly easily. A ticket costs about 25 cents. You can buy tickets from newsstands or from machines at the main stops. Parking is close to impossible in downtown Milan, so leave your car in the hotel garage and proceed by public means or on foot.

Walking is the best way to see the city, in any case; and the visitor who takes the usual urban precautions— stay out of parks after dark, avoid lonely side streets— need have no fear. There is no word for "mugging" in Italian, though there is a special one for "pursesnatching." Red Brigades and other terrorist organizations are not interested in foreign visitors. Taxis are not expensive by New York standards and can be ordered by phone (though it may take some patience in rush hours or on rainy days).

MUSEUMS

In addition to those mentioned above, Milan has several small specialized collections that repay a visit. The **Civica Galleria d'Arte Moderna** (Via Palestro 16) is in the neoclassical Villa Comunale, once inhabited by Napoleon and then by his stepson and viceroy, Eugene de Beauharnais. A modern art pavilion, to the right as you enter, features temporary shows; the permanent collection includes some fine nineteenth-century Italian pictures and some twentieth-century French ones. The villa itself should not be overlooked.

The **Museo di Milano** and the **Museo di Storia Contemporanea** are in the same building at Via San Andrea 6, just off Via Montenapoleone. The former sponsors temporary shows illustrating the city's past (a typical series presented little-known, gifted photographers of the turn of the century). It also has a collection of paintings of landmarks and festivals, testifying to a long-vanished Milan.

The Contemporary History Museum has mementos of both World Wars, the Fascist period, and some affecting documents of the Milanese Resistance.

Most of these museums are closed on Monday, but unlike museums in many other Italian cities they are open in the afternoon. In many cases admission is free. The **Museo Teatrale alla Scala** is open on Monday (Sunday is its closing day).

SHOPPING

The most fashionable street, a synonym for chic in Milan, is **Via Montenapoleone.** It leads to Piazza San Babila, from which other streets of smart shops branch out. For antiques, the Brera quarter is becoming more and more a center; many dealers have moved there. For music, records (and instruments), **Casa Ricordi**—publisher of Verdi, Puccini and the other great Italian composers—has its main shop at Via Berchet. For food, the most tempting shop is **Peck** in

Via Spadari. Around the corner, in Via Cantu, there is the **Rosticceria Peck,** for take-out cooked food, ideal if you're planning a picnic.

If you're in a hurry, go to an **Upim**—the Italian Woolworth's—which has several downtown branches (good for shaving cream, postcards and other humble requirements); or go to the more expensive **Rinascente,** under the portico on Piazza del Duomo, which is the closest Italy comes to Bloomingdale's. In the basement of this big department store is a section of Italian crafts where you may find suitable presents to take home. —W.W.

Light and Shadow in Brittany

JOHN RUSSELL

WHEN PEOPLE GO ON AND on about their last vacation, as they often do, I have a three-word rejoinder. "Brittany is bliss," I say, and no sooner is that said than heads are bowed in disbelief all round the table.

I persevere. I tell them about the iodized offshore breezes, the microclimate so temperate that it fosters camellias in midwinter, the standing stones that in their way are as grand as anything in Egypt, the white-painted cottages that make us reach for our dark glasses, the vertiginous rock structures on Belle-Île that Claude Monet never forgot, the versatile and innovative cuisine that draws upon raw materials as fresh as any in the world.

I tell them of august little towns like St.-Cado, where there are noble town houses that almost sit in the sea. I tell them of the Château des Rochers, where Madame de

Light and Shadow in Brittany

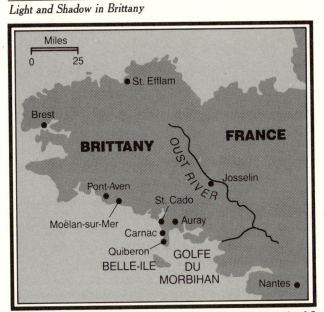

Sévigné wrote some of the very best of her letters. And I tell them of the isolated chapel at Trémalo, near Pont-Aven, where the wooden crucifix that prompted Gauguin's *Yellow Christ* hangs high on the wall and you can count on having the place to yourself with never a sacristan in sight, let alone a fellow visitor.

I tell them how the Breton sunlight makes the tiny and unhurrying river Oust look like a length of khaki-colored silk as it passes the colossal castle of the Rohans at Josselin. I tell them of the Moulins du Duc at Moëlan-sur-Mer, with its landscaped water garden, its outsize mill wheel continuously turning, its optimum comfort. I tell them how the new roads run like velvet beneath the rented Mercedes, and how whole communities vie with one another as to which has the highest standard of housekeeping.

I tell them about the Golfe du Morbihan, an archipelago that yields not at all to the Cyclades when it comes to the intermingling of land and sea. I tell them about the sweet alyssum, which gives off a smell of honey as it bends beneath my tread, and about the highly characterized rock faces, which are just as they were when an American painter from Philadelphia called Earl Shinn described one of them in 1866—"a mass of gray lichen, very pure Courbet in color, plenty of silvers along the gray, with some faint malachite reflections from the trees, and a good bit of burnt umber where they had a fire against it." I tell them about the caramel store called LeRoux in Quiberon, which is by common consent the best thing of its kind in all France. "That's the way it is," I say. "Brittany is bliss."

I must admit that there was a time when I would never have expected to say such a thing. In the England in which I was reared, we did not dream of Brittany when the talk turned to France. We dreamed of putting on the Ritz in Biarritz, playing the horses in Deauville, climbing one of the more taxing faces of Mont Blanc, checking out the folk songs of the Auvergne or paddling our own canoe along the Canal de Bourgogne. Brittany was nowhere.

Then, as now, people craved good weather. Sunlight on moving water was the most beautiful thing there was, and we couldn't get enough of it. Brittany to us was a barbaric and inhospitable countryside, all thorn hedge and upended wet stone, where raincoats were mandatory 365 days of the year and just about every place name began with a "K." We had a litany of such names. "Keremana'ch!" we would croak to one another. "Kermariaan-Iskuit! Kerminauouet! Kersaint-en-Landuves!" And for a final salvo: "Kerjouanno! Kerambosquer! Ker-

penhir! Kezhero!" At the very thought of those unlikely vocables, we cracked up.

Breton and Bretonne meant nothing to us, though we
knew that they were big on ethnic costume and that many
of them were separatists, ready to do battle with the central government of France on any and every pretext.
That Brittany was the homeland of the buckwheat pancake did not seduce us, since the fashion for crêpes still
lay many years in the future. And since schoolboys don't
usually like oysters, it said little to us that the Belon
beds were some of the most famous in France. The food
in Brittany was famously awful, people said.

Not so today. Dinner and an overnight stay at the
Moulins du Duc in Moëlan-sur-Mer, not far from Pont-
Aven, are as agreeable in their way as anything that
France has to offer. Moëlan itself is nothing much, and
the winding lane that leads to the hotel is wild country—
all oaks and chestnuts twisted by the wind—that also
promises little. But when the little yellow signposts give
over pointing and you pull up beside the duck-loud lake,
you can be in no doubt that a remarkable experience is at
hand.

The hotel is an ancient mill, as its name suggests, with
an ancient mill wheel that still turns. It has a large and
well-thought-out landscaped garden that is completely
replanted four times a year. Woodshed and cowshed
have been turned into dens of luxury, so that you are
likely to have a cottage all your own. The service is
about as good as it could be, whether by strong-thewed
young women from Moëlan or by a senior staff whose
ways are anything but rustic. ("The only way to keep
my staff," the owner told us, "is to close for the entire
winter and take them all to the Caribbean. That's why I
opened a restaurant [Le Pelican] on St. Bart's.") Hardly

has the meal begun before we have a sense of disorienta-
tion. French materials of the very top class are clearly
being used, but the result is not quite French. Where else
in France does an enormous dorade come to the table
baked in a thick winter overcoat of heavy rock salt crys-
tals? The coat cuts like armor, and yet the fish, when revealed, turns out not to be salty at all.

And what about that fig tart, with the thinnest imaginable slices of fresh figs spread like dark petals on the
thinnest imaginable slivers of pastry? And just a glister
of raspberry sauce on those petals? No Frenchman would
think of just that combination. And, sure enough, the
chef at the Moulins du Duc is a young Japanese named
Shigeo Torigai. He loves France, he has married a
French woman, he adores working with local French materials (as against working in St. Bart's, where everything
has to come from a million miles away). It is for him, as
much as for Mr. and Mrs. Questrebert, the innovative
owners, that people come back and back to the Moulins
du Duc—which, I may say, is by no means the only remarkable restaurant in an area where "ethnic" was once
the only polite word for the food.

Elsewhere, Brittany can still be rough. The wind
alone can beat a man down. When allied to the mud, the
featureless moors, the huge new constructions devoted to
the short and dull life of the battery hen, that wind
brings out in the Bretons a trait that they call *startijenn*
in their native language, which is related to Gaelic. A
synonym for physical and moral exuberance, *startijenn*
is in shorter supply among foreign visitors.

Yet even then there are compensations. Adam Nicol-
son, in his book *Long Walks in France,* tells us in memorable terms how the dipping path through the dense wet
bracken can lead in the end to "fields of early cauliflow-

ers and artichokes growing on the sea-edge like transplanted sea anemones . . . [and] at slate-blue bays
banded by quartzite where the sand is poured between
the stepped and shattered rocks like cream."

The bays in question are close to St.-Efflam, on the
north shore of Brittany, but my own conversion was ef-
fected in the area around Quiberon, to the south. Quiberon is a long way from Paris, but a train ride in which
Versailles, Chartres and Le Mans all make cameo appearances has much to recommend it. Besides, there is a
certain magic in the name of St.-Gustan, not far from
Quiberon, where Benjamin Franklin made the most discreet of landfalls when he arrived in France in 1776 on a
visit that was vital to the well-being of the infant Republic. And when we get into a taxi at the train station of
Auray and the straight road streaks southward, with the
ocean on one side and the bay on the other, we can al-

most feel the vibration of one of the most impressive of all surviving prehistoric monuments—the standing stones of Carnac.

What those stones mean, and how they got to be on that remote peninsula, are questions too complex to be unriddled here. But even if we ignore them and regard Carnac simply as the world's first and greatest sculpture park, we shall have an amazing time. *Les alignements* is the French name for these prodigious formations, and they indeed do have a perceptible geometric layout. Initially bunched together in a semicircle at the top of a very long and gentle slope, they gradually form up in more or less straight lines and become smaller and fewer as we walk downhill and away from Carnac itself.

Several things about the alignments should be noted. Unlike Stonehenge, they do not have to be fenced in. Unlike so many of the monuments of ancient Greece, they have never been vandalized. No names are incised, no fragments stolen. Such is their scale that even on a summer Sunday the crowd is almost invisible. No one talks much at Carnac either. An attentive awe comes over even the most convivial visitor as he feels himself in the presence of an order of things that is vast and mysterious beyond everyday understanding.

The visitor may also notice that the light at Carnac comes and goes in a most extraordinary way. Clouds move fast in this part of Brittany, which is no more than a mile or so from the famously wind-swept stretch of coast called the Côte Sauvage. The sun comes and goes, too, in ways unknown to the Côte d'Azur and the Caribbean. Nowhere is it more mercurial. What looks to be a terrible day turns into paradise in less time than it takes to sneeze, and vice versa.

This changeability is not to everyone's taste, but the

Light and Shadow in Brittany

very fugacity of the sunshine in this part of Brittany
heightens expectation. The visitor feels himself a gam-
bler for whom in time, and with no warning, the cards
will suddenly run the right way. It drove Monet to distraction when he stayed on Belle-Île and tried to fix the
giddying perspectives of promontory and inlet, high-
flung needle of rock and bottle-green inbound wave. (After the relatively placid coast of Normandy, he felt like a
man thrown into a den of tigers.) On the Côte Sauvage
outside Quiberon the racing torrent of seawater has still
its primal urgency, and anyone who ventures into it at
the wrong time is unlikely to come back alive.

My own recent visits to Brittany have revolved around
the Institute of Thalassotherapy in Quiberon. This is not
what is usually called a "fat farm." What it has to offer
is a general bodily rehabilitation, based primarily on the
potential of seawater to make one feel better and better,
inside and out. The patient experiences a sea change
(and for once that Shakespearean word is the only one
that fits) that makes him feel twice his old self.

Hosed with seawater, drenched and doused with
seawater, massaged in seawater and fresh from jumping
up and down in seawater, the patient is led to the gym,
fed with delicious (though fat-free, sauce-free and nonal-
coholic) lunches and dinners and laid to rest from time to
time in a silence room. At the institute, no one is more
equal than anyone else. Even if your name is Gérard De-
pardieu and you are in just about every film that is
playing in the town, everyone will feign not to notice
you, just as they feigned not to notice Max Ernst when he
paid his annual visit and went back to Paris with a
whole new exhibition of little collages under his arm.
When we step into the Porthault bathrobes (nicely
graded in color from yellow through rust and back again)

that are our daytime uniform we leave our identity behind us, and very pleasant it is, too.

Made over, the regenerated patient delights more than
ever in a countryside that has made the most of a
newfound prosperity without losing out to suburbia.
Bagpipe and clarinet—long fundamental to every Breton
wedding party—may have given way to a disco trucked
in for the occasion. Country inns where a private bath
was unheard of and all needs had to be satisfied down the
hall have given place to luxurious hostelries. The great
forests have dwindled. The sardine catch is in decline.
But the harborside of Le Pouldu, a fishing village near
Pont-Aven, is still recognizably the place where Gauguin's clogs once struck sparks from the cobblestones,
and when the enormous stretch of sound turns pink and
vanilla at low tide, I, for one, decide all over again that
Brittany is bliss.

PLEASURES OF A ROCKY COAST
COUNTRY RETREATS

Château de Locguénolé, 56700 Hennebont (telephone: 97-76-29-04). Situated in a 250-acre park on
the Blavet River, the hotel has a pool, twenty-three
rooms (double with bath, about $70; single with bath,
$40) and three suites ($100), breakfast $5 extra. Dinner
with wine starts at about $35 per person. Specialties:
red mullet and mussel soup, salad of sweetbreads with
sorrel, roast farm pigeon, fricassee of cod in garlic. The
château is open daily. Closes on November 15 and re-
opens on March 1.

Résidence de Kerniaven, Route de Plouhinec,
56700 Hannebont (97-76-29-04), about a mile and a

half from the château, and under the same management. The Résidence has twelve rooms (double with bath, about $65; single with bath, $40), and no restaurant.

Les Moulins du Duc, 29116 Moëlan-sur-Mer (98-96-60-73). Rates for the twenty-seven rooms are: double with bath, about $65, and single with bath, $45; breakfast is $5 extra. Dinner with wine begins at about $25 per person, thanks to the very strong dollar at this writing. Specialties: crayfish with mushrooms, red mullet with fennel, saddle of rabbit with noodles, duck fillets in ginger. Closed November 1 to April 1.

RUSTIC RESTAURANTS

Moulin de Rosmadec, 29123 Pont-Aven (98-06-00-22). In an old mill filled with bibelots and traditional furnishings, this restaurant specializes in such dishes as prawns à la nage, suprême of sole in champagne, duckling with fresh pepper and other regional specialties. Dinner with wine is about $30 per person. No credit cards. Closed Wednesday and from October 15 to November 15 as well as twelve days each February.

La Taupinière, Route de Concarneau (98-06-03-12), Pont-Aven. A regional restaurant installed in a thatched-roof house. Specialties include ragout of shellfish, bass in court bouillon, fresh Brittany ham grilled on a wood fire, hot apple tart. Dinner with wine begins at about $30 per person. Closed Monday and Tuesday from September 15 to October 15.

TAKING THE WATERS

Thalassa, 56170 Quiberon (97-50-20-00). Two people can undergo thalassotherapy at the **Hôtel Diététique** for about $190 a day, including double room, special meals and the cure (single room, $125 a day); there is a six-day minimum. (Closed during January.) Or they can stay at the 113-room **Sofitel Thalassa,** associated with the Institut de Thalassothérapie. Double room and full board (nondietetic meals), about $160;

single room and board, $110. Double room and half board (breakfast only), $140; single room and half board, $100. Closed during January.

The low-calorie menu at the Hôtel Diététique, available only to those taking the thalassotherapy, lists such specialties as turbot with hot oysters, lobster stew, tournedos with scallops and artichokes, lemon tart soufflé. The **Thalassa Restaurant** at the Sofitel Thalassa serves traditional French cuisine with an emphasis on seafood. Dinner with wine starts at about $25 per person.

Flaubert's Europe

FRANCIS STEEGMULLER

ROUEN, CAPITAL OF THE old province of Normandy, where Gustave Flaubert was born in 1821, figures, almost as a personality, in his first published and most famous novel, *Madame Bovary*. It remains a noble and picturesque city today, the more poignant for its sufferings in two world wars. Aerial bombings during World War II did much damage; the sixteenth-century Palais de Justice is an eloquent ruin; but the Cathedral of Notre Dame, gravely wounded in 1944 and since restored, is still one of the most splendid in France, its fine stained glass intact. Rouen's other Gothic churches, half-timbered houses and the magnificent illuminated manuscripts in the Municipal Library make the city a virtual museum of medieval art and architecture.

For Flaubert in his youth, however, Romantic though he was—and thus enamored of the Middle Ages—the Gothic allure of his native city was obscured by the heavily bourgeois aspect of its citizens. (Flaubert loved

his parents, and admired his father, who was head of the
municipal hospital; but he detested the class to which
they belonged.) In *Madame Bovary,* the scene of the lovers' meeting in the cathedral is satirical, and only in two
of his latest works did he pay tribute to details of the
great building: in his *Herodias,* to the celebrated figure
of Salome dancing on her hands; and in *St. Julien the
Hospitaler,* to one of the windows.

Friends and relatives of the Flaubert family lived in
various parts of Normandy. Today's visitor who passes
through the town of Les Andelys in the Seine valley will
be treading in Gustave's footsteps: It was the home of his
closest school friend, Ernest Chevalier, and together they
explored the Château Gaillard, the nearby ruined castle
of Richard the Lion-Hearted, on its height overlooking
the river. At Trouville, on the English Channel, where
the Flauberts had a summer cottage, and where the ado-
lescent Gustave first met and adored Elise Schlesinger
(the Madame Arnoux of *The Sentimental Education*
—which many think his greatest novel), there is a commemorative statue of Flaubert on the waterfront. In
neighboring, more fashionable Deauville, Flaubert in
later life sold a large tract of farmland, inherited from his
mother, to help pay the debts of his niece's husband. The
Deauville racetrack now covers the old Flaubert farm. In
Rouen itself his parents' apartment in the hospital can be
visited; and a mile or so down the Seine, at Croisset,
there is a small Flaubert museum in the remaining pavilion of the country house where he did most of his writing.

But to "get out of Rouen" was always the young Flaubert's restless wish, and eventually, as a reward for
passing his baccalaureat, he was allowed by his parents
to make his first long journey—to Corsica, via the Py-

renees and Provence. Even in the careful, sedate company of family friends, what a revelation it was of what
life in the sun could be: a glimpse of Spain, land of his
hero Don Quixote; in Corsica, certified ex-bandits; in
Marseilles, at night, the company of Madame Eulalie
Foucauld, the amiable, erotically accomplished mana-
geress of his hotel in the Rue de la Darse. Today there is
still plenty of life around the Vieux Port in Marseilles,
though less color than there was before 1943, when the
German occupants systematically destroyed, with explo-
sives, the notorious *quartier réservé.*

After these glimpses of the Midi, Rouen was more dis-
mal to the young man than ever. Even Paris itself, where
he enrolled at the Law School, held few pleasures for a
student with a limited paternal allowance and frequent
examinations to be passed. For a twenty-year-old Romantic, already the author of countless stories and plays
(all of these early works carefully preserved, but unpub-
lished in his lifetime), the prospect of life as an attorney
became intolerable. Literally so; and when Gustave collapsed during one of his vacations, struck down by a
kind of epilepsy, even Dr. Flaubert seems to have accepted the disappointment that this son was unfit for any
of the true professions, and must be allowed to live as the
mere scribbler he so curiously wanted to be.

By the spring of 1845 Flaubert had recovered suf-
ficiently—or rather he had become practiced enough
in preparing himself against the now diminishing attacks
of his illness—to travel once more; and with his parents
he accompanied his newly married sister, Caroline, and
her husband on their wedding trip down through France
to Italy. All went badly almost from the beginning.
Everyone except Gustave proved to be a bad traveler,
prey to various ailments; the bridegroom was under-

standably resentful of his in-laws' presence; and to
Flaubert's dismay plans to visit Florence, Rome and
Naples were canceled, and the party turned homeward
after going no farther than Genoa, Turin and Milan. The
young Flaubert was enraptured by what he did see, but a
passage from one of his letters to his best friend, Alfred
Le Poittevin, written from Marseilles early in the trip,
reveals that he had learned a basic requirement of proper
travel: solitude, or very carefully chosen company.

"By everything you hold sacred, dear Alfred, I con-
jure you in the name of heaven, in my own name, never
to travel with anyone! Anyone! I wanted to see Aigues-
Mortes, and I did not see Aigues-Mortes nor the Sainte-
Baume with the cave where Magdalen wept, nor the
battlefield of Marius, etc. I have seen none of those, because I wasn't alone, I wasn't free. . . . At Nîmes I saw
the Arena again. On the way to the Pont du Gard, two or
three wagons of gypsies. . . . Here in Marseilles I've
been unable to find that admirable big-breasted female
who gave me such blissful interludes. She and her
mother no longer have the Hôtel Richelieu. I passed it,
saw the steps and the door. The shutters were closed, the
hotel is abandoned. I could barely recognize it. . . ."
The party went on to Italy along the Côte d'Azur and the
Italian Riviera:

"I have seen a truly beautiful road, the Corniche, and
am now in a beautiful city, a truly beautiful city, Genoa.
You walk on marble; everything is marble—stairs,
balconies, palaces. The palaces touch one another; walking in the street you look up and see the great patrician
ceilings, all painted and gilded. I go into many of the
churches, listen to the singing and the organ, watch the
monks, look at the chasubles, the altars, the statues. . . . This is the place to come and think about Don

Flaubert's Europe

Juan: one enjoys imagining him as one strolls in these Italian churches, among the statues, in the rosy light coming through the red curtains, glimpsing the shadowy necks of the kneeling women. They all wear great white veils and long gold or silver earrings. . . . How is your novel?. . . Think only of Art, of that and that alone, because that's all there is. Work! God ordains it. To me that seems clear. . . ."

Like most tourists, Flaubert visited picture galleries, and a canvas he saw in one of the Genoese palaces was to be the inspiration for an important part of his life's work: "[In Palazzo Balbi] I saw a picture by Breughel, *The Temptation of Saint Anthony,* which made me think of arranging it for the theater. But that would require someone very different from me." Flaubert did "arrange" the story of the Temptation of Saint Anthony in dramatic form, in three different versions spanning several decades of his life. The definitive version was published in 1874, when he was fifty-three. It was at last performed in a theater—the Odéon in Paris, directed by Maurice Béjart and acted by the Compagnie Renaud-Barrault—in 1967. Between covers, although far less read than *Madame Bovary,* the *Temptation* is still very much alive. A new English translation, by Kitty Mrosovsky, complete with informative introduction and notes, was published as recently as 1980—135 years after Flaubert saw the picture in Genoa.

Then on to Milan, where Flaubert, a good Latinist (though a poor Hellenist), breathes out his love of the classical world in another letter to his friend Alfred: "Once again I have left my beloved Mediterranean! At Genoa I bade it farewell with a strange sinking of the heart. I carry the love of antiquity in my entrails. I am moved to the utter depths of my being when I think of the

Roman keels that once cut the changeless, eternally un-
dulant waves of this ever youthful sea. Ah! When will
you and I stretch out on our bellies on the sands of
Alexandria or sleep in the shade of the plane trees of the
Hellespont?" From Geneva, in that same 1845, Flaubert
wrote about sights well known to visitors to Switzerland
today:

"Two days ago I saw Byron's name on one of the pillars of the dungeon where the prisoner of Chillon was
confined. The sight afforded me exquisite joy. I thought
more about Byron than about the prisoner. . . . All the
time, I thought of the pale man who came there one day,
walked up and down, wrote his name on the stone, and
left. One would have to be very daring or very stupid to
write one's own name in such a place after that. . . .
Among all the obscure names there I saw those of Victor
Hugo and George Sand. . . . Byron's name is scratched
on one side, and it is already black, as though ink had
been rubbed into it to make it show. It does in fact stand
out in the gray column, and one sees it the minute one enters. Below the name, the stone is a little eaten away, as
though the mighty hand that rested there had worn it
with its weight. I was sunk in contemplation before those
five letters.

"This evening, just now, I lit my cigar and walked to
a little island attached to the shore of the lake opposite
our hotel, called the Île Jean-Jacques because of
Pradier's statue [of Jean-Jacques Rousseau] which is
there. This island is a favorite promenade, where there is
music in the evening. When I arrived at the foot of the
statue, the brasses were playing softly. . . . Old
Rouseeau, on his pedestal, was listening to it all. . . .
At the two extremes of Lake Geneva there are two gen-

iuses who cast shadows loftier than those of the mountains: Byron and Rousseau. . . ."

In his letter to Le Poittevin from Marseilles, Flaubert
had written: "This is the second time I have seen the
Mediterranean like a grocer on holiday. Will the third
time be better?"

The "third time," four years later, did indeed prove to
be not only better, but the best—a marvelous, leisurely,
eighteen-month tour of Egypt, the Near East, Greece and
Italy with his friend Maxime DuCamp. (Le Poittevin,
with whom he had once hoped to travel, had died in the
interval; and dead too were Dr. Flaubert and Caroline.
Madame Flaubert gave only reluctant consent to
Gustave's long absence.) The "third time" is notable,
particularly, for its Egyptian phase—eight months spent
in Cairo and exploring the valley of the Nile by daha-
beah as far south as Nubia, with a side trip on camelback
across the desert to the Red Sea. Flaubert's letters from
Egypt, written chiefly to his mother and to his friend
Louis Bouilhet, have been translated into English, German, Italian and perhaps other languages, and are
carried by many modern travelers as an informal supple-
ment to their guidebooks. Flaubert's Egyptian tour,
recorded also in photographs made by his companion
—Maxime DuCamp was a pioneer of the camera—has
become one of the most celebrated of nineteenth-century
journeys. It was one of the highest points of Flaubert's
life before the writing and publication of *Madame
Bovary,* which took place during the years immediately
following his return to France.

In Constantinople (as Istanbul was still called in the
West), half in Europe, half in Asia, Flaubert was much
struck by a "tourist attraction" no longer visible today,
the sultans and their suites having long departed:

"I saw the mosques, the seraglio, Santa Sophia. In the seraglio, a dwarf, the sultan's dwarf, was playing with white eunuchs outside the throne room; the dwarf was hideous, expensively dressed in European style— gaiters, overcoat, watch chain. As for the eunuchs . . . I wasn't prepared for them. They look like nasty old women. The sight of them makes you nervous, and torments the imgination. You find yourself devoured by curiosity, and at the same time the bourgeois in you makes you loathe them. The antinormality of their appearance is a shock to one's virility. Explain that to me. No question, though, that they are one of the most curious products of the human hand. What wouldn't I have given, in the Orient, to become the friend of a eunuch! But they are unapproachable." Today the halls of the former seraglio in the Palace of Topkapi contain neither sultans nor eunuchs, but collections of art, jewels, and antiquities that make it one of the great museums.

From Greece, Flaubert wrote ecstatically: "Even after the Orient, Greece is beautiful. I was immensely moved by the Parthenon. It's as good as the Gothic, whatever anyone may say to the contrary; and above all, I think, it is harder to understand.

". . . Nature did everything for the Greeks— language, landscape, anatomy, the sun; even the forms of the mountains, which are as though sculptured, with lines more architectural than anywhere else.

". . . The choice of Delphi as the abode of the Pytho- ness was a stroke of genius. The landscape is one to inspire religious terrors—a narrow valley between two nearly perpendicular mountains, its floor a forest of dark olive trees, the mountains red and green; precipices on all sides, the sea in the distance, and snow-capped peaks on the horizon."

Flaubert's Europe

Today's traveler to Delphi will recognize the dramatic landscape that Flaubert describes. Eagles swoop down from Mount Parnassus and wheel overhead; far below are the sea and Flaubert's great olive groves—some of the trees ancient, perhaps the very ones he saw; up the hill, above the Castalian Spring, the Sacred Way winds to the theater and the stadium, the place of the Sacred Games.

"Among the pieces of sculpture found on the Acropolis," Flaubert wrote in the same letter, "I noticed especially a bas-relief representing a woman fastening her shoe. There remains only a fragment of the torso, just the two breasts, from the base of the neck to above the navel. One of the breasts is draped, the other bare. What breasts! Good God! What a breast! It is apple-round, full, abundant, widely spaced from the other: you can feel the weight of it in your hand. Its ripe maternity and its love-sweetness make you swoon. The rain and sun have turned the white marble to yellow, a tawny color, almost like flesh. It is so calm, so noble! It seems about to swell; one feels that the lungs beneath it are about to expand and breathe. How well it wore its sheer pleated drapery!. . ." And his letter to Bouilhet from Naples and its region would be approved by present-day Neapolitans:

"Ah, poor fellow, how I missed you at Pompeii! I enclose some flowers I picked in a lupanar. . . . There were more flowers in that house than in any other. . . .

"I saw Pozzuoli, Lake Lucrinus, Baiae—each of them an earthly Paradise. The emperors had good taste. I melted with melancholy in those places.

"Like a tourist, I climbed to the top of Vesuvius and arrived exhausted. The crater is strange. Sulphur has accumulated around the edges in weird growths, yellow and purplish-red. I have been to Paestum. I was set on going to Capri; and very nearly remained there—in the deep. Despite my prowess as a boatman, I thought my last hour had come, and I confess I was worried and even afeared, much afeared. I was within an inch of annihilation, like Rome at the worst moments of the Punic wars. . . .

"Naples is a charming city thanks to its great numbers of pimps and whores. One quarter is garrisoned with girls who stand in their doorways: it's like the antique world, a real Suburra. . . .

"Naples is the place to come for a bath in the fountain of youth and to fall in love with life all over again. The sun itself is enamored of the place. Everything is gay and easy. The ears of the horses are decked with bunches of peacock feathers.

"The Chiaia is a long shorefront promenade, rows of live oaks arching overhead and the sea murmuring alongside. The newlyweds sitting there on moonlit nights warm their behinds on benches made of lava. The immemorial heat of the volcanoes reaches their hearts by way of their buttocks: they squeeze each other's hands and choke with emotion. I envy them their sensations." Since Flaubert's day, the Riviera di Chiaia, the "long shorefront promenade," has been separated from the sea by a narrow landfill along which runs the boulevard called Via Caracciolo; and there is a notable addition to the scene—the famous Naples Aquarium, founded in 1872 by Anton Dohrn and deserving of a visit by any tourist. But the "rows of live oaks," or their beautiful descendants, remain; as do the benches—made of concrete, today—and the lovers seated there.

In Rome, Flaubert was joined by his mother. His sightseeing became respectable, and together they returned to Croisset. Almost immediately he began to write

Flaubert's Europe

Madame Bovary. No greater contrast can be imagined than that offered by the stark novel of provincial Normandy and the great exotic sights he had just seen.

Flaubert's later life was devoted almost entirely to the long, sedentary labor of writing his novels, at Croisset or in his apartment in Paris, with occasional explorations of the French provinces for purposes of documentation. Probably his happiest French journeys were the two visits he paid his friend George Sand at her charming country house at Nohant, south of Bourges (open to the public today), where the two writers filled their days with conversation, readings from each other's works, parlor games, and watching performances by Maurice Sand's marionettes. There were occasional trips to England, to be with Juliet Herbert, his niece's former governess— visits regarding which he was always discreetly evasive. On one occasion—unwillingly, on doctor's orders—he spent a few weeks in Switzerland. "I'd give all the glaciers for the Vatican Museum," he wrote George Sand from Kaltbad Rigi; and to his friend Ivan Turgenev:

". . . I'm colossally bored. . . . I'm no man of Nature—her 'wonders' move me less than those of Art. She overwhelms me, without inspiring me with any 'great thoughts.' I feel like telling her: 'All right, all right, I just left you, I'll be back with you in a few minutes; leave me alone, I need other kinds of amusement.' Besides, the Alps are out of scale with our little selves. They're too big to be useful to us. . . . And then my fellow vacationers—the honorable foreigners living in this hotel! All Germans or English, equipped with walking sticks and field glasses. Yesterday I was tempted to kiss three calves that I met in a meadow, out of sheer humanity and a need to be demonstrative. . . ."

This account of Flaubert's European travels may be

closed with a little-known letter he wrote not in Europe but on shipboard after setting out from Marseilles for North Africa in April 1858. He had begun his second novel, the Carthaginian *Salammbô;* it was not going well, and he felt a need to see the site of the ancient Punic city, destroyed by Rome. On the steamer *Hermus* that was taking him across the Mediterranean, he wrote to Bouilhet:

"It's a beautiful night, the sea flat as a lake of oil, old Tanit [the moon] is shining, the ship's engine panting, the captain smoking beside me on his sofa, and the deck packed solid with Arabs Mecca-bound. Barefoot, swathed in their white burnouses, their faces covered, they look like shrouded corpses. There are women, too, with their children. The entire lot are sleeping, or wretchedly vomiting. We are skirting the coast of Tunisia, visible in the mist. Tomorrow morning we'll be at Tunis; I'm not going to bed—I want to miss none of this lovely night. Besides, my impatience to see Carthage would keep me awake."

And he goes on to share with Bouilhet what we have seen to be one of his earliest travel memories—in his erotic initiation by Madame Foucaud at her Marseilles hotel:

". . . All is changed! The ground floor, then the salon of the hotel, is now a bazaar, and upstairs there is a barbershop. I went there twice to be shaved. I spare you any Châteaubriandesque comments and reflections on the flight of time, on falling leaves and falling hair. No matter: it's a long while since I have thought—or is it felt—so deeply. . . ." Each man remembers his own particular Madame Foucaud. Flaubert forgot nothing; and much of his life's work has its origins in his earliest experiences, including the traveling he did when he was young. As with all reflective travelers, it was not only the memory of the sights themselves that he took away with him but the thoughts and expanded tastes that these gave rise to. It was after Flaubert returned from his second journey—the one in which he saw the picture of St. Anthony—that he came to his famous conclusion: "The three finest things God ever made are the sea, *Hamlet*, and Mozart's *Don Giovanni.*" Jottings in travel diaries and letters can be fascinating—sometimes as an involuntary sketch for the enriched personality already developing as a consequence of the journey.

TOURING THE NOVELIST'S NORMANDY

ROUEN

The city where Flaubert was born is eighty miles northwest of Paris, an easy drive from the capital on the Autoroute de Normandie. By train it is a journey of about an hour and fifteen minutes from Paris St.-Lazare station and the fare is about $11 one way in first class, about $8 in second class (double these fares for round trip).

SIGHTSEEING

Flaubert was born at the **Hôtel-Dieu,** where his parents had an apartment and his father worked as a surgeon. The building, at 52 Rue de Lecat, a few blocks north of the Guillaume-le-Conquérant Bridge, is now a museum devoted to Flaubert and to the history of medicine. Family souvenirs and nineteenth-century surgical instruments are among the exhibits.

The city's vast architectural heritage can best be appreciated by wandering through the narrow streets. The **Cathedral of Notre Dame** has an impressive façade

covered with detailed decoration and statuary dominated by two towers. There is a lofty spire. Rouen is
still, as Flaubert knew it, a city of churches and spires.
Though the cathedral and many of the churches have remained intact, much of the city has been rebuilt.
Rouen's history is, of course, linked with Joan of Arc,
and Flaubert must have often walked along the Rue du
Donjon past the Tour Jeanne d'Arc, where she was imprisoned.

ROOMS AND MEALS

The 125-room **Frantel Rouen** is in the old town
and close to the cathedral; double room, about $50;

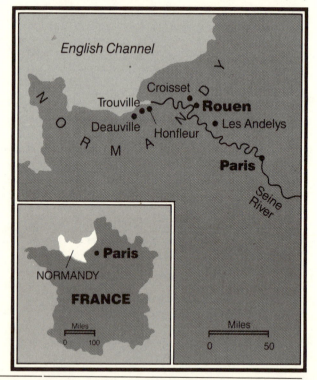

breakfast, about $5 a person. Another central hotel is the smaller **Hôtel de Dieppe,** about $35 for a double, breakfast about $3 a person. The **Novotel,** which has 133 rooms, is about three miles from town in the Parc des Expositions; about $35 for a double, breakfast about $3 a person. **La Couronne** occupies a fourteenth-century Norman house on the Place du Vieux-Marché. Specialties: *filets de sole Normandie* and *caneton à la Rouennaise* (roast duckling, mustard, spices and red wine). There are three set menus, ranging from about $15 to $25.

NEARBY

Four miles west of town, at **Croisset,** is a pavilion, now a museum, that is all that is left of the country house where Flaubert wrote *Madame Bovary* and did much of his other writing. It contains many personal souvenirs. Hours: 10 A.M. to noon and 2 to 6 P.M. The museum is closed all day Tuesday, Wednesday morning and occasional days in winter. There is a small admission fee. Flaubert's library is preserved in the mayor's office at neighboring Canteleu-Croisset and can be seen by arrangement. From the high ground in this area there is a fine panorama of Rouen.

Les Andelys, twenty miles southeast of Rouen, is dominated by the ruins of the Château Gaillard, which Flaubert liked to explore as a boy. The fortress was built beside the Seine by Richard the Lion-Hearted in 1196 for the defense of Normandy. The highest of the five towers remains. Michelin gives the ruins two stars as an attraction. There is also a thirteenth- to seventeenth-century Gothic and Renaissance church.

DEAUVILLE AND TROUVILLE

These neighboring resorts on the Channel coast can be reached by taking the autoroute from Paris, a journey of about 130 miles. By train from the Paris St.-Lazare station it is an hour and a half, but time must be added for

·the connection made at Lisieux. Fare: about $20 one way first class; about $15 in second.

Deauville, the larger and more fashionable of the two, is the leading bathing resort in Normandy, and it has fine gardens, beach, racecourse and yacht club. Visitors like to stroll—as in Flaubert's day—along the two-mile-long boardwalk. Many French families spend vacations at Trouville, which has a boardwalk as well as a casino.

ROOMS AND MEALS

At Deauville, major hotels include the **Royal** and the **Normandy,** both of which have more than 300 rooms and some apartments. Both overlook the sea. At the Royal, a double room on the sea side is about $115 in the high season, about $80 in the low season; on the land side, the range is about $95 to $65. At the Normandy, a double is about $95 to $85, depending on the season.

There are other, smaller hotels. The well-regarded **Ciro's,** on the boardwalk, serves lunch only (about $20 a person). Trouville hotels are generally smaller. The three-star **Bellevue,** which is open from June to October and has sixty-seven rooms, charges about $50 for a double room with bath. The St.-James charges about $60 for a double, including partial board, in the high season, and about $90 for full board; in the low season the prices are about $60 and $75, plus a 15 percent service change. The **Maison Normande** charges about $20 for a double without board.

Visitors in search of superior dining can drive about ten miles along the coast to Honfleur and the hotel called the **Ferme St.-Siméon**. The specialties are *navarin de homard* (lobster), *râble de lapereau* (saddle of young rabbit) and *feuillete aux pommes* (apples in puff pastry). Dinner: about $30 a person. In Trouville, **Le Provençal** (about $15 a person) and **La Petite Auberge** (about $10) are favored restaurants.

D-Day Plus 40 Years

JOHN VINOCUR

OINTE DU HOC IS A knife, stood on its edge, pointed into the sea. It looks lethal, a palisade of boulder and mean rocks where Normandy's green softness has reclaimed nothing. Battlefields: You could walk them from Gettysburg to Waterloo, and go back to your car, thinking of lunch. But not at Pointe du Hoc. The brightest morning roughens there, the wind working like a rasp, still scoring cruel edges on the sheer cliffs. On D-Day, the U.S. Army's Second Ranger Battalion had to climb the knife's blade through bullets and shells. Today, looking down to the sea from the viewpoint of the German machine-gun emplacements, imagination becomes superfluous. The emotions are all immediate and distinct: My God, they made it to the top; this is still a cruel place; it holds the mark of a killing ground.

Pointe du Hoc is special. For the most part, the pastoral blanket of Normandy covers over any sense of the fury, the dying, and the scale involved in the thrust of 180,000 Allied troops into Europe on the sixth of June 1944. The pastures are too lush, the land too rich with apple orchards and rose arbors. In Normandy, near the beaches, the war burned fast. There is no complaint, of course—the Allies rushed through the nearby countryside, and were soon gone; eleven months after D-Day, Hitler's Europe fell. Occasionally, a speech will resemble the regrown landscape and turn the invasion to whole glory, leaving the dead as a detail. Reality was something else. In the first twenty-five hours, the U.S. First Army had 6,603 casualties; two months later, the Americans had to use bulldozers to clear a passage through the 40,000 German corpses at Chambois to the south.

Normandy, its landscape healed, soothes mostly, and holds tightly to its emotions. They are there, although not much at Utah or Omaha beaches, or in the invasion museums, where models of the engineering feats have the look of Erector sets, and the old uniforms seem like rock band gear from costume shops. The sense of war, the extraordinary bravery of the Allied armies, the numbers, the losses, the real suffering that disappears in time and commemorative oratory, are not marked out in any red guidebook of the emotions, but they are present if you look.

I went to the D-Day beaches for the first time in May 1969, expecting no feelings at all. Europe seemed so rich and self-content that it was hard to believe that the United States had to come to help. World War II felt terribly long ago then; in 1969 there was too much war going between my own contemporaries, all of it bad, the just cause not having leaped the generational gap. I had just returned from Biafra reporting on a ghastly and lunatic war of starved children and big oil interests, and the news in the papers was of Hamburger Hill, the tag name for a place the U.S. Army was having trouble capturing in Vietnam. The stories made clear that there were grunts who did not want to go into the fire, and the accounts, I thought, were written with the sympathy of the times, and probably often read that way too.

I got to Pointe du Hoc mostly by accident then because the road was not well marked and seemed to peter out in the fields. The wind jumps up from the sea as you get closer, and the fields begin to roll and dip, cratered by the Allied offshore bombardment. At the edge of the cliffs, the wind is a smack, and D-Day becomes wildly clear: climbing that cutting edge into the bullets. The first men came up on rope, and then ladders belonging to the London Fire Department. The Germans, firing down at them, even rolling boulders over the precipice, killed more Americans in the first wave than those who got to the top.

The day I was there, a man paced around Pointe du Hoc as if he were taking measurements for a linoleum company. His name was Robert Fruling, he worked in a spare parts department in West Palm Beach, Florida, and he was looking around because he had come up the cliffs as a Ranger. I heard how he got hell for losing the radio he was toting, and how a bullet went through his helmet, kindly following a path that avoided his head. He talked about the place with a kind of chirpy good humor for a while and then he stopped. About 75 men in the 235 he came ashore with survived. "We got it, and we got it," he said, and turned away. He bent over, shaking with sobs.

There is as much death as glory now at Pointe du Hoc, and somehow, in a recriminating Europe of the 1980s, a continent of disenchantment, the battlefield and D-Day seem more real than in 1969. Do we discuss going up the cliff? Not here. Pointe du Hoc offers its own conclusions, a battlefield never gone quite still.

The quiet lies elsewhere, its emotions strong. The American cemetery at St.-Laurent-sur-Mer is a great lawn at the edge of the sea, white marble crosses and Stars of David against an open horizon. It is a graceful, light, uncomplicated place. I think of it as very American in the best sense: no phony piety, simple, easy. The graves are the message, and they are left alone: long rows, long rows, long rows. Unequivocal. The monument is inscribed with monument-inscription language, but minus the tremolo, it is right: "This embattled shore, portal of freedom, is forever hallowed by the ideas, valor and sacrifice of our fellow countrymen." At Cambe, near Isigny, away from the sea, and off a main road, there is a German cemetery. It is a very different place, a powerful one, not so simple, not so certain, one that is more of this than the other time. The headstones are low and dark, almost black, looking like Knight's Crosses. The grass is let to grow high, and it moves in the wind against the dark stones. The Germans executed scores of French hostages at Caen, nearby, the night of the invasion, but no one has ever touched, tried to vandalize, these graves. They have extraordinary dignity. As much as St.-Laurent seems American in its emotions, as much as it seems to reflect the right war and its cost, La Cambe strikes me as German; it has real beauty, and a dark, melancholy strength.

How do you mark the graves of a defeated army, fighting for monstrous goals, on the land of a country it had conquered? "Here lie German soldiers," one inscription says. On a pedestal in the same dark stone, old parents huddle and grieve. And this, chiseled deep: "God has the last word."

The Sevillano Spirit

V. S. PRITCHETT

NOT LONG AGO I WAS again in Seville, the most sparkling and intimate of Spanish cities. I have been there many times in the last sixty years. My vanity is that I am pre-mass-tourism, pre–Civil War, pre-Hemingway; I even wrote my first short story in Seville.

Ancient now, I sat on the terrace of the Río Grande restaurant, looking across the river, the Guadalquivir, trying to identify the quarter where I stayed when I was young.

Old Seville is a tangle of red roofs and low white houses in the main, out of which a few tall palm trees like mad pashas wag their heads, but it masses at the center round the gigantic cathedral—the third largest in the world. The tall Giralda tower, the minaret of a mosque that was destroyed in the early thirteenth century, rises high above the flamboyant temple. The city has a fine Moorish Alcázar, dozens of sedate churches, but in fact it is a place of secret gardens, a city of flowers, clean, bright, gay and crowded with lively people as it has been for centuries. Around it are new high-rise suburbs.

In sixty years Seville has doubled its population, and since my early times there it has leapt out of the Middle Ages and into the modern world. As I sat by the river I could hear the noise of bulldozers and drills; Seville is building a Metro! What a typical bombastic, theatrical gesture of the incurably theatrical city, trying to catch up with Madrid, even Moscow!

But why not? In the great century of Columbus, Magellan, Cortés and Amerigo Vespucci, when the Dutch, British and Spaniards were fighting for sea power and a share in the rape of the New World, Seville was one of the richest cities in the world, rich on the trade and the gold the conquistadors brought back to the elegant little tower, the Torre del Oro, on the waterside opposite where I was eating. Here the discoverers had embarked, here they had returned.

Near the cathedral stands the grand Archive of the Indies where exhaustive histories of the discoveries and the colonizing of Central and South America are stored. Cervantes himself was allured by the boom. There is a letter from him applying for an official job abroad. He was turned down, perhaps because he was in prison for dabbling in public funds.

Seville is a nocturnal city; its narrow streets, its grilled and shaded windows were built to keep out the intolerable sun of the hot months. Gardens or patios were placed in the cool center of the houses and even public buildings. You cool off in two pillared courtyards before you get to the official buildings. Formal from the outside, these places are intimate within. Even the open gardens of the Alcázar are designed in shrub-boxed patios where a little fountain tinkles, where the seats are done in pretty tiles. The palms, the lemon and orange trees, the flowering shrubs, the tall trees with the jasmine entwining their trunks create a lacework of scented shade.

The Sevillano Spirit

The same genius for creating outdoor rooms and halls can be seen in the superb María Luisa Park. The talkative Sevillano loves his privacies. One is so often near the sound of talkative water, for the Moors taught the Christians the art of irrigation. Even Andalusian speech —which is loud—has a mystifying, chattering, spurtling flow to it, for the Sevillanos throw out most of the consonants of their words and leave only the vowels running together like marbles or pebbles in the mouth. Or, to change the metaphor, one might be listening to one of those long fast runs of the gypsy's guitar. It is hard to get one's foreign ear into this accent. (It is mocked as a farce in precise and classical Castile.)

My first landlady in Spain was an Andalusian and broke me in to this talk, and indeed the women's voices manage to ripple with more sweetness than the men's. The Sevillano, though good at the rhetorical shout, relieves the tension by a passion for the diminutive ending. A flower is a little or tiny little flower, a dog is a tiny little dog, a glass, a little glass. Even a bull can be teasingly and affectionately called *torito.* Perhaps the habit springs from the love of minute embroidery or decoration, a love of the ingenious, fantastic and the clever little detail. (Think of Velázquez's treatment of every thread of silk in the gorgeous clothes of Philip IV; the minute care for the wrinkles on a hand or the shape of a fingernail.) The delight in detail is a kind of visual wit.

The ordinary Sevillano is a natural fountain of wit and ingenious jokes; he longs for you to cap them, to vie with his vanity—even to the point of putting on a poker-faced show of sly stupidity as he speaks. You'll never match him, for you haven't his native gift of momentarily taking leave of himself and becoming a little universe. And he is notorious for his childish jokes. I have seen the most respectable member of one of those clubs in Sierpes, the pedestrian street, stealthily approaching a dozing old gentleman and slowly trickling a bowl of sugar over his head. Such things (as they say) "pass the time."

Two mythical figures emerge from popular fantasy: the boasting Don Juan, who, if he had an original, may have come from the Spanish colony in Naples, and Figaro, the witty, even revolutionary barber. (I myself had the best haircut of my life this time in Seville—I have little hair left, and it calls for the artist in arabesque and trifles.) But there is a point at which the *burla,* or jest or trick, becomes licentious or wicked. So, in the myth, Don Juan is called the *burlador* of Seville because he is the brawling jester, but *"burla"* is also the sexual act, the deceit and seduction of women. There are two paintings of a part-Corsican, Don Juan–like gentleman, Miguel de Manara, in the Hospice for the Poor, which he founded after a licentious life. He repented and, in remorse, ordered two supposed portraits of himself by the Sevillian artist Valdès Leal. One represents a richly dressed skeleton, dangling a pan of jewels in one hand and a collection of bones in the other; on his velvet cape cockroaches are crawling. Manara's tomb is inscribed with a boast: "Here lies the worst man in the world."

Romantic Spanish writers, and foreigners, too, have written about the Spanish preoccupation with love and death. There are other interpretations of the Don Juan myth. In the 1920s, the dramatist Benavente wrote an anti–Don Juan play in which he is presented not as the Prince of Seducers but as a boaster who holds his strictly male cronies spellbound with fantasies of successes they themselves have failed to achieve.

In my young days, the males of Seville were noted for

their shouts of gallant or not so gallant remarks about the women. At the sight of a woman on the street they passed remarks like "What a tall one!" or "Look at this fat one" or "Here comes one with the salt in her! What a jewel." Foreign tourists were often annoyed or scared (or slapped the jesters down), and the city even passed a law against these salutes. Spanish women loved them and laughed at the fusses of timid northerners. In modern Seville, where the southern, almost Oriental segregation of the sexes has been dead for a generation, there are no more *dueñas.* The sweet, demure, dumpy Sevillanas, who used to seem like copies of the sentimental Virgins painted by Murillo, and who went out only in twos and threes with their very proper friends between five and seven o'clock in the evenings, have gone. The girl student, dressed in jeans and chattering with young men, is the changed creature of today. A handsome woman in a well-cut uniform controls the traffic near the Plaza Nueva.

Seville itself has changed. There are far fewer beggars—or the profession has become more sophisticated. The begging gypsy girls with their babies are scarce. One I did see had moved with the times. Her beat was not at a church or hotel door: She stepped into the traffic as it stopped at the lights. Stately, and a dyed blonde, she put her hand into the open windows of the cars. At the same time her young man, who had a long stick capped with a rubber swab, deftly bent forward and cleaned the windshield. No taker that I ever saw, but patiently the couple tried every day.

Another change, since the Spanish Civil War, is that the large population of strolling priests, often fat, shabby and smoking cigars, has gone from the streets or is in mufti.

Again, the food of Seville was never good, except for the fish that came up from Cádiz; canned paella was terrible, meals dragged on. Now, there are good restaurants tucked away in the little streets. In the old days, the reek of rancid olive oil and the charcoal stove used to pour out of the doorways; now electricity has killed the charcoal. An elderly Spaniard summed it up by saying gloomily, "Seville is, alas, no longer medieval. Now it is modern, anonymous. The twentieth century has killed it. The old Spain is dead."

This is not quite true, at any rate, of the supreme moment of the city's life, the fiesta of Holy Week and the Feria of horse-riding that follows it. Holy Week is still one of the world's extraordinary pieces of theater. The whole population is out on the streets day and night in a week of processions from every quarter, watching the images of the Virgin or of the Christ, followed by the brotherhoods of *cofradías* of their parish churches. Forty-five images of the Virgin, some of great beauty and extravagant in ornament, do their twelve-hour journey to the cathedral and then back to their parishes. There are forty-five floats carrying the Christ. Escorts of military bands and soldiers are followed by the members of the *cofradías* in their frightening tall slit-eyed conical hats. We are back in the times of the Inquisition. The public emotion is immense, very pagan and personal. Cries of amorous love are shouted at the Virgin. "I love you! You are my sweetheart! Throw me one of your jewels as a keepsake, darling," even, "The others are whores compared with you." La Macarena is the goddess of the city.

In all Spanish ceremonies the actors are casual. A man in that Inquisitional hat will slip out for a quick beer and race back when the cortège rests for a moment. The crowd rushes to give food and drink to the exhausted bearers who, concealed beneath curtains, carry the floats, which weigh tons.

I shall never forget my first sight of Holy Week back in the twenties. My landlady and her son, a young doctor, were passionately determined that I should hear the *Miserere* sung at the cathedral. A complete Sevillano, the doctor set out with me lazily, telling me he had scores of friends in high places who would see that I got the best place in the cathedral. We went from plaza to plaza, running into dozens of these special geniuses who knew how to bring off his "impossible" plan.

Suddenly, we were making our way through the dense crowd outside the cathedral and were at a little door at the side of it. I was pushed up a steep staircase in the dark; there was a sudden blaze of golden light and I found myself in the choir and in the ranks of the priests in their gorgeous vestments. They were mainly old men, chanting with their huge parchment books before them, and I saw I was within a few yards of the archbishop standing before the high blazing sheet of gold that seemed to rise behind the altar to the top of the cathedral. Was the archbishop staring at the young heretic in mufti, the blot on the scene, the one who couldn't chant?

I was terrified. The doctor had pushed me in and left me. Every now and then he poked his nose in to see how I was doing. I have never felt so alone in my life. I was in the situation of Don Quixote when he found himself among the Enchanters and went finally mad. My memory wavers—was it at this moment I heard suddenly the voice of the famous tenor of those days, Tito Schipa, rise to the high moment of Eslava's *Miserere?* That was unforgettable. At last the doctor got me out and we walked the streets for the rest of the soft night.

On my most recent visit I contented myself with the high mass to celebrate a Jubilation of the Family. The families and their children, in their thousands, rambled about during the service, crowding round their favorite side chapels, trooping into the sanctuary where the treasures of the cathedral are on show and where Columbus is said to be buried. The cathedral with its vast aisles was their common plaza and they crowded also into the cloisters, where the oranges hang on the trees. Small groups listened to the sermon coming out in a lordly nasal voice over the public address system. We might have been in a grandiose railway terminal waiting for the excursion train to take us all to heaven.

I did find the quarter where I first lived, after a search. It lay downriver, well past the bullring that looks like a pretty, deceiving cake outside, in a quiet district near the art museum. The museum, one of the happiest small galleries I know, was a suitable ending for my pilgrimage. The attraction is not only in its Murillos and Zurbaráns but in that they hang in a serene and intimate little place built round two pillared patios (it was once a convent, then a Jesuit seminary). One can *see* the pictures. No mustiness, no gallery feet here. Seville now considers the dignity of its pictures, gives them space and air to breathe in. And, for myself, it is these painters that in the end tell most about the untroubled domesticity of a city whose people are so given to the fantastic.

SEVILLE À LA CARTE
  HOTELS AT THE CENTER
  Alfonso XIII, San Fernando 2 (telephone: 22-28-

50), is a Moorish-Spanish fantasy, complete with pool and gardens, built in the 1920s. Some rooms overlook the gardens of the Alcázar. Double rooms are about $85, suites about $150. The bar is a fashionable meeting place.

Colon, Canalejas 1 (22-29-00), is another 1920s building, this time in the modern style, situated near the bullring. Double rooms are about $35, suites about $75.

Doña María, 19 Don Remondo, in the Barrio Santa Cruz (22-49-90), is installed in a building that dates from the turn of the nineteenth century. Each room is decorated differently and some have views of the Giralda; there is a roof garden with a swimming pool. Double rooms are about $50 to $55.

Macarena, San Juan de Ribera 2 (37-57-00), was built in the 1970s and has an inner courtyard with a fountain. One of the quieter places to stay during Holy Week, except when the image of the Virgin of the Macarena leaves or returns to her shrine just across the street. Double rooms cost up to $85, suites from about $170 to $200.

TYPICAL TABLES

The hotels listed above, with the exception of the Doña María, have restaurants serving Andalusian specialties. Other choices for catching some of the flavor of the city:

Río Grande, Betis (27-39-56), with a riverside terrace facing the Torre del Oro, has such specialties as *frito variado sevillano* (five different kinds of fried fish) and *toro la cucho* (bull's tail stew with potatoes); dinner for two, with wine, is about $30.

La Albahaca, 12 Plaza de Santa Cruz, in the Barrio Santa Cruz (22-07-14), has such regional dishes as garlic soup, *salmonete río viejo* (red mullet) and tournedos Albahaca; dinner for two, with wine, is about $20.

Rincon de Curro, Virgen de Lujan 45 (45-02-38), lists Andalusian-style bull's tail stew, *entrecôte al plato* *caliente* (steak served on a sizzling clay plate) and sliced tongue in sherry; dinner for two with wine is about $35.

Casa Senra, Becquer 45 (37-03-38), in the Macarena quarter, serves such simple regional fare as *punta de solomillo senra* (loin of pork), *frito sevillano* (fried fish) and gazpacho; about $20 for dinner for two, with wine.

El Rinconcillo, 42 Calle Gerona (22-31-83), has been an inn since 1670. For drinks and *tapas,* the Spanish hors d'oeuvres; about $10 to $15 for two.

The Ghostly Glory of Vienna

ANTHONY BURGESS

I HAD PREVIOUSLY KNOWN Vienna in spring and autumn—the right seasons for, respectively, Johann and Richard Strauss (*Voices of Spring;* last act of *Der Rosenkavalier*). This time I arrived just before Shrove Tuesday and in the bleak fag-end of the Central European winter. I'd traveled by train from Hamburg, by way of Cologne, Stuttgart, Zurich and Munich. German trains are wonderful, dead on time to the second, their efficiency unimpaired by strikes or the bloodymindedness of railroad scrimshankers, their shining galleys ready all journey long with anything from a sausage to a carpetbag steak.

But in winter it is perhaps better to travel than to arrive. It was not Vienna's fault if the weather was chill and dank and the Danube looked like gray dishwater. It is, of course, unfair to Vienna to expect it to fulfill dreams about love under the lindens and open-air string orchestras dispensing schmaltz salted with the faint clang of the zither. There is the city of *The Third Man,* where it is too cold for pigeons to brood on the head of a statue of Franz Josef. (Anton Karas, by the way, who played the zither music for that film, for a while had his own restaurant, called inevitably, Der Dritte Mann.) The winter city looks grim, but it knows how to keep carnival, which starts well before Christmas. I got to Vienna in time for the sumptuous pre-Lent ball held in the State Opera House.

This was an affair of white tie and tails, pearly bosoms, flashing jewels, with the whipped cream of Central European society sweating under the chandeliers as they jigged to rock or swirled to Strauss. Yet there was something artificial and nostalgic about it. It evoked a dead empire, when the imperial metropolis Vienna was a point of the triangle completed by Budapest and Prague. Prague does not glitter these days: Under the empire, the elite thought nothing of going there for the premiere of Mozart's *Don Giovanni.* Budapest, which is only a brief drive away, opens ready-enough gates and is perhaps the most tolerable capital of the whole Communist bloc.

Nevertheless, one is aware of a cold eastern wind blowing on to Vienna. Losing its empire, it went into a decline. With Hitler's Anschluss, it participated in the prospect of a world Reich. After Yalta it became, like the imperial port Trieste, a door opening onto the Russian steppes. Sightseeing in Vienna is mostly snooping on the glorious past. The good architecture is impressive baroque and wedding-cake rococo, and it all celebrates the Hapsburg dynasty. The modern age is typified by anonymous office blocks, which dimly glorify commerce, and by the statue to the Red Army, an onerous gift from the Soviet Union, whose liberation of the city (the Viennese called it looting and raping) the Russians will not allow the Viennese to forget.

The Austro-Hungarian Empire was, some of us believe, far superior to the Roman or the British. By its fruits shall ye know it—Metastasio, Haydn, Mozart, Beethoven, Schubert, all the Strausses; Hofmannsthal and Rilke and Schnitzler; Freud and Adler; the uneasy Jewish atonalists. Joyce's *Ulysses* was perhaps its last great literary product—started in Trieste as it was, at the edge of a crazy elegant ambience where the secret police were omnipresent but inefficient. Vienna thrilled all Europe and was a staple of popular ballads. It jetted out the spicy aroma of goulash or Turkish coffee. The goulash is still there, flavored with caraway, and the coffeehouses are crowded, but you will find no new Freud at a *Stammtisch,* nor see a new Schubert scribbling songs on the backs of menus.

Still, a coffeehouse is a fine place to be in snowy weather. It is a typical Viennese institution, springing from two unexpected sources. The first was the old apothecary's trade, which held the medicinal monopoly of sugar: This became the stuff of exquisite pastries, once munched only by the aristocracy but later, as the revolutionary spirit blew in from France, turned into a democratic right. The second dates from the seventeenth-century Siege of Vienna, when the retreating Turks left a sack of coffee beans behind, which spilled their heady scent onto the cobbles. The breakfast croissant is more Viennese than French: It has rendered the once threatening moon of Islam merely succulent. Viennese pastries are too good—the heart and soul of the *Jause,* or snack, they silt up the arteries very satisfactorily, abetted by the *Schlagobers,* or whipped cream, that crowns the coffee.

We had better dispose of the Viennese cuisine before

we go any further. It's a heavy cuisine that renders Viennese evenings quiet and torpid: After the meal, the soldier-citizens climb slowly to bed. Soup is a meal in itself. Take *Brandteigkrappeln,* with its milk, butter, eggs, flour, semolina and nourishing floating bits of fat meat. Or *Brösel* or *Gries* or *Leberknödel.* There is a fine *Gulaschsuppe,* which you can eat at five in the morning if you have been out on the town. You can eat *Apfelstrudel* after dinner, but you can also have bits of *Strudel* (salted, not sweetened) floating in your soup. The greatest of the main dishes is the beefy *Tafelspitz,* which seems purely Austrian—a necessary thing to say when you consider that, like most imperial capitals, Vienna has drawn on the provinces or even outlying foreign territories for its kitchen. Thus *Wienerschnitzel* comes from Milan, and paprika from Hungary. The Austrians don't like to serve things without sauces, whose spiciness points eastward when they're not homely compounds of chopped leeks or onions, dill or gherkin.

You can still eat well at the old places—the Weisser Rauchfangkehrer in Weihburggasse, in the center of the city, or, of course, the Sacher, whose *Tafelspitz* is superb and expensive: The Sacher gives its name to the delectable *Sachertorte,* which those with circulatory problems ought merely to gaze upon. The Drei Husaren, also on Weihburggasse, is pure Hungarian, and the Zum Stadtkrug, just across the street, has light music, which you've a right to expect in a Viennese eating house. The conservative, if cosmopolitan, cuisine of the city and its environs (Grinzing, for instance) has not been severely dented by the fast-food cult (which is aflame in Paris) or the impatience of the young, who see food only as instant fuel.

Vienna displays charm still, even in winter, though

capitalist pragmatism and socialist dogmatism alike regard charm as old hat and time-wasting. This means, I suppose, that charm has something to do with flirtatious leisure, a property of the pretty ladies in Schnitzler's novels, and that Vienna, like Paris but unlike London, is a woman's city.

Vienna's women are aware of the reality of sexual magnetism. It would be dangerous to think in terms of a *type* of Viennese woman, though I carry away with me, now as before, images of svelte dark-haired sirens rather than big-boned Brünnhildes. This, after all, is not Germany. The men, like everybody in Europe these days, look Irish or Turkish and probably are; the women are not quite Slav and not quite Italian. You will see them shopping in Kärntnerstrasse, which leads from the opera house to the cathedral, or in the Graben, just off St. Stephen's Square, where there are boutiques and fashion stores. This is still a city where women buy evening dresses or ball gowns, and one that still manufactures top hats for men. It is also a place where striptease cabarets are not picketed by women's groups, and where the advertisements for escort services (some of them in Arabic) promise, perhaps, more than you will get. "If you wish nice company?" says one coyly. "Come and meet the most charming and elegant ladies of Vienna." This invitation is illustrated by a charmer too nude to be elegant. Oh, I don't know, though.

The masculine aspects of the city can, as a prelude to wandering, be best seen from the belfry at the top of the cathedral. I climbed up there and agonized in a shark-toothed wind. There it all is to the west—the Ring and the Hapsburg palaces, the Rathaus and the Burgtheater, the Staatsoper and the museums. And to the east is the Danube Canal and the Franz-Josefs-Kai. To the north-

northwest is Black Spaniard Street or Schwärzspanier-strasse, leading into Freud territory. No. 19 Berggasse (a *Gasse* being smaller than a *Strasse*) is the Freud museum. The street, with its parked cars and gaudy sport shops, is not what the master knew. The master, exiled from a city that he had always regarded as anti-Semitic and obscurantist, died in London, and you can buy a phonograph record in which he speaks from the dead in precise English tortured by the clicks of his prosthesis. But he is alive, more alive than ever, though the museum was empty when I went to see it.

I said earlier that Vienna is not, despite the memory of the Anschluss, Germany territory. Austrian is not High German, and Germans need a glossary to tell them that *"a,"* as in English, means *"ein"* and *"eine"* alike, and that an *"achterl"* is *"ein kleines Glas Wein."* With an Austrian ruling the Third Reich, the Viennese could feel they had a stake in it; now they joke about sending to Berlin an Austrian they didn't particularly want. There is the kind of perky inferiority complex, expressed as contempt, toward Germany that Australians feel toward England. The Austrians are not as efficient as the Germans, and they know it: They have too much charm, a concern with *dolce far niente,* and they are still touched by the breath of a great dead civilization. But they are aware of no longer being in the middle of things, of that cold Soviet blast from the East. The native name for Austria, Österreich, like the Nazi Östmark, refers to an eastern empire, but the Latin name Austria, like Australia, refers to the south wind, which is warm and ripens the grapes. Incidentally, Anglo-American spelling is becoming sketchy: too many letters intended for Australia end up in Austria, and the Viennese are getting tired of saying that they have no Alice Springs or Wagga Wagga.

Perhaps there are so many Australians in the city because they have come for their mail.

English is a second language there, and the Blue
Danube radio discourses in English. There is an English
bookshop called, like the Left Bank protonym in Paris,
Shakespeare and Company. There is even an English
theater. But the Viennese patois seduces even anglo-
phones, who will call for a *Mokka* (black coffee) while
they sit in a *Café-Konditorei* with a *Funsn* or a *dumme
Frau*. It was, I think, pleasant for this particular
anglophone to go back to Vienna, but I needed the spring
or autumn and my own language of nostalgia, which is
also the language of Vienna's past. It's a pretty old
past—the Romans called the city Vindobona and Marcus
Aurelius died there—but one segment of it crowns the
rest: the period that began with the Haydn symphonies
and ended with the exile of Arnold Schönberg and
Sigmund Freud. And, whether we like it or not, we can't
separate even the high literary and musical achievements
of the city from the schmaltz of throaty tenors burbling:
"Call, call, Vienna mine."

Vienna ends up as a congeries of flavors and memories; the reality of stone and lime tree and river is somewhat insubstantial. We can thank God that it didn't join
the new Russian Empire and become grim and purposeful. It belongs to the capitalist West, with all its self-
indulgence, consumerism and sensuality. But, even in
summer, we're aware of that chill wind.

GRAND HOTELS—A VENERABLE QUARTET
Imperial Hotel, 16 Kärtner Ring (telephone: 65-

17-65), an antique-filled, converted nineteenth-century palace, is two blocks from the Vienna State Opera and one block from the Musikverein; the concierge and ticket agent are particularly adept at securing tickets for performances and galas at either establishment. Double rooms are about $150; the royal suites, with three or four bedrooms, sitting rooms and painted ceilings, can run up to about $2,000 a day.

Hotel Bristol, 1 Kärtner Ring (52-95-52) is another former nineteenth-century palace with touches of Art Nouveau and Biedermeier furnishings in most of the bedrooms. Double rooms are about $110 to $150 for two, about $325 for a suite with two bedrooms and a salon.

Hotel Sacher, 4 Philharmonikerstrasse (52-55-75), just behind the State Opera, is decorated with antiques, oil paintings and sculptures; the dining room has red silk brocade walls. Doubles are about $140 to $150; suites range from about $300 to $450 a night, for the largest available, with two bedrooms and a salon.

Hotel im Palais Schwarzenberg, 9 Schwarzenbergplatz (78-45-15), is installed in a wing of an eighteenth-century baroque palace with gardens and mirrored galleries. There are only forty-four rooms; reserve well in advance. Rates vary with the season; doubles average about $165.

All of the hotels have restaurants with Viennese specialties; that of the Hotel im Palais Schwarzenberg has been awarded a Michelin star for its version of Viennese nouvelle cuisine, with seasonal game preparations a specialty. Dinner for two, with wine, is about $80.

Snug Little Bergen

JAN MORRIS

T HE TRAINS FROM OSLO, and, for that matter, the buses from the municipal airport, seem to skulk into Bergen, that ancient and famous seaport on Norway's western coast—surreptitiously through tunnels, laboriously over hill passes, as though they were allowed to enter the town only by special permit from the burgomaster.

A century ago indeed there were no trains from Oslo, and hardly a proper road either ("allow seven miles," says my grandfather's old *Handbook to Norway,* "as a good average 12 hours' journey"). In those days the formidable ridges that surround the port, hemming it in upon its waterfront, were more or less impassable except to the hardiest of travelers. Even now it does not feel altogether natural to be approaching Bergen from the landward side, and your first glimpse of the place, as you cross the last crest or emerge from the final tunnel, is distinctly a backdoor view—every house, it seems, looking the other way, every road leading downhill toward the distant sliver of the sea beyond the rooftops.

For nearly a thousand years, since King Olav Kyrre the Viking founded it, Bergen has been standing there like that, back to the mountains, face to the sea, and though it is spilling out nowadays in suburbs and satellites over the surrounding hills, it remains fundamentally private, compact and self-sufficient, like an opinionated little city-state of the north. Bergen people do not say they come from Norway; they say they come from Bergen.

I like Bergen best in the summer, and then the best introduction to the city is to find yourself a modest pension in one of the residential districts. Then you will feel all around you, sober, plump but somehow secretive, like the *mise en scène* of an Ibsen play, the tight continuity of the place. Look out of your window in the warm evening and all is bourgeois order—lace curtains, brown front doors, decorous window ornaments, hooped iron fencing around gardens of hydrangeas. Somewhere somebody is practicing the piano. A woman in a brown felt hat is exercising her terrier on a lead. A casement opens, and a hand with a watering can emerges to sprinkle the potted plants in the window box.

In a swath all around the city center this comfortable stability is solidified, in row upon row, terrace upon terrace of immaculate housing, some in an early nineteenth-century style, painted clapboard on cobbled alleys, some solidly *fin de siècle,* all snug, a little complacent and I dare say rather gossipy. It is the true ambience of a merchant city, enriched by generations of steady enterprise, clannish, comradely and unostentatious. It makes you feel, as you close the window, that you have entered the living quarters of some immemorial guild or all-embracing family business.

The piano practice ends with a flowery if smudged arpeggio. High on the mountain ridge above the city a warning light appears upon a television mast, as though to announce to the hinterland behind that Bergen's gates are closing for the night.

In the morning it is probably misty, and the television mast is veiled from sight, but it will not last for long. Either it will rain, washing every vista clear and clean, or the pale and limpid summer sun will presently appear. Bergen's climate is unexpectedly mild, because the Gulf Stream loiters somewhere near; even in winter the snow seldom lies in the streets for long, and now, if you are lucky, a marvelous goldenness bathes everything, picking out vivid green patches on the forested hills around, glinting on weathercocks and encouraging the grass to sprout between the cobblestones.

By the time the mist has cleared the focus of the city has concentrated itself, out through the brown front doors, along the alleyways, down to the waterfront market. There on the quayside last night's woman-with-the-dog, still in her hat, is earnestly inspecting a twitching and gasping sea trout, just netted out of its great stone tank by the fish merchant. All around, the market bustles like an allegory of Scandinavia. There are stalls of prawns, pickled herring and smoked trout, there are trestle tables piled high with potted plants and cut flowers, there are lobsters scuttling around tanks, there are men gutting huge salmon in the sunshine, there are women selling reindeer pelts and cucumbers and boxes of mountain berries and hideous ceramic trolls for the tourist trade.

Immediately beside the market is the inner harbor, Vagen, the vortex of Bergen since its beginnings. The scene is dominated by a white full-rigged training ship, the municipal flagship since 1922, but otherwise all is functionally modern: trawlers, their crews lounging beside their wheelhouses, yachts with inflatable dinghies, spanking blue-and-white hydrofoils, coastal freighters unloading sacks and barrels on the quay and, tied up near the harbor entrance, perhaps, a great white cruise liner, all flags and parasols, its passengers even now crowding down the quayside toward their sightseeing bus. A quaint little ferryboat, like something from a fairground pond, trundles ceaselessly back and forth across the harbor, and sometimes a seaplane comes swooping down to alight in a froth of spray beyond the entrance mole.

The ships have changed, of course, but in all essentials this is how Bergen's inner harbor has looked since the Hanseatic merchants from north Germany established their trading colony here in the fifteenth century and made it one of Europe's great entrepôts. Though Bergen has been repeatedly ravaged by fire and war, still those old stalwarts from Lübeck and Bremen would easily recognize the scene. There by the harbor mouth is the fortress of Bergenhus, with its King's Hall and its burly Rosencrantz Tower, and there are the gaunt twin towers of Mariakirk, and along the northern quay stand the pointed gables of the Bryggen, the surviving offices and warehouses of the Hanseatic merchants, tumbled wood and crooked balconies and bright-painted boards.

The purpose of the place, too, remains what it always was. Bergen is a hardworking, hardheaded seaport, proud of its past but eager for profitable progress. A

Snug Little Bergen

powerful conservation movement keeps a gimlet eye on everything that happens around that harbor—it is called Det Nyttige Selskab, the Useful Society, and since 1774 it has been defending the constancy of this city, its style and its architectural honor. (On the other hand, when I remarked one day that I would like to live in one of those picturesque old Hanseatic houses of the waterfront, my companion was horrified by the thought—no electric light, no central heating, imagine!)

Buildings around the port are of our own century. Yet somehow it manages to preserve the spiky, uneven, lopsided feel of Scandinavian antiquity. Our woman in the hat, having decided that none of the man's sea trout are up to scratch, stalks off among the market stalls looking notably Nordic; and all around Vagen the rubber-tire fenders, some big, some small, hanging in long irregular rows along the barnacled wharves, look as medieval as anything. I was standing one morning in the Bryggen Museum, one of the handsomest small museums in Europe, when the curator drew my attention to a gray-haired man in a reefer jacket walking by outside. He was the architect of the building, Oyvind Maurseth. I was struck that he did not give his creation a second glance, but good gracious, said the curator, he walked by there every morning—what could you expect?

Bergen is very familiar with itself. Its people know each other well, its celebrities stroll by each morning. It is provincial in a way almost inconceivable in modern America, or in most of Western Europe—still self-contained there between the mountains and the sea, with only a single television channel to preoccupy its evenings, and all the appurtenances still of a prosperous nineteenth-century city. It has a splendid concert hall and a symphony orchestra to play in it. It has agreeable modest restaurants, not of your coq au vin and Burgundy kind, but of your comfortable beer, fish and smorgasbord variety. It has a grand theater, its foyers lavish with oil paintings of inexplicably theatrical theater folk, impresarios in tall silk hats, leading ladies in shimmering satin. It has a daily newspaper, and a university, and a celebrated aquarium, and it is littered all over with memorials to its own heroes and worthies.

Of course, there are a few discos in town (even a homosexual one at weekends) and the odd busker strums and an occasional layabout relieves himself against the memorial to the medieval saga writer Snorri Sturlason. Mostly, though, Bergen's manner is thoroughly old-school and respectable. Bergeners are said to be adept at Norwegian repartee, but they are reserved with strangers and even their casual compliments are genteel: *"Der er solskinn i hatten din!"* a man said to me one day as I walked by in my yellow terry cloth hat from Sydney, but all he meant was, "The sunshine is in your hat." It takes a moment or two to thaw them, and by then, one feels, they have pretty well got the hang of you and decided whether or not you are the kind of person the City of Bergen has a right to expect.

For its standards are very high. Bergen's roster of distinguished citizens is impressive. Ibsen himself learned his trade as a stage manager in this city, and for many years one of the everyday figures of the place, one of those civic celebrities passing by outside, was Edvard Grieg. Everyone knew Grieg in Bergen and nothing is more absolutely of this city than his house, open to visitors nowadays in the suburb of Troldhaugen; not a showy house, but homey and assured—agreeably full of bric-abrac, secluded in its gardens, with a wooden pavilion among the trees in which the composer, warmed by a big iron stove in the corner, would settle at his worn old table to write his melodies.

And ah, what themes came to him through the trees, from the still water of the fjord in front of his windows, from the wooded hills behind. Bergen may be mercan-tile, but it is also intensely romantic. It may have got rich by business, but in its time it has known the high passion and melodrama of the Norsemen. Here Magnus Sigurdsson was blinded by Harald Cille, here Sigurd Mund was murdered on the quay, here Birkebeiner fought Bagler savagely for possession of the town! The northern grandeur of Bergen's setting, the intensity of its ancient meaning, its history all combine to make it just the place for writing A-minor piano concertos.

If the city feels introspective at first through the pen-sion window, over the days it develops a grander excite-ment. The sea wind blows the lace curtains, and braver allusions emerge. The ghosts of great captains, you be-gin to see, haunt those conventional promenades; some-times a face in the street, or the posture of a man hunched over his outboard in the harbor, reminds you that this was the coast of the Long Ships. Half the men of Bergen turn out to be former merchant seamen, and their city, which seems so isolated, is really in touch with all the world.

The United States? Why, there is hardly a soul in Bergen without an uncle in Montana. The East? Ha, Olav Nilssen here could tell you enough about Calcutta to make your hair curl. There are Bergeners who speak English of an Oxonian perfection almost forgotten in its homeland, and every winter a sizable proportion of the city's population moves as in a mass migration to its wintering grounds in the Mediterranean south.

For if that mountain wall looks like a rampart to the east, to the west, beyond the harbor entrance, you can see the wide blue space of deep water. True, it is bounded by the long line of an island beyond, speckled all over with bright houses, but still it seems to beckon the Bergeners away from their ordered streets into wilder parts. From the west come the sea winds and the Gulf Stream; to the west, day after day, century after century, the ships of Bergen sail out past the Bergenhus. The *chug-chug* of freighters, the *plomp-plomp* of fishing boats, are the truest sounds of Bergen; and the very best way of spending a summer afternoon in this city is to take a picnic to one of the waterside parks, lie in the tree-dappled green, let something from *Peer Gynt* stream through your memory and watch the ships go by.

And in the end, to do justice to the fine old place, you must board a ship yourself; and sailing out of Vagen past the fortress wall, past the cluttered warehouses of Nordnes and the aquarium on its headland, find yourself at last in that open sea beyond. Then you realize that Bergen's bourgeois isolation was all illusion after all. The mountains may seem to enclose the city protectively behind you, but in front, the wide free waters sweep this way and that, full of sting and space and vitality, out to the open sea, down to mighty Sor Fjord and the fruit groves of Ullensvang, up to Sogne Fjord, narrow beneath its ice-capped mountains, to Laerdal, and Kristiansand and all the glimmering water-world of the north.

COMFORTABLE IN BERGEN
Selected Summer Hotels

It was once difficult to obtain a hotel room in Bergen during the summer without booking long in advance. New hotel construction, however, has largely remedied the problem, except during the festival season (late May till early June) when the city—and the hotels—are often crowded. If you are planning to be in Bergen at this time, make your reservations early.

First-Class Choices

The **Hotel Norge** (telephone: 323-000), Ole Bulls Plass 4 (mailing address: P. O. Box 662, N-5001 Bergen), and the **SAS Royal Hotel** (318-000), Bryggen, a fairly new hotel designed to blend in with the old wooden buildings on the nearby Hanseatic quay. Both have several cafés and restaurants. The **Hotel Neptun** (326-000), Walckendorffsgate 8, is also well situated, not far from Torgalmenningen and close to the harbor. A double room with bath is about $70 to $90 at the Norge, about $90 at the SAS Royal and about $70 to $80 at the Neptun.

Other Good Bets

The **Bergen Center Hotel** (232-300), Torgalmenningen 11, next to the information center; the **Park Pension** (320-960), Harald Harfagresgate 35, in a quiet location, and the **Augustin Hotel** (230-025), C. Sundtsgate 24, some of whose rooms overlook the harbor. A double room with bath is about $80 at the Bergen Center, $45 at the Park Pension, and $65 at the Augustin. Prices include a hearty Norwegian breakfast.

Smorgasbord and Beyond
The Real Thing

Like other Scandanivian countries, Norway specializes in enormous smorgasbord tables groaning under the weight of hot and cold preparations of meats and fish—

especially herring in many guises—and salads galore. Both the **Norge** and the **SAS Royal** offer smorgasbords for about $12 or $15. The smorgasbord at **Bondeungdomslaget Karristova,** a small café near the fish market, is notable for such specifically Norwegian declicacies as *kreps* (freshwater crayfish) and sour cream porridge, about $10 a person.

CONTINENTAL TOUCHES

The Neptun's **Le Restaurant** is one of Bergen's best dining spots. Budget $40 and up for two, for a meal of such dishes as fresh oysters, pheasant in port wine sauce, fillet of reindeer with cherries and orange soufflé. The **Restaurant Bellevue** (310-240), Bellevuebakken 9, offers a panoramic overview of the city, weather permitting. A full-course dinner of such specialties as carp roe on parsley mousseline, dogfish with salmon-roe sauce and cloudberry parfait should be about $50 for two. **Villa Amorini** (310-039), a small restaurant in the same building as the Bergen Fine Arts Society in the center of town, has a reputation for inventive cooking. Its specialties include reindeer pâté, poached monkfish in white wine sauce, raspberry surprise. Dinner for two is about $50.

LIGHTER FARE

For lunch and snacks, there are several cafés and cafeterias around the harbor and along the old quay. These serve inexpensive if not particularly exciting Norwegian food (fish and meat puddings, open-face sandwiches). At **Bryggestuen** and **Bryggeloftet** (ground floor and first floor respectively), a tasty fish meal for two is about $15 to $20. Also popular with Bergen regulars is **Bryggen Tracteursted,** tucked away between the old warehouses on a small square. Well worth a visit, at least for a glass of beer or lunch outdoors on a sunny day. Close by, at **Enhjorningen** (327-083), a luncheon buffet of various preparations of seafood is the specialty (about $25 for two).

Snug Little Bergen

CAVEAT DRINKER

Quoted meal prices do not include wine or drinks. Alcoholic beverages are a state monopoly in Norway, and tariffs are high. A medium-quality Bordeaux in a Bergen restaurant will command about the same price as a fine vintage wine in New York. Smaller cafés often serve only beer and wine; there is also a hefty tax on beer, so a pint costs up to $3.

Afoot in London's Theaterland

BENEDICT NIGHTINGALE

AYBE THE QUEST SHOULD
begin beside the Thames in Southwark, where a bright
young upstart from Stratford-on-Avon made a name for
himself as an actor and playsmith in the 1590s and
1600s. But one can spend hours scouring those dowdy
streets for a sign, symbol or residual sniff of the Swan
Theater, the Rose Theater, or Shakespeare's Globe, and
find little but desolate warehouses and decaying red-
brick walls with racist graffiti daubed on them.

Better to jump a century or two forward and a few
miles west, let's say to **St. James's Square.** This area
is pleasant in itself, with several of the old Georgian
buildings still overlooking a leafy little park in the center. It's where I usually park my car if I'm booked into a
play on or around Shaftesbury Avenue. It's also a good
point from which to start a nostalgic ramble through the
highways and byways of modern theatrical London,

meaning the theatrical London reactivated by Charles II after his restoration in 1660.

Let's not look westward too long. That grim-looking office building just off the Square was once the St. James's Theater, the last of London's great playhouses to be thus rudely transmogrified. There, an unknown actress named Mrs. Pat Campbell achieved overnight renown with her disconcertingly honest performance of a demimondaine in Pinero's *The Second Mrs. Tanqueray.* Her leading man was the actor-manager George Alexander, the first of many to incur her dislike and her barbs. In a later play at the same theater he surreptitiously flashed her a look of such loathing during an amorous embrace that she burst into giggles, a breach of decorum that provoked him to send the stage manager to her dressing room to tell her not to laugh at him onstage. "My compliments to Mr. Alexander," answered Mrs. Pat, "and please inform him I never laugh at him until I get home." Much later, Vivien Leigh played Cleopatra there to Laurence Olivier's all-electric Antony, and headed a national campaign to save the St. James from demolition. Alas, it closed in 1957, another reminder that much of London's theatrical past lies buried beneath concrete or tarmac or, quite often, reconstructed versions of the same playhouse.

The **Haymarket Theater,** for instance, is the third theater of that name on the same site, though its famous Corinthian portico, designed by John Nash in 1821, survived its rebuilding sixty years later. Stand in St. James's Square, look straight east, and there it is, one of the sweetest sights in London. The theater itself is a bit staid and respectable in its offerings these days, which was not always so. The novelist Henry Fielding was manager there in the 1730s, and wrote stage satires so scathing that theatrical censorship was introduced, not to be abolished until 1968. In 1805, it took redcoats with bayonets to quiet a huge mob of tailors who had invaded the Haymarket, howling and hurling shears and threatening arson in their rage at a play they thought discourteous to their profession.

Five years later, there were scenes scarcely less uproarious when the celebrated eccentric Robert Coates came with his vanity production of *Romeo and Juliet.* He arrived at the door in the vast horse-drawn scallop shell he called his "triumphal car," then strutted onstage in blue-spangled coat, full wig and opera hat, and proceeded to express his adoration for the dead Juliet by dragging her round the tomb by her hair, splitting his red pantaloons in the process. And wild was the hilarity when Coates laid down an enormous silk handkerchief, explaining to the audience he wasn't going to "spoil my nice new clothes," and extravagantly died once, twice, three times, to cries of "encore."

Almost opposite the third Haymarket is the fourth **Her Majesty's,** a bulky architectural extravaganza dating from 1896. This is where Handel established himself with a group of Italian opera singers, and Jenny Lind, "the Swedish nightingale," made her London debut, and, in our time, *West Side Story* captivated a rather wider audience. But the theater has seen its straight plays, too. Here, Shaw's *Pygmalion* had its famous first performance, with Mrs. Campbell's Eliza Doolittle reducing a fashionable audience to ecstasies of nursery mirth with her cry of "not bloody likely," and Sir Herbert Tree playing Higgins, so terrified of forgetting his lines that he had copies of them pinned all over the stage furniture and a squad of prompters stationed behind the doors, the windows, even the sofa. For him, the performance was the uncomfortable climax of two spectacularly successful decades in which, since he was its owner, manager and principal actor, his name was permanently plastered outside Her Majesty's. Sir Henry Irving, it's said, once caught him raptly staring up at it. "Hello, Tree," he remarked. "Working?"

Almost too many stories, too many distracting anecdotes are to be found behind the wrought-iron filigree, the quaint statues of muses, the fake Grecian pediments and columns embellishing the façades of the playhouses that have collectively become known as **Shaftesbury Avenue.** Collectively and, let me add, somewhat inaccurately. In fact, there are hardly more Shaftesbury Avenue theaters directly on Shaftesbury Avenue than there are Broadway theaters on Broadway, and they aren't the oldest and most historic ones in London, either. Lyric, Apollo, Globe, Palace: They and most other theaters west of Covent Garden date from the 1880s, 1890s, 1900s. It was then that wide new streets, subway stations and other such proofs of progress permanently altered the higgledy-piggledy area to the west and south of Covent Garden. Along with the slum housing, tacky shops and brothels torn down around Drury Lane have come much of what had become the center of London's theaterland, to be gradually replaced on supposedly more salubrious sites farther to the west.

Not that the newer theaters don't have their attractions and their memories, too. A personal favorite of mine is the tiny **Criterion** on Piccadilly Circus. This was built in 1874, when it was proudly described as an "underground Temple of Drama into which it is necessary to pump air to save the audience from being asphyxiated"; the theater was remodeled and more sensibly ventilated a decade later; and these days it's still much as it was a century ago. Down, down and down one walks, past period tiles solemnly commemorating composers famous and obscure, Bach to Boildieu, Verdi to Flotow, and into an auditorium whose Victorian-rococo charm has managed to survive a recent redecorating in pink and mauve. Even the upper circle is still below the level of the passing pedestrians on the sidewalk outside.

The Criterion has so far evaded the recurrent threat of demolition made in successive plots and plans for the renewal of what has become a pretty seedy Piccadilly Circus. Wander down Coventry Street to Leicester Square, and the story is less happy. Several of the movie houses here were once live theaters, and busy bustling ones. The Odeon was the Alhambra, where "the Marvellous Eccentric Musical Spider, the Laughter Demon of Paris" amazed audiences with his contortions in 1864. The Warner was Daly's, opened by the American producer Augustin Daly in 1893, and almost as famous for its musicals as another lost London theater, the Gaiety. And the Empire cinema was the Empire Theater, notorious in the Gay Nineties for a promenade in which dandies and women of the town brazenly held their trysts. Thanks to the American social reformer Mrs. Ormiston Chant and her supporters, popularly known as "prudes on the prowl," canvas screens were eventually erected between the offending walkway and the auditorium. They were then torn down and paraded through London by the youthful Winston Churchill and some fellow military cadets, but the Empire lost its old allure, and was never as interestingly wicked again.

Pressing on eastward, one finds theaters that are, thankfully, still theaters. Here's the **Garrick,** put up by W. S. Gilbert, who rediscovered a river known to the Romans beneath the foundations and said he didn't

Afoot in London's Theaterland

know "whether to continue the building or let the fishing." Here's the **Duke of York's,** behind whose fine
Regency-style façade *Peter Pan* first saw the footlights.
Here's the **Albery,** where Sybil Thorndike created
Shaw's St. Joan and Olivier and Gielgud alternated Romeo and Mercutio. And here is the little **Ambassadors,**
outside which I myself recall sitting perched on one of a
row of canvas stools, in hopes of securing a cheap seat
for a brand-new play called *The Mousetrap* by Agatha
Christie, starring Richard Attenborough. I got it, too, on
a bench at the back of the orchestra, in those days still
known as the pit. Thirty-two record-splintering years
later, *The Mousetrap* is still on West Street, though now
shifted to the adjoining St. Martin's Theater.

Stand outside it, swivel round, and there's the long
green façade of the **Ivy,** as popular a restaurant among
theatrical folk in the 1930s as the Café Royal or Rules in
earlier times or the Caprice and the Savoy Grill in later
ones. Noel Coward made it a rule to take lunch at his pet
table near the door after one of his first nights, especially
if it had been a flop. You can still get a solid meal there
or, for something cheaper, stop off in one of the pubs
with theatrical associations in Covent Garden, such as
the **Lamb and Flag** in Rose Street, where the poet and
playwright John Dryden was cudgeled almost to death
for libeling a mistress of Charles II. Or try the **Coalhole**
on the Strand, where Edmund Kean formed the Wolf
Club, an organization dedicated purportedly to charita-
ble deeds but actually to drink, lechery and staggering
out en masse to barracking the great tragedian's rivals at
Drury Lane or Covent Garden.

Drury Lane, Covent Garden. Their majestic por-
ticos continue to dominate Catherine and Bow streets,
respectively, and their elegant nineteenth-century foyers

are still there to be relished. The Lane, now in its fourth incarnation, is mainly given over to American musicals these days, and the Garden, in its third, is of course the Royal Opera House. But for nearly two centuries they were *the* London theater, often in bitter competition with each other. That was because they shared a monopoly over the production of drama that had been granted by Charles II and, though it was repeatedly and often illegally challenged elsewhere, that monopoly was not officially broken until 1843.

Hard to believe it now, but they were rowdy places in their time, the regular rendezvous of beaux and women of the town, and packed with jostling crowds apt to quarrel, heckle and throw orange peels and worse at those whose faces displeased them. Repeatedly, unruly behavior would erupt into riot. One riot, at Covent Garden in 1809, lasted for sixty-one nights when the management incautiously raised prices. Yet, somehow, plays managed to get themselves heard and performances seen. Quin, Cooke, Kemble, Macklin, all great names in their day, appeared at the Garden. Master Betty, whose thirteen-year-old Hamlet took the town by storm, made his first appearance there, and there Mrs. Siddons, most famous of all Lady Macbeths, gave her last performance of the part.

The history of Drury Lane is richer still. Dryden and Congreve wrote for it, and Sheridan also owned, managed and reconstructed it, only to see his new building burned down. "Cannot a man take a glass of wine by his own fireside?" he is said to have asked, as he sat in a nearby coffeehouse, watching the end of his income and the ruin of his theatrical career. Earlier, the Lane was the home of David Garrick, a Hamlet so real that women fainted and men cried out when he first saw his father's ghost, and later that of Macready, the most celebrated of all Macbeths. It was also the place where Kean, conceivably the greatest actor who ever lived, made an astonishing London debut as Shylock, and went on to triumph after triumph, moving Lord Byron to suggest that watching him was like reading Shakespeare by lightning. Even in his years of decay, when he was drunk, gouty, hoarse of voice, half demented with paranoia, Kean could perform Othello with such power and pathos that, in the words of a contemporary, "men leaned their heads upon their arms and fairly sobbed."

His ghost doesn't haunt the Lane, except metaphorically, but a gray gentleman in wig, cloak and riding boots can sometimes be seen stalking across its upper circle. The pub opposite, the Opera Tavern, is said to have its own specter too, a man who was murdered and buried there and still makes the bottles rattle in the cellar. More benign presences have been recorded elsewhere. Some have heard the footsteps of Buckstone, a much-loved manager of the nineteenth century, echoing round the Haymarket's dressing rooms. Fanny Kelly, actress, militant feminist and manager of the Royalty about the same time, was regularly spotted wandering happily round her old playhouse before it was destroyed by the Luftwaffe. So many London theaters have vanished, and with them even some of their ghosts.

Take the **Lyceum.** Its hefty, looming columns are still in Wellington Street, not far from the Royal Opera House; but behind them is a dance hall, not the theater where Irving flamboyantly earned the first knighthood ever given a British actor. And just around the corner is the **Aldwych,** still open, still an attractive building, but to me not the place it was, now that the Royal Shakespeare Company has moved out, ending two decades of often astonishing achievement on its pleasantly shabby stage. Any *Nicholas Nickleby* of the future will presumably be found inside the vast caverns of the Barbican, the company's new home in the City, as unprepossessing a building as London has ever seen. It's there, and in the all-concrete National Theater south of Waterloo Bridge, that the best of British performance is to be found these days, not in the traditional West End. It's there that history is being created right now.

But meanwhile there's still much to be discovered, especially if you're willing to substitute wheels for feet. Take the subway to Sloane Square, where you'll find the **Royal Court,** probably the most important British playhouse this century, at least as far as serious drama is concerned. A famous season in the Edwardian era regalvanized a moribund theater with work of Shaw, Galsworthy and others, and fifty years later the same stage saw the first performance of John Osborne's *Look Back in Anger,* from which critics usually date a dramatic renaissance many feel still to be in full flow. Take a cab across Waterloo Bridge to the **Old Vic,** in the early nineteenth century a respectable enough place, later the shoddy and shambling home of "blood-tub" drama, then a music hall and eventually as distinguished a classical theater as our era has seen.

What major British performer hasn't played there? That's where Olivier was Hamlet, and where he went on to establish himself in the theatrical pantheon. That's where Richardson created his great Falstaff, Gielgud his Romeo and Richard II, Guinness his Hamlet, and Burton his blazing Coriolanus, the performance that left many wondering if the British stage hadn't acquired another Kean. There, as a boy in the 1950s, I discovered Shakespeare, and there I saw classic after classic in the

1960s and 1970s, when Olivier's new National Theater company first proved itself at that theater and Olivier himself played Othello, Shylock, James Tyrone in *Long Day's Journey into Night.*

The Old Vic has its anecdotes too, many of them involving Lillian Baylis, the doughty maiden lady who transformed its fame and fortune by replacing vaudeville with Shakespeare. In the middle of meetings or interviews with members of her company, she would often sink to her knees and launch into blunt business conversations with God. Would He kindly ensure her latest production was a success? Would He please send her some good actors? Then she would pause. Would God be careful to make them cheap? No doubt she's still somewhere in the London ether, still trying to make London's present and future as memorable as its past. Certainly we can never have enough people, or ghosts, like her.

EATING AND DRINKING THEATRICALLY

If you want good French cooking and a bit of atmosphere—indeed a lot of atmosphere—head for the **Café Royal's Grill Room** at 68 Regent Street (437-9090), and gourmandize amid the gilded caryatids in what Cecil Beaton once called "the most beautiful room in London." In the Gay Nineties, the time of its greatest fame, dinner guests included kings, princes, statesmen and artists of every kind. Here Oscar Wilde held court, and here he was advised by Shaw and others to escape the country, thus avoiding the trials that landed him in prison, convicted of gross indecency. Try *tournedos flambé aux poivres verts* at about $16, *croustade de langoustines sauce d'homard* at about $18 or *suprême de*

volaille Guiliana at about $10. The wines are outstand-
ing if sometimes expensive; but a good meal for two
shouldn't cost more than about $80 or $90.

These days, however, theatrical people are more
likely to go to **L'Escargot** at 48 Greek Street (437-
2679) in Soho or **Joe Allen's** at 13 Exeter Street
(836-0651), not far from Drury Lane and Covent Garden. L'Escargot changes its menu regularly, and today's
wild duck with green peppercorns or saddle of lamb
with spinach may tomorrow be roast woodcock or gratin
of salmon trout with scallops in mushroom sauce. The
cost for two, with wine, will be about $50, less if you
elect to eat more modestly in the brasserie downstairs.

Joe Allen's may be precisely what American visitors
don't want, being a conscious replica of its namesake
on West Forty-sixth Street in New York, down to the
checked tablecloths and menus chalked on blackboards.
But it undeniably offers excellent value, with black
bean soup at about $2.20, a decent chicken teriyaki at
$8 or so and hot fudge éclair at $2.50. Besides, that
lean, worried-looking figure over there is probably
Trevor Nunn, director both of the Royal Shakespeare
Company and the musical *Cats,* and the man he's talking to may be playing Hamlet or Lear at the Barbican.
Two can eat and drink amply for about $30.

Almost any pub of any age in the Covent Garden area
can claim some theatrical associations. The **Lamb and
Flag** on Rose Street (where Dickens drank, like Dryden
before him) has good beer, and sausage and mash for
about $2.50 at lunchtime. The **Opera Tavern** on
Catherine Street, where you're liable to find the chorus
of *42nd Street* before it begins that evening's performance at Drury Lane, has equally cheap steak pies. A
favorite of mine in this area, though not especially theatrical and often very crowded, is the **Marquess of
Anglesey** on Bow Street. You can drink Young's
Special Bitter, probably London's best beer, and up-

stairs there may be pork and chestnut pie or ratatouille and rice; each is about $2.50. Unlike many pubs, the Marquess of Anglesey sells good, hot food in the evening.

Half a mile east is the **Old Cheshire Cheese,** quaintly nestling in Wine Office Court, off 145 Fleet Street. You're more likely to find lawyers or journalists than theatrical people standing on the sawdust sprinkled around the winding stairways and musty, paneled bars; but there's compensation in both the age of the building, which was built soon after the Great Fire of 1666, and in its literary associations. Congreve was here, and Dr. Johnson, and more recently Yeats and his fellow members of the Rhymers Club.

Or take a taxi out to the **Anchor** at 1 Bankside in Southwark. The present building was erected in the eighteenth century but has plenty of atmosphere, and it's difficult to resist the legends that Shakespeare drank here or that Pepys stood at the door, watching the Great Fire rage the other side of the Thames. Both pubs include restaurants that offer traditional English food at sensible prices. Roast beef and Yorkshire pudding costs about $10 at the Anchor; a whole meal for two with wine is about $40. Dinner at the Cheshire Cheese, perhaps with steak and kidney or mushroom and game pie, should be about $30.

No London hotel is especially rich in theatrical associations, but one or two are rich in rich theatrical people. One such hotel is the **Savoy** (836-4343), which has its entrance on the Strand and many undeniably luxurious rooms overlooking the Thames. That Broadway producer in the lobby, on the hunt for plays to take to New York, is paying between $150 and $200 a night for his double room, or, if he's feeling especially confident, between $300 and $440 for his suite.

Should you want somewhere a little less grand, but also a little further from the theaters, try **Brown's** on

Dover Street (493-6020). Brown's was founded by Byron's gentleman's gentleman in 1837, and still has the look and feel of a distinguished and comfortable club. A double room here is about $120.

Cheaper places are obviously also available, especially if you're prepared to stay still further from Shaftesbury Avenue. The **Cadogan Thistle** at 75 Sloane Street (235-7141) has a paneled entrance hall, well-furnished rooms and was, as it happens, the hotel where the doomed Wilde waited to be arrested by the police. A few minutes away, at 8 Basil Street just behind Harrods department store, is the elegantly old-fashioned yet cozy **Basil Street Hotel** (581-3311). A double room there costs about $90; the Cadogan is a little less. —B.N.

Churchill's Command Post Beneath London

DREW MIDDLETON

IS THERE A FAINT WHIFF
of cigar smoke in the corridor? Does the shuffle of tourists' footsteps still the memory of those lambent phrases
that were the sword of freedom when freedom's swords
were few? Perhaps so. It is nearly fifty years since Winston Churchill first entered the bunker known as the
Cabinet War Rooms, from which he conducted Britain's
war. But the flavor of the man and the period are alive in
this place.

Hitler died in his bunker in Berlin. Churchill fought
from his. Today, after extensive and careful reconstruction, the visitor to London can see the rooms from which
a war was fought during its most desperate period.

The war rooms lie some ten feet underground in the
basement of the Government offices at the western end
of Great George Street, a few steps from Parliament
Square. Construction began in the summer of 1938,

when the thunderclouds were rising above Europe, and the rooms became operational on August 27, 1939, a week before Britain and France declared war on Germany.

Churchill, the War Cabinet and the Chiefs of Staff used the bunker most frequently from September through November 1940. This was the period of the Blitz, the name the British public gave to the protracted bombing of London by the Luftwaffe. The Cabinet Room also was used extensively from June to September 1944 and from January to March 1945, when German V-1s and V-2s rained on London.

The Cabinet Room seems almost too small—about eighteen by twenty-one feet—to contain the leadership of a nation at war. The visitor sees the room as it was on October 15, 1940. Churchill's chair is in the center of the back row. The chair on his right was reserved for Clement Attlee, the Deputy Prime Minister. The other chairs were occupied by men, great in their day, who are a memory now: Anthony Eden, Ernest Bevin, Lord Beaverbrook. A staff officer's cap hangs on a peg.

In the middle, facing their formidable master, sat the chiefs of the three armed services. Who can name them now? Certainly not the awed little boys who survey the room.

An air of timelessness hangs over the room. A visitor remembering those days half expects Adm. Sir Dudley Pound to stamp into the room, fling himself into his chair and begin to tap the pale green blotter impatiently. Or for Anthony Eden, always elegant, to murmur a few words to the attentive Attlee.

In 1940 when the War Cabinet met in the bunker it was reasonably secure. The concrete slab above the Cabinet Room was proof against a 500-pound bomb and

Churchill's Command Post Beneath London

there were few bombs of that size at that time. Above the door on the left are two electric bulbs painted red and green that indicated whether an air raid was in progress. Cabinet meetings began about 10 P.M. and lasted until business was done. A participant remembered that the Prime Minister refreshed himself from a tall glass of whiskey and water.

A board indicates the weather above. During air raids it frequently read "Windy," in British usage meaning frightening.

Security was one thing, comfort another. Sir John Colville, Churchill's private secretary, has recorded that "The Prime Minister much disliked the place, which he found ill-smelling and claustrophobic." Churchill worked at No. 10 Downing Street by day and in the bunker by night during the worst of the German air raids.

Churchill much preferred a bedroom built on the floor above, but he slept in his bunker bedroom three or four times, and from the table that faces the bed made four of his wartime broadcasts, one of them the declaration of war on Japan. A storm lantern stands on the table next to his bed, sharing the space with an ashtray for his cigar butts. A cigar humidor is within reach.

Churchill, like Hitler, was prepared to die in his bunker. After warning the British of the dangers of invasion in July 1940, he looked around the Cabinet Room and, according to his associates, said, "If the invasion comes, that's where I'll sit. I'll sit there until the Germans are driven back or they carry me out."

Throughout the bunker there are reminders that this was the nerve center of a nation at war. On one wall of the map room hangs a blackboard reporting the state of the Luftwaffe and of the Royal Air Force's Fighter Command on September 15, 1940, the critical day of the Battle of Britain.

Not unnaturally, the figures represent the inflated British claims of the day. These were later revised, but even the revision showed that the R. A. F. had mauled the Germans to the point that they began to withdraw from the daylight air battle.

The map room was the nerve center of the bunker. Staffed around the clock throughout the war, every piece of information from every battlefront, every air strike and every convoy was logged and recorded on the maps. The room rings with history. Here are the Japanese moving into northern Burma toward India. There are the Germans fighting the Allies in Normandy with heroic desperation. All the maps were left in place when the bunker closed in August 1945. Dusty pigeonholes near a green scrambler telephone still bear their labels: "Se-cret," "Most Secret" and "The King."

Perhaps the most important room in the bunker is the transatlantic telephone room from which Churchill spoke directly to President Franklin D. Roosevelt in the White House. At the outset of their conversations, the calls went by radiotelephone and scramblers were used. How-ever, no absolutely secure link existed until the middle of 1943 when an advanced scrambler developed by Bell Laboratories was shipped to Britain. This machine, code-named Sigsaly, was too big for the Cabinet Room in the bunker and was installed in the basement of Selfridge's de-partment store in Oxford Street, with an underground cable connecting it with the terminal in the bunker.

Rooms 62, 62A, 62B were taken over from July 1940 to January 1941 by Advanced Headquarters and it was from these rooms that the defense of Britain would have been coordinated in the event of invasion. Room 62B was allocated to Gen. Sir Alan Brooke, commander of Home Forces.

Sir John Colville recalls that when the invasion scare was at its height, Churchill frequently would visit this Advanced Headquarters, marching over from Downing Street to "see what progress they are making."

Living conditions within the bunker were in keeping with the austerity of the times. Canned soup, sardines and sausages were the staple diet for those living in the bunker, with brown ale to wash it down. The visitor see-ing the confined quarters allocated to the typists who worked for the military staff and studying the menus may ask how people could put up with such conditions for working days that stretched to fourteen or fifteen hours. The answer was then that "the game is on the table"—in other words, the British had to choose between survival and defeat. Business in the bunker did not focus solely on defense. Every night during the winter of 1940–1941, the military planning staff, a special unit created to mislead the Germans, and the Joint Intelligence Committee met there to discuss means of carrying the war to the enemy.

Inevitably the visitor is drawn back to Room 65A, the Prime Minister's bedroom. Here, more than elsewhere in the bunker, one feels the flavor of those times. In the mind's eye, one can see that short but strangely commanding figure seated before the microphone and hear the matchless prose.

But to many of the thousands who visit the bunker, it is just a place where people lived and worked at a precarious period in the island's story. Emerging, there is the sunlight, the noise of traffic on Whitehall and the bobby who announces he intends to bring the wife and nippers to see the bunker soon.

Like the Tower of London, the bunker's message is from the past, but a not-too-distant past. The visitor may emerge with a clearer view of what a people may have to endure to preserve their freedom.

IF YOU GO

There are twenty rooms in the bunker. Five of them had been open to visitors on a severely restricted basis in years past. Ten more, which had been used by senior staff officers and typists during the war and were later used as a storage area, have recently been restored and furnished with wartime memorabilia. A further two are now used as exhibition rooms for documents and photos and a changing series of period objects.

The bunker is open Tuesday through Sunday from 10 A.M. to 5:50 P.M. with the exception of Good Friday, Christmas Day and the May Day holiday, May 7, plus the few occasions when a state ceremony is held and the whole area is cordoned off. On these occasions it opens at midday and close at the usual time. The phone number to call for information is 930-6961, but reservations are not necessary. Admission is about $2.50, children and students, about $1.50.

TOURING THE BATTLE SITES

A variety of World War II battlefield tours are available from both England and France. All are by bus.

ENGLAND

Major and Mrs. Holt's Battlefield Tours, 15 Market Street, Sandwich, Kent (telephone: 0304-612248). There is always a Normandy beach tour on June 6 and several others are scheduled in July and August. Trips to sites in the Netherlands are scheduled in September. The cost is about $200 a person in a room for two, an additional $40 for a single, including breakfast and dinner. The Holt tours, which each last four days, give a great deal of background information on the buses.

Summerfield Coaches, 247 Aldemoor Road, Southhampton (0703-778717). Normandy beach tours in June, July and August last five days and cost from about $230 a person in a twin room. All their tours are accompanied by an experienced historical guide.

Townsend Thoresen Holidays, P.O. Box 18, Tonbridge, Kent TW9 1TW (0732-365437). Four-day tours of the Normandy beaches are offered in June and July at about $185, to Arnhem in August and September for about $200, and to the site of the Battle of the Bulge in September for about $235.

FRANCE

Cityrama, a French organization, operates one-day bus excursions from Paris to the battlefields and landing beaches in Normandy. English-speaking guides accompany the tours, which cost about $75 a person. The main Normandy battle sites are also included in several two- to four-day circuits going to Mont-St.-Michel or the Loire Valley. Transportation is by air-conditioned motorcoach. Prices (about $160 to $350) include transportation, admission fees, meals and, in the case of extended tours, accommodation in double rooms with bath. Drinks not included. Cityrama has offices in New York, Suite 607, 276 Fifth Avenue, New York, NY 10001 (212-683-8120). Bookings can also be made in France through a travel agency.

Seeking the Soul of Derbyshire

ALAN SILLITOE

TO BE APPEALING, landscape should have a mixture of soulful subtlety that comes about through the thumbprints of human activity, and visual grandeur produced by the growing pains of an infant earth that had no one to control its geological tantrums. There is no possibility of exploring Derbyshire and being bored, for it has both of these qualities. Byron assured us that there are things in that county "as noble as in Greece or Switzerland." Though poets exaggerate, much like everyone else, I would tend to endorse his opinion.

For me, Derbyshire is Matlock, a ribbon of resorts in the winding Derwent Valley. I first bicycled there one summer from Nottingham (a round trip of fifty miles) when I was sixteen years old, with a group who worked in the same factory. We hired a boat on the Derwent River, roistered about the tea shops, and shinned up the Heights of Abraham—an ideal Sunday outing.

Forty years later I go alone by car in the early spring, and randomly select the Temple Hotel for a night's lodging. Queen Victoria stayed there when it was an annex to the New Bath Hotel, and Lord Byron left his mark by scratching a poem on a windowpane. A large room with shower and four-poster bed cost me a reasonable $28 and an evening meal (minestrone soup, steak and mixed vegetables, and coffee cake) added another $7. After breakfast (corn flakes, bacon, egg and sausages, toast and marmalade and coffee), which was included in the room charge, I went out to find that my car wouldn't start, owing to the freezing all-night mist, so I decided to leave it for a while and revisit the Heights of Abraham.

After paying about eighty-five cents to get into the area I went through woods and followed the track to Prospect Tower, built in 1844. The door was open, and stone steps led to the viewing platform. I heard traffic from 800 feet below. Ridges and the tops of hills came into sunlit view between gaps in the heavy mist, which still hung over the valley. A cable-car system connects with the opposite hill, and just below the tower, beside the green and yellow station, three tiny cars were threaded onto the cable. Each had a bulbous glass window at the front, so that they looked like the heads of bluebottles, one behind the other, the result of some ferocious decapitation hung on the wires as a warning to others. Around the tower the olive greensward sloped toward Masson Hill. Bits of crest line to the south stuck up like an old sailor's teeth, making the area seem much grander and more precipitous than it was, though the hill behind was barely 1,200 feet. Clusters of houses became visible on the hillside, and through a hole in the mist a bus went along the main road.

Seeking the Soul of Derbyshire

Four miles southeast, beyond the neighboring Heights of Jacob, Crich Tower stood on a shelf of cloud like a rocket ready for blast-off, blue space waiting for it to come roaring up, as if Derbyshire had secretly prepared a space program, and today was the day. But the tower is a monument erected "in the memory of 11,409 men of all ranks of the Sherwood Foresters (Nottinghamshire and Derbyshire Regiment) who gave their lives for king and country in the Great War of 1914–1919." Both counties from which the dead men came were visible: an enormous patch of dark wood in Derbyshire shaped like the horseshoe of the Carpathians on a layered map; and the colliery villages of Nottinghamshire on the opposite skyline.

Matlock was started on its career as a spa by John Snedley, a hosiery manufacturer. His health broke down in 1849 because of worry and anxiety and, scorning doctors' remedies, he built a series of opulent hydros at which people could be treated with cold water. The Romans were drawn to Matlock by its lead mines, but now excursionists come from nearby industrial cities to enjoy the scenery and pure air. Mr. Smedley's buildings are used for offices or for educational purposes.

Visitors in his time may have been impressed by a local character, Phoebe Brown, the so-called Amazon of Matlock Green who, in her time—she died in 1854 at eighty-two years of age—was a carpenter and mason who defended herself with fists as well as with weapons she made at her blacksmith's forge. She could walk forty miles a day and do any kind of labor, which included breaking horses at a guinea a week. She also read Milton, Pope and Shakespeare, and played the flute, violin or harpsichord in church.

Back at the hotel the car still wouldn't start, so I sat on

the terrace in the sun and drank coffee until a Royal Automobile Club mechanic came in his van to set me once more on the road.

My next outing was to Chatsworth, the home of the eleventh duke of Devonshire, which is near Bakewell ten miles north of Matlock. It is a grim-looking building but the grounds are of lavish style and stunning beauty. For about $4 you are allowed to walk around the great house and linger unescorted. The route is cleverly arranged between roped-off areas and closed doors so that there is no chance of getting lost in its 175 rooms, or of disturbing the duke at lunch.

The paintings stop one's progress: Poussin's *Landscape with Settlers Hunting*, *A View of Tivoli*, attributed to Salvator Rosa, and Veronese's *Adoration of the Magi*. I carried binoculars, with which to bring close the lovely and pleasing flesh on the painted ceilings far above. A notice in the library warned against touching the books, so someone must have seen me coming. My fingers itched to examine the exquisitely bound volumes impossible to buy on a writer's income. Views from the windows are almost as inspiring as those on the walls and tapestries within. Rivulets and lawns sweep away against a background of gentle hills. A great cascade of water comes down in clouds of soft foam from the hillside. Other windows show ponds, fountains and delicate stone bridges.

After wandering around as if you owned the place you may buy, if you can tolerate the sight of such plebeian items, maps and postcards in the shop, as well as cakes, honey, pottery and ornamental trays.

A different kind of landscape is found north of Buxton, where huge crows on fence posts survey empty moors on every horizon. There is no subtlety here as around Matlock, at least not until the valley of Edale is seen from the Castleton Road. A grand circus of beige hills is broken by the gray paneling of cliffs. In the fields, newborn lambs totter after their ewes. For several miles the road winds by hamlets and farms. The valley seems like a cul-de-sac, which only the working farmer and summer moor-walker know about. The Pennine Way begins here, a long-distance footpath ending, after 250 miles, at the Scottish border.

Walking was not always allowed in the area. Grouse-shooters objected to ramblers on their land but, in 1932, 400 people met for a demonstration on the wide table-land of Kinder Scout. Newsreels of the time make the foray look like troops going over the top in World War I. But the ramblers were advancing against police and gamekeepers, and five of the so-called ringleaders were sent to prison. The Pennine Way was opened in 1965, though complete access to the moors is still forbidden.

The way to the village of Eyam leads through a wooded valley, a river glinting between trees. The switch from dramatic to subtle scenery comes with little warning. Part of the road overhanging an escarpment has crumbled away, so only one car can pass at a time. Eyam seems as cut off now as during the incidents that gave it fame during the Great Plague. A man who opened a box of clothes sent from London in September 1665 infected the whole of his family. Before the end of the year 46 people had succumbed. Snow and frost were credited with checking the disease, but it broke out again and killed another 152. At the end of the outbreak 90 inhabitants were left. Some say only 30 survived out of 350.

Many more might have perished if the Rev. William Mompesson hadn't talked his parishioners into sacrificing themselves by staying in the village. A cordon was drawn, beyond which no one was to stray, and the out-side world, happy at such an arrangement, left supplies of food at certain points along the boundary. Money for payment was placed in a shallow trough of running water, since known as Mompesson's Well, to cleanse it of infection.

Mr. Mompesson and his wife sent their children away before the blockade began. Mrs. Mompesson perished, but her husband lived until 1708. Every cottage in which people died still has its plaque, and the village has ever since been visited by the plague of notoriety, of which I was a part.

According to all accounts, Mr. Mompesson had no easy task persuading people to remain in the infected area. In those days the parson's word was law, but two men made a run for it, and got away. I only hope they were among the survivors.

There is still an eerie aspect about Eyam. I felt goulish walking around with map in hand, tramping the fields, and studying the graveyard. Without the plague Eyam would have been one of the many pretty villages in the area, and no more.

Gray stone walls and green banks on either side of the winding lane took me south again. The car splashed through a ford and went over open country to Tissington, until the jagged green shape of Thorpe Cloud Hill marked the beginning of the valley called Dovedale. What nature makes, man will praise, and Izaak Walton said much for the area in *The Compleat Angler*. Even Dr. Johnson, who preferred towns, and was shocked by Derbyshire's "horrid hills," said: "He that has seen Dovedale has no need to visit the Highlands of Scotland."

A path goes three miles up the glen, and you can take

your lunch, of cheese and ham perhaps, available at village shops, to the packhorse bridge at Milldale, and then walk back. Those engravings of the spot in Victorian guidebooks seem realistic, for the enclosed glen, where the sight and sound of running water are always present, has a romantic and Gothic charm, like the scene of some doomed love affair or dastardly crime.

An escarpment lifts to the sky, rags of cloud floating above. Dead trees are wreathed in anacondas of ivy, and winter catkins hang in isolation, but at the next curve of the path a woman is pushing a pram, and her husband has a geologist's hammer swinging from his belt. (The last bear seen in England was said to have been killed near Dovedale.)

Sixty children's parkas make a moving rainbow farther along the river, before they coagulate at a stile. Outcrops are so rectangular they look as if built of small bricks that have been crumbling for a hundred years. A splash of sun reflects trees and pinnacles in the water, giving a view downward as well as up. One outcrop resembles an enormous chisel-blade poised to scrape the sky. On the way back, a sweep of green hillside is divided by the faint letter L of a stone wall going to the summit. Above the wood individual trees are scattered as if held by soldiers advancing toward Macbeth's castle.

But Derbyshire is in the middle of England, and a fifty-mile stretch from the Vale of the Trent to the High Peak repays exploration. I wouldn't liken it to Greece or Switzerland, however, for Derbyshire is unique, and needs no such comparison.

GETTING THERE

Buxton, Bakewell, Matlock and **Dovedale** lie along the A6 road, an easy and uncongested drive (to Buxton, about 160 miles, or three and a half hours from London). Trains to Buxton and Burton-on-Trent leave regularly from London's Euston Station. The run to Buxton takes four hours. Round-trip fares from London to these towns are from about $35 to $40, depending on the destination; fares are cheaper on weekends and for one-day excursions, and children travel for half price. Trains to Derby, Matlock and Chesterfield run from London's St. Pancras Station. It is also possible to travel to Burton-on-Trent from St. Pancras Station. For train times from both these stations, which are next to each other, telephone 387-7070. Connections by bus to Dovedale and Bakewell are available but so infrequent that it would be advisable to visit these villages by car.

MATLOCK

SIGHTSEEING

Above Matlock Bath and adjacent to the railway station, thirty-five acres of wooded slopes form the **Heights of Abraham.** A visit to the Heights can be made by cable car. Round-trip tickets are about $2 for adults and $1.30 for children. The cable car operates daily from April through September and weekends only during the winter (telephone: Matlock 0629-2365).

EATING OUT

Riber Hall Restaurant, Riber, Derbyshire (telephone: Matlock 0629-2795) is open for lunch from noon to 1:30 P.M. and for dinner from 7 to 9:30 P.M. The dishes are mainly French inspired. The set lunch price is about $10; dinner for two including wine is about $65. The **Courtyard,** Dale Road, Matlock (0629-5650), a bistro-style restaurant, is open for lunch from noon to

2 P.M. and for dinner from 7:30 to 9 P.M., Saturday from 7:30 to 9:30 P.M.. Closed Sunday for dinner and all day Monday. The set dinner is about $12. Dinner ordered à la carte is about $35 for two. Just down the street is the **Riverside Food and Wine Bar,** 1 Dale Road, Matlock (0629-56061). Home-cooked dishes are served on a terrace looking over the river Derwent. Open daily from 10 A.M. for coffee and from noon to 2:30 P.M. for lunch. Dinner is served Friday and Saturday from 7 to 10 P.M. and Tuesday from 6:30 to 10 P.M. Af ternoon teas are served from 3 to 5 P.M. from June through September. Closed between Christmas and New Year's.

WHERE TO STAY

Riber Hall, Riber, Derbyshire (telephone: Matlock 0629-2795). The extensive grounds of the manor house include an orchard and a walled garden. Bed and breakfast for a single is about $55; doubles, about $75. **Temple Hotel,** Matlock Bath (0629-3911) is on a wooded hillside. The hotel has thirteen bedrooms with singles from about $25 including bed and a good English breakfast, doubles from $35. Lunch is served from noon to 2:30 P.M. Monday through Saturday and from noon to 2 P.M. Sunday. Dinner is from 7 to 10 P.M. every night. Light meals such as hamburgers also are served in the bar. Dinner for two with wine, service and tax is about $30.

BAKEWELL

SIGHTSEEING

Two miles south of Bakewell on the A6 is **Haddon Hall** (062-981-2855), possibly the most complete and authentic example of a medieval and manorial home in England. Open Tuesday through Saturday from 11 A.M. to 6 P.M. in July and August, and Tuesday through Sunday from April 1 until September 30. Admission is about $2.50, half that for children. **Chatsworth** (telephone: Baslow 024-688-2204) lies four miles east of Bakewell. The house and gardens are open daily from March 27 to the last Sunday in October from 11:30 A.M. to 4:30 P.M. Admission is about $4.

EATING OUT

Fischer's, Bath Street, Bakewell (062-981-2204). Closed Sunday evening and all day Monday. Also closed the last week in September and three weeks in January. Reservations necessary. Lunch for two, about $20; dinner for two, about $55 with wine. Seasonal menu with typical dishes such as quail terrine, saddle of venison and crème brulée. The **Country Kitchen,** 5 King Street, Bakewell (062-981-4100), features homemade scones, tea cakes and fresh cream cheese cake. Open from 10 A.M. to 6 P.M. Monday to Wednesda y and Friday to Sunday. Closed Christmas Day plus three weeks in either November or January. Open sandwiches at about $2.

WHERE TO STAY

The **Rutland Arms Hotel,** the Square, Bakewell (062-981-2812). Renowned as the birthplace of the Bakewell pudding, this nineteenth-century hotel still has many of its original features. Singles are about $35; doubles, about $45. Continental breakfast is about $3 and full English breakfast about $6.

BUXTON

SIGHTSEEING

The scenic 17.5-mile **High Peak Trail** links Cromford with Buxton. Originally part of the train route in 1830 through the Derbyshire dales, the old **Station House** and a **Rail Museum** are on the trail. Buxt on is host to the annual **Buxton Festival,** which takes place in late July and early August and follows a different literary theme each year. For reservations and more information, write or call **The Festival Box Office,** Opera House, Buxton, Derbyshire SK17, 6XN (0298-71010).

EATING OUT

The **BULL I'th Thorn,** Hurdlow Town (029-883-348), on the A515 a few miles south of Buxton. This pub is open from 11 A.M. to 3 P.M. and 6 to 11 P.M. Monday through Saturday, and from noon to 2 P.M. and 7 to 10:30 P.M. on Sunday. Bar meals served, such as chicken and chips, about $2.50, and cottage pie, $1.50.

WHERE TO STAY

The **Old Hall Hotel,** the Square, Buxton (0298-2841), dates back to the sixteenth century. Singles are about $25 and doubles $40, including a full English breakfast. Lunch is served from noon to 2:30 P.M., dinner from 7:30 to 10:30 P.M. Hours are extended during the Buxton Festival when a pre-theater supper and an after-theater dinner are offered. Dinner for two with wine is about $35. **Mary's Wine Bar** is part of the hotel and is open from 10 A.M. to 11 P.M. ever y day. Coffee is served there in the morning, a large snack menu all day and tea in the afternoon. The **Sandringham Hotel,** Broad Walk, Buxton (0298-3430). An old country house overlooking the Pavilion Gardens. All the rooms are doubles with bath at about $25, including breakfast.

DOVEDALE

SIGHTSEEING

Along the dale northward from the town are the **Twenty Stepping Stones** that link Staffordshire on the west bank with Derbyshire on the east. Nearby **Eyam** has its well-decorating festivities in late Augus t. Free.

WHERE TO STAY

Peveril of the Peak Hotel, Thorpe Cloud Hill

(033-529-333). An extended rectory set high in the Peak District with spectacular views from picture windows in the bar. Singles are about $40; doubles, about $55. A full English breakfast is about $6; a Continental breakfast, about $4. A set dinner in the dining room with wine is about $30.

Voices of
England's Past

PAUL WEST

KID" OR "SQUIRE"
is what Mr. Gaunt the butcher calls you when you buy
his sliced ox tongue, a squashed-pea paste called mushy
or shoulder pork baked in a pastry case. "Kid" is informal, implying perhaps that meat can keep you young.
"Squire" is for when he is feeling a bit subserviently
medieval, though in a mutinous way. He will even say
"sir" or "madam" with a rich man's leer under his Ron-
ald Colman mustache, but his most outrageous mode of
address is "darling," popped at either sex with a mixture of sangfroid and prankish insolence befitting a
stand-up comic.

Somehow, in rosy-cheeked Mr. Gaunt (what a name
for a butcher, anyway), a highly developed sense of station has gone awry in the age of unisex, punk, and socialist peers. He finds all salutations equally valid,
equally silly. He does the honors at his shop in different

voices, only truly at home with the cut-up hogs, cows and sheep that cross his threshold fresh from the back-yard cooler.

Mostly, the bluff, cordial folk of Eckington, a Derbyshire mining village, address strangers as they have addressed them since Shakespeare's time. "Eigh-up, serry," they call out to you, as to one another, meaning: I have noticed you, sirrah (an Elizabethan word). Or, regardless of sex, they call you "love" or "duck," reserving for intimates such words as "flower" or "bonnie." Sometimes you need an interpreter. A man is a mester. Busy is throng. A candy is a spice. Food is snap. To be jiggered is to be tired out. And to cut cake or carve roast untidily is to chavel it. This rough-and-ready society has words for things unfussed about elsewhere. Among so many words that sound like gongs, there lurks a sly finesse, a cryptic delicacy, you would never guess at if merely passing through rather than spending a week.

Eckington, the locus of these linguistic time warps, was founded by the Romans in the middle of the land now known as the Midlands, D. H. Lawrence and Byron country. The local dialect is close to Old Norse and Anglo-Saxon, but one village only a mile away is called Frecheville, while twenty miles west lies Chapel en le Frith and, some sixty miles to the south, Ashby de la Zouch, in Leicestershire. Normans as well as Vikings came here and stayed. Roman logic survives at the village center ("The Cross"), from which branch out two opposite thoroughfares called Northgate and Southgate. The crossroads' other limb does indeed run west, uphill to the Top End, and east, down to the Bottom End, but there was never a Westgate or an Eastgate. The vital artery was north-south, a point renewed and made large when British Railways revised its system by abolishing cross-country services galore but leaving the north-south ones largely intact.

Here, in the middle of England, just about as far from the sea as you can get, you are between the Derbyshire dales to the south and the Yorkshire moors to the north. You are among symbolic roses too. Not far away, they fought the Wars of the Roses (Lancaster versus York), a sporadic fifteenth-century rivalry perpetuated in dour cricket matches between the Red Rose county of Lancashire and the White Rose county of Yorkshire. The rose of Derbyshire happens to be yellow, and Derbyshire disdain for the things of Lancaster or York is chronic; the natural affiliation of Derbyshire folk is with Robin Hood and Sherwood Forest, which lies across the Nottinghamshire border. People come here to walk, to admire country mansions such as Chatsworth and Haddon Hall, to watch the local wells being decorated with flowers or local hearties playing Shrovetide Football, a pagan ceremony marking the end of winter, but possibly a violent echo from a Saxon victory over the Danes or the Romans, in which event the ball was someone's head.

Or you come here to savor famous quotations, from Sir Arthur Conan Doyle, who said the whole county was hollow from mining ("Could you strike it with some gigantic hammer it would boom like a drum"), to Jane Austen, who reported that there was not a finer county in England. Daniel Defoe, however, called it a howling wilderness, and Byron said, "There are things in Derbyshire as noble as in Greece or Switzerland," as if that mattered at all to people who right in their midst have the weird stone circle at Arbor Low, the chambered tombs on Minninglow Hill, and from the Stone Age hunters of Cresswell Crags a horse's head engraved in bone, Britain's first artifact.

The prehistory is there, all right, but you might think yourself among Quakers, with "thee" and "thou" as common as "you." If you are lucky enough to hear a street quarrel, you will witness one of those weird throwbacks to French mentality when a twentieth-century English villager objects to the second-person singular pronoun as too familiar. (In France you never tutoyer a stranger.) In Eckington the same breech of etiquette attracts the following retort: "Don't thee thou me, thou tharrer," a hilarious formula that might have delighted the linguistic philosopher Ludwig Wittgenstein for its truculent use of what it fiercely rejects. A tharrer (rhyming with Lara) is a thou-er, a tutoyist, denounced.

Like Prospero's island, the village is full of noises, especially on Saturday night after the pubs expel their patrons at closing time toward the Cross. Such times apart, life in the village is sedate and even humdrum. In summer, if you are watchful, you will see scores of families dragging back from their seaside holidays, all having come on the same train or coach, all having been given the same check-out time by the boarding houses. Always on Saturday.

Or, if you are only merely observant, you can see the pubs' car parks fill up just before eleven in the morning, and there the drinkers wait in neatly outlined lots until opening time, patient and dry, but with many calls to make if they want to do a crawl, working their way from the Moss Brook at the Bottom End to the West End at the Top. In between thrive the lordly, heraldic central array of The White Hart, The Prince of Wales, The Angel, The Duke of York, The Royal, The George Inn, The Bird in Hand, The Rose and Crown, and The Lion and Lamb.

Gone are The Coach and Horses, The Brown Bear, The Moulder's Arms, and The Crown and Cushion. Who needs them? The West End has a beer garden and, says a guidebook, "a warm welcome for visitors," The Rose and Crown is the main haunt of local pigeon fanciers, and The White Hart sits next to the warmly glowing granite of the village church, named for St. Peter and St. Paul. Long after you leave, the buttery-heathery tang of the hops from which the beer is brewed will tickle your nose, whether you have paid local or what the locals sardonically call "Nottinghamshire" prices.

Few tourists blur your view of the village's uncontrived, dim pageantry. Men in flat caps and collarless shirts wander around with a sprig of hawthorn between their teeth, their hands clamped behind them. "Aaahhh," says one to another as they meet, summing up all the pain and contrariness of the world. "Ah," answers the other in absolute assent. There is no need to talk it out. All you have to do is say "Ah," mingling pity, rage, and stoicism in one breath, and everyone within earshot will echo you.

Gaudy ribbons dangle the full length of summer doorways to keep out wasps and flies. The windows are screened with billowing muslin. To bake bread, buy a paper twist of "balm," known elsewhere as yeast. The mailwoman whistles past on a red bicycle, its frame festooned with parcels. An aroma of hot fat wafts from the fish-and-chips shop, which also sells Chinese food. The street reeks of vinegar as folk stroll and eat their chips from nests of sodden newspaper held on the palm of one hand. Two children toot past, their arms linked behind them in an ancient game known as Belthorses. Most of those not eating are sucking—mintoes, caramels, pear drops, acid drops, mint imperials, Pontefract Cakes (pastilles of embossed licorice), fish-shaped sweets, or jelly babies. "Nice spice," they murmur to one another as they walk, almost lisping in the suck. And some of them, as they bite into a succulent portion, slow and halt as if to concentrate, frozen in the chomp.

The men's voices are either percussive, crude, and low, full of lurking testosterone, or shredded and hoarse as in certain caricatures of the Mafia. Everyone has a cough, not as in the old days from coal dust but, as someone told me, "just from being out too much." Fresh air is deadly, they say here. But then, what does outside mean? They always knock and enter in one movement, so the interiors of others' homes belong as much to neighbors as does the outside world itself. If the falsetto of some men is full of menace, or old-style silicosis, the women cluck, cackle, and curse, Junos all, every bit as big and strong as the men, and two thoughts arrive. If the Vikings and Romans had seen these, they would have quit to begin with. But these are the Vikings and Romans, in physique anyway.

Quaintly enough, although there are a hundred reasons for getting to know the village, it also happens to be Lady Chatterley's village, Tevershall, although (understandably) Lawrence's villagers talk with a Nottinghamshire rather than a Derbyshire accent. Close by is Renishaw, site of Renishaw Hall (Wragby in the novel), the ancestral seat of the Sitwell family, whose literary and extraliterary antics amazed a generation. Like a stranded, gorgeous cormorant, Dame Edith Sitwell opened and presided over local garden parties on St. Peter's cricket ground here, well aware that none of the locals except for a few grammar school kids knew her flamboyant poetry or her subjective, histrionic life of Alexander Pope.

Sir Osbert patroled the woodlands, which belonged to him, with a stout stick and a courteous, braying hello as the miners and farmers tugged their caps to him—Lord of the Manor—and little knowing that, soon, Flight Lieut. Eric Plumtree, Battle of Britain ace, would zoom low over these trees in his Spitfire, where once an es-caped tiger had roamed. Sacheverell, the other brother and the only member of the trio still alive, is also a poet and the author of some eighty books; a grave soul, some-thing like a Sibelius to Osbert's Sousa. Talk to Billy Cooper, whose sister, Gertrude Stevenson, has looked after the Sitwell family for half a century, and he will tell you of "Sasha's" latest doings: an essay on the sea-side resort of Scarborough, where the Sitwells often lived.

Once upon a time, special trains ran from London to Renishaw, to either of its train stations, bringing famous names for a country weekend. Evelyn Waugh, the pho-tographer Cecil Beaton, the composer Sir William Walton, the painter John Piper and a host of others wan-dered the streets of this robust village in a time when children thrashed tall thin tops called window breakers and sooty miners in wooden clogs clopped home from shiftwork to a metal bath filled with hot water ladled from a copper boiler heated by a small coal fire.

In those unprosperous times before bingo and video-cassette rentals, the editor of the literary magazine *Life and Letters*, Robert Herring, lived on Station Road with his German shepherd dog and shopped with a deep wicker basket. While these luminaries edited, composed, painted and wrote out at Renishaw, playing erudite party games, kazoo bands marched the streets, the names of those chosen to play cricket appeared in the tripe shop window, and the ice cream man drove a pony cart and crammed cold yellow custardy stuff into a customer-provided glass. Boys scurried from door to door with basin, knife and lambswool rug, performing the mumming play known as the Derby Tup or the Derby Ram, in which the Old Tup goes on the rampage before being ritually killed. A pair of horns strengthened the illusion. The cut throat was that of a Scandinavian giant, Ymir, also a Norse invader.

Versions of the Tup can still be found, and each bunch of boys has its own variants, but none of them know that the ballad "The Derby Ram" was the favorite folk song of George Washington.

Failey, failey, fol-da-riddle-da-ray,
As I was going to Derby upon a market day,
I met the finest tup, sir,
That ever was fed on hay.

Such is the local version, the heritage of small unliterary boys to whom Ymir is not half so imposing as the Jedi; but they can still be seen aping their elders, pretending to walk with lighted cigarettes cupped in their hands held together behind them. Their legacy is richer than they know, still including the Tup, the six bombs that hit the village in the Second War injuring no one at all, and Renishaw Hall, with the piano that plays itself at night, the ghost of Lady Ida Sitwell that walks, and the haunted room that chills you from the waist down. Alas, the Hall is hardly ever open to the public anymore. Only the other day, there was a garden fête in its not overmanicured grounds, but the Hall was off limits although the posters said otherwise. The new generation of Sitwells is not flamboyant or, indeed, half as much away as the famous trio was. The legend lives on in local mouths, of course, not only of the Billy Coopers, but of the Sitwell-fanciers who still keep alive tales of how Edith slept in a coffin, wore an iron mask, and could fly like a bat.

The Hall, for all its Gothic transfigurations by John Piper, has become another house. Eckingtonians now marvel at a town called Eckington, near Washington, D.C., founded in the eighteenth century by emigrants from here, and one wonders at such marveling, for that is how foreign places get their names. The mood of this ancient, Roman one is something like Bizet mixed with Rabelais and Hogarth: vivacious, bawdy, blunt. Get into it by sampling a Bakewell tart (a jam tart with a marzipan lid), oatcakes and pikelets (made from special flour and smothered with butter when hot), or the sticky sweetmeat called a brandysnap. Try the local potted meat with its curd of yellow fat on top. Ask if you can still buy a donkeystone to whiten your doorstep with.

When I do these things, I half hear a birth cry on a snowy day in Market Street from a time when the post office was candlelit and doctors wore fur-lined gloves and the midwife in gaiters and starched cuffs rode a bicycle with a crossbar through the drifts. In that room whose windowframe some stranger has repainted purple I was born on the day my mother's doctor died, into a timeless place that changes only to remain itself.

IF YOU GO TO ECKINGTON

To get to Eckington, take an X50 or X53 bus from the Pond Street station, Sheffield. Bus fare is about twenty cents. If you want to stay in the village, you could try one of the pubs for not very much, but expect incessant din and the constant smell of beer. One mile away, a much better bet is the **Mosborough Hall Hotel,** which offers not only a "Fourteenth Century Cocktail Bar" and from its roof a view of seventeen churches, but also four-poster beds, color television, central heating, and mainly French cuisine. The site dates from 1066. Double rooms are about $55, Monday through Thursday, and $40, Friday through Sunday, including breakfast and V.A.T. Dinner for two, including wine, tax and service charge, is about $30 for table d'hôte menu, $65 à la carte. Address: High Street, Mosborough, Sheffield S195 AE. Telephone: 0742 484353.

Nearer Renishaw Hall, a mile from Eckington, try **The Sitwell Arms,** doubles, about $55 during the week, $35 on weekends, breakfast not included. Dinner for two, including wine, tax and service charge, about $35 for French cuisine. Telephone: Eckington 435226.

French's "news shop," in the village's Bottom End, offers a good range of local and national periodicals; the lending library is excellent, and bus service up and down the village is frequent. If hungry, try black pudding or a chip-butty, a sandwich with French fries in it. To be truly local, you should smother all you eat in thick brown sauce, Daddie's or H.P. Most pubs provide a snack, from pork pie or a sandwich to a plate of meat and two vegetables. More expensively, and more formally, there is the medieval "banquet" at **Eckington Hall** (two minutes' stroll from Mosborough Hall and served on Fridays and Saturdays at 7 P.M.), costing about $20 for two, and this provides more than you can eat of lamb, steak-and-kidney pie, pike, roast potatoes, cauliflower in white sauce, rhubarb tart, and sherry-drenched English trifle. Telephone: Sheffield 485811. The English, especially in the north, eat nonstop, even though a full English breakfast, if you give it the time it deserves, will get you through to dinner with scarcely a pang. —P.W.

An Old Oxonian's Oxford

A. L. ROWSE

Everyone knows that Oxford is not only one of the most historic but also, in large part, one of the most beautiful cities in Europe, a treasured possession of the English-speaking world. There is something in it for everybody—history and architecture, ancient colleges and gardens, picture galleries and museums, science and music—to say nothing of its magical situation between two rivers, the Thames (locally called the Isis) and the Cherwell; its old city girdled by parks and meadows; its hills within view and walking distance.

Sir Nikolaus Pevsner, the architectural historian, has described the High Street (the High), spine of the university town, as one of the world's great streets. The beauty of it is the long curve that goes all the way from the tower of St. Martin's church at Carfax to Magdalen College tower, reflected in the river near the bridge at the bottom.

The curve is so gentle that it presents changing vistas wherever one stops; it is bordered on either side by historic buildings, colleges and churches of various periods, providing visual interest at every point.

Pevsner makes a further point of importance: Oxford has centricity. The city has a nodal point in the splendid Radcliffe Camera—a dome like St. Paul's (though more Roman in inspiration)—with a large square all round it. One side is dominated by the medieval university church of St. Mary the Virgin, with a decorated fourteenth-century spire; the opposite side has the big Jacobean Schools building, now occupied by the Bodleian Library. The eastern side is faced by the eighteenth-century Gothic of All Souls College, the western by Brasenose College and a glimpse of Exeter's garden; a corner of the Georgian Hertford College shoulders its way in. Façades, towers, battlements, parapets, traceried windows, a grand spire and magnificent Roman dome—this is the heart of the university. What could be more picturesque?

It takes the inside of a week to see Oxford properly. But one of the joys of living in such a place is that there is always something new for one to see—though when I say "new" I mean "old," just as New College is one of the oldest colleges, new only in 1379, when it was founded. Though I have lived in Oxford most of my life, there are still corners and crevices into which I have not even yet penetrated. Not only those: I have never been into the grounds of the Radcliffe Observatory, an eighteenth-century Tower of the Winds, which Pevsner calls architecturally the finest observatory of Europe, whose interior is also a delight. I have seen only the outside, from over the walls along the Woodstock Road.

Since there is so much to see and enjoy—and it takes

whole books to cover it all—I must be unashamedly personal and say what I myself like best: There is no other
way of dealing with such richness in a single piece.

The grandest and biggest buildings are not necessarily
my favorites. The largest and most splendid of the colleges is Christ Church, founded by Cardinal Wolsey and
Henry VIII. Though I was proud to be an Eng. Lit.
scholar there, it is not the most congenial to me—I fancy
something smaller. Tom Quad is the biggest of quadran-
gles, dominated by Sir Christopher Wren's gatetower; it
contains Great Tom, the heavy bell from Osney Abbey
that reverberates over the roofs of the city with 101
strokes at five minutes past nine to call the original number of students home within the walls at night. Within
the great gate, Wolsey's Tudor hall rears up on the right
to recall Matthew Arnold's "line of festal light in Christ-
Church hall."

Farther beyond is the cathedral, anciently the priory
of **St. Frideswide,** whose most remarkable feature
is the rich fan vaulting of the choir, though the place
is crowded with every kind of interest, medieval and
Pre-Raphaelite stained glass, sculpture, monuments,
brasses.

I graduated from Christ Church to become a fellow of
All Souls—lucky topographically as well as in other
ways, for the fifteenth-century front faces on the High,
while the inner quadrangle looks grandly up to the dome
of the Radcliffe Camera. One got the best of both worlds:
from my back windows I looked across small enclosed
gardens to the splendid long line of Queen's College.
Pevsner is positively enthusaistic about Queen's, which
he styles the grandest piece of classical architecture in
Oxford. Its library is my favorite interior. That noble
room has the finest rococo plasterwork and decorative

bookcases of any; while the chapel, with its coved ceiling and superb screen, is hardly less fine. Altogether, Queen's College makes a baroque palazzo worthy to be compared with Blenheim Palace, just outside town.

The interiors of colleges—especially the chapels, dining halls and libraries—offer a subject in themselves. I recognize the interior of the Radcliffe Camera as the finest—it is like looking up into the dome of St. Paul's Cathedral. I must also speak up for the Codrington Library at All Souls, longer and simpler than Queen's, but no less elegant with its tall line of windows. Dr. Johnson said that it was a fine place to prance in, but I don't suppose he ever pranced in it by moonlight, as I have often done, with its ghostly shadows and one's tread reverberating behind one. Other library interiors I admire are those of Christ Church, ornate and grand, and Oriel, built in 1788, plainer but with scagliola columns.

All these libraries have wonderful treasures to show to those specially interested. All Souls, for example, has a collection of rare Americana, including such illustrated eighteenth-century books as Catesby's book on the Carolinas and marvelous prints of exotic birds, beasts and flowers. (We also have five folio volumes of Wren's drawings and plans for palaces, houses and churches, among them all his designs for St. Paul's.)

One must appreciate the range and variety of these interiors—all the way from the almost barnlike thirteenth-century Merton library to the great hall of twentieth-century St. Catherine's. (I do not so much care for this last; and after all, one does not come to Oxford for modern buildings, not very good anyway—one can see them anywhere.)

Let us go back to the earliest and rarest. St. Michael's Church in Cornmarket Street actually has an Anglo-

Saxon tower, from before the Norman Conquest; Oxford Castle has a fine Norman tower from not long after. In the shadow of that tower was written a book that has in-fluenced European literature perhaps more than any book except the Bible: Geoffrey of Monmouth's *History of the Kings of Britain*, from which the whole of Arthu-rian literature has flowed, from the French romances and Sir Thomas Malory right up to our day with Edwin Arlington Robinson. From that same time we have the Norman work in the cathedral.

Merton, with its beautiful thirteenth-century chapel and splendid early glass, was originally intended to have a long nave, but stopped short at the transepts; this T-shaped building set the pattern for others. The plan was followed in the next century at New College (which has the largest medieval chapel, with magnificent stained glass and a fine collection of brasses in the tran-septs). All Souls has the most characteristic of fifteenth-century chapels, with all its original woodwork, most notably stalls, undisturbed—there are no pews for un-dergraduates, since the college has only fellows, as was originally the case with all medieval colleges.

Externally, most people would agree, Magdalen is the ideal college. Presided over by Wolsey's splendid tower, the college has the finest situation beside river and bridge. Within, all is spacious and eye-catching: green lawns and gray cloister, a grove for the fallow deer, Addison's Walk, named for the poet, around a park bounded by the river, red chestnuts in bloom in June and the scent of balsam carried on the breeze.

College gardens are a special feature of Oxford, and I am particularly fond of Worcester garden, on the western edge of the university, because it has a lake, swans, ducks, moorhens and a good long walk around. Beyond

the trees is the Byzantine-style campanile of St. Barnabas, Thomas Hardy's "ritualistic church of St. Silas" in *Jude the Obscure.* Merton's garden is smaller, but with a raised terrace over the ancient city wall that bounds it. During the civil wars, when Oxford was the royalist capital, Charles I's Queen held court here, while the King occupied Christ Church: One sees the doorway cut in the wall to give access from one to the other.

The nearest garden for my afternoon walks is at New College, next door to (and mother of) All Souls. A leading feature here is a long stretch of the inner city wall, quite high with defensive bastions; a tall mound in the middle of the sunken garden punctuates the scene. St. John's has a very large garden, with a rock garden with rare plants. Neighboring Trinity and Wadham are also well-off for space; colleges in the very center are apt to be cramped, but even so, there are patches of green lawn and flower borders everywhere. At the bottom of the High, opposite Magdalen, is the university's botanic garden, entered through a grand Caroline arch. It was first of its kind in England and a gift from Henry Danvers, intimate friend of Shakespeare's patron, Southampton. (In the Middle Ages it was the Jews' burying ground.)

I have a special feeling for the smallest, most intimate spots: for example, diminutive St. Edmund Hall, last of the medieval Halls, with a pretty chapel and a tiny library with a gallery. This college has now been able to annex the finest of the medieval churches, St. Peter in the East, for its library; Lincoln College has made similar use of All Saints, with its fine eighteenth-century interior. I also particularly like Pembroke College, with its small eighteenth-century chapel, and its front quad bright with window boxes full of flowers.

We must not forget the university institutions as such. First and foremost the Bodleian Library, one of the greatest and earliest of European public libraries; the oldest part is Duke Humphrey's fifteenth-century building, with the Divinity School beneath, whose vault, "one of the marvels of Oxford," is one of the most richly carved in the country. From the window embrasures—so pleasant to work there—one looks down on the garden of Exeter, where I remember a telling performance of *Samson Agonistes*. (The gardens of Oxford lend themselves to this; the finest performance I have ever seen of *The Tempest* was by the lake in Worcester Garden, with Prospero's barge sailing away from the magic island and Ariel tripping out over the water to say farewell while the moon rose over the trees.)

In this ancient center is Wren's first experiment in architecture, the Sheldonian Theatre, where degrees are conferred. Next door, something of special interest to scientists: The Old Ashmolean, a seventeenth-century palazzo with a fine portico and a museum of ancient scientific and medical instruments. Some way farther out is the big Natural History Museum, important as both the first demonstration of the importance of nineteenth-century science and a portent of its growth, for it has eaten up a large section of the University Parks beyond.

Oxford is a perfect treasure house of works of art— paintings, drawings, monuments: so many that it would occupy a lifetime to become acquainted with them all. I am happy that from my Oxford years I still carry so many of them in my head.

The Ashmolean is one of the most charming picture galleries in Europe, strong in seventeenth- and eighteenth-century Italian paintings, though it also has the most famous picture of Paolo Uccello, a forest hunt scene, five

Pre-Raphaelites and the ancient Arundel marbles. From early Virginia, among other relics, it has Powhatan's ceremonial mantle of deerskin, with wampum decoration.

The Bodleian Library houses scores of portraits of historic and literary interest, with fine bronze busts of Charles I, Archbishop Laud (not much loved by the Puritans but the greatest benefactor to the university) and Sir Thomas Bodley himself.

All the colleges, too, have portraits, busts or monuments of their famous alumni—we may take the monarchs and divines as read. The grandest college, Christ Church, has a whole picture gallery of its own: a fine collection of paintings, of mainly eighteenth-century inflection, and an extraordinary gathering of more than two thousand drawings. Among the former one should look out for a majestic Piero della Francesca of the Virgin and Saints and a Hugo van der Goes of Jacob and Rachel (though I carry in my head from undergraduate days a Carracci *Butcher's Shop*).

Christ Church's great hoard of portraits is mostly concentrated in Cardinal Wolsey's great hall (there is, of course, one of Wolsey himself, as founder, along with Henry VIII). Among all those pompous grandees and bishops, look out for John Wesley and William Penn. There are other fine portraits of Gladstone (by Millais) and Canning (by Sir Thomas Lawrence); and, among literary figures a good Millais of Ruskin and a posthumous one of Lewis Carroll—he was too shy to allow anyone to paint him in his lifetime.

Portraits and busts of writers proliferate: Dr. Johnson at Pembroke, Shelley at University College (which sent him down), Matthew Arnold, Charles Reade, Cardinal Newman. (Yet I do not know whether Magdalen has yet acquired a portrait of its alumnus, Oscar Wilde.)

Music? Three or four colleges have choir establishments, so that one can always hear choral music from all periods in their chapels. (Large-scale concerts take place in the big Town Hall and the Sheldonian.) Next to Wadham College, on Holywell Street, is the Music Room of the 1740s, said to be the earliest building in the country dedicated solely to the performance of music. Holywell itself is one of the oldest and prettiest of Oxford's streets; it is lined with seventeenth- and eighteenth-century façades, though the houses behind them are often much older, Elizabethan or earlier Tudor.

I have said nothing of the townscape, the old streets, of Oxford. Merton Street is my favorite, the old houses mostly undisturbed, the upper stories all looking over into Merton Garden. Beaumont Street is late eighteenth century, formal and classic like Bath, and built of fine Bath stone. Broad Street (the Broad) offers a fine broadening prospect to the east, colleges on either side, and pretty streets nearby: Turl Street (the Turl) and Ship Street, both of which have kept the distinction of an earlier society and time, when the works of men's hands were still in proportion and had not outrun the human scale.

And such, providentially, is the ancient center of the university city still.

SUSTENANCE IN OXFORD AND ENVIRONS

The colleges are usually open to visitors in the afternoon, from 2 until 5 (although some close at dusk). There is no central information office for the university, but the **Tourist Information Center,** St. Aldate's (telephone: 726871) can generally answer questions. The center is open from 9 A.M. to 5:30 P.M. Monday through Saturday, and, from the end of May to the first week in September, from 10:30 A.M. to 4 P.M. on Sundays and holidays. From April through October, the Tourist Center also offers walking tours of the colleges; the hours vary, according to demand, and the price is about $2 for adults, about $1 for children.

IN TOWN

Le Petit Blanc, 272 Banbury Road (Oxford 53540). Both lunch and dinner are prix fixe; the menu changes every day. Lunch is about $15, and might begin with fillets of mackerel or rillettes of pork. Main courses include grilled breast of pigeon, served with a white wine sauce, and pork stuffed with prunes in a wine and cream sauce. Half a carafe of house wine is included in the price. The dinner menu, at about $25, includes such traditional French country fare as onion soup, baby lamb, and *boudin noir* (black pudding), as well as a range of seasonal specialties. Open from 12:15 to 2:15 P.M. and 7:15 to 10:30 P.M., closed all day Sunday, Monday for lunch and holidays. Reservations are essential.

Heroes, 8 Ship Street (723459). For a quick, cheap bite, Heroes offers a choice of twenty sandwich ingredients which can be combined in any permutation. A sandwich will cost about $1.50, homemade soup about 75 cents and homemade cakes from 50 cents to $1. Breakfast is about $2.25. Open from 9 A.M. to 5 P.M., Monday through Saturday, closed holidays. No alcohol is served.

Bacchus Wine Bar, 29 George Street (241127). For a quick bite with a glass of wine: salads and quiches and pâtés, all around $5. Wine is about $1.50 by the glass, $5 to $6.50 by the bottle. Open Monday through Saturday from 12:30 to 3 P.M. and 6:30 P.M. to 2 A.M.; closed Christmas and New Year's.

St. Clements Coffee Shop, 43 St. Clements Street (726286). For a quick bite in a worthy cause—the proceeds from the shop go to charity. A snack of homemade soup and quiche should cost about $2.

Ladbroke Linton Lodge, 9–13 Linton Road (just off Banbury Road, the central road into Oxford; 53461). The restaurant has both an à la carte and a set menu. An appetizer of mushrooms stuffed with Stilton and fried with tarragon (about $1.60) sounds heavier than it is; duck with black cherries and cherry brandy sauce (about $11) is a recommended main course. The basic table wines cost about $10. Lunch is served from 12:30 to 2:30 P.M., dinner from 7:30 to 9:30 P.M. Double rooms are about $80, without breakfast, from Monday through Thursday, about $50 Friday through Sunday. Special weekend rates of about $60 a person, with breakfast, are available for stays of two nights (one must be a Saturday).

Cotswold Lodge Hotel, 66A Banbury Road (512121/9). Fish is the specialty, although you can begin with fresh asparagus (about $2), or melon and strawberries (about $2.50). Unusual offerings are monkfish with green peppercorns or skate in black butter (both about $7). The house wine is $6. Lunch is served from 12:30 to 2:30 P.M., dinner from 6:30 to 10:30 P.M. Double rooms are about $70 during the week, while two nights over a weekend cost about $100 for two; both rates include breakfast.

VILLAGE RETREATS

Feathers Hotel, Market Street, Woodstock (812291). The village of Woodstock is eight miles from Oxford, at the gates of Blenheim Palace. The restaurant of the Feathers has such specialties as an appetizer of brie in puff pastry ($3) or lobster soufflé ($4.50), and such main dishes as smoked leg of English lamb marinated in cider with yogurt and cream ($6) or brill wrapped in lettuce and poached in white wine ($15). The house red is a Côtes-du-Rhône ($9), and the wine list contains such entries as a Nuits-Saint-Georges 1979 at $25. Lunch is served from 12:30 to 2:15 P.M., dinner from 7:30 to 9:45 P.M. Double rooms cost from about $50 to $90, including breakfast.

Bear Hotel, Park Street, Woodstock (811511). Appetizers include Cornish crab and prawns in a white wine and tomato sauce ($4.50) and smoked Scotch salmon ($8), as well as poached rainbow trout and lemon sole (both $8). A whole duckling flamed in Grand Marnier is served for two ($20). Lemon mousse and pastry swans filled with strawberries are among the desserts ($3 each). Lunch from 12:30 to 2:30 P.M., dinner from 7 to 10:30 P.M. Double rooms are about $90 a night, but special rates are available for longer stays. Check with the hotel.

COUNTRY INN

Le Manoir aux Quat' Saisons, just outside Oxford in Great Milton (8881). The restaurant was given two Michelin stars before it even opened in its present location. There is a weekday set lunch for about $21 (excluding drinks) and three- and five-course Sunday lunches at about $30 and $40; an à la carte meal with drinks, wine and service will average $60 a person. Starters include asparagus tips in puff pastry with a chevril sauce or langoustine with Pernod; main dishes might include medallions of veal with truffles. Desserts run to the lavish—a baked apple filled with Calvados soufflé with an apricot coulis, for example. The extensive wine list holds a number of bottles for less than $15 (Cahors or Rully, for instance). Lunch from 12:15 to 2:15 P.M., dinner from 7:15 to 10:30 P.M. Closed for Sunday dinner, all day Monday and Christmas. A double room costs from $125 to $200, including breakfast.
—Sheila Gruson

Journeys Through Wales: An Ancestral Land Discovered

EMLYN WILLIAMS

P*LENTYN CYMREIG YDWI,
a plant Cymreig oedd fy rhieni.*" Which is Welsh for "A
child of Wales am I, as my ancestors were too." My
mother used to advise me never to talk about myself in
front of strangers. But when the subject is Wales, I have
to: Wales and I are bound together. And since I'm not
talking face to face, but on paper, perhaps my mother
would forgive me.

As a child, at home and in the village I spoke nothing
but Welsh, until I went to school and learned English,
which, of course, is still a normal procedure. And that

makes me realize something I've never thought of: That is, the fact that to the visitor, Wales presents an advantage not shared by any other "foreign" country. While it retains its own language and all the unconscious and arresting "quaintnesses" of a strange land (we even boast a patron saint, David, celebrated in song and poetry and festivity every March 1) we suffer from no language barrier. Everybody—except, very occasionally, the very old inhabitant of a remote countryside—speaks fluent and often colorful English.

Another advantage: When I was a child, Wales—to me—was an immense country surrounding me on all sides. But as I grew bigger, Wales grew smaller. And smaller. Because it is small—on a motoring holiday, you can drive right round it in a couple of summer days; in a leisurely two weeks, you can see everything, and there's a lot to see.

Small, yes, but small can be beautiful. You might say I sound prejudiced, like somebody who says "My mother's a beauty"—but Wales is beautiful. And I'm not prejudiced.

I'll tell you how I know: because I didn't discover Wales till I was twenty-one. Which meant that it was revealed to me as if to a tourist. I was born in Flintshire, a pleasant but unspectacular county in the northeast corner next to (English) Chester. When, at the age of ten—a moment to start appreciating the magic of travel—I read *Wild Wales*, the classic written by George Borrow in 1862, I thought . . . he makes my country sound exciting, but nothing to do with this part of it . . .

The exciting part started not more than ten miles from where I lived, but there were no buses or coaches, and I didn't have a bicycle. Going straight from school to Oxford, I saw nothing of Wales, and so had been unable to

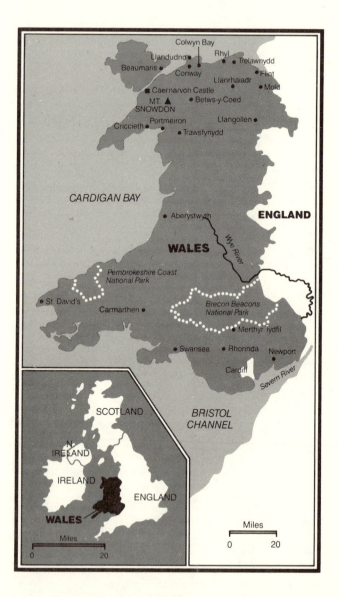

absorb, gradually from birth, the natural richnesses of my country, so as many children do, taking them for granted and looking back on them later with nostalgia. I could only read about them. And when I found myself an Oxford undergraduate roaming round Italy on a traveling scholarship, I thought, Wales can't be as romantic as this . . .

Then, after Oxford, marking time before confounding my parents by "going on the stage," I got a temporary job teaching Italian to young Megan Lloyd George, daughter of the great Welshman of that time. I had to cross North Wales to Criccieth, the village where the family had their Welsh home; and that meant traveling westward, by train, across the breadth of North Wales, more than fifty incredible miles, as far as Cardigan Bay, facing Ireland.

It was a fine afternoon in September 1926, and as the train edged leisurely along the sea, in a late golden light over a landscape as enchanting as the Roman Campagna, my excitement at meeting Lloyd George's daughter gradually mingled with my other thrill: the pleasure of discovering Wales.

I can never forget the train gliding round a curve, and then the slow swing into view of the great majestic mass of Conway Castle. I was back in the Middle Ages, as the venerable stones glowed warmly in the evening light, as they had glowed since the thirteenth century. Signposts and advertisements told me of inland valleys, which I sensed to be of the greatest beauty: Betws-y-Coed, the Llanberis Pass, Llanrhaiadr (the Village of the Waterfall) . . .

Then came the mountains. Not anything like as spectacular as the Alps, but not so forbiddingly glacial either. Friendly mountains. Even towering Snowdon does not frighten as it watches over green pastures dotted with stone farmsteads a hundred years old, some older than that. A variety of landscape is enhanced by the fact that the sea is never out of reach: the tawny sands of Rhyl, Colwyn Bay, Llandudno, Beaumaris . . .

Then Caernarvon Castle, even more proudly imposing than Conway: a historic stronghold which, forty-three years later, was to become newly historic with the Investiture of the present Prince of Wales. No one who was there for the ceremony—I was a radio commentator—can forget the sight of the great age-old citadel, floodlit and reflected in the sea: a reminder of endless Celtic romance, before even the Saxons arrived, from the mythical Druids through King Arthur and his knights to the heroic wars of Llewelyn the Great, of Owen Glendower, and of Llewelyn the Last . . .

Back to 1926. In the weeks to come, in the Lloyd George motor car, I was to savor my fill of the delights I had not known till then—pleasures that persist unchanged to this day, the only innovations being better roads, television and comfortable guesthouses.

So many pictures and sounds are still in my mind. Breathtaking mountain sunsets, blazing behind peak after peak, you could imagine a line of warrior horsemen with their banners red in the dying light. . . . And when I say "sounds" I mean singing, which is as much a part of Wales as the trees and the rocks: wonderful impeccable harmonies, often accompanied by the harp, floating unexpectedly from any quarter, from old country pubs, village street corners, barns, cottages, bustling marketplaces, even from historic little mountain railways.

I may have seen nothing of the real Wales till I was grown up, but I have certainly made up for it since, what with family visits and professional forays.

Journeys Through Wales: An Ancestral Land Discovered

For instance, three times in the last few years I have returned to Flintshire to play in Theatr Clwyd, a remarkable arts complex, strikingly set on a hillside overlooking the rustic town of Mold. With each visit, as I grow older, I am more and more poignantly aware of my roots—more and more firmly imbedded in the soil of a warmhearted life-enhancing little country.

All these visits of mine are vividly jumbled in my mind. I remember . . . a trip to Cardiff, our capital city, to cast Welsh parts in a comedy of mine, *The Druid's Rest*, when I auditioned a seventeen-year-old grocer's assistant from outside Swansea named Richard Jenkins, then in the process of changing his name to Burton.

On this and later trips I took the chance to explore, and to discover that Cardiff, while a typical modern city teeming with industry, has a rich heritage: There is a castle, a stronghold with 1,900 years of history, involving a siege in the Civil War—and a roof garden! A few yards away stands one of the handsomest civic centers in the world, in Portland stone, including a National Museum. Just outside, at St. Fagan's, is a museum in the shape of a Tudor mansion "as it used to be," restored and furnished and costumed, an uncanny pilgrimage into the past. And right on the outskirts of the urban mass, ancient Llandaff Cathedral houses a startling modern sculpture, Jacob Epstein's huge figure of Christ.

Excursions outside Cardiff confirmed for me that South Wales is not composed entirely of slag heaps. To the west of Cardiff lies the Vale of Glamorgan, and there I found beaches both rocky and sandy, topped by limestone cliffs. Farther west again, Dylan Thomas country (*Under Milk Wood*'s Laugharne with his much-loved boathouse home) and at the farthest west point, the

Pembrokeshire peninsula with, at its tip, facing the Atlantic, the Cathedral of St. David's.

And higher up in the map, the lyrical Wye Valley and the great national park known as the Brecon Beacons. For there, as in North Wales, rise the mountains; and among them I encountered a sport I had never heard of and which is remarkably popular—pony-trekking.

I saw famous Portmeirion, in Meirionethshire, the pocket Italianate villaggio created (concocted?) by Clough Williams-Ellis and—I have no doubt—labeled by the present generation as "high camp." Less amusing but rather more real, I remember a tiny village named Trawsfynydd ("Across the Mountain") with, at its center, a lone proud stone figure. The young poet Hedd Wyn, killed in World War I. How many villages, in England or America, are grouped round the statue of a poet?

I remember . . . 1952. After a season as Dickens at the Golden in New York, I played a month of benefits, for the Youth Clubs, through Wales—in cinemas, town halls, chapels, barns. Sheep and lambs at the stage door, a stray bird in the rafters, horses neighing in the adjoining field . . .

August 1953. The event of the year in Wales, the National Eisteddfod, this time at Rhyl: a unique and age-old summer institution of culture and entertainment to which, for generations, the American Welsh have flocked—and indeed Americans not Welsh—for a week of song, poetry, oratory and dance. I went through an exciting ordeal; at one of the sessions as President of the Day, I had to make a twenty-minute speech, in Welsh.

Another year, as narrator for Honegger's *King David*, I appeared at the annual Musical Festival at a venue as picturesque as Shakespeare's Stratford: Llangollen on the Dee, near the romantic ruins of Valle Crucis Abbey.

Incredible as it may sound, not only does this tiny community house—every summer—a celebration second only to the National Eisteddfod itself, it is an event to which flock singers and dancers from all corners of the world. On a sunny summer morning the spectacle of hundreds of competitors in their national costumes, strolling along the riverbanks and over the bridge—Serbo-Croat, Spanish, Turkish mixing with the native Welsh—is a painting of an out-of-doors opera.

Finally, a special memory. I was playing, again at Rhyl, in my own country, as *Dylan Thomas Growing Up*. Trelawnydd is a minute hill-village near my old home, and as president of the Trelawnydd Male Voice Choir, I was invited, on the Sunday morning, to a rehearsal in the Village Hall, for a forthcoming tour of the United States.

I took with me my American stage manager, Bob Crawley, on his first visit to Wales. As the group of dedicated, unpretentious countrymen rose to their feet, and those voices soared up into the sleepy Sunday air, I was proud to see Bob fascinated by the old folk songs sung in Welsh—"All Through the Night," "Gathering the White Wheat." Then suddenly—a gesture to the America they were about to visit—the familiar harmonies of "Shenandoah." The sophisticated man of the theater had tears in his eyes.

"Well," he said at last, "here's a country with glorious scenery, poetry and music. I'm not surprised at what you feel about your part of the world."

I am not surprised either. I salute my friendly mountains.

JOURNEYS THROUGH WALES

What follows is a highly selective list of hotels, restaurants and attractions in a few cities and tourist areas in Wales. Many events are free or require only a nominal admission fee.

The **British Tourist Authority,** 40 West 57th Street, New York, NY 10019 (telephone: 212-581-4700), has useful free brochures, among them *Wales: Where to Go and What to See,* which contains maps, descriptions of castles and industrial archaeological sites and lists of accommodations and regional and municipal tourist offices. Other publications are devoted to regional attractions, farm and country holidays and, especially, festivities.

CARDIFF

Cardiff Castle was built in the Victorian era to the design of William Burgess, who was also responsible for nearby Castell Coch. Its opulent state rooms are decorated with scenes that range from Greek mythology to the Canterbury Tales. The grounds incorporate the remains of a Norman fortress built on the site of an earlier Roman fort.

The **National Museum of Wales,** in the Civic Center, depicts the story of Wales from the earliest times; exhibits include a simulated coal mine. There's also an important collection of modern European art, including French Impressionist works. Open daily, but afternoons only on Sundays.

Llandaff Cathedral, on the west side of the city, was established in the sixth century by St. Seiriol and contains a late thirteenth-century Lady Chapel and Jacob Epstein's *Christ.*

St. Fagan's, Welsh Folk Museum, also on the west side of town, incorporates old buildings from all parts of Wales that have been reconstructed stone by stone. Besides the furnished cottages and farmhouses there is a working woolen mill and corn mill, a barn, tannery, smithy, chapel, tollhouse and cockpit. Open daily, but afternoons only on Sundays.

Among Cardiff hotels, the **Park Hotel,** Park Place (222-383471), is a beautifully restored establishment with a restaurant (meal for two with wine about $22), grill room and 108 rooms for about $65 for a double. The **Angel Hotel,** Castle Street (222-32633), is a portly nineteenth-century building with about 100 rooms starting at about $50 and spacious public rooms (the crystal chandelier in the hallway is reputedly the largest in the country).

Restaurants include the **Welsh Room,** 74 Whitchurch Road (222-42317), with such Welsh specialties as laver bread (made from seaweed), Welsh lamb, trout and even Welsh wine; about $10 to $13 a person for a three-course meal, including wine. **Gibson's,** 8 Romilly Crescent, Canton (222-41264), specializes in the cooking of a different region of France each week; a five-course dinner is about $16, a three-course lunch is about $9 to $13.

CRICCIETH

Perched on a rocky peninsula above this seaside town are the remains of a thirteenth-century native Welsh castle, later strengthened by Edward I. It commands fine views over the Tremadog Bay.

The **Bron Eifion Hotel** (76671-2385), five minutes' walk to the west of the village in a large estate, is known for its manigificent wood paneling. Its kitchen runs on the simple formula of plenty of fresh food (menu changes daily); a room, an English breakfast and dinner are about $45.

CAERNARVON

The **Castle,** probably the most famous of Welsh fortresses, was built by Edward I as part of his great chain of fortresses. The Regimental Museum of the Royal

Welsh Fusiliers is situated in the Queen's Tower and an exhibition of armor and of the history of the Castle in the Eagle Tower.

CONWAY

The castle and walled town, built in the late thirteenth century, together present an almost perfect example of medieval fortification. The castle follows the contours of a narrow strip of rock, and its eight towers dominate the estuary of the river Conway. The town wall, flanked by twenty-one towers and pierced by three gateways, is virtually intact (you can walk around the top).

Follow the river upstream on the B5106 road and, just ten minutes from the castle, you'll come to **Tal-y-Bont** and **The Lodge,** a modern restaurant (49269-534) set in peaceful surroundings just inside the National Park boundary. Specialties are fresh fish, and vegetables and herbs straight from the garden. Set menus are about $12. There are also ten simple bedrooms, about $20 a person, including breakfast.

In nearby **Llandudno** (Llandudno Junction is the railroad station for Conway), the **Bodysgallen Hall Hotel** (492-84466/7) has deep, dark oak paneling, heavy drapes and carpets, a profusion of antiques, stone mullioned windows and massive fireplaces. These, together with its gardens backed by moody views of Snowdonia, make it one of the finest places to stay in all Wales. Its restaurant serves "countryhouse cooking," with an emphasis on old English recipes (the menus change weekly). Room prices begin at about $60, while dinner is about $17, excluding wine.

SNOWDONIA

Cenedlaethol Eryri, the "Land of the Eagles," is the Welsh name for the 840 square miles that lie within the boundary of the **Snowdonia National Park.** There are National Park Information centers at Llanrwst,

Llanberis, Blaenau Ffestiniog, Harlech, Bala, Conway, Aberdovey and Dolgellau.

BETWS-Y-COED

At one of the gateways to Snowdonia, the **Henllys Hotel** (6902-534) is housed in the former courthouse overlooking the river Conway. A small, family-run hostelry with home cooking ("nothing out of a packet or a tin"), the Henllys has double rooms beginning at about $23, including breakfast, and a three-course dinner for about $10. The **Park Hill Hotel** (6902-540) is a small Victorian establishment on the outskirts of town, with views over the Conway Valley; there is an indoor heated pool and spa. Double rooms are about $35 and dinner (which may include pheasant, jugged hare or Conway salmon) about $12.

A mile or so away, in the middle of the village of **Penmachno**, the **Penmachno Mill** (6902-545) produces tweeds for ties and hats and brushed rug cloth and mohair wool for scarves and stoles, all on sale at the mill shop, which is open daily from April to October. At the top of the village, **Eagles** (6903-203) is a small restaurant with good, traditional cooking; everything is homemade, steak and kidney pie is a specialty, and a five-course dinner for residents is about $7. Rooms are about $11 a person, including breakfast. Dinner for nonresidents is about $8.

LLANGOLLEN

In the village, the **Canal Museum**, in an early nineteenth-century warehouse, uses working models, slides and films to show the importance of waterways in British history. At **Llangollen Weavers**, in a former corn mill on the banks of the river Dee, visitors can watch the manufacture of distinctive tweeds and tapestries.

At **Glynceiriog**, near Chirk, Llangollen, the **Golden Pheasant** (69172-281) allows you to combine eavesdropping on local gossip in the stone-flagged bar with dinner and a room for the night. Horseback riding, golf, fishing and pheasant shooting can also be arranged (in advance). A room with breakfast and dinner is about $40 a person; dinner alone—which could be homemade soup, then scampi in a Pernod sauce followed by a double helping of dessert—is about $12.

BRECON BEACONS

Near Libanus, on the edge of Mynydd Illtud Common, the **Brecon Beacons Mountain Center** provides an informative introduction to the National Park through interpretive displays, photographs and leaflets.

In **Crickhowell,** Powys, the **Bear Hotel** (837-810408) is an eighteenth-century coaching inn with simple rooms and a reputation for good local food. Double rooms begin at about $32, and dinner at less than $12.

ABERGAVENNY

The **Angel Hotel,** Cross Street (873-7121), is a handsome seventeenth-century coaching inn where Queen Victoria once watered her horses and the Beatles once stayed. Double room prices begin at about $50, excluding breakfast. Nearby, at **Llandewi Skerrid,** the **Walnut Tree Inn** (873-2797) has a French and Italian menu that changes daily; specialties are fish and game preparations, and meals are about $20 a person, including wine.

LAUGHARNE

The **Boathouse,** Dylan Thomas's home from 1949 till his death in 1953, is now a small museum. In the village you can enjoy a drink at Thomas's favorite watering hole, **Brown's Hotel,** visit the churchyard of **St. Martin's** where he is buried and buy copies of his works in the local greengrocery.

ST. DAVID'S

Founded in the sixth century, St. David's cathedral is one of the great historic shrines of Christendom. Its rich interior includes fine examples of carved wooden choir stalls and ornate stonework. On its grounds are the ruins of a bishop's palace.

The **Warpool Court Hotel** (437-720300) overlooks the usually gray Atlantic. Comfortable rooms and local fish and produce; from about $40 a person for a room with breakfast and dinner. —David Wickers

In the Lowlands of Scotland

RUMER GODDEN

WHERE IS DUMFRIES and Galloway? Remarkably few people know: It sounds Irish but it is in southwest Scotland, running along the border to the Solway Firth and the Irish Sea, perfectly accessible yet talked of as if it were remote. Perhaps it is, in terms of comprehension, because it is as unexpectedly different from the rest of Scotland as Scotland from the rest of Britain.

If you come up the main motorway from England, just after the river Esk you reach the border crossed by the Tollbar Bridge, and on the bridge is a sign surmounted by Royal Arms (of Scotland): a lion rampant on a shield of gold; above it is the Cross of St. Andrew, Scotland's patron saint, a diagonal cross of white on a blue background, flanked and headed by three thistles, its traditional and prickly flower. The Scots are prickly about their homeland, which is not an extension of England;

In the Lowlands of Scotland

you are entering a different country with different ways; different speech—though few Scots now speak Gaelic. The turn of phrases and many words are "foreign" to English ears, but they are as individual as the Scots themselves, the only people who can spend years overseas and yet remain completely themselves.

The one country that has ever influenced them is France; their courts are run in the French pattern but their laws are their own, which is why, just beyond the bridge you find the hamlet of Gretna Green, where runaway couples, often desperately chased, used to race to the old smithy, the blacksmith's forge, where they could be married "over the anvil." They had only to make their promise in front of witnesses and they were man and wife, the pursuing father or brothers arriving too late. Unfortunately, Gretna marriages are no longer valid but it is still lucky to make promises over the smithy's anvil, and almost every car, coach, cyclist or walker, as soon as they have crossed the bridge, go the short distance to Gretna Green, drawn by the romance.

We have all heard of the beauty of Scotland, but romance? It seems the last quality to be expected in this reputedly dour bleak country of sturdy hardheads, yet it is steeped in it.

> *O, my luve's like a red, red rose*
> *That's newly sprung in June.*
> *O, my luve's like a melodie,*
> *That's sweetly play'd in tune.*

A poem so simple that it seems to write itself, which is the art of the true poet, but it throbs with feeling because it comes truly from the heart—of Robert Burns. The romance of Scotland, as compared to, say, England, is like comparing the wild lament of the bagpipes, their turbulent skirls—the pipes can indeed skirl—with the ordered melody of a violin. The pipes may be too harsh for some ears, but they can have a haunting sweetness, a call that lingers, a beckoning as if to draw the stranger away into unknown worlds.

Few listen: Almost all the cars, coaches, walkers, on leaving Gretna Green, turn north to the Scotland they know—or think they know or at least have heard about—the Highlands. If they turned west they would reach the largely unknown Galloway, the region that holds the wild tracts of the counties of Kirkcudbright-shire and Wigtownshire, incorporated now with a third county, Dumfriesshire, and the Dumfriesshire districts of Nithsdale and Annandale. (The county capitals are the towns of Kirkcudbright, Wigtown and Dumfries.) What lilts of names! Galloway is perhaps so little known because until some twenty years ago all the main Scottish motor roads ran south to north, not east to west. Its appealing landscapes, even its beaches, were unexplored, except by locals.

Galloway and Dumfriesshire have no mountains as high as Ben Nevis in Inverness, but rather hills, many forested, snow-covered in winter and often capped with the mounds of old Roman encampments not found in the north. There are rivers well stocked with salmon and trout, but the area's lochs are smaller than Loch Lomond. The cities are not majestic like Edinburgh, Stirling or Aberdeen—the towns are plain, solid worka-day market towns. Of course it has castles—this is still Scotland—but it holds no royal Holyrood or Balmoral. Its moors, though carefully kept for grouse and heather, are fewer. The natural stone is not only granite and whinstone but often the softer sandstone that, given centuries, can mellow to a muted rose color.

In the Lowlands of Scotland

No one can deny the beauty and grandeur of the High-lands. Dumfries and Galloway can offer nothing as mag-nificent as that: Its charm is more subtle. It is a land of wide glens, hills with scattered white-walled farmsteads, their fields divided by "dykes," those gray rough dry stone walls, hand built—a dyker is a most skilled crafts-man. There are fishing and coastal villages like Kipp-ford and Southerness where locals moor their yachts and fishing boats and where the young John Paul Jones, the American naval hero of the Revolutionary War, who was born in a cottage at Kirkbean, would have sailed. The beaches, of course, have caravan parks and camping grounds, but even on the busier coast there is still space.

Anyone coming to Scotland is prepared for cold and rain—how lucky that it is the center of the wool trade. Galloway has plenty of "smurr," that Scottish word for fine mist drizzle, but its weather is milder; indeed, along the Solway, warmed by the Gulf Stream, are semitrop-ical gardens like the beauties of Logan and there are days—often weeks—of such warm balmy sunshine as would shame southernmost England. The air is clean, and there is a wonderful softness in the water—middle-aged women here have complexions like young girls; the water, too, makes tea such as you have never tasted.

Visitors will be offered plenty of that—it might be the poet Burns's "cup of kindness." Lowlands people are friendly and hospitable and above all give value for money—the farm and small house "bed and breakfast" places are justly renowned, and there is always time for talk because the way of life seems curiously unhurried. It is kindly, purposeful yet slow, and never dull, be-cause all Galloway, perhaps all Scotland, has a touch of the magical.

"My grandaddy saw a watermaid sitting starkie on

Scroggs Bridge," a small girl assured me and I can believe it. The Lowlands have no Loch Ness Monster but there are dragon pools still said to be inhabited (the curator at Dumfries Museum is an expert on dragon lore). It was in Dumfries, too, that J. M. Barrie wrote *Peter Pan*, at Moat Brae House; he was at school at Dumfries Academy. There are water "kelpies," strange will-o'-the-wisps called "spunkies" or "fire-flauchts," who help you to get lost at night, an easy thing to do in the myriad twisty lanes. Halloween is a great night in Scotland and people still plant the bright-berried rowan trees in their gardens to keep witches away.

With all the witchery, or because of the witchery, the real charm of Galloway is its gentleness. "Peace unsurpassed in any other part of Scotland," the guidebooks rightly say, which is a paradox because in no other part were more battles fought: bloodiest of battles against the English or between Scot and Scot—for the Crown; battles and feuds about love as in the ballad of young Lochinvar, who stole his bride away at her own wedding from under the noses of her kinsmen and bridegroom. Galloway ballads are true; Lochinvar is buried at Glenluce Abbey in Wigtownshire, but one thinks of him as perpetually young.

The bitterest wars were about religion. It was St. Ninian who brought Christianity to Scotland, and at Whithorn near Wigtown Bay there is a cave that was his hermitage. Every August on the Feast Day of St. Ninian, people from miles around make a pilgrimage to hear mass said in that cave, with the sounding background of the sea. Hundreds of Roman Catholics—some from the oldest families in Scotland—take communion kneeling on the rocks and sand. It is a harmonious scene—St. Ninian might have had a vision of it—but could he have

envisaged something you often see as you drive through
Galloway: a lonely cross on the hillside, a cairn of small
stones in a field, to mark where a Covenanter was shot or
cut down, one of the brave men who signed a Covenant
at Greyfriars in Edinburgh to resist the, to them, "embroidery" of the English Episcopal liturgy that Charles I
was trying to force on them with the Book of Common
Prayer.

The Covenanters were martyred, many at work on
their farms, or fishing boats; their women were tied to a
pole in the Solway and left to drown when the tide came
in. The battle between Protestants and Catholics had begun long before that, notably between the followers of
Mary, Queen of Scots, and the stern John Knox, and it
was not until the Yorkshire battle of Marston Moor that
Presbyterianism was declared the official Church of
Scotland. The Covenanters had not died in vain.

It is strange how these bloodiest of wars have left behind them castles of beauty and peace. Just south of
Dumfries lies the **Castle of Caerlaverock,** which
guarded the Scottish shore from the invasions from
Cumberland, the English mainland. Caerlaverock is
shaped like a shield, having only three sides with a tower
at each corner, one from which to scan the Irish sea, one
to scan the Solway across to Cumbria, the third looking
over moors and farmland. The drawbridge was hidden,
the moat around it deep, but now the drawbridge is
down, and though you can still walk into Caerlaverock,
climb some of the old steps, gaze up at the arches, it is
surrounded by smooth sward and this once ferocious castle is a favorite place for picnics.

In autumn the quiet of the sky of the marshes is often
broken by an eerie wild honking and soon an arrowhead
appears, as the wild geese home in to winter in the

Caerlaverock Wildlife Bird Sanctuary, which stretches along the Solway. People are allowed to go into the sanctuary before the short dusk closes in, and watch from the keep or, for privileged persons, from a "hide," where they can see birds in their thousands alighting for the night: geese, both graylag and barnacle, duck and widgeon, gulls, tern and whooper swans, herons wading in the shallows. At dawn, high over the quiet domesticity of farms and houses, you will hear that wild honking again as the geese fly out.

The geese are only seeking their feeding grounds, but this mixture of the uncanny with the canny is, to me, typical of Galloway. The small village of **Ruthwell** (pronounced Ruffle), also on the Solway coast, has, for instance, a unique place in the world of finance because it was here, in a whitewashed cottage in 1810, that its minister, the Rev. Henry Duncan, founded the first savings bank—it would be Scottish! Yet he was more than a financier: He saved one of Britain's oldest treasures, the Ruthwell Cross, now in the apse of the parish church. It dates from 700 and, as well as miniature sculptures of the Gospel stories, like Mary Magdalene drying Christ's feet with her hair, it is carved in ancient runic script with Caedmon's "Rood Lay," the song or lament of the cross on which Christ was crucified.

It is awesome to see and touch that ancient cross with its immortal message. It is difficult to imagine, too, anyone who would not be moved by the story of **Sweetheart Abbey,** whose sandstone shell stands amid low hills, fields and farms in the village of New Abbey in Kirkcudbrightshire. Most of the abbey's walls are still there, its arches, the stone pattern of its great rose window, the foundations of the cloister, parlor, novices' room, kitchen, storerooms, but it is not those that draw the people: It is the grave of Queen Devorguilla, who built the abbey in 1273 in memory of her lord, John de Balliol—and founded Balliol College, Oxford. John de Balliol, briefly King of Scotland, was defeated by Edward I of England and eventually usurped by Robert the Bruce. He spent three years imprisoned in the Tower of London, then exiled himself to his lands in France where he died, but he and Devorguilla loved one another so much that, on his death, she had his heart embalmed and put in a casket of ivory. This that she called her "sweet silent companion" went with her on all her travels; it is buried with her, and the monks changed the name of the abbey to Dulce Code or Sweetheart Abbey.

Perhaps even more poignant is **Dundrennan Abbey,** also a gracious pink sandstone ruin. It looks over the sea and it was here that Mary, Queen of Scots spent her last night on Scottish soil. She must have gazed over to the English shore, hoping—in vain—for the mercy of her cousin, Elizabeth I.

Perhaps it is because of all the blood, pain and sorrow of their history and balladry that the Scots love their poet, Burns, so much; he is so incorrigibly cheerful, ribald as well as tender, and filled with such zest for life. Burns, born in 1759 and dying when he was thirty-seven, had, too, the true poet's genius for putting a world in a nutshell. He loved Moffat, a small wool and weaving town in Dumfriesshire, set in glens and hills culminating in a fine waterfall called the Grey Mare's Tail, and all over Moffat and the Lowlands are rocks on which Burns sat to write his poems, walks where he paced, inns where he drank.

You can visit the tenant farm at Ellisland where he wrote "Tam o' Shanter" and his tiny house in the town of Dumfries, kept exactly as it was in his day. Its frugality shows how little money he made, but then he was no use at anything except making love, drinking and writing poetry. Burns is to Scotland what Shakespeare is to England. "But at least we can read Shakespeare," most people complain; so they can Burns if they persist and especially if he is read aloud.

On Burns's Night, held, at his favorite haunt, Dumfries's Globe Inn, on his birthday, January 25, scholars and admirers come from all over the world to pay him tribute. The chief dish on Burns's Night is haggis, piped in with ceremony by a piper playing a march. Before the haggis is cut, a guest of honor stands up and "addresses" it; and part of his speech must be from Burns's own "Address to a Haggis." Then toast after toast is drunk with dram after dram of Scotch whiskey.

Haggis is a sheep's maw, stuffed with minced sheep's lights mixed with onions and oatmeal, heavily spiced. It should properly be eaten with "tatties" (potatoes) and "neeps" (mashed turnip) and is unexpectedly good, though many shrink from it. It must be admitted that Galloway is not a place for gourmets—the ultimate horribleness I have met was cold porridge in sandwiches served in Stranraer—but there are compensations: The plain home cooking and baking is usually excellent. Those drop scones hot from the griddle! It's often the man of the house who makes the best porridge, smooth and hot, and it should be eaten with salt, not with "fancy" milk and sugar. Oatcakes are crisp and the Scots have fine cheeses. A specialty is smoked fish, all of it good, from the humble kipper—a smoked herring —to the perfection of smoked salmon and, of course, there is the unequaled Scottish beef, especially Angus. What in most countries is ranked as a luxury is here home grown: fresh salmon and trout, game, venison,

grouse, pheasant, but these come mostly from the big estates.

Not all the castles and great houses of Galloway are
ruins. It is still a region of large estates, some even vast,
each with tenant farms, cottages, its "great house" or
castle and, often, other sizable houses as well. Even the
manses are spacious.

Maxwelton House, at Moniaive, is not a castle: It
was the home of the Lauries, one of whom, Sir Robert,
had a daughter, Anna, born on December 16, 1682.
There are no Lauries at Maxwelton now but it is still a
family house and has been meticulously restored, even to
the little chapel in the grounds. Its "braes are more than
bonnie," but it is not for its beauty that people flock to
Maxwelton; they come because of Anna, Annie Laurie,
and her romance with William Douglas. It is popularly
supposed that he wrote the song we all know, but in fact
he wrote a poem:

> *Maxwelton braes are bonnie*
> *Where early fa's the dew*
> *And it's there that Annie Laurie*
> *Gie'd me her promise true.*

The poem was not adapted into the song until Victorian times and, sadly, Annie's promise was not true—or
else her father overruled her. She married Alexander
Ferguson of Craigdarroch (another lovely house), had
four children and lived till she was eighty-one, and
Douglas did not die. He married too.

Greatest of all the estates, though not one with romance attached, is the realm—no lesser word fits—of
the Duke of Buccleuch and Queensberry. The Buccleuch
Estates are run as a flourishing company, employing
hundreds of workers, many of whom are a part of the

family, having been "attached" for generations. The Buccleuch's Dumfriesshire home, **Drumlanrig,** is the most important lived-in castle in southern Scotland. Drumlanrig was rebuilt in the seventeenth century of pink sandstone, centered around a courtyard with four towers, its roof ornamental with lead-topped turrets carved with stone garlands, gargoyles and the strange crest of the Douglases—a heart with wings.

It is filled with treasures: paintings by Holbein, Murillo, Reynolds and, chief of all, Rembrandt's masterpiece, the *Portrait of an Old Woman Reading.* There are rooms of exquisite French furniture, hangings, tapestry, porcelain and silver, including the 136-pound silver chandelier, made in 1680, in the hall. Yet, with all this splendor, Drumlanrig is a family house. The parlor is the present Duchess's sitting room; all the rooms are used when the family arrive. There are bowls of flowers, books, magazines, games and parties.

There is so much to do and see in Dumfries and Galloway that the best thing to do is shut your eyes, take a pin and go where it pricks. I can only give a taste, but the name Douglas takes me back down the centuries to what, though it is so small, is to me the pearl of Lowland sights, the little castle of Threave on an islet of the river Dee, near the town of Castle Douglas and the National Trust Threave Gardens. **Threave Castle** is really a keep, four stories high, with rounded towers protecting its outer walls. It was built by Archibald the Grim, perhaps the blackest of all the Black Douglases—they got their dark name from their evil, treachery and cruelty. Most met violent deaths and finally the ninth Earl was overthrown. Now Threave stands in utter peace; not even a car can come near. To reach it, you have to take a rough path through fields and woods and ring the ancient bell

In the Lowlands of Scotland

for the ferryboat, a cockleshell rowed by a man who takes you across the water, among rushes and wild swans, to the island and its honey-colored tower—open these days to nothing more fearsome than water and sky.

My acquaintance with Galloway is anything but "auld," only five years, so I am still a stranger but, even if I went away tomorrow, I should not forget the crystaline air, the space, the strange stories and the magic, the friendliness, the unhurried freedom, the peace.

Come to Gretna Green and don't turn north, turn west.

Where Mystery Is Commonplace

RACHEL BILLINGTON

IRELAND IS A MYSTERY.
Ireland is beyond reason. The Irish love it fiercely—
particularly those who have left it. It's called the Emerald Isle, but vast areas are mauve or brown or gray with
barren rock. The greenest expanse is the sea that rips at
its every edge. But even that is not constant, changing
with the moods of the sky that sucks clouds in and out
like the breath of a god.

Gods are easy to imagine in parts of Ireland where ancient forts and crosses mark a gaunt survival against
winds and rain. The people near them, those who
haven't left, wear the same granite weather-beaten features. Yet inland on the lush grasslands of Meath or
Tipperary, the large herds of cows in the fields are rivaled only by the long columns of cars in the towns. And
in the grand old cities of Dublin, Cork or Galway, there

are people and hotels and theaters as sophisticated as any in the world. Ireland is a land of contradictions. A place where the past seems to dominate, yet the future is grasped with both hands.

The past of the last few hundred years has been shaped by the English. They have left a legacy of grand houses, or castles, as they are more often called— Tullynally Castle, in County Westmeath, has been owned by my family, the Earls of Longford, for 300 years. At first these great white elephants impress with their size and grandeur, their libraries and corridors, their paintings and their pillars. But in Ireland nothing is quite what it seems. The sharp-eyed will soon discern, on back passage walls, the damp-induced mushrooms that threaten constantly to move forward into splendid dining room or hall. Romantics should like them all the more for this.

But the English were only the last in a series of foreign invaders. Ireland was unfortunately placed for indepen-dence, with the wild barrier of the Atlantic on its west and a host of energetic seafaring nations, including Picts, Gaels, Vikings and Normans, to its east. When the great poet and dramatist W. B. Yeats (whose youth, incidentally, was spent in London) set out to restore for Ireland a sense of its own essential nature, he looked back 800 years or more to an ancient country of myths and legends. There Irish was the national language and even Christianity, when it arrived with its mighty miracle-working St. Patrick, did not extinguish a wor-ship of tree and stone. Yeats was my literary intro-duction to Ireland. His poetry, both descriptive and pro-phetic, his nationalism, his energetic battle to create a public Irish literature both in theater and books, inspired me—sitting snugly as I was in my Oxford college.

An ancient bridge, and a more ancient tower,
A farmhouse that is sheltered by its wall,
An acre of stony ground,
Where the symbolic rose can break in flower . . .

One can visit Thoor Ballylee at Cort, County Galway, where Yeats spent his summers from 1919 to 1929. It is a Norman thoor, or tower, now sitting solidly on the edge of a tranquil river, but when Yeats discovered it, it was crumbling fast into the mists of time. His work of loving restoration has been continued by the Irish Tourist Board.

The ancient world that inspired him also survives. Anyone traveling across Ireland will be struck by the number of stone crosses, formed in the complicated pattern called Celtic. They often stand in the middle of a field grazed by cows—like the one above Bantry Bay, which has lost its top but is worth a visit for the boat carved into its side. The crosses are, obviously, symbols of the Christian faith, but the remains of even older cultures, often still unexplained by historians, abound, particularly on the West Coast and its islands.

Ireland is already such a small island that it may seem perverse to suggest that its mystery might be explained by visiting as many of its own islands as possible. Certainly, this is the best way to appreciate the extraordinary beauty of the jagged, and therefore very secretive, coastline. One of the strangest experiences is to fly into Shannon Airport, which lies on the estuary of the river Shannon, take a small diversion past Bunratty Castle for a look at the beautiful old town of Limerick, with its churches, courthouse and river walks, and then head sharply west. Soon the expected Irish greenness disappears and you are into the Burren of County Clare, mile after mile of limestone rock where nothing grows but shallowly rooted flowers creeping forth from concealed crevices. Eventually you arrive at the great fishing port of Galway, from which boats go out to the Aran Islands. The chances are that wind and rain will make the crossing seem a lot longer than it really is.

The Aran Islands are a desolate and humbling place. From the sky each island looks like a patchwork, for every tiny field is bordered by the stones picked laboriously out of its soil. Here are the coracle boats, made of skin and immortalized in Flaherty's documentary, *Man of Aran*. Recently I stayed on the biggest island, Inishmore, for a night or two. The rain fell continuously. On the second morning I walked to Dun Aengus, an ancient stone fort that peers out from the island to the desert wastes of sea and sky. There are other forts of its kind in Kerry and Clare and Galway, but there is nothing so impressive as this. Michael MacLiammoir, the actor, accurately described it as "monstrous and magnificent." It makes a mere human being feel very small indeed.

This becomes a fairly usual sensation if you travel down the west coast. In Clare there is the grandeur of the Cliffs of Moher, whose dark rocks drop down into a continuously tumbling sea. Even the two great peninsulas, the Dingle and the Ring of Kerry, are crisscrossed by mountains that, even if providing some sheltered sandy beaches, as at Inch, still break out at their tips into jagged and threatening rocks. At the end of Dingle, a boat leaves for the Blasket Islands, and nearby there is the forbidding stone fort of Dunquin. From Waterville, in the west of Kerry, you can get across to the ancient island kingdom of the Skelligs. On Skellig St. Michael, or Great Skellig, there is a whole colony of the extraordinary early buildings known because of their shape as beehives. Sometimes it seems as if the ancient Irish wanted to lose themselves in sea and sky.

More ordinary mortals might be tempted to take the mountain road from Killarney and aim for the luxury of the Kenmare Park Hotel. The road winds high into the mountains, passing through walls of dark and glistening rhododendrons until the rich soil is left behind and once more the rocks close round. There, far too high to be anything but a bit of Irish magic, is Upper Lake, a pool of watery silence. Finally the road makes a tortuous descent through the mysteriously named Moll's Gap and almost runs straight into the hotel's nine-hole golf course. Ireland is a land of contrasts indeed!

Farther south in Cork County, the western winds are not quite so strong and the mountains not quite so high. But that's only relative. A drive down from Skibbereen to Baltimore (it was there first) takes you as far southwest as you can go, were it not for the little island of Clear just a few miles out. There always seems to be one more island, and always a ruin on it of a fort or an unexplained collection of stones like the Drombeg Circle. It seems these older inhabitants were not afraid of their environment, indeed felt a particular attraction for its most exaggerated and rugged expressions.

It is in these areas that Irish is still spoken. The man selling me picnic cheese tossed a few authentic words over his shoulder. If Yeats tried to restore Ireland's history, Synge and O'Casey did the same for its people. Synge traveled around the west and the Aran Islands taking notes on the speech and the life of its inhabitants. The voice of the man from West Kerry, Mayo or Wicklow speaks in his plays. Not that he attempted to solve any mysteries in their character. In Kerry I overheard a farmer describe his neighbor as "a typical Kerry man, he answers a question with a question." He said it with a mixture of pride and resignation.

I sometimes think all Irish national characteristics can be explained by climate and geography. Nothing is ever certain—except change and a very high proportion of rain. It can be as cold as December in June and hottest of all in April. A few days of the wet westerly winds is enough to make one understand the joys of a pint of draught Guinness drunk in front of a sweet-smelling peat fire. (Again, it is typically perverse that the most gloomy of all areas, the peat bog, should produce the most comforting and glowing of all fires.) Alcohol has always been a peculiarly Irish weakness, as if being on an island surrounded by water, with water falling constantly from above, gave them an enormous thirst. The opposite might have seemed more logical. Some regions are famous for their capacity to down alcohol more or less continuously. Cork is one such place.

Cork is in a very favored position on a natural harbor in the south of the island. But it has never quite equaled the

success of its eastern rival, Dublin. Since they are traditional rivals, it may be a consciousness of failure that
makes it drown its sorrows. Or it may be, on the other
hand, simply a nasty rumor put about by Dubliners.

Dublin was designed as a grand eighteenth-century
city. There are still well-preserved districts like Merrion
Square. Sadly many of them have been neglected or torn
down. Nevertheless, a drive out to a suburban area like
Rathmines will take you through forgotten rows of classical façades in which it is easy enough to imagine the
splendors of the past. The splendors of the present or recent past can be found in O'Connell Street, the central
thoroughfare of the town, which leads toward the dark
waters of the Liffey. The main post office still shows
bullet wounds from the Easter Uprising, but the web of
streets linking it are filled with shops as glittering (and
expensive) as any in Europe.

Cork rose to prominence later than Dublin and is a
predominantly nineteenth-century city. However, unlike
Dublin, Cork remains largely unaltered. It is built
around a large harbor, a wide canal and up the slopes of
a steep hill. The number of churches, the oldest and most
graceful being St. Anne's, Shandon, is rivaled only by
the number of bars. In the small street facing the church,
I counted The Shandon Arms, The Steeple, The Chimes
and, last but not least, Pat O'Brien's. Presumably not
for this reason, Cork is also a city of the arts. There is a
film festival and sometimes a film industry. Kinsale, a
small fishing village nearby, caters to day visitors from
Cork with a selection of bars and restaurants, selling
lobster and oysters and crabs and Guinness. Or just
Guinness. Among the many deserted beaches nearby I
found one entirely made of tiny seashells.

Within the city, the beauty of the surroundings seems

reflected in the many small art galleries, usually in buildings a hundred years old or more and showing paintings of local scenes by local painters. There is also the large city art gallery, which has some romantic portraits by Sir John Lavery and landscapes by Jack B. Yeats, the poet's brother. (The most impressive building, however, is the lunatic asylum on the outskirts of town, supposedly the biggest in the world.) Cork also has a culinary tradition, with superb fish constantly available. The Arbutus Lodge, a small hotel in the smart hillside area of Montenotte, has a menu that embraces both French sauces and Irish soda bread. It is always full.

It was while sitting in the Arbutus Lodge that I realized how very like the Americans these Irish seem to an English eye. It is a matter of style, a kind of natural exuberance. The exuberant Irish, of course, are the successful ones who have got as far away as possible from the desolation of clifftop and rainswept pasture, to a brave new world of deals and development. Originally, they benefited from the Common Market agricultural policy that at last made farming profitable rather than a grim battle against the elements—profitable on fertile inland soil, that is. County Cork, like Meath and Tipperary, is a glorious pastureland. But now they run companies or manage small factories. Or become lawyers, doctors or shopowners. Just like any other modern country, in fact. The only difference is that in Ireland it has all happened rather suddenly, and the old still exists side by side with the new.

It is the new sort of Irishman who now runs the country—although he must take into account the others. In St. Mary's, Cork, there is a little miracle-working ivory carving of the Madonna and Child that is still well attended. The day I was there, a man and his dog occupied the front pew. But these new Irishmen have to look to the future. Recently there was much excitement over the new oil wells being drilled near the south coast. When I flew into Cork during this time, a chauffeur waited, holding a placard saying, "Oil Man." But during my visit the scene changed. Headlines in the *Irish Independent* read, "Oil Well Runs Only Water." Not, you might say, the luck of the Irish. Or perhaps they should say a few more prayers at the shrine of Our Lady of Graces.

Although, speaking as a Catholic myself, I could hardly complain of a lack of worship. In Castlepollard, a village near my own family's castle, there are two fine granite churches, almost identical in appearance. In fact, the only difference is on Sunday, when the Catholic church is full to overflowing and the Church of Ireland (Anglican) is scarcely inhabited. On the other hand, the old abbeys took a British beating in the seventeenth century. A ruin fancier might start with Muckross Abbey, situated just outside Killarney on the edge of Lough Leane. Its cloister is still in perfect condition, although it now has a roof made by a huge tree that must have been planted as a piece of ornamental greenery several hundred years ago. Fore Abbey, near my family home, sits among three lakes, including the mysterious Lough Derravaragh, where, according to legend, the children of Lir were turned into swans.

Lakes are an important part of Ireland. One recent summer I swam in three different lakes on successive days. Those cowards who don't like clear, ice-cold water might prefer to take a boat and fish. A dawn rise and a couple of hours among the reeds waiting for duck was always a childhood treat, although more coot seemed to appear than duck. Ocean fishing tended to the same kind of problem. One outing from Tralee became known for the superabundance of dogfish. "Oh," smiled the Irish fisherman who had accompanied us, "it's a fine thing to think of all those happy sole and cod and turbot you haven't caught."

The other day I lay on my back above a 200-foot drop and kissed the Blarney Stone for the first time. That night I lay awake in my hotel bedroom while two Irishmen in the room above me talked without cease till 4:45 A.M. They then woke up at seven and began again. In my sleepless exhaustion, I tried to imagine what they could be talking about, in that insistent melodious rhythm, that was so much more important than a night's sleep. I failed. So has anyone else I've asked. "Perhaps they were drunk," someone suggested. But they weren't. And I was the one who'd kissed the Blarney Stone.

My mistake, of course, was to look for a rational explanation. Stone forts on bleak islands, a miracle-working image in a Cork church, intricately carved crosses in the middle of nowhere, all retain their mystery—and so do my Irish nighttime conversationalists.

Ireland is a mystery which only a fool would try to unravel.

A GATHERING OF GREAT HOUSES

Ireland's great houses, once owned by landlords across the channel, are now mostly permanently inhabited and, because of a recent tax concession, also mostly open to the public. Many grounds and gardens are always open; advance permission is occasionally required to visit a house itself.

For very different reasons, the following four houses, spread as they are across Ireland, illustrate for me the romance, and sometimes the sadness, of Ireland.

Glin Castle stands like a sugar birthday cake on the estuary of the river Shannon. It is owned and run by the Knight of Glin, who is the twenty-ninth holder of the title, and Madame Fitzgerald. Inside, it is as elaborate as the most elegant townhouse, with fluted pillars, decorated ceilings and some commanding portraits of Fitzgerald ancestors. One, a colonel of the Royal Glin Artillery, leans nonchalantly against a cannon.

Tullynally Castle, in County Westmeath, was originally square, but was Gothicized in the early nineteenth century by the addition of a forest of meaningless turrets and castellations. It was also expanded around two additional courtyards, so that there are now 130 rooms. This is only a little exceptional in a country where space is about the only thing never in short supply.

Bantry House, in County Cork, stands in a wild Italian garden (always open) where hundreds of crumbling stone steps lead up to a breathtaking view across Bantry Bay to the distant Caha Mountains. Owing to the warm water of the Gulf Stream, semitropical vegetation flourishes, half burying the house, which was built about 1750 and has the eighteenth-century virtue of being spacious and airy without being in any way formidable.

Lissadell, in County Sligo, tall and gray, is also set at the edge of a bay, Drumcliff Bay, and looks toward the Ox Mountains with the 1,078-foot Knock Narea. The house contains relics of W. B. Yeats; its rooms and halls echo with the ghosts of the two beautiful Gore-Booth sisters, one of whom, Countess Markievicz, was imprisoned for her Republican sympathies.

SOJOURNING IN IRELAND
STYLISH DIGS

Arbutus Lodge Hotel, Montenotte, Cork (telephone: 501237), is set in its own garden in an inner suburb of the city. There are twenty rooms; a double costs about $65, with full breakfast. The restaurant menu has such local specialties as Cork drisheen (blood sausage), sea bass with ginger and saffron and Tipperary lamb with herbs; dinner for two, with wine, begins at about $60 to $70. There is an extensive wine list.

Kenmare Park Hotel, Kenmare (41200), is a Victorian structure overlooking the sea and mountains, with marble fireplaces, damask curtains and family portraits. There are fifty rooms, of which nineteen are completely furnished with antiques (three have four-poster beds), and six suites, two with four-posters. A double room is about $105, with full breakfast; suites are about $145. Restaurant specialties include chicken stuffed with salmon in prawn sauce, roast Kerry lamb with honey and thyme sauce, and poached sole with lobster sauce; dinner for two, with wine, is about $60 to $70.

FISH DINNERS

Blue Haven Hotel Restaurant, Long Quay, Kinsale (72209), serves a casserole of prawns, scallops, mussels and monkfish (called a Molly Malone), as well as braised monkfish and Queen Maeve's breakfast, a composition of prawns, cabbage, shrimp and Irish Mist liqueur. About $35 for a meal for two, with wine.

Vintage, Main Street, Kinsale (72502), has wild rabbit provençal and pigeon breast in pastry with duxelles, as well as seafood. The house specialty is hot-smoked local salmon. About $40 for two, with wine.

Skipper's, Lower O'Connell Street, Kinsale (72664), has prawn cocktails, seafood soups, monkfish or plaice and poached salmon in cucumber sauce, as well as meat dishes. Dinner for two, with wine, is about $30.

Man Friday, Scilly, on the outskirts of Kinsale (72260), serves baked black sole stuffed with seafood as well as an eclectic sampling of international dishes. Dinner for two, with wine, is about $40.

Dublin's Timeless Trinity

P. D. JAMES

IT MUST BE A RARE visitor to Dublin who does not place the College of the Holy and Undivided Trinity—Trinity College—high on the list of sightseeing priorities. Some national monuments are difficult to find; Trinity is impossible to miss. There can be few universities that occupy so privileged a site, forty secluded acres of harmonious stone, grass and trees set in the very heart of a capital city.

To return to Trinity as a visitor after more than thirty years is to feel an immediate sense of recognition. One comes back to loved buildings as to old friends; they change in externals but not in spirit. The long Palladian west front facing College Green seems a little grubbier, perhaps, in contrast to the gleaming sweep of the recently cleaned Bank of Ireland; the traffic is busier, the city seems to press more insistently against Trinity's railings. But John Henry Foley's statue of the statesman

Henry Grattan still stands on its island above the swirl of traffic, holding out its hand toward the college as if to proclaim that here it still is.

The entrance is flanked by statues, also by Foley, of two of Trinity's most illustrious graduates, the poet Oliver Goldsmith and the statesman Edmund Burke. Goldsmith in his breeches and buckled shoes stands, left foot forward, in insouciant ease, reading from a book held in his left palm. Burke, hand on hip, has a more resolutely aggressive air. Their plinths stand on twin lawns behind the railings and on land first leased to the college in the 1680s for half a crown a year "and a couple of fat capons at Christmas, yearly to the Lord Mayor." Behind them the arched portico seems physically to draw the city's traffic (and no buses grind more than the yellow and green buses of Dublin), through Theodore Jacobsen's west front, and into the austere and harmonious peace of what must be one of the most impressive academic squares in Europe.

This magnificent courtyard of cobblestones and lawns was a nineteenth-century innovation formed by the merging of Parliament Square (so called because it was funded by the old Irish Parliament) and Library Square. Trinity is cruciform in shape, the cross formed by six squares. The visitor passes through Front Square to this immense area. To the north is Botany Bay, a residential square named for the Australian penal colony, so it is rumored, because of the unruliness of its former student inhabitants. To the south lies Fellows Square, containing the Arts and Social Science Building, opened in 1978 when the cruciform design was completed. To the east is New Square, which contains the museum, arguably the most beautiful building in Trinity.

But it is the merging of Parliament and Library

squares with the great campanile, with its two ancient and sonorous bells, rising from the center that is perhaps Trinity's most successful architectural innovation. Here buildings and cobblestones, lawns and carefully tended trees under the ever-changing Dublin sky, combine to form an impression of austere but totally satisfying peace and harmony.

To walk here is a joy in almost any weather. Dublin can experience the four seasons in one day. The morning may bring driving rain, which bounces against the cobbles as if to dislodge them. Then the clouds move across the mountains with purposeful majesty, the sky becomes a limitless translucent blue and the grass in New Square burns so green that it stings the eyes. The quality of the light in Dublin is unique, just as the sky there seems closer than it does in any other city.

Dublin's Timeless Trinity

Two identical templelike buildings, each with four Corinthian pillars, face each other across Parliament Square, both the work of the eighteenth-century architect Sir William Chambers. To the north is the chapel; to the south the theater, usually known as the Examination Hall. Inside, too, they are similar in design, with a barrel-vaulted ceiling and long apsed auditorium. But they are totally different in mood. The theater is the more immediately spectacular with its decorated ceiling by one of Dublin's finest stuccoers, Michael Stapleton, its carved organ case, its gilded oak chandelier, its nine large portraits of college worthies. But I prefer the simplicity of the chapel. I like the way in which the curve of the gallery echoes that of the apse, the fine carving of the paired pilasters, the tall collegiate pews so reminiscent of Cambridge college chapels. Nothing is superfluous; all is order and proportion.

There is, of course, nothing here of the original Elizabethan Trinity. Those who seek some trace of those early origins can find it hidden away behind the chapel in the simple memorials to some of the men connected with the foundation of the college. The stone was laid on March 13, 1592, on the site of a suppressed Augustinian monastery that lay to the east of medieval Dublin.

It is appropriate that its sponsor should have been the first Elizabeth, easily the most learned of English queens. But her motives were not entirely academic. The intention was that "knowledge and civility might be increased by the instruction of our people there, whereof many have usually heretofore used to travaill into ffrance, Italy and Spaine to gett learning in such foreign universities, whereby they have been infected with poperie and other ill qualities and so become evil subjects."

But this was also the Queen who proclaimed that she had no wish to make windows to pry into men's souls, and we can, I think, assume that she would have approved the decision in 1793 to admit Roman Catholics and would welcome the fact that Trinity is now a nondenominational college interested in the scholarship of applicants, not in their religious allegiance. But it has nevertheless been in its time the academic and spiritual home of the Anglo-Irish—"no petty people," as W. B. Yeats said of them—and these squares have been walked by distinguished representatives of the breed: Swift, Congreve, Berkeley, Oscar Wilde, J. M. Synge.

For me the most exciting building in Trinity is the museum. It is best viewed, preferably on a fine day, from the south across New Square. It was begun in 1853 and completed three years later, and the architects, Sir Thomas Dean and Benjamin Woodward, were responsible also for the successful alterations to the interior of the library. Despite the range of tall chimneys thrusting low on the roof, the first impression of the museum is almost entirely Venetian. With its narrow, rounded windows formally arranged and its marble discs adorning the façade, it looks like a particularly well-preserved palazzo; half closing one's eyes, it is possible to imagine the shimmer of water flowing through New Square and see the gondolas rocking at the steps. The ground floor is open to the public, but as the door is usually closed one should press it boldly. Too many casual visitors, I suspect, miss the interior of this remarkable building.

Inside the door the two flanking skeletons of prehistoric beasts and the display cases make the function of the building immediately clear. But I could wish them away, the better to relish the ambiguities of the interior. Outside all is symmetry; here all is rich variety. A profusion of color, carving, pilasters, columns and arches, of changing light and vistas are held in marvelous balance so that the whole is totally harmonious. The twin domes patterned in blues, pink and cream, the arches with their alternately colored bricks, the rows of pillars hinting at mysteries half concealed are Islamic in style and spirit; the building could be a mosque.

But the pillars and their fine capitals, the formally patterned floor and the wide, branching staircase remind one of some great department of state. And yet there is something, not exactly domestic, but companionable about the building. It invites, it does not intimidate. And the carving is magnificent, a profusion of naturalistic foliage, fruit, flowers and animals. The records show that it is an Anglo-Irish cooperation, the work of a Mr. Roe of Lambeth and of the O'Shea brothers of Cork.

The brothers were employed by the two architects to work also on the Oxford museum, but are said to have been sent back to Ireland because of drunkenness. But drunk or sober their work here is one of the delights of Trinity. No wonder John Ruskin described the museum building as an architectural masterpiece; much of the design of this monument to Victorian ebullience and craftsmanship was taken from his book *The Stones of Venice*. But it is his in spirit as well as in design.

The building to which the majority of Trinity's visitors first make their way is the old library, not only for its own splendor but because it houses a treasure, the marvelously illuminated Gospel Book of Kells dating from the early part of the ninth century and reputed to come from the monastic center of Kells in County Meath. For such a treasure the Long Room of the library is an appropriate setting. The entrance is in New Square adjacent to the modern Berkeley Library, the first major building

project undertaken by the college after 1900. The impo-
sition of the modern on the old is always controversial.
But unless architects are to be restricted to producing
buildings that are copies, good or bad, of past glories, the
additions must reflect the needs, the aspirations, the
spirit and the technical achievements of their own time,
and Paul Koralek's prize-winning, solidly horizontal
design makes its statement with confidence. The wide
steps that lead to it lead also to the old library, which is
approached through the library shop. This is a well-
arranged and agreeable place in which to find souvenirs:
books and prints, woven scarves, posters, pewter, jewelry and an excellent series of postcards of the Book of
Kells. But it is still a slightly incongruous entry into the
marvels above.

To mount the final stairs and stand at the entrance of
the Long Room is to experience that quickening of the
blood which is the response to wholly successful architecture. The arched nave stretches in seeming infinity,
cathedral-like in its majesty and dignity. Yet this is no
church; the atmosphere is at once secular and academic,
Hellenic rather than Christian. Its deities line either side
in a series of eighteenth- and nineteenth-century busts by
Peter Scheemakers, Louis François Roubillac, Simon
Vierpyl and others. Their seemingly severed heads
gleam pale against the richness of the paneling in symbolic potency: Greek philosophers, writers, scientists,
statesmen, administrators, former provosts of the college, arranged in impressive solemnity.

The foundation stone of this building was laid in
1712, and the architect was Thomas Burgh. But, astonishingly, the high arched roof that is such a feature of the
room was an 1860 addition when the gallery was continued upward to branch into this great barrel vault. So per-

fect is this synthesis of eighteenth-century classicism and nineteenth-century Romanesque that it is hard to believe that the interior was not originally designed as it now stands. On a sunny day in particular the whole nave glows; the spines of the leather-bound books, mounting tier on tier, gleam against the rich and varied browns of the wood so that the gallery seems like a gigantic treasure chest lined with strips of golden mosaic.

And so to the treasure. I first saw the Book of Kells nearly forty years ago and can remember that it was then open at the page showing a stolidly seated Virgin holding on her lap an astonishingly mature and adolescently long-haired Christ. The symbolism of these iconlike figures, so important to an understanding of the work, must then have escaped me: that the size of the Mother represents her majesty, the maturity of the Child His innate wisdom and power. Each of these full-size pages showing scenes from the life of Christ and the Evangelists is framed by a brilliant and intricately designed border of interlacings, circles, swirls, design within design.

Every page is a wonder. The initial letters are almost obscured by the intricacies of the decoration: brightly colored peacocks, tumbling figures, inquisitive angels, grotesque monsters with protruding tongues. One visit is not enough even to begin to penetrate the mystery of this extraordinary book. One sees in imagination that long-dead hand moving slowly across the vellum. And it must, surely, have been a young hand. Old eyes working by candlelight could hardly have produced such fine and intricate detail. And there must have been more than one illustrator, not only because of the sheer size of the work—340 pages have survived—but because of obvious differences of style and workmanship.

The result is a manuscript that combines remarkably

the skills of superlative craftsmanship with inspired creativity. To see the faint lines scored on the vellum as a guide to the letterist is to experience an almost physical sense of contact with the mind and spirit of those patiently laboring ninth-century monks.

Dublin is a friendly, walkable city, set between the mountains and the sea, its pleasures the greater because they are unostentatious. Its Georgian elegance is a reminder of that golden age when it was known as the most brilliant of European cities (although as with so many other historic cities, one must now avert the eye from some examples of what seem almost wanton despoilation of its heritage).

Dublin's museums and art galleries are the more satisfying because they are on a human scale like the city itself, uncrowded and with helpful custodians. And although the weather is unpredictable and one does not come to Dublin to sunbathe, there is always the promise of marvelous translucent light and ever-changing skies. For me, the city's satisfactions were not immediate; one grows into Dublin as into well-loved clothes. But the tedium and rigors of modern transatlantic jet travel are more than repaid by Trinity alone, its great squares, its museum, the glorious Long Room of its library and the treasure it holds.

NEARBY REFRESHMENT

After touring Trinity College you may be in the mood for sustenance. Here are some nearby pubs: **The Bailey,** 2–4 Duke Street, (telephone 773055 or 770600). The bar lunch is served from 12:30 to 2:30 P.M. and offers a choice of hot and cold food. **Blooms Hotel,** 6 Anglesea Place, serves a good buffet lunch weekdays. **Mooney's,** at the corner of Abbey and O'Connell streets, is across the bridge and one block north of the river. It is a huge, lively and popular luncheon spot and was visited by Stephen Dedalus in *Ulysses.* Lunch is served from noon to 2:30 P.M. at modest prices.

Possessed by
Epirus

NICHOLAS GAGE

WHEN THE POET BYRON, at the beginning of his first visit to Greece, stepped onto the soil of the nearly unknown province of Epirus in 1809, he fell instantly under the spell of its stark mountain scenery, inhabited by nomadic tribes and steeped in history. It was after visiting Ioannina, the province's capital, that Byron began "Childe Harold," which would bring fame both to him and to the isolated province, enticing such notables as Gladstone and Disraeli to venture into its wilderness. Byron contended that no other part of Greece could match these towering peaks and steep ravines where "roams the wolf, the eagle whets his beak, birds, beasts of prey and wilder men appear."

I was born in Lia, a mountain village near the Albanian border, in 1939 and nine years later was sent away with three of my sisters in an escape planned by our mother, Eleni. She acted to save us from being abducted with other village children by the Communist guerrillas who had occupied the village during the Greek civil war.

At the last moment, my mother was prevented from going with us. As she embraced us in farewell, she warned us to throw a black stone behind us when we left, a charm to ensure that we would never return to a place that had been plagued by famine, war and hardship for a decade. We did as she said, but the vow not to return was one I couldn't keep.

I went back to Lia fourteen years later and have gone nearly every year since, although until 1974, Lia was still in a "forbidden zone"—so close to Albania that a special pass was needed to enter. Almost half of the Epirus that Byron visited is still inaccessible because it fell inside Albania when the boundary with Greece was arbitrarily set by a commission in 1923. The current rulers of Albania won't let anyone in or out.

Until recently plumbing was unknown in Lia, electricity was a novelty and the single road was unpaved. Today the harshness of life in Epirus is only a memory, although mountain goats still leap the vertiginous cliffs and wild boars roam the high plateaus. In Lia there is not only plumbing but also a small hotel, scheduled to open in the summer of 1985, with a bathroom for each of its ten rooms.

Civilization, in the form of the great homogenizer television, has invaded the most isolated corners of Epirus, but for the fleeting present the province still offers scenes that would have been familiar to Byron or even Olympias, the mother of Alexander the Great, who was born there. Mountain pastures dotted with goats and sheep are watched over by grizzled shepherds in the hooded capotes admired by Byron. Black-kerchiefed women spin wool on their hand-carved distaffs or bend nearly double under towering piles of kindling. In Ioannina, storks still nest atop minarets inside the ancient walled city; in the mountain town of Metsovon, bearded men in black kilts gather daily in the square to play backgammon while the women, in bright hand-woven skirts and embroidered aprons, sit chatting at their looms in the front windows.

"Where'er we tread, 'tis haunted, holy ground," Byron wrote. Epirus is rich in evidence of all phases of Greece's history. The mystic Acheron of mythology, the river the ancient Greeks believed flowed to the netherworld, runs through the region. Dodona, the ancient oracle of Zeus mentioned in both the *Iliad* and the *Odyssey*, is fourteen miles from Ioannina. Monuments of the powerful Molossian tribes are all over the region. Olympias was a Molossian, as was King Pyrrhus, whose victories over the Romans were so costly they left us the term Pyrrhic victory. The ruins of Nicopolis, built by Octavian, dominate the plain north of the Bay of Actium. Churches and monasteries throughout the area offer a panorama of Byzantine architectural styles. Ioannina is one of the few areas in Greece where evidence of the long Turkish occupation has not been obliterated.

In Lia, scarcely a pinprick on the map of Greece, it's hard to plow a field or dig a cellar without stumbling over the relics of the Hellenes and invaders who have passed this way. When the Germans burned my grandfather's house in 1944, he dug a new foundation and unearthed a Roman sword, which now rests in my office. At the top of the mountain stands a Molossian acropolis from the fourth century B.C. It formed a link in the chain of fortresses stretching from the seaport of Himara (now in Albania) to the ancient site of Dodona to the south.

Possessed by Epirus

Signal fires could be seen from one acropolis to the next—a pre-Christian telegraph system.

When I was a child, storytellers peopled the acropolis above Lia with medusas and chimeras, minotaurs and griffins—fantastic creatures whose legends were passed down orally through hundreds of generations. The inhabitants of Lia still refer to a plateau near the acropolis as the "agora"—the ancient Greek word for marketplace—even though no one passes through it but wild boar and the occasional shepherd. The memory of pagan rituals is still woven into the daily life of the Epirotes. In many villages they put coins on the eyes of corpses before burial, as the ancients did, to pay the boatman Charon for passage to Hades. The survivors dig up the bones of the dead several years later and wash them in wine (wine stains were found on the bones in the tomb of Philip of Macedon). Once a year, on July 20, villagers climb from Lia to the highest peak to light fires to the prophet Elias near his small white chapel. They have no idea that this is a Christianized version of the worship of the sun god Helios, whose temples were reconsecrated in the name of the prophet. Fires have been lit on this peak to invoke good weather and crops since time immemorial.

The mountains of Epirus have been trampled by every invader of Greece—Crusaders, Bulgars, Slavs, Romans —and the inhabitants have for centuries withdrawn into their caves and fortresses in an attempt to save themselves. My mother nursed me in the caves above our village while hiding from the invading Italians in 1940. Generations before, the villagers hid in the same caves from the Turks. The Ottoman Empire held Epirus captive for 482 years, until 1913, and the sign of the crescent can still be found. My father left Lia in 1910

wearing the red fez and pantaloons of the Turkish over-
lords. His first gesture on boarding the steamer for
America was to throw the fez into the sea. Until his death
at the age of ninety-two he liked to chuckle over the passport that listed his nationality as Turkish.

Lia is in the section of Epirus called Thesprotia,
which Aristotle considered the cradle of the Greek race
and language. So isolated are the people that intermar-
riage has preserved the fair coloring, blue eyes and classical Greek features of Pericles' time as nowhere else.
Byron's remarks about the people of the region are not
entirely inappropriate today: "They are cruel, though
not treacherous, and have several vices but no mean-
nesses. They are, perhaps, the most beautiful race, in
point of countenance, in the world, their women are
sometimes handsome also, but they are treated like
slaves, beaten and, in short, complete beasts of burden."

Those traveling by sea from Italy generally enter
mainland Greece at Igoumenitsa, the port where ferry-
boats from Corfu and Brindisi dock. The bustling but
unprepossessing seaport is lined with souvenir shops
hoping to lure the tourists before they board buses, cars
or rented motorbikes and set out toward Ioannina, sixty-
five miles away. There is little to charm a visitor into lin-
gering at Igoumenitsa except the prospect of good
swimming and the evening promenade along the quay.

It was there that my sisters and I were housed in a large
refugee camp. We cooked at an outdoor fire, used the ravines for a bathroom, screened our living quarters from the
others with a hanging sheet. My most vivid memory of
Igoumenitsa is one of the sea, an incredible prospect for a
child who had always lived on a mountaintop.

The winding road from Igoumenitsa leads over the

mountains to Ioannina, which my sisters and I visited shortly after escaping from Lia. I recall gaping at the shop windows, the beggars and peddlers selling every kind of marvel, the crowds of soldiers and curious civilians who stared at us escapees from the Communist territory. A sympathetic bystander bought me an ice cream cone. Never having eaten anything frozen, I dropped it at the first taste, crying that it had burned my tongue.

Much of Ioannina remains unspoiled, with storks flying over the walled Turkish city and its minarets, tiny cobblestoned streets, baths and fortresses. The ancient city contains a synagogue built in 1790, one of the four that once served the large Jewish community. The Turks were driven out in 1913, and the Jewish population was rounded up and shipped off to concentration camps in 1944, but their influence lingers to give the city an Oriental flavor.

Byron was fascinated with the rich panoply of the court of the Turkish ruler Ali Pasha in Ioannina and quickly affected the gold-embroidered native costumes. The silver and gold filigree work is still a specialty of the area. Gold is a bargain in Ioannina, and many jewelers, including the founder of the house of Bulgari, who went on to Rome to make his fortune, learned their trade in this region.

Byron wrote to his mother that he was graciously received by Ali Pasha, but he was aware of the Pasha's reputation as a brutal despot: "He has the appearance of anything but his real character, for he is a remorseless tyrant, guilty of the most horrible cruelties."

Today's legend holds that the ghosts of concubines drowned by Ali Pasha hover in the morning mists over the lake bordering Ioannina. At sunset the water reflects the minarets of the Turks' past glory as pedestrians stroll

along the lake past outdoor cafés and, in summer, carnival rides and shadow puppet shows. Ferries dart back
and forth to the island in the center where Ali Pasha met
his death at the hands of one of the sultan's emissaries.
The seventeenth-century monastery where he was shot is
now a museum containing engravings of the period.
Nearby are outdoor restaurants serving frog's legs, crayfish, eels and trout pulled fresh from the lake.

About three miles along the eastern road out of the city
is the hill of Perama, hiding one of the most dramatic
caves in Europe. A well-lit concrete path meanders
through the cave to an exit at the opposite end, making it
possible to explore the whole forest of stalactites and stalagmites without retracing any steps.

Metsovon is a town hidden among the snow-covered
peaks of the Pindus Mountains—a fifty-five-mile side
trip from Ioannina toward the east on a serpentine but
well-paved highway. Almost unknown to Americans,
Metsovon is well worth the detour, for it provides a
glimpse into a part of Greece's past never pictured on the
travel posters.

Cut off from the rich plains of eastern Greece by a
breathtaking pass called Katara—the Curse—Metsovon
nestles high among forests of fir, looking more Swiss
than Greek. It includes a ski jump and chalet and cheese
and woodworking factories and produces the best red
wine in the country. Like a Greek Williamsburg,
Metsovon is preserved as it was in its glory. Its wealth
resulted from a special dispensation from Turkish taxes
and restrictions because in the sixteenth century a peasant from Metsovon gave sanctuary for a year to a Turkish vizier, in disgrace with his sultan, who promised on
his return to power to grant the peasant any wish. As a
result of its special privileges, Metsovon attracted rich

Christian families, who built magnificent walled mansions, designed to be self-sufficient during the harsh winters and safe from attacks by marauding brigands.

The citizens of Metsovon belong to a tribe called the Vlachs and speak not only Greek but also their own tongue, a Rumanian dialect closely akin to Latin. Their ancient crafts, skills, lore, even recipes, have been rescued from oblivion by Evangelos Averoff, one of Greece's leading political figures, and his nephew, a former mayor of Metsovon, Yiannis Averoff. The Averoff family has also restored several old churches and chapels in the area, with priceless icons, carvings and altar screens.

The Museum of Metsovon is a restored eighteenth-century mansion, with stables, storerooms and fountains within the building's walls on the first floor. Higher floors contain the winter and summer bedrooms (with grilles through which the secluded women could watch the comings and goings of visitors) and rooms for cooking, weaving, listening to musicians or attending to business. All are filled with the rugs and tapestries, handicrafts, arms, silver and gold and carvings for which the region was famous. Even the wardrobes are full of richly embroidered garments.

In Metsovon most inhabitants wear hand-woven costumes and practice the ancient crafts of embroidery, woodcarving and weaving. But unlike the inhabitants of Williamsburg, the Metsovites are not playacting. They dress that way all the time.

Most visitors to Epirus never suspect the existence of Metsovon but head instead from Ioannina southward toward Athens. On the way they may stop at the ruins of Dodona, the most ancient oracle in Greece, compared to which Delphi is an upstart. Herodotus believed that

Possessed by Epirus

Dodona was founded by one of two kidnapped sisters from Egypt—one taken to Libya and the other to Dodona, where each created shrines to Zeus. The priests were called *Helloi*, from whom, according to some historians, the Greeks, who refer to themselves as Hellenes and to their country as Hellas, got their name. The priests interpreted the words of Zeus in the rustling leaves of the sacred oak. The Argonauts were said to have fitted a piece of wood from this tree into the keel of the *Argo*, enabling the ship itself to speak at critical moments.

One day I stood watching the plateau where the temples stand turn from silver to gray as the sun sank behind the mountains and the shadows of the columns crept down the slopes like fingers. An evening breeze swept through the trees that stood like sentinels around the temples and echoed against the sheer stone cliffs of Mount Tomaros. I could easily understand how the rustling leaves of a giant oak could be accepted by my ancestors as the voice of God.

Thirty miles below Ioannina, travelers must choose either the western branch, leading to Nicopolis, Preveza and Actium, or the eastern branch to Arta. Either choice is studded with rewards. Arta, surrounded by orange groves, was twice the capital of Epirus. On the site of the ancient capital of King Pyrrhus, Arta reached its zenith in the thirteenth century when some of the most magnificent Byzantine churches in Greece were built there. It is now most famous in the legends and folk songs of Greece for its graceful arched bridge. According to legend, when the bridge was being built, the arches would collapse every day. A bird told the chief mason that it would stand only if he sacrificed his young wife in the foundations. She was lured onto the spot and, as she realized she was being buried alive, she placed a curse on the bridge. Eventually the chief mason committed suicide. Yet the bridge still stands.

The ruins of Nicopolis, on the route to Preveza, are all that remain of the cosmopolitan city founded by Octavian to commemorate his victory over Antony and Cleopatra at the nearby Bay of Actium, "where once was lost a world for woman," as Byron wrote. There, when it was a metropolis of 200,000 people, St. Paul preached and wrote his Epistle to Titus and the philosopher Epictetus had his school. Today the ruins stand like gravestones as hawks wheel overhead.

Beyond the ruins of Nicopolis lies Preveza, on the Ambracian Gulf. The city was founded by King Pyrrhus, occupied by the Venetians, ceded to the Turks and then the French, and retaken by Ali Pasha. Now, amid olive groves and orchards of lemon and orange trees, it provides a pleasant respite by the sea, with modest seafood restaurants, a colorful evening promenade and quiet swimming. Preveza provides a look into the heart of Greek life largely unaffected by foreign visitors as well as a magnificent view of the "dark mountains" of Epirus.

Like Antaeus, whose strength depended on his touching the earth, most Epirotes, however far they are scattered, feel a need to return to the land of their birth. Every Greek goes home to his village, if only in his thoughts, on its name day. When Lia celebrates its annual festival on the day of the prophet Elias, July 20, emigrants come from as far away as Australia and Chicago. They climb the highest peak to worship at the prophet's chapel, then descend to the agora to dance, eat and drink below the ruined acropolis in festivities that last for three days. It wasn't until 1963 that one of the old village women told me the actual date of my birthday (I knew it was in July). She recalled how, on the third day of the prophet's festival, July 23, 1939, my mother sent for the midwife and I was born—the long-awaited son—setting off more days of feasting and celebration.

I'm glad that black stone we threw behind us in 1948 failed in its spell. Nowhere else do I have such a sense of place, such a feeling of being part of the continuum of life. Nowhere else but in Epirus would my birth be remembered in connection with a festival that has been celebrated since pagan times. The first thing one Greek asks another upon meeting is the name of his region, because the place of one's origin explains so much. Harsh as it may be, I expect to go back to Epirus for as long as I can make it up those mountains, and each time to draw new strength from its soil.

VOYAGE INTO EPIRUS

In the less-traveled parts of Greece, **Xenia** hotels, a chain run by the government, offer clean and comfortable lodging. During the high tourist season, half board —breakfast and one other meal—is usually obligatory.

Meals in Epirus are modest and inexpensive; such Greek specialties as shish kebab, cheese and meat pies and fresh seafood are served in simple tavernas throughout the region. (It is usual to walk into the kitchen and point at what appeals to you.) Unless otherwise specified, a meal with local wine will cost no more than about $5 a person.

ARTA

The **Xenia** (telephone: 27413) has double rooms for about $15 and charges about $7 a person for breakfast and lunch or dinner. For dining, try the seaside tavernas in one of the fishing villages—perhaps **Menidi**—on the road to Athens.

IGOUMENITSA

The **Jolly** (23970) charges about $20 for a double room, with breakfast at about $2 a person; no restaurant. The **Xenia** (22282), with its own beach, has doubles for about $15; add about $7 more a person for breakfast and one other meal. Both have balconies from which one can watch the bustling port and the townspeople taking their evening stroll along the harbor, where there are several tavernas.

IOANNINA

The **Xenia** (25087) charges about $15 for a double room, about $7 a person for breakfast and either lunch or dinner. All rooms offer a view of the gardens and a glimpse of the lake; on warm evenings, dinner is served on an outdoor terrace. The **Palladion** (25856 or 34601 for reservations) is older and nearer the center of town; doubles range from about $15 to $20, depending on season. Breakfast and another meal cost about $8 extra a person.

For dining, the **Periptero,** or Tourist Pavilion, has a few German and Russian dishes, as well as Greek specialties, and a terrace with a sweeping view of the city. The **Litharitsa** restaurant complex, installed in the restored residence of one of the sons of Ali Pasha, overlooks the lake and the old Turkish city; there is a taverna, a discothèque, a cafeteria and a restaurant. **Limnopoula** is on the lakeshore; **Gastra** is on the road to the airport, and specializes in meat dishes cooked in a covered pot that is buried in coals.

LIA

The **Xenona** inn, with restaurant, is scheduled to open in 1985.

METSOVON

The **Hotel Diasselo** (41895 or 41719) is decorated

with local embroideries and antique hanging lamps; a double room will cost about $30. The most traditional taverna is the **Averoff,** whose owner tends to serve customers whatever he thinks they should have. A newly opened taverna, **O Costas,** specializes in charcoal-grilled meats.

PREVEZA

The **Margarona Royal** (24361), just outside town, is decorated in Italianate rococo style with crystal chandeliers and flocked wallpaper. A double room, including half board, can cost up to about $35; suites can cost up to about $60 with half board. The hotel's restaurant, the **Santa Lucia,** has Italian and Greek specialties; dinner with wine is about $8 a person. The **Zikas** (27505) charges about $18 for a double in the high season and about $7 a person for half board. Both overlook the water.

Good tavernas on the seaside road west of the port are **Panorama** and **Katsoularis. —**Joan Gage

In Search of
the Ultimate Island

FREDERIC RAPHAEL

I WISH I WERE IN
mine island," Byron used to wail when things were not
going to his poetic, or lordly, liking. He was not the first
man to imagine that isolation would be blissful, and he
was certainly not the last. Getting away from it all is, if
we are honest, much the same as getting away from them
all. And what keeps other people away better than a wall
of water? In Shakespeare's chauvinistic speech about
England, John of Gaunt talks in precisely those terms
about the moated demi-paradise of "this scepter'd isle."
He was, of course, referring to the same place from
which Byron later longed to escape. One man's meat is
another man's prison.

I have never been too sure precisely which island
Byron had in mind. In one of the most quoted repetitions
in all verse, he apostrophized "The isles of Greece, the
isles of Greece," and seemed to single out Lesbos, where

burning Sappho did her memorable stuff. However, I doubt if he ever went there, though he probably did go to Naxos, which once sported a Jewish duke.

The Greeks themselves were fascinated by islands from the beginning of their mythology. Other races imagined paradise to be a garden—to the Persians, paradise simply was a garden—but the Greeks dreamed of a heroic afterlife on the Isles of the Blest, where the happy few would enjoy the eternal amenities of a select Club Méditerranée. There they would be lulled by the Lydian mode rather than by hard rock, something of which, in their mountainous land, they would have had rather more than enough during their mortal lives.

The idea of a select society—though not so choosy as to exclude oneself—ensconced in inaccessible beauty has always excited the fantasist. *"Odi profanum vulgus et arceo,"* sang the Roman poet Horace, snobbish arriviste that he was. "I hate the common crowd and keep it at a distance." The Emperor Tiberius endorsed this sentiment so ardently that he packed up his purple, so to speak, and went on permanent vacation to Capri. The whole world was his oyster, but he chose to be a crabby hermit. He was, of course, soon accused of indulging in all kinds of questionable activities, a lot of them in the swimming pool. The malice of Suetonius, the gossipy historian of the Caesars, was almost certainly tainted with envy, but sensuality—like virtue—has to be its own reward.

Doubtless it is evidence of European narrow-mindedness that I think largely of the Mediterranean when it comes to islands. The South Seas are glamorous with coral strands, and the Caribbean is ideal for those who want to swim in warm soup while being jostled by the wake of some showy boat, but I never tire of the land-locked sea in which Greeks and Egyptians, Jews and Arabs, Persians, Turks, Phoenicians, Franks, Romans and Visigoths have rubbed shoulders for five millenniums and more.

Here are islands for all tastes and all seasons, of all colors and contours, shapes and sizes. The most improbably and (forgive the solecism) most manifestly unique city in Europe was described by Byron as "throned on her hundred isles." What is Venice but an archipelago laced together with bridges? An anthology of retreats and secret places, it was devised by fugitives in the midst of a lagoon, somewhere to give them breathing (and breeding) space when the mainland proved too hot for them.

From their island base, the Venetians set out to build an empire, paving the Mediterranean with a glorious sequence of refurbished steppingstones that enabled them to hold the gorgeous East in fee. Corfu is still majestic with their confident mansions, from whose balconies Englishmen (and Corfiots) can be seen playing cricket in the noonday sun, vestiges of another vanished supremacy. As for Crete, which the Venetians yielded so reluctantly, it is almost an independent country—Cretans call it simply *to nisi,* "the island"—and remains so charged with history, pride and tragedy that a lifetime could not pick the locks of all its treasuries.

Cyprus, too, so elegiacally celebrated by Lawrence Durrell in *Bitter Lemons,* carries its harsh past like an unhealing wound that cannot mar its beauty. Rhodes, too, knew the Venetians, as it knew everyone, standing there at the crossroads of Homer's pathless sea, its manners rubbed smooth by passing trade, its bazaar plausible with souvenirs. Do not be deceived, will you, by those that show the Colossus with his legs astride the harbor. He was indeed gigantic—more than one hundred

In Search of the Ultimate Island

feet tall—but he neither straddled the waterfront nor, if I am right, wore that tactful loincloth (it is there to spare the Bishop's blushes). The monumental tribute to the sun god stood adjacent to the port, advertising the wealth of an island which, for my taste, still carries more traffic than the escapist can relish. Yet Lindos remains a pretty, vertiginous curiosity, and the colorful Valley of the Butterflies (*petaloutha* in Greek) promises that Vladimir Nabokov was right when he spoke of the prettiest of all nature's iron laws, the survival of the weakest.

In Search of the Ultimate Island

What attracts me more than any island where one hires a car is one of those increasingly rare ribs of rock where not even Avis can try harder because there are no roads, not even—if you are very lucky—any wheels. (To invent the wheel is talent; to ignore it is genius.) When we first went to the island which I think of as "mine island," there was no way of reaching it except on a ferry that arrived at three in the morning, after fourteen hours of bucking the Aegean. When the creaking tub nudged its way into the black harbor, the only sign of life, at first, was a little red glow, no bigger than the rosette of the Legion of Honor on a funereal Frenchman's lapel. It turned out to be the end of the lighterman's cigarette as he pulled toward us. (Talking of the French, the only undoubted island hater among such-traveled celebrities was Napoleon: He left Corsica to become Emperor, fled Elba to resume his interrupted career and ended up on St. Helena, where he took a poor view of the accommodation.)

Once ashore on our island, the musky sweetness of the herbs drugged the nostrils. One thought of Odysseus and his companions as they landed on Circe's beach and tried to remember what was so wrong with a diet of lotus. Cavafy, the great Alexandrian Greek poet, wrote a sly poem about Odysseus, the island hopper, and his long-delayed return to Ithaca. Cavafy did not question the hero's appetite for home, but he advised the frustrated traveler not to be in too much of a hurry:

> . . . *pray that the road be long.*
> *That the summer mornings are many,*
> *That you will enter ports seen for the first time*
> *With such pleasure, such joy!*

Direct flights are neat, but they lack magic. Sometimes only a detour can take you where you want to go.

In Search of the Ultimate Island

Luck can take the island hopper—and the island hoper —to places where vanity alone will later prompt them to disclose, where the water and the welcome are both warm, but do not cloy, where neither the fish soup nor the music is canned. My ideal choice has a long, obscure history: I could not easily enjoy somewhere totally unrecognized in literature, though a footnote will be enough. (One of the Seven Wise Men, the great Solon, sneered—unwisely—at humpbacked Sikinos, in the Cyclades, on account of its dull remoteness, which sounds like commendation to me.)

The greatest charm of islands is that they can seem unchanging: They promise that things can be the same again, that life can almost stand still, or come round again. The nicest of all tributes to isolation was written, inevitably, by a modern Greek called Odysseus—Odysseus Elytis, a recent Nobel laureate—who once said, *"Oles tees idees mou enesiotisa,"* which you might translate as "All my ideas come out as islands." Everything the poet stands for is expressed in his love for the Cyclades, that string of pearls on the throat of the Aegean. He loves their mystery, their discreteness, their enigmatic simplicities. On our favorite island, we can raise the drawbridge, however briefly, and refute John Donne by believing, albeit selfishly, that a man can be an island and that solitude (in the right company) is the most humane of all states.

THE MIDDLE EAST
AND AFRICA

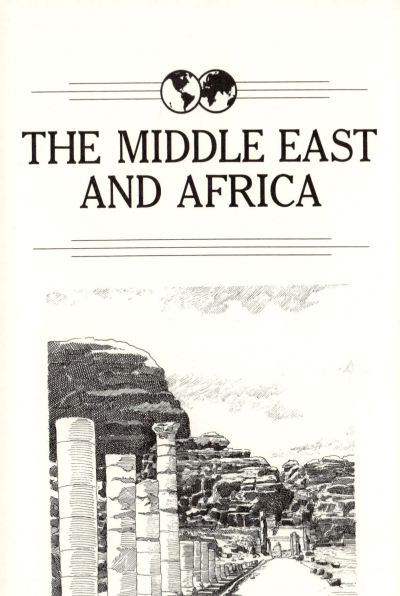

Footsteps of Abraham

MALACHI MARTIN

THE HEAVY CURTAINS of far-distant time part upon an unlikely stage whose name is Ur. Today, Ur is a desert scrubland with miserable ruins jutting from terrain of sand and mud. It is about 120 miles northwest of the Persian Gulf, in the country we now call Iraq. Unlikely or not, however, very nearly forty centuries ago, here began a journey that transcended history, and whose arc etched a crescent of hope and faith so indelibly that it determined the motive and course of events for centuries down to this day and far beyond the borders of the nations that were in its path—places we know as Iraq, Turkey, Syria, Lebanon, Israel, Egypt, Jordan.

The traveler who undertook that momentous journey was Abraham, claimed today as physical ancestor and as archpatriarch of faith and unity by great peoples who, though scattered wide, have long memories. He was

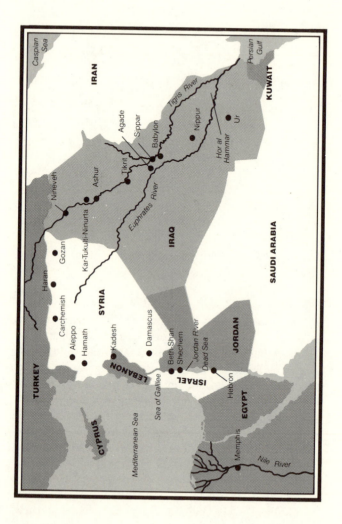

claimed earliest by Jews, as tenaciously by Christians, belatedly by Moslems. Each religion claims priority, and, largely because of their different faiths, members of all three are locked in a bloodstained struggle that rages intermittently over the lands he crossed.

From Ur, Abraham traveled 700 miles to the borders of present-day Iraq, another 700 miles into Syria, another 800 down to Egypt by the inland road, and then back into Canaan—what is now Israel. It is a journey that today's pilgrim, for reasons of international polity, cannot easily replicate. But even though much of the route is difficult of access, and although many of the cities Abraham knew are now only ruins, there are nonetheless rewards for today's traveler, spiritual monuments to the man and his faith. Begin, then, in the Ur of history and imagination, and end at Hebron, where, under Israeli protection, the faiths, however briefly, meet.

When Abraham strode upon the stage at Ur, he was by Semitic reckoning already a man of seventy-five. And Ur was then a capital city of more than 100,000 inhabitants, a place of beauty, graced with towers, palaces, temples, law courts, market squares, statues, shrines, gardens, mosaics, friezes, reliefs and monuments. It was divided into rectangular blocks by paved streets lined with two-story houses. It had its own seaport and man-made canal giving access to the Persian Gulf and the Indian Ocean, opening it up to lucrative foreign markets in the areas we call Africa, India, Malaysia and the Arabian peninsula. Ur was, in fact, part of an empire ruled by a written code of law drawn up by King Hammurabi. The civic order and public glory of that empire, Babylonia, are legendary.

We know some personal details about Abraham. He belonged to a race of Semites who traced their ancestry

back to the dawn of human existence, and who had settled at Ur some one thousand years before his time, a
race the local Sumerians called Chaldeans. His was
probably a family of merchant traders, buying and selling in Ur's rich markets. All his long life, Abraham
loved one woman, Sarah. He spoke four or five of the
main languages of his time. He was a skilled rider,
hunter and fighter. Fiercely independent and an inveterate haggler (he even bargained with God), he had one
central quality: faithfulness. And, if even one quarter of
the words ascribed to him are authentic, he must have
had as large a mind as any man ever born.

By the same Semitic reckoning of age, we are told that
when Abraham was 75, his father, Terah, was over 200
years old. Yet it was Terah, the Bible records, whom
God rather suddenly impelled to move on with his son
and family toward an ancient promise of land and blessing for his race. That promise would not be found at Ur,
where more than five hundred different gods and goddesses were worshiped. Terah and Abraham and their
fellow Semites worshiped one god—the only god, they
said. God.

If not at glorious Ur, then where? To the west, in the
land named after its marvelous purple dye: Canaan.
Terah and Abraham knew their route. Then, as now,
there was only one way by land to Canaan, an arc of fertile terrain, a long finger of rice and cotton and citrus and
melon, corn and dates, figs and grapes, a curving miracle of green, arching its way in the midst of impassable
desert wastes: the Fertile Crescent.

And so, one fine day, when the winter rains were almost over, they packed all their goods and chattels onto a
few dozen four-wheeled carts drawn by oxen. They liq-
uidated their merchandise, or most of it probably, and

converted it into chits of value and exchange, made of baked clay. All along their route they could obtain funds and food and every material necessity with those chits.

We, in our unpeaceful world, are apt to imagine all sorts of dangers that Terah and Abraham must have faced—bands of roving robbers, murderous cave-dwellers, ravenous wild beasts. What is hard for us to understand is the reality: the remarkable security in which they actually made the trek. In fact, they traveled every inch of the long way by established trade routes complete with milestones, armed patrols, river fords, guardhouses, food depots and secure cities. The only serious enemies they might face were disease and the dreaded dust storm, the *idyah*, that came every spring and summer from the western desert, bearing a fine powder that blocked eyes, nostrils, ears and mouth, ultimately choking the unprotected. It was the same *idyah* that helped doom the effective use of helicopters in the abortive American attempt to rescue the embassy hostages in the Ayatollah's Iran.

When he left Ur, then, and traveled up through the territory of modern Iraq, Abraham set out upon a "royal highway" through an area governed by civil law, bristling with trade and communications, inhabited by populations who enjoyed music and painting and sculpture and a written literature of plays, poems, epics, songs and novels. And, as he passed slowly on the road northward, at the sufferance and under the protection of great imperial authorities, he was carrying destiny away with him in his very person, as surely as he was carrying his worldly possessions in his ox-drawn carts.

As long as the caravan was on the first leg of its journey north over what was called Mesopotamia, the travelers never lost sight of the works of man. Apart from cities, they could always see at least one of those most visible objects in that land, the ziggurats. Each ziggurat soared skyward from a gigantic broad-based pedestal of brick and asphalt, rising sometimes to hundreds of feet, and always topped with a shrine to a god upon its pinnacle. Traveling through what we know as the Iraqi provinces of Muntafiq, Diwaniya, Hilla, Baghdad and Mosul, Abraham passed at least thirty-five of these monuments gleaming in the sun on either side of his route. Today, only squat piles of ruins are to be seen.

Their first important stop after leaving Ur was Babylon. Abraham knew it as Bab-Ilu, the most renowned of ancient royal cities. Its site lies just north of the town of Hilla in southern Iraq. Rectangular in shape, it was protected then by moated walls with nine gates. It was bisected by the great Euphrates River. It had eight urban and seven suburban districts whose paved streets were everywhere enlivened with many-colored friezes and reliefs and lined with palaces, temples and luxurious houses. Abraham and Terah led the way through the Litamu suburb and, as all northbound travelers did, entered central Babylon through Urash Gate. They went up Nabu Street, turned east at the temple of Ninurta, then north by the main street and past the sacred area of Esagila where the royal palace stood. There, two extraordinary buildings loomed: the Temple of Marduk, with its frightening gold-sheathed, winged statues of that god, and the Eteme-an-ki (House-of-the-Foundations-of-Heaven-and-Earth) ziggurat, which rose to a height of 296 feet. All of Abraham's descendants down to our day would remember it as the Tower of Babel.

Most of Abraham's Babylon lies buried today beneath a deep bed of silt, some of it beneath the water table. Of the original ziggurat, only one small island of worn brick surrounded by a moat remains. But you can still see enough to imagine the glory, and a smaller-scale reconstruction stands nearby. You will marvel even today at the remains of the huge fortifications, the skillful use the Babylonians made of water channels to enclose the city, the still awe-inspiring remains of temples and palaces and statuary. Even the piles of rubble mixed with sand and broken mud brick set the imagination whirring.

After Babylon, there would have been nothing remarkable for many weeks of travel. Some fifty miles north, they might have stopped just beyond a wide curve of the Tigris River, at a little village of mud huts called Baghdad, but that place became a great city only some 2,500 years later; and it is far more likely that the caravan paused at such big, busy, prosperous cities as Sippar, Agade or Tikrit, now in ruins. About ninety miles from Babylon, Abraham and his family tramped over a spot in the road where the pipeline now passes, bringing oil from the Iraqi fields of Kirkuk south and west to Dulaim and beyond.

It was not until they reached Ashur that they saw another extraordinary city. Ashur, on the bank of the Tigris, was as holy in the eyes of the Akkadian, Assyrian and Babylonian people of Abraham's day as Rome, Mecca and Jerusalem are for modern Catholics, Moslems and Jews. Abraham would have entered the city by Gurgurri Gate, and ridden over paved streets through rich bazaars, past glorious temples and the huge royal palace. His progress would have been interrupted by nearly constant religious processions. But, tradition tells us, he refused even to dismount from his camel there, for in the thirty-four temples dedicated to the god Ashur, and in the sixteen dedicated to the goddess Ishtar, abominations were taking place daily: sacred male and female prostitution; sexual orgies in honor of Ishtar. Abraham ate and drank briefly, always in the saddle, and left the city as quickly as he could.

Within another four or five weeks, by overnighting at such minor cities as Kar-Tukulti-Ninurta and Nimrud, Abraham's family would have arrived at the most north- ern reaches of today's Iraq, and entered the city of Nineveh on the east bank of the Tigris. Travelers along the trade route that followed the Fertile Crescent, as surely as a river flows its course, had to pass through Nineveh to replenish supplies of food, water and medi- cines, because the next leg of the journey was the hard- est.

It was inevitable, therefore, that Nineveh grew later to be the capital of the Assyrian empire—a place so large that the prophet Jonah reckoned three days to cross it on foot. Today, its site is near the small town of Kuyunjik. And, even though most of the old city is now mounds of dust and sand with some remaining brickwork and soar- ing walls, the restoration of the original gate, with its fearful winged guardian deity, instills an immediate sense of the whole's original greatness.

From Nineveh, Abraham's little band at last took a westward turn, for a trek of 200 miles. Along this stretch, the vegetation was thinner, the water scarcer, the road bleaker and rougher and less well protected. Sixty miles along the way, the route left what we call Iraq, passing into Turkey. There was only one adequate rest- ing point, the city of Gozan—modern Tell el Halaf in Turkey—before Haran. Gozan covered 150 acres, was guarded by high mud-brick walls on three sides and by the river Khabur on the fourth. You can walk around the city limits today, noting the remains of houses and streets, and the remnants of a once beautiful building that rested on pillars fashioned in the shapes of divinities mounted on lions. You can still see samples of Gozan's painted pottery, decorated with animal and geometric designs—Abraham and his party surely traded for some of it, for it was renowned all through the Middle East. Gozan was welcoming; but still, having rested there, when travelers made it across from Nineveh to Haran, even the hardiest were generally as much in need of rest as of supplies.

It was at Haran that old Terah died, at the age of 205. The family mourned him and buried him there; and, tradition tells us, the caravan spent the winter there. But, as soon as the monsoon rains were finished, early in the new year, it was to Abraham that God spoke now: "Get thee out of this country . . . into a land that I shall show thee."

The way was still westward from Haran, and it was fifty miles to the high-walled, 250-acre city of Carchemish, near a place in modern Syria called Jerablus. There were huge defense towers in the walls of Carchemish. The city had a powerful police and security force, and a monopoly in the transshipment of copper and timber; merchants from all over the north willingly paid the upkeep for that protection. Pausing at Carchemish today, we can admire still the statuary of lions, the reliefs of wild boars, of charioteers and archers, of soldiers in battle; and we can trace the outlines of the ancient sawmills and warehouses and examine the remains of Carchemish's great palace and temple, its citadel surrounded by moat, fosse and towers.

Carchemish was a dual turning point in Abraham's journey. From here, the way was south. And from here, the caravan traveled among Semites.

Sometime in the late spring or early summer, the caravan entered a long descending valley. Whoever leaves Syria for the south must pass through this valley. From remotest antiquity, it had been called the Womb, and so it is called today: the Beka. One spring season, a shade less than 4,000 years ago, the Beka valley, where in recent times Israelis and Syrians have fought with missiles, supersonic jets and tanks, was happier witness to the caravan of carts and camels that bore Abraham and his household southward.

Their first important stop was Aleppo, where Abraham grazed his herds of cows. Today, the Islamic citadel sits on the central hill, and beneath it are the streets where Abraham walked. On the spot where now you see the minaret of Jami Zakariyah mosque, named after a descendant of Abraham, there once stood a ziggurat. After Aleppo, it was on to Kadesh, today called Tell Nabi Mand. When Abraham entered this fortress-city, Kadesh was the center for all the throbbing, hyperactive Syrian confederacies of his day. The buildings he saw were made of basalt; there are now few traces of them. After Kadesh, he traveled in a southeasterly direction; and so he reached Damascus.

Damascus was the home of warrior-princes and rich merchants who lived in buildings of fairyland architecture, enjoying the plethora of food and luxury goods that poured into this place from every direction. The city (its name means Sackful of Blood) grew to glory on waves of perpetual strife and war. Then, as now, the city appeared suddenly in the middle of the desert, beckoning to the traveler like a distant jewel glistening on brown velvet. In Abraham's day, it was almost 3,000 years old. Buildings we moderns regard as ancient marvels— the seventh-century Ummayad Mosque, the sixteenth-century Suleimanieh Mosque, the eighteenth-century

Azem palace—had of course not yet been built, nor the reasons for their existence even dreamed of. Still, Abraham made both dreams and buildings possible by his obedient journey of hope and belief.

Abraham and his caravan would have stayed in Damascus for some time, even wintering there. The old city, where Abraham tarried, lies south of the Barada River; its center—containing citadel and palace and temple—was on the escarpment overlooking the river. Take some time to walk along Suk al-Tawilah (the Long Bazaar) until you come to that street called Darb al-Mustakin (Straight Street). Beneath the stones your feet tread lies an older street, but with the same name; Abraham walked that more ancient street called Straight—it existed in his time—where, centuries later, his fiery descendant, Paul of Tarsus, was cured of his blindness. The squat houses and archways and tiny shops of today stand above those Abraham saw and perhaps entered.

God is patient; but still Abraham would have left Damascus at the end of the rains, passing over the Bashan road, across the Golan Heights that are today manned by watchful Israeli troops, east of the Sea of Galilee, covering terrain that, it seems, has never been unknown or unimportant in the destinies of men and nations.

Slowly, Abraham led the way down the eastern bank of the river Jordan, past the place where the fortress-city of Beth-Shan peered across the water; 1,000 years later, on its walls the bodies of King Saul and his son Jonathan would be nailed as trophies by the Philistines. Finally, where the river Yarmuk joins the Jordan, an ancient ford carried the caravan across to the land of Abraham's very great destiny: Canaan.

The Canaan of that time corresponded very closely to

the present boundaries of Israel and the territories it controls. The land was 50 miles at its broadest points, and stretched almost 120 miles south, from the Wheel of Galilee's mountains to the Bag of Sand—the Sinai.

It was at Shechem that Abraham first stopped, and he made of it the most venerated shrine of his race. He built an altar—his first, but far from his last in that land. Five centuries later, Joshua stood where Abraham had; he built another altar from a pile of stones, and spoke his final words of commendation and exhortation to the gathered tribes of Israel. And, after fifteen centuries more, not far from there, Jesus met the woman of Samaria at the well dug by Abraham's grandson, Jacob. Today, it is the remnant—only the merest signs are visible—of Joshua's pile of stones that marks the place where Abraham's altar had stood. Surely, though, it is not stones, but Shechem, the place itself, that will speak to you of all of Israel's dreams, all of its promise, all of its pain.

Though he had entered Canaan at last, Abraham's traveling was not yet over. In a sense, it had only begun. He was in the promised land, but not yet of it. This land did not possess him, nor he it. "Walk through this land in its length and its breadth," the Ancient Voice told him. "All of it will be yours." Early on, he judiciously picked out a spot as his permanent home: Hebron, in the fertile, sunny south. And then he did again as God said; he traveled his land, as if the very condition of its belonging to him and his descendants was that he cover every square inch of it, live in every quarter of it, journey to the lands bordering it—Egypt, the territories of modern Jordan, of the Gaza strip, of Lebanon, of Syria.

Nowhere can you travel there that he didn't. Nowhere do modern Israelis live that he didn't. Nowhere do they fight today for survival that he didn't. He talked with God, with angels, with Pharaoh, with kings, with princes, with Bedouins, in palaces, in towns, in huts, in tents, in the open fields. He could use honeyed words, the subtle understatement of bargaining, the diplomatic lie, the threat. He arbitrated the division of vast properties. He accumulated gold, silver, copper, real estate, herds of cattle. He led his own army, fought pitched battles, asked for no quarter from lethal enemies and gave them none, although he pleaded naggingly with God to have compassion on men whose vile wickedness he deplored. For he hated human waste. At the age of 100, he fathered a famous son, Isaac, and fetched a bride, Rebecca, for him from 2,000 miles away. When his own wife, Sarah, died, for the sake of more children he took a second wife and fathered whole tribes that still live on today in Jordan, Syria, Libya and North Africa.

Yet there are no monuments or shrines of the usual sort to Abraham along the route he followed from Ur to the land of Canaan. There are several wadis—dried-up river beds—named after him. One of the Anatolian foothills in modern Turkey bears his name. An ancient mosque in Aleppo and a very old synagogue in Damascus were named after him, but they were both destroyed in the latter-day hostilities between Arab and Israeli. All through Iraq and Syria and Lebanon, there are certain places where local tradition has it that Abraham rested, or fought a battle, or built an altar, or spoke with God.

But the realization that overtakes you finally is that Abraham's "shrine" is of a different sort: Every place he built an altar to God, there some of his illustrious descendants would later plant a memory still living today for us—Joseph in Egypt, Joshua in Shechem, Samson in Philistia, Ruth and Naomi and Booz in Jordan, Samuel at Shiloh, Jacob and Saul at Bethel, David on Moriah, Solomon in Jerusalem, Jesus at Sichar, Paul at Damascus—as if he had presanctified all these places for all of them, for Israelite holy man and warrior, for modern kibbutznik and sabra and pilgrim.

For Sarah's burial, Abraham had purchased an expensive plot of land, the field of Mamre, in the shade of the immemorial oak trees at Machpelah near his chosen Hebron. When he, too, finally died at age 175, there beside the wife he had loved uniquely, they buried this man who had never made a mistake with God and who had traveled so far, so long, so boldly, to seal promises and blessing, land and destiny, race and religion.

Should you visit Hebron today, approaching from the north, you will pass through a ring of Israeli settlements surrounding what is now a densely populated city of 70,000 people, most of them Arab Moslems. The Israelis who live in the city itself—about 100 of them—are in the old Jewish quarter where they returned in 1967 for the first time since they were expelled in the bloody riots of 1929, when 67 of their number were killed and many more were wounded. Whether in settlements or in the old quarter, Israelis are protected now round the clock by armed reservists.

To the east, you will find the Capital Vista, as it is called, and it is a perfect place from which to get your bearings, to survey in a moment of relative serenity, and in one sweep, the monuments of Hebron that you came here to see. They are scattered over tens of acres that seem to breathe history as we breathe the air. From the vantage point of the Vista, you can see Ramath el-Khalil's oak trees where Abraham pitched his tent. The oak where Abraham accosted the Three Angels—the Moslems say that the Holy Family rested in its shade

Footsteps of Abraham

during the flight into Egypt. The pool of Hebron over which King David hanged the murderers of Ishbosheth, the son of his beloved Jonathan. Eshtemoa village, where the probable remains of David's treasure were found not long ago. And there, straight ahead of you, the deceptively plain limestone walls that enclose Hebron's central monument. It is in reality a magnificent shrine—compound would be a better word—built over the caves where three patriarchal couples are buried: Abraham and Sarah, Isaac and Rebecca, Jacob and Leah.

If Israel and Judaism have a central shrine anywhere on the face of this earth, surely it is here. It is the only standing structure that exhibits today the Herodian architecture of some 2,100 years ago. Later, when you enter, you will be in the only religious edifice in this world within whose walls Jews and Moslems worship at their respective synagogues and mosques. The great Isaac and Rebecca Hall is an ornate mosque often filled with Moslems, barefoot, kneeling on prayer mats, facing Mecca, eyes closed, hands outstretched, barely audible Arabic syllables pouring from their lips. The Abraham and Sarah Chamber and the Jacob and Leah Chamber are synagogues where modern bronze arks house the Torah scrolls and Jews come in endless numbers to stand, heads covered, bodies bending and bending, over and over again, in reverence, as their lips move to the rhythm of Torah verses and their faces seem misted over with ancient memories and the ever-present hope. Dark steps lead to the cave where Abraham and Sarah are buried; one imagines descending into a space hallowed by the intangible and eternal sleep of Abraham, but reverence and tradition bar the visitor and pilgrim alike from penetrating there.

Discreetly behaved but well-armed Israeli guards and

Moslem overseers keep a sharp eye at every turn and tourists shuffle through, gathering in all there is to see. But for worshipers, those jarring elements seem not to be there at all as they lose themselves in prayer to the God who called their common father, Abraham, out of distant Ur of the Chaldeans to claim this land for his faith and for his race of believers.

When, from the Capital Vista, you have surveyed all the monuments and are ready to descend to visit each one in turn, pause for just a moment more. Raise your eyes. Gaze in any direction—and you will be looking where Abraham walked. He didn't merely cover the territory as a matter of course. He stamped it indelibly by an activity that was as dazzling in its variety and prodigious in its extent as his hopes and ambitions had been far-reaching and unstoppable. For he had not quit his beloved Ur and come all of 2,000 miles to see any obstacle overturn his God-given destiny to be the father of millions in this land. "Look up!" God commanded him once in the silence of a far-off midnight. "Count the stars in the sky! As numerous will be your progeny in this land!"

And, still today, be they Israeli or Arab, Christian or Moslem or Jew, whether living in Israel or in its surrounding countries from Algiers in the west to Iran in the east and beyond, all claim Abraham as their prophet, their archpriest, their patriarch. Indeed, we all do. And that is Abraham's enduring shrine.

FOLLOWING IN THE FOOTSTEPS

Although borders and politics impede the casual traveler who wishes to follow the whole of Abraham's route today, **Hebron,** the historic and cultural culmination of the journey, is easily accessible. Here is the shrine of all the People of the Book, the common heritage of Jew, Christian and Moslem.

GUIDANCE

Hebron is not noted for touristic comforts, and visitors will prefer to make their base in Jerusalem. Several companies in that city can supply chauffeur-driven cars and English-speaking guides for the excursion to the Tomb of the Patriarchs. Three of these are **Eschcolot Tours,** 36 Keren Hayesod Street (telephone: 665-555); **Travex,** 8 Shamai Street (223-211), and **Shalom Tours,** 23 Hillel Street (245-770). Eschcolot charges a rate of about $90 for a five-hour trip for four people, or about $150 for ten hours. Travex can arrange excursions to Hebron for about $100 for a half day and $150 for a full day. Shalom's tours to Hebron are $90 for a half day and $140 for a full day.

Another alternative is hiring a taxi to stay with you for the length of the tour. The average charge is about $10 an hour before bargaining. It is about a forty-five-minute drive from the heart of Jerusalem to Hebron.

LODGINGS FIT FOR A KING

Jerusalem's most opulent hotel is the **King David,** with its huge lobby and decor reminiscent of a Cecil B. De Mille epic, overlooking the walls of the Old City. Rates range from about $100 for a standard double to about $135 for a deluxe room with a view of the Old City, breakfast included. Telephone: 221-111.

The more modest **American Colony Hotel** on Nablus Road was once a pasha's palace; double rooms, with breakfast, are about $50 to $100; the former are merely adequate but the latter are enormous, high-ceilinged chambers facing a cool and verdant courtyard. Telephone: 285-171.

SHIRT-SLEEVE DINING

Most Jerusalem restaurants are casual; the local cui-

.

sine reflects its Middle Eastern origins, and fresh fish is always a good bet. Some recommended establishments, in addition to hotel restaurants, are:

For seafood, especially the local St. Peter's fish, the **Dolfin Restaurant,** Alrashid Street (reservations: 282-788), is open daily for lunch and dinner, with entrees in the $10 range.

For dinner only (and never on Fridays), try **Fink's,** at 2 Histradrut Street in West Jerusalem (reservations: 234-523), which features seafood and steaks (beginning at about $10). The atmosphere is informal, even for Israel, and there is a bar popular with visiting journalists.

The view of the Old City is the thing at **Mishkenot Sha'ananin,** just below Montefiore's Windmill on King David Street (reservations: 233-424). Open daily; closed Friday evening and midday Saturday. A la carte specialties with a Continental accent include beef stroganoff and veal with mushrooms; dinner for two with wine averages about $60.

The Crossroads of
Three Faiths

MALACHI MARTIN

APPROACH JERUSALEM,
if you can, from the western plain and when dawn is
about to break. As you climb, you will catch a first
glimpse of the city up ahead of you, set among the hills
"as a queen surrounded by her courtiers."

Jerusalem in our time is actually two cities. The new
city, at least ten times bigger than the old, has been built
largely since 1948. The Old City, the goal of your pilgrimage, nestles deep in the new like a diamond-shaped
kernel within the fresh young fruit it has produced.
Driving along Derech Shechem in the new city, you realize that its slim symmetrical lines, its transparent glass,
its angular shining steel, its glossy chrome, have been
merely draped around the cavernous bulk of the Old.
Your eyes already search, then focus on those high cren-
ellated walls.

A quick drive brings you up directly to the Damascus

Gate, yawning its limestone yawn in the early day. This gate, one of seven, is a high-vaulted, solid stone passageway through the walls that takes an almost right-angle turn at midpoint. A few short moments through its semidarkness, then out again into the brilliant sunlight. You are there! And now, everything will conspire to hold you.

Dawn over Jerusalem is incredibly beautiful. It starts with a radiant whiteness and then a kaleidoscope of colors. "Ten measures of beauty descended upon the world at creation," the Talmud says; "Jerusalem received nine of them." Jerusalem's heat is dry, its air freshened by gentle breezes, the light of its sun softened and mellowed by reflection off the Judean limestone from which most of its buildings are made.

Within these walls, you soon discover, there lie four distinct quarters: Jewish, Christian, Moslem, Armenian. It will take you at most two hours to walk through them cursorily.

From the Damascus Gate, follow Khan ez-Zeit Street, branching out everywhere, packed with vendors and shops (there are over eight hundred merchants here), thronged with visitors (about a million a year). Make your way among a dizzying variety of Arab headdresses, desert robes, veiled Moslem women, armed Israeli soldiers in battle fatigues, tourists in every kind of garb, small carts pulled by donkeys, pack-camels with sweating drovers, beggars, rabbis, nuns, priests, street urchins, Orthodox bishops wearing tall *kallimaski*, Jewish seminarians wearing yarmulkes. Here, over this sea of bobbing heads, the babble of Arabic, Hebrew, English, Turkish, Greek, French, Spanish, Russian, desert dialect, the pealing of church bells, the booming voice of Islam's muezzin calling the faithful to prayer five times a day and the cries of persevering hawkers and peddlers.

Glimpse everywhere through the eddying crowd the graceful minarets, lonely crosses, worn stone plaques bearing the Star of David, squat towers, humped monuments, rugged pavements, fading icons, flaming mosaics, street names—traces of the nations who tramped these streets claiming them for their own. First the Jews, then Arabs, Greeks, Romans, Byzantines, Persians, Moslems, Norman-French Crusaders, Venetians, Genoese, Ottomans, Mamelukes, Turks, English. And, in full circle, the Jews. Jerusalem has been the object of all their desires. It remains, while many of them have passed into mute history.

Yet, even in that amazing hurly-burly, you will soon realize the essential quality of Jerusalem is its association with the God worshiped by Jew, Christian and Moslem. All have their sacred shrines here.

Jesus was born near here, off to the south, in Bethlehem, the village of David. Within these walls, he was tried and condemned. Within these walls runs the Via Dolorosa, the path he followed to his execution. There also is the site of the Temple where as a child he listened to the Jewish scholars and was found by his anxious mother; and there, as a man, he taught, prayed, disputed, drove out the money-changers, forgave sins and cured the sick.

Going westward from there, the Christian pilgrim will seek out the three places where Jesus was tried. The house of Caiaphas, the palace of King Herod and the fortress of Roman Governor Pontius Pilate. These places are in ruins now. But you can still see the Roman flagstones on which the blood of Jesus ran when they punished him with leaden-tipped Roman whips.

With the help of a guide, you can follow on foot the remaining spots, or "stations" as Christians have always called them, where Jesus walked carrying his cross: the places where, tradition says, he met his mother, where he fell beneath the weight of his cross, where he was helped by Simon of Cyrene, by Veronica, where he spoke to the bystanders—until you come to Calvary where he was nailed to the cross and left to die there in the sight of all. And the tomb in which his body was laid after death. Both Calvary and the tomb are now within the Church of the Holy Sepulcher.

Do not be shocked at the contrasting, sometimes clashing sentiments you will notice in the Church of the Holy Sepulcher. At least four main Christian groups—

Roman Catholic, Eastern Orthodox, Coptic and Armenian churches—have been occupying and disputing ownership of this sacred site for over 1,200 years. Brown-garbed Franciscans with booming voices sing the Latin Gregorian chant. Bearded and long-haired Greek and Russian priests pour out age-old Eastern hymns. Coptic and Armenian bishops and priests repeat the old Abyssinian and Central Asian invocations. Each group has its carefully watched privileges within the building, its jealously guarded time to perform in faith its rituals at the site of Jesus' death and burial. The division of Christians within these ancient walls depicts in microcosm the shattered unity of Christians all over the world. Sometimes, you feel only the appearance of Jesus himself would suffice to heal the animosity.

At every one of these "stations," no matter how pitiful the modern remains, the pilgrim is not surprised, not astonished, when he realizes that, in some mysterious way, he is reaching with the hand of his faith to touch a grace that claims him as surely as it hallows these places.

This is even more palpable in two of the remaining and most important sites for the Christian pilgrim. East of Jerusalem, separated from the old walls by the Kidron Valley, is the Mount of Olives. Here you stand upon one of the surest locations in the life of Jesus: the Garden of Gethsemane, in which Jesus spent his last night in agonizing prayer and decision. Lawrence of Arabia wrote to a friend that merely to sit in the Grotto of the Betrayal, where with a kiss Judas betrayed Jesus' whereabouts to his enemies, and to listen to the late afternoon wind soughing plaintively in the olive trees, was "to feel the approach of something hideous and uncouth coming through the trees to desecrate all that quiet beauty and holiness." Such, Christians have always believed, must have been the inner foretaste Jesus had, there in the dark of the quiet night.

Climb then up above the Garden of Gethsemane. Stand overlooking the Old City, as Jesus' followers did, at the place where, we are told, he ascended into Heaven in their sight.

Surprisingly, it will not be jarring when you plunge back into the Old City. Walk through the narrow, stepped streets and passageways, tasting again their welcome that never is old. This place has already laid claim to you. There is already a resonance of spirit between you and Jerusalem. For, sometime, during your walking, your viewing, your pilgrimage, the Old City has revealed the first eight measures of its being. You savor its grace, peace and sense of perpetuity. It calls mysteriously for justice and proclaims holiness. You feel part of one family. And everywhere it speaks of God.

Once you have tasted those eight measures of its beauty, you will pick time and place carefully to perceive the ninth. Sometime close to sundown most of the sky is a deep, cooling bronze, with an off-white light seeping from beneath the horizon. Wander out by that eastern wall along the Kidron Valley. At dusk, you will never see elsewhere such a white-gold moon riding in the orange-pink of a smiling, restful sky. Stand facing south, a little distance—about twenty or thirty yards— from the Golden Gate where Jesus entered in triumph on Palm Sunday.

That wall is lined on both sides with tranquil, centuries-old tombs; and, in the life-death paradox of Jerusalem, it is alive with an undulating patchwork quilt of green laurel, hyacinth, iris, anemone, myrtle, poppy, cassia, sweet storax, lilies-of-the-field. Behind you looms the pinnacle of Herod's Temple on which Satan tempted Jesus. Down this southern road, around the Mount of Olives, lies Bethany where Jesus raised his beloved Lazarus from the corruption of the grave.

The day will be over before you have half begun your pilgrim musings. Take one last look at the city that is yours now, too. Nightfall. The sky is from the Arabian Nights. It is a curving dome made of black-blue velvet, its stars shining with a silvery patina, tempting you with the idea, the certainty, that you can simply reach up and touch it—or that it is embracing you gently.

Across the Kidron Valley, from Jerusalem's lighted walls, there comes lilting desert music blending with the Gregorian chanting from nearby monasteries. The raucous day-sounds, the voices of Jerusalem's children, are more subdued now, are a little weary. They may differ in religion, these children, but they are all there because Jerusalem has always promised its ninth measure—salvation.

It was the noblest human ancestor of Jesus who perhaps supplied every pilgrim, Christian or other, with the most suitable words for these moments. Whisper them over Jerusalem as it sinks gradually into sleep for just another of its thousands of nights: "To Jerusalem, which gathers all its children together," David sang in his psalm, "the peoples of the Lord go up in order to worship Him."

The Jerusalem
of David

ELIE WIESEL

HILLS AND SPARKLING
domes, the sounds of the marketplace at the gates of the
Old City, monotonous, melancholy singsong voices from
houses of study, homeless beggars, newly arriving
pilgrims—the human tumult made of so many religions,
so many nations, so many memories: Jerusalem holds
you and never eases its grip. No other city in the world
exerts such a hold on a visitor. You plunge into it as into
a poem, you depart reluctantly and with a sad heart.

Is it its past, crossed by so many tempests, battles and
challenges, that forms its allure? As a Jew, you wander
in the streets and alleys, toward the Wall, in the steps of
ancient kings and prophets who still walk with you. You
cannot be conscious of this feeling of a living past, of
this millennial presence, anywhere else. Knowingly or
not, you move beyond time.

Outwardly, the visible City of David astonishes you

with its harmonious beauty. One can sense the mystery behind each edifice, one glimpses the force of history in each encounter. There, everything is majestic. Even the suffering? Even the suffering.

Of course, it is the Jew in me who speaks, but it is the Jew who remembers. What would a Christian say in my place? Or a Moslem? I have no right to speak for them. I observe their churches and mosques, the holy places of the one or the other, and I visit them respectfully, and it is from respect that I do not tell their stories. I speak only of what is mine, of what is in me.

I love to linger in this city where I feel close to my an-cestors, and, through them, to all beings who share my faith in mankind. I always discover a new depth there, a sense of a deeper secret, a more urgent meaning. Seven-teen attempts to destroy this city have been made. Built and rebuilt with determination and hope, it has grown like a monument straining to the heights. As the work of man, it rises above mankind as a symbol of pride and triumph.

Let us take a walk. It is my favorite pastime in Jerusa-lem. I walk from morning to night, and deep into the night. I stop only to admire a landscape that stands with-out comparison in the world.

I admit that the modern sections move me less. The luxury hotels with their pools and restaurants, the rich shops with their electronic gadgets remind me too much of commercial strips in certain Western capitals. I prefer Meah Shearim, the place known as the Hundred Gates.

It's true that the inhabitants there will strike you as strange and even fanatical. They flee from cameras, dis-trust your appearance and behave rudely, but still I have a weakness for their presence: They bring back for me, in their way of life, the exile of my childhood, somewhere in the Carpathians. These children, already so pious, so fragile, remind me of the others, those whom the world had abandoned on the other shore, over there.

Let us continue to the Old City where, since the destruction of the Temple, there has always been a man, or a child, to lament the tragedies of the Jewish people, and when there was no one, the Shekhina—the divine presence—herself would appear among the ruins to repel forgetfulness with her tears.

Let us stop here. Before the Wall, we must be silent in ourselves.

Those men kissing the stones, those women caressing them, those children confiding their dreams to them—you see them, and thanks to them, you are reconciled to humanity.

I might as well say right out what you have already guessed: I love Jerusalem, I love it deeply, I have always loved it. I know and yet do not know why my love is ignited by it. A simpleminded attitude, or childish? In Jerusalem, I become a child once more.

When did I first go there? I cannot remember. I often have the feeling that I have never left. As the Israeli Nobel laureate S. J. Agnon put it, in his speech in Stockholm, "The truth is, I was born in Jerusalem, only the Romans invaded Judea two thousand years ago and pushed my cradle all the way to Poland." That goes for all Jewish children, especially the children of the shtetl, vital and picturesque villages in central and eastern Europe where the longing, the thirst for Jerusalem helped us survive. So we do not inhabit Jerusalem: Jerusalem inhabits us. We turn toward Jerusalem to pray, to sing, to dream. We invoke its name like a blessing and as a consolation. To the orphans of misery, we speak of it in quiet voices.

The Jerusalem of David

Before the pogroms, during the massacres, after the trials and lasting torments we make ourselves drunk on its glory and its suffering.

And then, one beautiful morning I rediscovered myself in it at last. It's silly, it's romantic, I admit, but I was seized by an irresistible weeping—I, who detest all traces of sentimentality. But I could not help it: In discovering Jerusalem, the Jew in me could not restrain the tears for himself, for us.

And the non-Jews? I don't know. I have put the question to close friends of mine, Catholic and Protestant; if they are devout they, too, are moved by the city. But if they are not, they are not. Such are the conclusions of my private survey: Jerusalem responds only to a spiritual need. An agnostic sees in it a city like so many others, perhaps more beautiful, but no more stirring than the rest. It exerts scant attraction to the irreligious. But for the Jew, Moslem, Bahai, Christian or Buddhist, Jerusalem resonates like a deep, mystical chord in us all.

If not for the spiritual dimension of the city, it would be little more than a big little provincial city, or a little big city. For Jerusalem is all that, too. Everyone knows everyone else. Various clans are formed to combat rival clans. Young boys and girls, children of the bourgeoisie or the intellectual elite, gather in the evening to dredge up each others' lives, to have a little fun in having fun, to build up and tear down careers, so and so's career, so and so's reputation, from envy or malice. They take off for Arab restaurants for food, the sacred places for a little local color. They talk politics, poetry and the cost of living. Like everywhere else, the writers envy each other, the politicians lie to each other. Ah, yes—it is unthinkable but true: Jerusalem is not always, and not everywhere, a sacred, a divine city. It possesses not only its sages and its choristers but also its fools and its thieves, its amateurs of idolatry, and its sex maniacs.

I found it shocking. If I had been told, in my childhood, that there were, that there would be thieves in Jerusalem, I would have replied with a burst of laughter.

Was I wrong? Had I confused the heavenly with the earthly Jerusalem? Now I know that there are in Jerusalem several cities at once, or more exactly, several communities united within a common space. Christians, Arabs, leftists, intellectuals, politicians, artists, merchants, the crazed and the princely: They live separately, they mingle but rarely. What do the Hassid from Bratzlav and the soccer player imported from Europe have in common? The messianic dreamer and the professional athlete—what unites them?

Once again I owe a confession: I am more at ease among the pious. Those who observe the Sabbath (Shabbath). Who believe still in the coming of the Messiah. Who are open to fervor, to prayer, to waiting.

I am not talking about the fanatics, the Neturei Karta, those "Keepers of the Gate" or "of the faith," rigid and inflexible, for whom the smallest deviation from the Torah constitutes an unpardonable sin and who refuse to recognize the state of Israel; I am talking about those who marry orthodoxy with tolerance. Pay them a visit: They will greet you warmly and without judging you; they will explain to you why God is God and why He has the right to chastise those He loves. They are sincere, devout, pure; their enthusiasm is contagious.

For that matter, there is a whole movement of repenters and penitents—the Baale Teshuva, raging through Israel, especially in the Bohemian crowd. Old stars of the stage, from music halls and the movies—you come across them suddenly in some yeshiva, dressed in

Hassidic clothes, their eyes burning with fire or religion. Some have become rabbis, others are steeped in the Talmud. Speak to them, and they will explain their metamorphosis: One morning, one evening, they realized that they were wasting their days away, and so they decided to remake their lives by returning to the source.

At first, people thought that it was all just another publicity stunt, people mocked them, but no one mocks them now. Their movement has become a real force, a source of disquietude to some and a sign of hope to others, a yearning for certainty, for passion? A fear of tomorrow? Disenchantment with the illusions, the facile success of artistic life? How can we know? A friend of mine, a reporter, told me: "My best friend, a famous actor, is part of it. The binges, the crazy fun we've had, all the joy, it's all changed for him. He's changed, he has aged. And he's positive that in a little while I'll be there with him, like him. It frightens me. . . ."

Yet not all inhabitants of Jerusalem consider themselves exclusively the servants of God. You will meet the

same sort of people everywhere, preoccupied with the same worries. The quotidian haunts them more than the metaphysical. How to make ends meet? Illnesses, vacations, jobs . . . security. And then, of course, war or peace, or both? It blows in gusts, ecstasy and anguish. Sadat? A distant memory.

What will tomorrow bring? In Jerusalem it is impossible to live without hope and so without patience. This city has suffered too much under the heel of war to aspire to anything but a reconciliation.

And when is it for, the true accord? I took a walk in the Old City, as I did on the morning after its liberation in 1967, and I saw the same stoic Arabs, the same Arab children with their same shy and sadly humble smiles. I observed their parents, the hard and angry faces of their older brothers. What do they feel toward me? What do they expect from me? What do I represent to them? And above all, how to extinguish the anger in this city whose name is, whose name demands, peace?

As a Jew, I belong to this city because its memory is mine. I listen to its subterranean rhythm, its beating heart, at dawn and late at night.

You should listen, too. Listen to the muezzin in his droning call to prayer. Lift your eyes, look at the sky's sober and shifting hues. Here and there, you will salute a young student or an old cabbalist heading for the Wall. Follow them. You will find men and women, come from afar, alone and in groups, starving for joy and serenity, and above all for memories. They spill their tears, in prayers or silently; each of their words is suffused by a dark and beautiful melancholy that is not of this world, not of our time.

At dawn, you will rediscover the city in its blinding timelessness, and it will never leave you.

Holy City of Islam

SARI NUSEIBEH

ISLAM CONSIDERS
itself to be rooted in Judaism and Christianity. "We believe in God and in what has been revealed to us," the
Koran says. "We believe in what has been revealed to
Abraham and Ishmael and Isaac and Jacob and the
tribes; we believe in what has been delivered unto Moses
and Jesus, and in what has been delivered unto the
prophets from their God." To be a Moslem is not to believe simply that Mohammed is God's prophet. Rather,
it is to believe in the revelations of God to all his prophets, of whom Mohammed is the last. Islam venerates
Isaac as it venerates Ishmael, and Jesus as it venerates
Mohammed.

It is in this sense that the Koran speaks of "the sancti-
fied land," referring to the arrival of Moses and his people to the borders of the Land of Canaan. It is probably
this, too, that explains why Jerusalem, before Mecca,

was chosen by Mohammed as the *qiblah,* or the place to which Moslems turn in order to pray. The Jewish and Christian love for Jerusalem runs in the religious blood of Islam. From its very roots, Islam venerates Jerusalem for the same reasons it is venerated in Judaism and Christianity. The pilgrim who wishes to visit Moslem holy places will pause in the Church of the Holy Sepulcher as well as wonder at such specifically Moslem shrines as the Dome of the Rock, a masterpiece of early Islamic architecture, and the Al Aksa Mosque.

Just as Dante's *Divine Comedy,* reflecting the classical Christian medieval tradition, portrays Jerusalem as the mystical meeting place of the earthly and the divine, so, too, did the earlier Moslem mystics and philosophers view it. This probably explains why Islam never accorded Jerusalem a political status or made it a political capital. This abstraction of Jerusalem from worldy affairs by Islam, and its veneration as a divine city, is reflected in the Islamic tradition that relates how Moslems first came to Jerusalem: Rather than overpowering the city by military might, Islam's second caliph, Omar, traveled by camel with his servant until they reached Jerusalem and entered it peacefully, receiving it into the custody of Islam. On the journey, the tradition relates, Omar and his servant took turns riding the caliph's camel, thus symbolizing Omar's human humility before the city. The story symbolizes Islam's veneration of Jerusalem as a city above men, rather than an earthly city that can be conquered by man.

The Islamic view of Jerusalem as a mystic city is not simply a view inherited from Jews and Christians, since Islam itself sanctifies Jerusalem. The major Islamic event with which the city is associated is the miraculous ascension of the prophet Mohammed to the heavens. The miracle is memorialized in two magnificent mosques on the Temple Mount.

The Dome of the Rock, built about 690 and the oldest existing Moslem monument, dominates the area. It stands on a plateau within an enclosed rectangular holy space, called the Haram esh-Sharif—the "Noble Sanctuary"—that, flanked by slender minarets, covers about a sixth of the Old City. The Dome of the Rock is octagonal in shape, covered with marble and glass mosaics in interlocking floral patterns on the inside and with blue and green ceramic tiles on the outside. The tiles, which range in color from turquoise to indigo, bear exquisite examples of the calligraphic art at which the Moslems excelled. Various verses of the Koran are set out; just beneath the dome is a verse specifically celebrating Mohammed's miraculous ascension. The dome itself, set on a high drum, gleams above the horizon; it is covered with a gilded copper sheath that reflects the rays of the rising and setting sun.

Farther to the south stands the second of the mosques, Al Aksa, which commemorates Mohammed's journey from Mecca to Jerusalem in preparation for his ascent to the heavens. Here the prophet is said to have left his legendary winged horse. The mosque is surmounted by a silver dome; in front of the main door is the fountain for ritual ablutions before prayers.

The Haram esh-Sharif and its holy places are no strangers to the violence that has marked Jerusalem. In 1982, an Israeli soldier was arrested after a shooting spree that left two dead and at least eleven wounded. In 1969, an arsonist set fire to Al Aksa, destroying a wooden pulpit placed there by Saladin after he recaptured Jerusalem from the Crusaders in 1187. (Saladin also restored and embellished other parts of the Haram esh-Sharif; during Crusader times, Al Aksa Mosque had been the headquarters and stables of the Knights Templars.)

The importance to Islam of the miracle the mosques commemorate cannot be overstated; it is, in fact, the only miracle associated with Mohammed. In Mecca and its environs, Mohammed was the recipient of revelation, when divine knowledge was indirectly transmitted to him through the Angel Gabriel. The Jerusalem miracle turns the tables, however, by providing Mohammed with a direct vision of the divine foundations of the universe. In Mecca, Gabriel descended to Mohammed, but from Jerusalem Mohammed himself ascended to the heavens. Jerusalem is thus the gateway to the heavens and to divine knowledge, the medium through which to reach the divine—in short, the spiritual threshold of the divine paradise.

The Jerusalem miracle has broad implications. Mohammed, according to his own words, was only a human being like other human beings, and his ascension reflects the ability of all men to attain transcendental and divine knowledge. The miraculous achievement of Mohammed could be regarded as an achievement attainable by the rest of mankind: If men apply themselves to a devout life and to religious learning, they, too, may be able to achieve knowledge of the divine mysteries of the universe.

Jerusalem thus developed into Islam's center of sacred learning. The area around the mosques, from which Mohammed ascended to heaven, became the focal point of contemplative and religious education. Other schools and study centers proliferated around this central area.

Today, the whole area is filled with domes and pulpits, ornamental fountains and arcades, pilgrims' sta-

Holy City of Islam

tions and square minarets celebrating various Islamic holy events. If a visitor stands in the center of the Haram esh-Sharif and looks west and north, most of the buildings he sees rising above the arcades will be those of religious schools, some of which are now private houses sheltering very old Moslem families. Due north, two still functioning schools occupy the greater length of the area; due west are vaults housing the tombs of Moslem religious teachers. One of these buildings contains the Aksa Library, with some very old and rare Moslem manuscripts; to the south is the Moslem Museum, with a collection of Islamic relics. The gate of the Haram esh-Sharif, with its archstones of alternate light- and dark-colored stones and its half dome set above a stalactite-decorated niche, is a good example of the eclectic Islamic architecture of the fourteenth century. (The entryway is often the most important element in buildings of this period.)

Outside the precincts of the mosques, throughout the Old City, lie no fewer than forty-nine religious schools and nineteen other establishments that doubled as schools and shrines or mosques. Most are now private homes, and visitors can glimpse only their embellished entrances as they stroll around the city.

Other evidences of Islamic Jerusalem are visible wherever one looks: The present city walls are Ottoman, built by Suleiman the Magnificent in the sixteenth century. Six of the present city gates, among them the Damascus Gate, the principal entrance to the Old City, were also built during this period. Throughout the city there are pilgrim caravansaries and schools, minarets and fountains dating from the Islamic Middle Ages. In Jerusalem, the paths of pilgrims, Christian, Jewish or Moslem, often cross.

The Sinai's Harsh Splendor

TERENCE SMITH

HE GOOD NEWS FROM the Sinai is that there is no news.

Despite the transition not long ago from Israeli to Egyptian stewardship, nothing important has changed in the "great and terrible wilderness," as it is so aptly described in Deuteronomy.

The essential Sinai is still there: the stark, spectacular mountains, the magnificent beaches, the deep blue waters of the Gulf of Aqaba, the lush, palm-fringed oases. All of these are the same, as is St. Catherine's, the sixth-century Greek Orthodox monastery-fortress nestled at the foot of the traditional Mount Sinai, which still retains its awe-inspiring, otherworldly isolation. The Bedouin are the same graceful, gentle enigma. The diving and snorkeling off the coral reefs along the Sinai coast are still beyond comparison.

The whole peninsula, in fact, remains what it has al-

The Sinai's Harsh Splendor

ways been: one of the last great wildernesses of the world, a place of stunning beauty and harsh reality where history, religion and modern politics come together as nowhere else.

The latest change of watch in the Sinai took place on April 25, 1982, when Israel returned the peninsula to Egypt in exchange for formal peace. It was a major event in world politics, but a mere footnote in the 6,000-year history of the Sinai. After all, this barren, seemingly worthless tract of real estate—some 23,500 square miles, about the size of West Virginia—has been conquered and reconquered by fifty different armies over the centuries. Little surprise, then, that it should survive this latest shift in the political winds.

But if the essence of the Sinai is unchanged, the atmosphere is noticeably different now that Egypt is once again in charge. This was apparent to three travelers who made a late-September journey through the eastern half of the peninsula two and a half years after Egypt regained control of the area. All of us had visited the area repeatedly during the Israeli years. Now we were going back to see what had changed.

The area has a distinctly different feel under Egyptian administration, a more languid, Levantine pace that becomes evident at the border crossing at Taba, a few miles south of the bustling, kinetic Israeli port of Eilat.

We had made the arrangements for our trip through an Israeli travel agent, Johnny's Desert Tours, based in Eilat. Johnny Lamm, the agent, had sent word across the border that we wanted a car and Bedouin driver for four days and bookings at the modest vacation hotels along the coast. His Egyptian counterparts had assured him that all was in order: An air-conditioned Peugeot and driver would be waiting at the border crossing, and the hotel reservations were made.

Thus encouraged, we set off on a trip that proved to be an almost comic series of foul-ups. Virtually nothing worked out as planned, yet in the end, everything worked out fine. That's not uncommon in the desert, but the trip served as a vivid reminder of the fragility of the lines of communication between Israel and Egypt these days. If the two countries fought wars the way they coordinate travel arrangements, peace would have broken out years ago by default.

Perhaps anticipating this, my two companions, Micha and Orna Bar-Am, brought basic camping gear, food and water as a precaution.

The first surprise came when we pushed our luggage and gear through the border crossing on carts. A travel agent from Carmina Tours, a Cairo-based agency, met us and cheerfully advised that the promised air-conditioned Peugeot was in Cairo. Instead, he offered a Toyota Land Cruiser, an elongated jeep whose air conditioning was provided by the canvas flaps on the sides. "It's a very beautiful jeep," the agent said encouragingly.

The three of us shrugged in resignation. After all, we reminded ourselves, this is the desert. We knew we had to adopt the philosophy Orna Bar-Am calls "Bedouism," the laid-back, fatalistic, come-what-may approach that the Sinai natives take toward life in general. Whatever the problem, the Bedouin motto is *"In-shallah"*—"If God wills."

"Bedouism is the key to a successful trip in the desert," Orna Bar-Am said, not knowing how right she was.

The Egyptian frontier at Taba consists of little more

than a series of wooden huts along the side of the road. The traveler arriving from Israel passes through a gentle gauntlet of sleepy bureaucrats who stamp passports, change money and sell seven-day visas to the eastern Sinai on the spot for $6.

Once inside the Egyptian Sinai, the pace seemed noticeably slower, the roads and beaches less crowded. During the fifteen years that Israel was in charge, from 1967 to 1982, the lovely beaches along the coastline from Eilat southward were frequently packed with tens of thousands of Israeli campers, especially during holidays. Over the long Rosh ha-Shanah weekend of 1984, however, only a few score Israelis decided to obtain a visa and cross the border to camp along the coast.

With darkness approaching, our "air-conditioned" jeep roared down the coastal highway toward our first stop, the Israeli-built guesthouse at Nuweiba. Looking at the mountains etched against the evening sky to our right and the lights of the Jordanian and Saudi coastline across the Gulf to our left, I was reminded once again of the extraordinary beauty of the Sinai. Very simply, there are few places in the world to compare with it.

Nuweiba, called Neviot under Israeli rule, is a splendid oasis on the beach about an hour's drive south of the border. The Israelis built a kibbutz-style guesthouse there that is now being run, like all the hotels in the Sinai, by an Egyptian concern, Sinai Hotels and Diving Clubs.

When we arrived, the small reception area was jammed with a busload of Coptic pilgrims who had come directly from Cairo. From the harried look on the face of the reception manager, it was obvious that there were not enough rooms to go around. Suddenly our confirmed, prepaid single room and double room collapsed into one triple. We shrugged again, reinforcing our "Bedouism."

Under the Israelis, the beach resort at Neviot was a freewheeling, casual escape from daily life. Nude sunbathing was common, and the smell of hashish frequently wafted across the beach from a small band of Scandinavian and European hippies who camped there more or less permanently.

Under the Egyptians, the atmosphere is almost prim. A sign on the beach implores: "In respect for our culture, please avoid nudity." The open-air disco on the beach still pumps out the same mix of Western rock and Arab pop, but now it is mostly men who take to the dance floor.

The hotel itself has gone to seed a bit. Israeli-built air conditioners still cool the individual units, but the door handles tend to come off in your hand. One Swiss woman who had been a guest under both incarnations summed up the difference this way: "Under the Israelis, the food was dreadful, but the rooms were spotless. Now the food is better, but the rooms are filthy." Under the philosophy of "Bedouism," of course, one shrugs at the difference.

After an early swim the next morning, we headed inland toward St. Catherine's. The route took us along a major new Egyptian addition to the network of modern roads started by the Israelis. It is a freshly paved highway that for the first time links the coastal road to the rugged, mountainous interior. A ribbon of black asphalt winding through the tawny brown landscape, the road is an adventure in itself. Now a drive that used to take hours in a jeep along a rock-strewn track can be traversed in an ordinary car in less than an hour.

But if the Egyptians have improved the road system, they have also increased the red tape and tightened restrictions on travel inside the Sinai. It is no longer possible, for example, for the foreigner to freely roam through the magnificent wadis, the steep-walled canyons that lace the Sinai. Instead, the visitor encounters bold signs in English and French every few miles that declare: "Foreigners Are Forbidden to Leave the Main Road." No explanation for this restriction is offered, but it seems to be part of the general Egyptian penchant for security. The authorities have also established checkpoints along the main roads manned by soldiers whose armbands read "Tourist Police." Unfailingly courteous, these soldiers nonetheless seemed quite determined to record the name, nationality and passport numbers of all who pass their way.

At the wheel of our jeep was Hamid, a twenty-one-year-old Bedouin of the Muzzeina tribe, who had managed to learn fluent Hebrew and some English while working for the Israelis at Neviot. His driving technique was uncomplicated: He put the accelerator of the jeep to the floor and kept it there.

The road to St. Catherine's winds through some of the most spectacular scenery in the Sinai and leads directly to the gate of the monastery. Visitors are allowed to enter from 9:30 A.M. to 12:30 P.M. daily except on Fridays and roughly a score of religious holidays. We arrived on a Thursday morning, only to discover that it was the Greek Orthodox Feast of the Cross. The monastery was technically closed, but we managed to talk our way through the heavy gate by asking for water—a request the monks always grant in the tradition of desert hospitality.

Once inside, we encountered a young priest, Father Makarios, who, despite his full beard, fluent Greek and flowing Orthodox robes, proved to be from Bingham Canyon, Utah. He said he had been living at the monastery for a year and a half and found it to be "a treasure of Orthodox spirituality."

When the Israelis ruled the Sinai, Father Makarios said, an average of 2,000 tourists visited the monastery each week. The average now is closer to 1,000 a week, he said, including large numbers of Coptic pilgrims from Cairo.

The number may rise again in 1985 when Egypt completes work on an ambitious new hotel complex near the monastery on the Plain of Raha where, according to the Bible, the Israelites danced around the golden calf while waiting for Moses to descend from Mount Sinai with the Ten Commandments. Plans call for 100 two-room bungalows, all in native Sinai granite that blends with the landscape, a swimming pool and restaurant. Visitors can already stay in several completed bungalows, including the three-room villa that was built for the late President Anwar el-Sadat of Egypt, who visited the site after the area was returned by Israel. The complex has a spectacular view of the monastery and the 8,000-foot peaks that surround it.

From St. Catherine's, we drove back to the coastal road and south to the Dahab oasis, another seaside resort developed by the Israelis. The familiar tumultuous scene was underway in the lobby, where dozens of Egyptians were clamoring for the last few rooms in the forty-one-unit complex. Our claim of advance reservations evoked a helpless shrug from a polite but overwhelmed room clerk. "Remember your 'Bedouism,' " Orna Bar-Am cautioned.

The crowded quarters were another reminder that the Egyptian tourist has suddenly discovered the Sinai. Prior to 1967, few Egyptians bothered to travel to the area they universally dismissed as "the desert." Then for fifteen years they were denied access to the territory that had been the scene of all their modern wars. Now, with the restoration of Egyptian sovereignty, thousands of middle-class Egyptians have begun to sign up for tours of the area. Traveling mostly in organized groups from Cairo, they have all but overwhelmed the limited tourist facilities in the scenic eastern half of the peninsula.

With Hamid as our guide, we retreated to a Bedouin encampment just down the beach. For $1 each, we rented a hut on the beach and spread our sleeping bags on the sand.

Our "innkeeper," a smiling, toothless Bedouin named

Ali, took some of the flour the Bar-Ams had packed and returned in thirty minutes with freshly baked pita bread from his fire. We augmented this with fresh lobster caught and boiled by a Bedouin fisherman and washed it down with a few cans of Israeli beer. Suddenly, roughing it Sinai style seemed downright luxurious.

After dinner, we crawled into our sleeping bags beneath a shimmering canopy of stars. A pale new moon rose out of Saudi Arabia across the Gulf. Not bad, I thought to myself, not half bad.

Our next and final stop was Sharm el Sheik, the strategic promontory near the southern tip of the Sinai that has figured in every Arab-Israeli war. The Israelis built a town here, called Ofira, and developed a full-blown beach resort at nearby Naama Bay, complete with three hotels, a diving center, several restaurants and discothèques.

Once again the place was jammed with Egyptian tourists, but we managed to secure one room in the modern Marina Sharm Hotel.

At the Red Sea Diving Club, Ayman Taher, the Egyptian manager, said the coral reefs around Sharm had proved to be just as big a lure to foreign divers under Egyptian administration as under Israeli.

"We have many of the same divers from Europe and the United States who came here under the Israelis," he said cheerfully. "We are divers here, not politicians."

After a morning of snorkeling at Ras-um-Sidd, a nearby point, the attraction was easy to understand. The reef juts out a few hundred yards from the shore and then drops off suddenly, exposing a sheer wall of brilliantly colored coral 80 to 150 feet deep. The sunlight streaming through the warm, transparent water illuminates a vast

undersea panorama of breathtaking beauty. Many experts regard the diving here to be unequaled in the world.

The last surprise of our desert journey came as we prepared to return to Eilat. The jeep, which had carried us
hundreds of miles through rugged terrain, refused to
start. Hamid's native "Bedouism" took over at this
point. He simply leaned on the starter and waited for
God to intervene. The engine finally coughed to life.
Hamid smiled.

"Inshallah," he said.

SAFARIS INTO THE PENINSULA

Excursions from Israel into the Sinai are organized by
several travel agencies in Eilat and Tel Aviv. It is also
possible to make the trip on your own, crossing the border at Taba, where you may obtain an Egyptian visa
that is limited to the eastern sector, between Taba and
Sharm el Sheik. The visa costs $6 and no currency ex-
change is required. Since only vehicles registered to
individual Israelis are allowed through by Israeli authorities, rental cars must be reserved in advance and
picked up on the Egyptian side. **Johnny's Desert
Tours** (telephone: 76777 or 72608), Post Office Box
261, Eilat 88102, Israel, can make such an arrangement; a car and driver cost approximately $125 a day.
Johnny's also arranges safaris into the Sinai that range
from a half-day tour for about $30 a person to a five-
day tour that includes a visit to Cairo for about $300 a
person.

Naot Hakikar Safari Ltd., 36 Keren Hayesod
Street, Jerusalem 92149 (699385 or 636494), orga-
nizes one- and two-day camping excursions into the

Sinai from Eilat. The one-day tour, which includes a visit to St. Catherine's, costs about $60. The two-day tour, which includes an overnight stay near St. Catherine's and a predawn hike up Mount Sinai, costs about $125 a person; transportation, guides, meals and sleeping bags are furnished. The main office of Naot Hikikar Safari Ltd. is at 36 Keren Hayesod Street, Jerusalem 92149, Israel (699386 or 636494).

The resort hotels on the east coast are operated by the **Sinai Hotels and Diving Clubs, Inc.,** 32 Sabry Abu Alam Street, Cairo (7702000 or 770301). Prices range from $25 to $30 a person a day, including breakfast and one other meal. The resorts include the holiday villages at Nuweiba and Dahab, and three hotels at Sharm el Sheik: the Marina Sharm, the Aquamarine and the Clifftop Village. Reservations are essential.

Several Cairo companies offer both bus and air tours into the Sinai. Among them are **Spring Tours,** 65 El Gom Houria Street (9108730); **Travco Travel Company,** 3 Ishak Varoub Street, Zamalek (803448), and **Misr Sinai Tourist Company,** Misr Travel Tower, Abbassia (821061 or 831356). Misr is developing hotel and resort facilities on both coasts and at St. Catherine's, although several of the facilities have not yet been completed.

Petra, *Half* as *Old* as *Time*

R. W. APPLE, JR.

WHEN I WAS GROWING
up in Ohio in the 1940s, my most treasured possession
was a book with a dark-blue cover and impressive pictures of far-off places inside. It was called *Richard
Halliburton's Book of Marvels*, and it helped to give me
a case of incurable wanderlust. One of the places
Halliburton wrote about was Petra, the ancient Nabatean
capital in southern Jordan, to which he, like everyone
else, referred as the "rose-red city half as old as time."
(A stirring phrase, that, worthy of Ruskin or Words-
worth, but in fact the work of a feeble, long-forgotten
nineteenth-century English poet named John William
Burgon, who had never been there.)

Halliburton assured his readers that "in the years to
come, when the memory of the other wonders you have
seen has grown dim, you, too, will still recall clearly, as
one of the truly magic moments of your life," the sight of

Petra's majestic temples and tombs. I immediately resolved to get there as soon as possible, which turned out
to be roughly forty years later.

Petra came into being because of geography. It lies in
the great rift valley of which the Dead Sea and the Jordan
River and the Sea of Galilee also form a part, a north-south
trade route since time immemorial, and it lies at the only
really convenient pass through the mountains that blocked
land communications between the ancient civilizations of
the Nile and of the Tigris and Euphrates. It also had water,
a precious commodity in that parched region.

Through Petra, in the centuries before the birth of Jesus, flowed the wealth of China and India and Egypt and
Greece—gold, damask, pearls, spices, cotton, silk,
myrrh, ivory. On each shipment, the peoples who lived
there levied duty, and with the money thus earned they
built their city, culminating in the stupendous Hellenis-
tic monuments we see today. It was the Nabateans, a nomadic Arab tribe, who brought the city to its commercial
and artistic peak, but of them we know regrettably little.

What we do know is that they were sculptors of the
first order, capable of transforming, with simple tools, a
pink rock-face into a temple as tall as a ten-story building, adorned with graceful columns and wonderfully
delicate garlands and flowers and friezes, with an unem-
bellished rock hall behind it—a cube forty feet on each
side. This is the Treasury, the greatest of Petra's
2,000-year-old buildings. It is the first one that the visitor sees, and so perfect that I had often wondered how
the rest of the place could possibly avoid anticlimax.

I was not let down, nor were my wife and our traveling
companions (although one of them, a New York interior
designer who knows about such things, assured me that
most of Petra was not rose-red after all, but cinnamon-

colored). After seven hours in that hidden valley—not only dramatic, not only romantic, but only beautiful, but also essentially unchanged since J. L. Burckhardt, an intrepid young Swiss disguised as an Arab, rediscovered it for the West in 1812—two of us found ourselves

whistling, spontaneously and simultaneously, if comically, "When You Come to the End of a Perfect Day."

Of few places in the world would I dare to say that they would thrill any sane person, because I know people who hate London and Paris and even Florence, but I would say it about Petra. The world affords few travel experiences to rival the mile-long ride on horseback through the narrow defile called the Siq, the walls of rock rising 200 feet and more above your head, shutting out the sky, the sound of the horses' footfalls echoing about you, until suddenly, when it seems that the end will never come, you round a last corner and see beyond the mouth of the defile, glowing in the morning sun, the crisp Classical façade of the grandiose Treasury, hewn from the living rock.

"There is a fierce and tragic quality in the scenery," Margaret Alice Murray wrote in her book on Petra forty-five years ago, "which seems to have inspired the hymns to Jehovah which abound in the Bible."

It is possible to visit Petra in a single day. Travel agencies in Amman send buses down the bleak Desert Highway early each morning—four boring hours each way, with less than two hours in Petra itself, which is not nearly enough. If you are going to take the trouble to travel as far as Jordan, take the trouble to rent a car in Amman and devote at least two days to the trip. That way you can take the far more interesting King's Highway south, following in the steps of the Roman Emperor Trajan, visit Petra the next day, then head back up the Desert Highway at nightfall. Even better, spend three days, and use the third for a visit to Wadi Rum, the remote desert valley, filled with surrealistic rock formations of every conceivable hue, that T. E. Lawrence of Arabia celebrated in *Seven Pillars of Wisdom.*

The whole journey can now be accomplished in the kind

of comfort undreamed of only a dozen years ago. Both highways are now well paved and graded, and in 1983 a fine little hotel, the eighty-two-room **Forum,** opened in Wadi Musa, the village nearest Petra. Built in expertly dressed local stone by the Jordanian Government and superbly managed by Britain's Grand Metropolitan group, it is an outpost of civilization crouching at the foot of the savage mountains, offering everything that the wandering sybarite could ask for—clean, bright rooms (about $45 a night for a double) with well-stocked minibars; a big swimming pool; good meals, prepared by a German chef, including fresh seafood brought from Aqaba by truck (about $40 for two, including decent French wines); and even a quasi-discothèque inside a real Bedouin tent.

The best months to go are March and April, when it's not too hot, the crowds are still small and the fragrant oleanders are in bloom, but the fall is a good second choice. Take a hat, a wrap for the evening, a set of binoculars, insect repellent and a pair of stout walking shoes. In Amman, at your hotel or at any good bookshop, you should buy Iain Browning's *Petra,* which is indispensable despite an intermittently banal style, and the wonderfully relaxed and informative *Antiquities of Jordan,* by G. Lankester Harding, one of the greatest of Palestinian archaeologists.

We left Amman at about nine-thirty in the morning, taking a picnic, and headed southwest toward Madaba, about twenty miles away. Just at the edge of town, a spur road leads off to the right toward Mount Nebo, overlooking the Dead Sea, where Moses is thought to have sighted the Promised Land at last, just before his death. It is a barren site, but strangely stirring, like so many in the Holy Land, even for the irreligious.

The Madaba region was the home during the Byzantine period of a noted school of mosaic makers, and one of the finest of their works is on top of the mountain. Now sheltered by a building that looks like an aircraft hangar, it was the pavement of the north aisle of a basilica from which part of the apse, several chapels and bits of columns also survive. It shows hunting scenes and other scenes of country life, perfectly preserved and full of vigor, with delicious portraits of animals—buffalo and lions, boars and goats, zebras and dromedaries. There are other good mosaics at Mekhayyat, off to your right as you head back to Madaba on a well-posted road, and in Madaba itself. We particularly liked the sixth-century mosaic map of Palestine in St. George's Greek Orthodox Church, shown to us by an old man whose explanation was incomprehensible but who charmed us by dropping our tip into the church's poor box.

From Madaba to Wadi Musa is 150 miles, a comfortable four-hour run. That leaves ample time for a visit to the rugged hilltop citadel of Kerak, built by the Crusaders under Payen le Bouteiller starting in 1142 and rebuilt by the great Arab general Saladin. From the upper court, there is a glorious view over the Dead Sea, and a sickening one down into the valley. Prisoners used to be flung over the sheer precipice, Harding says, with boxes tied securely around their heads so that they would not be knocked unconscious before reaching the bottom. South of Kerak, you reach the awesome Wadi al Hasa, a vast dry gorge that marked the ancient boundary of the land of Moab. We ate our picnic on the north wall of the wadi at a spectacularly sited parking area; I don't know whether it was the setting or the cooking, but all hands agreed that the fried chicken (supplied by the Marriott Hotel in Amman) was world-class.

You should arrive at Wadi Musa just in time for the sunset. The next morning, it is only a short walk from the hotel down the hill to the visitors' center, where you buy your tickets and arrange to rent horses (about $7 a day each) for the ride into Petra. They are small, docile beasts, and young boys accompany you, holding the lead if you like. Try to start by about nine in the morning so you will reach the Treasury around ten, when the sun is shining on it and it is at its most glorious. Down you go onto the trail, passing the Obelisk Tomb and large rectangular funerary monuments on your way to the dam that closes the mouth of the Siq, the gigantic cleft in the sandstone barrier that leads to the city; before the dam was built, flash floods poured through the defile, endangering anyone trapped there. Once inside the Siq, you can see carved decorations on the walls, which are sometimes only five or six feet apart.

When the final bend has been rounded, you catch a first glimpse of the Treasury—a single column with its Corinthian capital, part of the drum on the top, half of the split pediment. It is hard to believe, even after all the photographs, that it is real; it looks too much like something on a Hollywood back lot. But soon you are off your horse (it will be returned to you at the end of the day near the center of the city), looking up, gawking, convinced.

Turning then to the right, you pass a wall of cavelike houses, decorated with ziggurats and pyramids, and then the theater, with a slot that allowed a curtain to be raised and lowered. We sat halfway up, all alone except for a few optimistic goats looking for green shoots on the stage, and drank a bottle of wine we had brought along, just to calm ourselves.

A few steps more, and you come out into the main valley—bigger than expected, dusty, rocky, with only the oleanders and some scrub for relief. There is another surprise, or at least there was for us: Up ahead was a

Bedouin tent, over on the left a clothesline strung between a stumpy tree and a boulder. Petra is still home to 150 families. Their children cluster around, asking for ball-point pens, offering shards of pottery for sale, but not in the maddeningly insistent way of Egyptian children.

Off to the right lies a series of façades, each worthy of a close inspection—the imposing Urn Tomb, high up on the hillside, once used as a Roman or Byzantine church; then, lower down, the Corinthian Tomb, so badly eroded that it looks like melting ice cream, with red and gray and blue and orange striations exposed in the rock, and the Palace Tomb, a broad building that is almost baroque in its uninhibited handling of the Classical vocabulary.

Farther on is the less interesting, heavily ruined center of the old city, where one should nonetheless notice the ancient paving stones and the inscriptions on the ruins of the Temenos Gate, carved with medallions representing some of the gods of the caravans that brought Petra its wealth. Just beyond is the small museum, which houses fragments of sculpture and a few examples of the elegant, miraculously thin Nabatean pottery, orange with brown and black overglazes.

The Forum will pack a lunch for you, as elaborate as you like (one called the Grand Explorer costs about $20 and includes, among other things, smoked salmon from Scotland, pâté and Danish pastries), but we had decided to eat in the new restaurant the Forum had opened near the museum. A handsome, low-lying building that blends perfectly into its surroundings, it has a sunny patio as well as immaculate toilets and everything else you wouldn't expect to find.

An assortment of appetizers, including minty tabbouleh, a kebab, drinks and coffee—all delicious—cost us about $12 a head.

Petra, Half as Old as Time

Then on to the climax of the visit—the hour-long walk up past the Lion Gate to the largest of all the buildings in Petra: El Deir, the Monastery. Ancient steps cut into the rock and modern stairways make the going easier, and there are benches where you can rest, but it is stiff going all the same, not for those who fear heights nor for those with heart trouble or other infirmities.

The path twists upward through a heroic landscape, much greener than the valley floor, with cactuses and broom and gnarled cedars, past rocks that look like stalagmites. Sometimes the stone resembles petrified redwood. Alone, except for the slight whoosh of the wind, the buzzing of bees and the occasional birdcall, we were exhilarated by the way the Nabateans had managed to impose order on nature without destroying it. Finally, puffing embarrassingly, we emerged into a meadow dominated by the huge façade of the Monastery (in fact a tomb), tallowy in the golden afternoon sun under an improbably azure sky. It is simpler than the Treasury, modified Doric rather than Corinthian, but no less striking; a grown man can barely see over the lintel under the front door, and the urn on the top is twenty-five feet high. It is the sort of thing that some German Romantic might have thought up, we decided; that inveterate traveler, Goethe, would have loved it, and so would that most melodramatic of painters, Caspar David Friedrich. So, in fact, did we.

The walk down took only thirty-five minutes, and a lot less energy. It ended perfectly. Just before we reached the bottom, we saw a herd of baby goats, sure-footedly standing on a steeply sloping rock. The old woman tending them snatched her scarf across her face when I approached, but not before I saw the blue tattoos around her eyes and nose, and she thrust out a grubby hand filled with what she hoped I would think were Nabatean coins.

GUIDELINES FOR VISITING JORDAN

One of the minor tragedies of the continuing strife in the Middle East is the inaccessibility of many of its outstanding archaeological sites. Except for the occasional businessman, journalist or diplomat, Americans are effectively barred from Persepolis in Iran, Baghdad and Nineveh in Iraq, Palmyra and the Krak des Chevaliers in Syria, and Baalbek in Lebanon. At the moment, Jordan is one of the safest and most hospitable places in the entire region, eager to prove its virtues to Americans. It is prudent, however, if you are going there or any place else subject to political upheaval, to have your travel agent check conditions with the State Department or other informed sources at the last minute.

Alia, the Royal Jordanian Airline (535 Fifth Avenue, New York, NY 10017; telephone: 212-949-0050 or 800-223-0470 outside New York State), has four flights a week to Amman via Amsterdam or Vienna. The flight takes about twelve hours, with an hour's layover in Europe. A ticket good for a stay of seven to sixty days, purchased two weeks in advance, costs about $800. Amman has a number of hotels designed for an international clientele, among them the Marriott (telephone: 660100), Holiday Inn (663100), Jordan Inter-Continental (41361) and Regency Palace (660000), all with double rooms beginning at about $65.

A visa is required for United States citizens wishing to visit Jordan. They are obtainable without fee from the Visa Section, Consulate of Jordan, 866 United Nations Plaza, New York 10017 (212-759-1950).

Eden on the Isle of Bahrain

PAUL LEWIS

THE LAND OF DILMUN is Holy, the land of Dilmun is pure.

In Dilmun no cry the raven utters,
Nor does the bird of ill-omen foretell calamity.
The lion kills not, nor does the ravening wolf
Snatch away the defenseless lamb.
Unknown is the wild dog who tears the kid.
The dove does not conceal its head.
No one here says, "My eyes are sick,"
No one here says, "My head is sick,"
No one here says, "I am an old woman,"
No one here says, "I am an old man,"
The maiden walks here in innocence.
No lustrations need to be poured.
The somber death priest walks not here,
By Dilmun's walls he has no cause for lamentations.

These words came from one of the world's oldest poems. It was first written down some 4,000 years ago in the ancient Sumerian city of Nippur near the Euphrates, using cuneiform wedge script on a clay tablet.

The poem tells about the doings of the gods at the dawn of time in a sacred island paradise called Dilmun, a place closely resembling the Garden of Eden, where death and sickness did not exist and sweet waters flowed.

Holy Dilmun is mentioned in many other cuneiform writings of that period. The epic hero Gilgamesh goes there to obtain the secret of eternal life from Ziusudra, who alone among mankind survived the Great Flood after building an ark on instructions from Enki, Lord of the Abyss and Ruler of the Sweet Waters Under the Earth.

Gilgamesh dives into the sea with stones attached to his feet and brings up the "Flower of Immortality." In a clear parallel with the biblical story of Adam and Eve, he allows a serpent to eat the flower, cheating mankind of immortality.

Other ancient records show that 4,000 years ago Dilmun was also a great trading center and the capital of an empire. Yet until 1857 when Sir Henry Rawlinson, a British scholar, discovered how to read cuneiform and the first references to this ancient island paradise were deciphered, the name of Dilmun had vanished from the collective memory of mankind.

That Nineveh, Babylon, Thebes and Ur had all once been great cities was never entirely forgotten because their names are recorded in the Bible, even if little was known about them. But for thousands of years the legend of Holy Dilmun, the island paradise where man lived forever, disappeared.

Eden on the Isle of Bahrain

The enthralling tale of how Geoffrey Bibby and other archaeologists from the Danish Museum of Prehistory at Aarhus identified the present-day Persian Gulf island of Bahrain as the site of the lost paradise of Dilmun has been told by Mr. Bibby in his book *Looking for Dilmun*. And it is one of the most gripping archaeological detective stories ever written.

But visitors to Bahrain today can still relive Mr. Bibby's search for Dilmun with the help of his book, visiting the major excavation sites, inspecting the most important finds and recapturing something of the excitement he felt as the pieces in the puzzle slowly fell into place and the ruins of "lost" Dilmun emerged from beneath his trowel.

Today this tiny, verdant island, with its copious freshwater supplies, still seems a kind of paradise in that parched, bone-dry region of the world. Lying just off the coast of Saudi Arabia, barely sixty miles long and thirty wide, Bahrain is the garden of the Persian Gulf, with shady palm groves full of bright-colored birds, fruit and flowers.

At several points around the coast, springs bubble up through the brine from the ocean floor with such force that you can drop a bucket into the sea and pull it up full of fresh water.

It remains a famous center for pearl fishing, where divers still weight their feet with stones just as Gilgamesh did. And how much more beautiful than modern white cultured pearls are the big, lumpy natural ones, with their luminous, greenish hue.

Emerald shoal waters surround the island. And at the end of the last century, Captain Durand, an early explorer, described daybreak on Bahrain in terms still true today. Nature, he wrote, seemed to have "exhausted every tint of living green in her paint box; and then, wearying of the effect, splashed a streak of angry purple into the foreground."

But Bahrain has a mysterious side. In the sandy center of the island lies a truly astonishing sight—thousands upon thousands of little hillocks each some ten to fifteen feet high and packed tightly together in an unending vista so that at first the visitor thinks they must be a natural phenomenon, like sand dunes. But they are not. The hillocks are man-made grave mounds. Bahrain, the original Garden of Eden, is also an ancient island necropolis.

In another sense, too, Bahrain remains a Persian Gulf paradise. For it is the only Gulf state that welcomes Western tourists and tries to make them feel at home. The island has been designated by its neighbors as the region's financial and services capital, the place where banks, accountancy firms and engineering companies working in the area are encouraged to establish their headquarters and base Western employees.

Although a Moslem country like other Gulf states, Bahrain tolerates a more easygoing life-style than do Saudi Arabia or Kuwait. Alcoholic drinks, pork dishes, magazines and books shunned elsewhere in the Gulf are all available in hotels and restaurants frequented by foreigners. Women are permitted to drive, and mixed swimming is allowed.

These days the hunt for Dilmun begins at Bahrain's National Museum, over the causeway from the capital of Manama on Al-Muharraq island near the airport.

This is an essential first stop because visitors need to get a pass from the director, Sheika Haya Al-Khalifa, to visit the Barbar Temple, a key Dilmun relic. But the museum also contains a splendid display of Geoffrey

Eden on the Isle of Bahrain

Bibby's major finds, telling the story of the discovery of Dilmun and its links with the Garden of Eden.

Here, too, is a replica (the original was lost in London during World War II) of the first major clue identifying Dilmun with Bahrain. It is a foot-shaped black basalt stone found by Captain Durrand in 1879 while survey-ing the island's antiquities and bearing the Sumerian in-scription "Palace of Rimum, slave of the God Inzak, Man of the tribe of Agarum."

In a masterly paper, Sir Henry Rawlinson, then seventy-five years old, showed that Inzak, or Enzak, was the titular god of Dilmun. After surveying all known references to Dilmun in ancient Sumerian literature, he argued for the first time that Bahrain must be the site of the island Paradise, last described by King Sargon of Assyria before it faded from human memory as "a fish in the midst of the Sea of the Rising Sun."

But if Sir Henry, working from written evidence, was right and Bahrain was Dilmun, then, Mr. Bibby rea-soned, remnants of its lost civilization must still be buried there. He had only to dig.

Besides the Dilmun antiquities, the museum has displays devoted to pearl fishing and local art and clothes. Particularly interesting are those devoted to women's clothing, showing the sumptuous traditional Bahraini marriage dress and the scarcely less magnifi-cent clothes worn in the old days by unmarried women. Of course, in the street, Bahraini women to this day con-tinue to be shrouded in black veils, but at home they look very different.

A fifteen-minute taxi ride from any of the big hotels along King Faisal Boulevard will take the Dilmun enthu-siast to the site of Mr. Bibby's first great find: Gala'at al-Bahrain, known in English as the Portuguese fort.

Only the tumbled-down walls remain, though inside you can see the remnants of the palm-leaf encampment Mr. Bibby and his Danish companions built there in 1957, the last vestiges of what the archaeologists dubbed the "Carlsberg Culture" after the Danish beer they drank.

But below the fort's southern walls lie remaining bits of the walls of the Dilmun-age "palace" they found, the first evidence that there was a thriving civilization on the island 4,000 years ago. Here were discovered the famous Dilmun seals and weights, which link the island with ancient Ur and the Indus Valley, confirming its importance as a trading center. But here Mr. Bibby also found astonishing evidence of a direct religious link between the inhabitants of ancient Dilmun in the third millennium B.C. and the much older legend of Gilgamesh's unfortunate encounter with the serpent—ritually buried rows of pots, each containing a snake's skeleton and a pearl.

The pearl Mr. Bibby identifies with the Flower of Immortality, recalling how in ancient Egypt Cleopatra drank an elixir of pearls dissolved in wine. "Here we have clear proof that the legend of Gilgamesh was still a living and integral part of the religion of Bahrain at the time the palace was built and inhabited," he writes.

Today, visitors can scramble into the pit and walk along the streets of ancient Dilmun, admire the great stone doorway of the palace, clamber through its rooms and recall how its inhabitants also commemorated man's fall centuries before Genesis was written.

A few miles west of the fort lies Mr. Bibby's second major site, the Barbar Temple. After their first exploration, Mr. Bibby and his companions re-covered the temple with sand to stop theft. But in 1983 the Bahrain

Eden on the Isle of Bahrain

Government re-excavated it, building a permanent site with concrete walkways and viewing points for visitors.

The first of three temples was built here nearly 5,000 years ago. But as the temple complex grew bigger over the centuries, a magnificent sacred well was always retained as its central feature. Well-trod steps lead down to a limpid pool of fresh, blue water contained in finely cut limestone blocks. Nearby stands a stone altar with a drain for the blood of sacrificial animals.

For most scholars the Barbar Temple was sacred to Enki, Lord of the Abyss and Ruler of the Sweet Waters Under the Earth, the god who saved mankind from the Great Flood and who lived in Holy Dilmun at the beginning of time. Its well was thus a sacred link with the god holding dominion over the fresh waters on which life depended.

And sure enough, an ancient Sumerian fragment refers to a great Temple of Enki, calling it "the far-famed house" that is "built in the heart of the Lower Sea," the name then given to the Persian Gulf. Bahrain is halfway down the Gulf, in "the heart of the Lower Sea."

Close by, near Diraz village, lies an intriguing mystery Mr. Bibby never resolved. The well here, once the biggest on Bahrain, was filled in around 800 by a Moslem ruler to punish the villagers for idolatry. Today, stone blocks used to seal the well litter the sand. Visitors can also see the "tantalizing stairway" Mr. Bibby found leading down into the well, and where he discovered two broken idols from Dilmun times. Was there another sacred well here where the villagers still worshiped Enki 3,000 years after the Barbar Temple was built and 800 years into the Christian Era? We don't know. The excavation was never completed.

Only two stops remain in the quest for Dilmun. First

to Ali village to see the "Royal Mounds," a cluster of unusually large grave mounds where Mr. Bibby found the cups and glasses he called "a table service worthy of the Kings of Dilmun."

Anywhere along the road, a visitor can stop and inspect the island's grave mounds, many now opened by archaeologists. They housed the dead citizens of Dilmun, and the discovery of similar burial mounds in Saudi Arabia, Gatar and Failaka Island off Kuwait helped Mr. Bibby establish the boundaries of Dilmun's empire.

After this long, hot tour, Dilmun enthusiasts may want to drive another few miles to the Emir's beach at Az Zallaq on the west coast. Here Bahrain's ruler, Sheik Isa bin Sulman Al Khalifa, keeps a marble summer palace on a silver beach edged with shady lawns and golden lampposts. He allows Western visitors to swim there free of charge, eat picnics under the palm trees and stroll on a black and gold pier above an emerald sea. It is a present-day paradise, a modern Dilmun.

WHERE TO STAY AND WHAT TO DO

The best time to visit Bahrain is early in the year, say from January to June, before the humid summer heat sets in. But try to avoid going during the holy month of Ramadan, when Moslems fast during the daylight hours. Restaurants generally close during the day then, and the sale of alcohol is forbidden until sunset. The pace of life slows down, and making business or other appointments tends to be difficult. Since Ramadan changes every year, check the dates with the local embassy or consulate of any Moslem country. In addition, United States citizens are granted seventy-two-hour visas upon arrival in Bahrain; permits for longer stays are given only to persons doing business in the country.

The easiest air connections are from London. Gulf Air flies direct to Bahrain seven days a week, leaving Heathrow at 10 A.M. and arriving at 6:35 P.M. local time. There are four direct flights a week from Paris. An alternative is to fly to Kuwait and take one of several Gulf Air flights a day to Bahrain.

Bahrain, like all Gulf capitals these days, is full of luxurious air-conditioned hotels. And for the visitor, there is nowhere else to stay.

All the big names are there: Hilton, Sheraton, Inter-Continental and several others. My recommendation is the **Inter-Continental,** also known as the **Regency,** a huge, gray concrete pile on King Faisal Boulevard, because it is within easy walking distance of the souk, or Arab market, and of the business center of Manama. The others tend to be a taxi drive away.

All the hotels have splendid swimming pools and lots of restaurants, serving mainly imported food. But they are not inexpensive. A double room in most is around $120 a night. An average meal easily runs about $60 a person.

There are very few Western-style restaurants outside the hotels. The **Wind Tower** (telephone: 243732) is a fine old Arab house, but the food is uncertain. Another, more modern, restaurant is **Upstairs Downstairs** (713093).

The main local dish is the old Arab standby of roast lamb and rice cooked with raisins and almonds. The Inter-Continental offers this as a regular buffet every evening. Otherwise, Bahrain's hotels offer classic Western cuisine made mainly with imported ingredients. Exceptions are the excellent local fish and big Gulf shrimp.

The island has several Chinese, Japanese and Indonesian restaurants.

The best way of traveling around the island is in a taxi or a chauffeur-driven rented car, making sure you get a knowledgeable, English-speaking driver. Theoretically, visitors can rent self-drive cars. But in practice the complications of getting a temporary driving permit are almost insurmountable and signposts are bad or nonexistent. So a local driver makes sense.

Again, it is not inexpensive. A half day with a rented car and chauffeur costs about $90. Taxis have no meters, so you haggle over the price. A trip to the airport is around $20 to $30; a half-day's driving around, about $60 to $75.

Visitors should plan to spend some time at the **souk,** a maze of narrow streets packed with tiny stalls where anything can be bought. In the middle stands the gold souk, a large, air-conditioned building where most of the island's jewelers are found.

Here you will find a glittering display of necklaces, earrings and bracelets, and usually crowds of black-veiled Arab women inspecting them. Don't miss the Bahrain pearls. A full necklace costs from $600 up. But a single pearl set in gold, which can be hung as a pendant from a necklace, costs about $180. Look also at the modern gold copies of the famous Dilmun seals, which can also be used as pendants; they cost about $100 each.

Al-Muharaq, across the causeway, contains several old Arab houses that are open to the public. Ask at the National Museum for permission to visit them. Sheik Isa's house is a nineteenth-century Arab prince's home that was the residence of the present Emir's grandfather. Not far away is the Siyadi House, the home of a rich pearl merchant, which contains a magnificently carved *marjlis,* or meeting room.

The **National Museum** is open from 9 A.M. to 2 P.M. every day but Friday, the Islamic sabbath. Admission is free. The telephone number is 320-283.

BOOKS ABOUT DILMUN

For any visitor to Bahrain, Geoffrey Bibby's book *Looking for Dilmun* is obligatory reading. It is available in the soft-cover Penguin edition at bookshops on the island and in the United States.

However, Dilmun enthusiasts probably will want to consult or acquire several other books about Dilmun that are interesting to nonspecialist readers.

Dilmun Discovered (Longman and the Bahrain Department of Antiquities and Museums.) is a fascinating collection of some of the major writings on Dilmun, which cannot easily be found elsewhere. Here is the complete text of Captain Durand's report, complete with his drawings of the "Rimum" stone and its inscription. The book also contains the text of Sir Henry Rawlinson's masterly essay on the inscription, setting out the written evidence for identifying Bahrain as Dilmun.

It also contains a curious essay by the Rev. Edward Burrows, reproduced in the original longhand from a copy deposited with the Pontifical Biblical Institute in Rome. It is a profoundly erudite study of the origins of the name Dilmun that concludes that Bahrain, Dilmun and the legend of the lost Paradise recorded in the Bible and the Epic of Gilgamesh are all the same.

The Temple Complex at Barbar (Bahrain Ministry of Information) tells the story of Dilmun in breezy, popular language and contains some magnificent color photographs.

Dilmun: New Studies in the Archeology and Early History of Bahrain, edited by Daniel T. Potts (Dietrich Reimer Verlag: Berlin. 1983.), is a collection of studies of various aspects of Dilmun in several languages. Particularly interesting for the general reader is Bendt Alster's paper on Sumerian myths about Paradise.

Finally, the real enthusiast should consult the annals of the Jutland Archeological Society, in which Bibby and his colleagues first published most of their findings. —P.L.

Discovering Immortal Dilmun

GEOFFREY BIBBY

ARCHAEOLOGICAL SITES are always full of ghosts. But it is disconcerting to find oneself among their number. It was thirty years, almost of the day, since we had first set spade in the city-mound of Gala'at al-Bahrain, and nothing seemed to have changed. The biscuit-brown sunbaked surface of the tell, crowned by the crumbling stone ramparts of the Portuguese fort, dipped down in the middle distance to the surrounding palm gardens, so that their feathery tips fringed the view on three sides. On the fourth side, to the north, the sea stretched to the horizon.

Nothing had changed. Even our diggings could not be seen—they were, of course, below ground level, and, now that the fences with which we had surrounded them were gone, they only appeared as we approached their edge. And, against the immensity of the tell, forty-five acres in extent, even thirty years of digging had made but little impression. Scarcely 1 percent of its area had been dug.

Our most impressive hole in the ground, though, was still impressive, as I climbed the slight rise and stood upon its brink. A rectangular pit some 100 by 200 feet, sheer-sided and 20 feet deep, it still looked as though someone had taken the lid off an enormous box to see what was inside. And the box was full of buildings, roofless admittedly, but with many of the stone walls reaching almost to the surface.

This was our "palace" site, a colossal structure of chiseled stone, built probably in the eighth century B.C. when Sargon was king of Assyria, but raised above, and in places incorporating the walls of, an even more massive building, erected some 700 years earlier. For me, the palace had always been haunted by the ghost of King Uperi of Dilmun, who at the beginning of the seventh century B.C. had sent a token force to help Sennacherib of Assyria raze the walls of Babylon.

But as I descended the steep entrance ramp to the excavation it was newer ghosts who crowded around, the archaeologists and the workmen who, year after year, had gradually deepened and widened the digging and gradually revealed the buildings. For this was apparently now also history. This too was part of the past. In popular parlance this ancient monument was not called "Uperi's palace." It was called "the Danish excavation."

Above the ruined walls of Assyrian Dilmun, within the ruined ramparts of the Portuguese fort, we had built, in 1956, our *barasti* camp, a neat square of huts with palm-thatched walls and palm-ribbed roofs, covered with mats and tarpaulins. And the camp still lay where we had built it three decades ago—but now it too had joined the ruins of successive cultures that surrounded it.

Discovering Immortal Dilmun

Nothing stands without constant maintenance in the exacting climate of the Persian Gulf, and in the six years
since last we had lived here the fierce summer sun, the
constant humidity and the abrasive sand-laden northern
wind had laid our camp low. A new layer of the many-
layered tell was in process of formation.

In many ways it was a pity, I thought as I sat on the
crumbling cement step that had borne our water tank,
that the Antiquities Department, which held our excavations so sand-free and was even now shoring up the ramparts of the fort itself, had not thought it worthwhile to
maintain our camp. For it, too, was an ancient monument; it, too, represented a vanished civilization.

When we built it, half of Bahrain's inhabitants lived
in just such *barasti* houses, frameworks of palm ribs
lashed together with fiber cord and thatched with palm
leaves. They were cool and pleasant dwellings, and most
attractive to the eye. Now they are gone, replaced by
solid cement houses with electricity and indoor sanita-
tion, with fans and air conditioning. Fair enough, for
one cannot air-condition a *barasti*, and even electricity
increases the fire hazard that was the main argument
against palm-leaf construction. When, seven years ago, I
had wished to show this traditional construction to Thor
Heyerdahl, passing by in his reed-built vessel, the
Tigris, on his historic (in more ways than one) voyage
from Mesopotamia to India and Africa, I had been unable to find a single specimen—except our own camp.
And now it too was gone.

It was a special occasion that had brought me back to
Bahrain, the bicentenary of the Al-Khalifa family who,
200 years before, had established themselves as rulers of
the island, freeing it from Persian domination. To celebrate the event they were holding a historical conference,

at which 200 of the foremost authorities on Middle Eastern history and archaeology were gathered to assess the place of Bahrain and the Persian Gulf in the history of the world.

That, I felt, was the measure of the changes wrought by thirty years of active research. For thirty years ago Bahrain and the Arabian Gulf had no history, at least none that stretched further back than the advent of the Portuguese in the early sixteenth century. Now we were debating details of a historical sequence stretching 7,000 years into the past, and discussing the interconnections between almost a hundred major sites on the shores and islands of the Persian Gulf and the Indian Ocean, demonstrating a millenniums-old network of trade from India to Mesopotamia. It was the father of the present Emir who had given the first grant-in-aid to the expedition that, in its first year, had discovered the first two sites, the city of Gala'at al-Bahrain and the temple-complex at Barbar, and it was fitting that his family's anniversary should demonstrate once more its interest in historical research.

We were lodged in one of the new luxury hotels with a famous international name, and I went out the first morning to renew my acquaintance with Bahrain's capital, Manama. And I was completely at a loss. This was odd, for Manama is not a large town, and I knew it backward. Besides, one could always tell one's direction by the sea—and there indeed was the sea, a hundred yards away, across a thoroughfare and a sweep of oleander-lined lawns such as existed nowhere in Manama. Then I realized. I was on made land, the land that they had been planning, six years ago, to reclaim from the sea. Manama had grown outward, across the shallows,

which, at low tide, had always been a mile-wide, malo-
dorous waste of sand and coral and rotting seaweed, dotted with beached dhows loading and unloading cargo by
donkey cart as they waited for the tide. The new Manama
now edged the deeper water, and along its new espla-
nades new tall buildings were rising, the banks and
offices and agencies of the international companies
competing for the new trade of the oil lands.

Such, I reflected as I strolled inland in the morning sunshine toward the former coastline, such had
Bahrain's role always been. Every 2,000 years or so
Arabia finds itself the producer of some commodity of
which the world stands in need. Now it is oil—2,000
years ago it had been frankincense—4,000 years ago it
had been copper. And Bahrain, strategically placed halfway up the Gulf, rich in fresh water and luxuriant vegetation off an otherwise desert coast, had been the natural
entrepôt through which the new products must pass. All
this had happened before.

I crossed a busy street that I thought I knew, the
former coast road, and a block farther on I was suddenly
in Old Manama, with its narrow alleyways between the
high, windowless façades of Arab houses, their carved
wooden doors securely closed with only a tiny portal
open in one of the massive leaves. Now I knew my way.
Along these alleys we had trudged thirty years before, on
our way from the old Imperial Airways hotel to the bazaar. And the bazaar was still there, unchanged, with its
open stalls selling ironmongery and coffee cups, shawls
and headdresses, spices and sandalwood and green tobacco. The number of goldsmiths had maybe increased,
the number of coppersmiths perhaps lessened. And the
merchants still sat cross-legged within their stalls, smok-

ing their water pipes, chatting with friends, drinking small glasses of sweet tea, sublimely uninterested in casual customers.

Bahrain has not changed with the times. It has not exchanged old lamps for new; it has accepted the new, and retained the old. And it is growing in both directions, incorporating into its culture both the new modernity and the new antiquity. You can stay at the Dilmun Hotel, or dine in the Gilgamesh Bar. The bronze doors of one of the largest banks are decorated with the impressions of Dilmun seals and beyond the Moharraq causeway lie the yards of the Dilmun Steam Navigation Company. Which would have delighted King Uperi.

Three days before we left I was taken to see the newest excavations of Bahrain's own Antiquities Department. Out beyond the suburbs, where the desert begins and where a new garden-city is planned, they were digging burial mounds. It was the first large-scale research project on the mounds, designed to classify their types and to attempt to determine more precisely the number of centuries their vast numbers covered. Beyond the thirty or so mounds that had been excavated the moundfields still stretched endlessly, an estimated 170,000 mounds in all, by far the largest prehistoric cemetery in the world.

But the thirty mounds, carefully chosen to give a cross section of types and sizes, were meticulously excavated, drawn and photographed. And their contents, laid out in an adjoining tent, showed clearly that the earliest civilization of Dilmun owed nothing to Mesopotamia. Here was the early painted pottery that we had first identified in the Oman peninsula far to the east, on the southeastern tip of Arabia, and which could be dated to about 2600 B.C. It was possible that the culture of the moundbuilders had come to Bahrain from Oman. But it had de-

Discovering Immortal Dilmun

veloped independently here, into the Holy Land of
Dilmun that had given the tradition of the Garden of
Eden to the world.

As I drove back to the hotel I reflected that we were
leaving the archaeology of Bahrain in good hands. And
that, if one is to haunt one's excavations, there are worse
places to be a ghost than in the Garden of Eden.

Congo on My Mind

ALBERTO MORAVIA

A WORD GIVES A NAME
to a place and can also transform the place into literature—which, in turn, is substituted for the place. After
Homer, in certain parts of the Mediterranean you are no
longer traveling in Italy or Greece but in the *Iliad* or the
Odyssey. And it could be said that today, after Conrad,
you are not just in Zaire, or Malaysia, but in *Heart of
Darkness* or *Lord Jim*. These things come to my mind
while I am seated on the deck of the *Colonel Ebeya*, a
small and ancient steamer that in eight days travels up
the River Zaire (it was called the Congo in Conrad's
time) from Kinshasa to Kisangani.

I have been traveling to Africa, a continent that fascinates me and to which I always long to return, for fifteen
years. It is my third voyage on this river, whose immensity is worthy of the country through which it flows.

Before me, immobile as a swamp under the gray

winter sky, stretches the river, plum colored, pocked as far as the eye can see by floating clumps of water hyacinths. In the distance, you can discern the hazy, melancholy outline of the forest. The day is hot, humid and oppressive. In the silence the regular, labored sound of the ship's engines suggests a heart that is giving out. Everything is still, inert, exhausted, like the first day of Creation. But this endless swamp is actually a gigantic stream that, with imperceptible movement, is flowing to the sea. I can sense the movement as I look at one clump of water hyacinths, bigger than the others. A few moments ago it was to the right of my eyes; now it's to the left.

So this is the river of *Heart of Darkness.* But there are significant differences between the river that I see and the river described by Conrad. For example, Conrad says that the boat, at a certain moment, comes upon a kind of sandy island that divides the river into two narrow channels. Conrad's ship enters one of these channels; and then, as it proceeds, very close to the shore (a distance of ten feet, according to Conrad), Africa suddenly bursts out. Savage and threatening faces appear amid the foliage, and a hissing rain of arrows falls on the deck.

Now none of these details seem exact. At this moment, the *Colonel Ebeya* is advancing along one of the channels, where an island, just as in Conrad's novel, divides the river; a short time ago we passed through another, similar passage. In fact, the entire river, at more or less regular intervals, is divided into two channels by long, narrow, sandy islands. But this doesn't make us navigate close to the forest; on the contrary, we are so far from it that we could never see faces among the leaves or be struck by arrows. At most, sharpening our eyes considerably, we could glimpse acrobatic monkeys over there, swinging from branch to branch. Ten feet, indeed! Between us and the forest, the shallow water must stretch for at least 150 feet. But why does Conrad exaggerate? Why does he transform the vast, majestic river into a narrow, menacing canal?

At this point I am distracted from my reflections by something that is happening before my eyes. Yesterday, at a stop, my cabin mates bought a monkey, already dressed, which is to say, headless, its fur singed, its arms and legs trussed up. Now a young woman crouching on the deck is chopping the monkey into pieces with great blows of a machete, and as she does this she throws hands, feet, legs, arms and sections of the belly into a pot boiling on a Primus stove. This sight fascinates me. I ask her if monkey is good to eat. She answers, laughing, that it is very good. I remember then that yesterday, in the captain's cabin, I saw a little alligator tied with a rope running between its jaws. The captain assured me that alligator, too, is very good to eat.

So Conrad exaggerates the narrowness of the river and makes it a cramped passage. Why? I think about it a bit and conclude that there's no understanding Conrad unless you bear in mind that he was a man of the nineteenth century, a former Pole, an Anglophile, or rather an Anglomaniac and, moreover, an old-fashioned gentleman with a strict code of honor. And, naturally, a great writer, of acute moral sensitivity. So then, once these qualities are taken into consideration. . . .

Another interruption. All of a sudden, there in the immense expanse of water, I see something surprising on this river where only our steamer and the pirogues are usually seen. Here is a great white vessel, apparently brand-new, all decked out with flags, proceeding slowly in the direction opposed to ours. It looks like a pleasure ship, and, in fact, when I question the captain, who comes along the deck at this moment, he tells me it is the private yacht of Mobutu Sese Seko, the President of Zaire. Then my imagination pictures the luxury of that ship, and I cannot help comparing it with the squalor of ours: drab cabins, with worn linoleum and noisy, ineffi-cient air conditioners; bath full of spiders, broken mir-rors and rusty faucets; stifling dining room, the radio blaring at full volume, army mess food (today it's water buffalo with potatoes, tomorrow potatoes with water buf-falo).

As to Mobutu and his yacht, I recall a brief dialogue in Kinshasa: "Mobutu? He's filling his pockets with money that belongs to Zaire. When the revolution comes, we'll settle accounts."

"How?"

"We'll kill his whole tribe!"

Obviously in Zaire, even today, revolution is a matter not of class but of tribe.

But back to Conrad. He transforms the difficult navi-gation on the Congo River into a kind of descent into the Underworld: ambushes, arrows, natural obstacles of every kind and, at the end, after two months of sinister journeying, the bloodied nest of Kurtz, the superman slaver and colonialist. All this has been said before, but it's worth repeating: The voyage of *Heart of Darkness* is a voyage to the depths of colonialism, which takes the form of an Inferno in which Conrad is the dubious and horrified Dante. And, as in the Inferno of Dante, at the end, there is the cave of Lucifer, so in the Inferno of Conrad, at the end, there is Kurtz's stronghold, sur-rounded by stakes on which the heads of disobedient na-tives are impaled.

I am distracted again. On the expanse of water a great raft appears; it seems to be made of huge logs bound together. Little black figures cluster on the raft around a hut from which a thread of smoke is rising.

I ask a fellow passenger what this raft is; she answers that those are trees cut down in the heart of the forest and then entrusted, in the form of a raft, to the river, which will carry them to the sea, where they will be loaded onto ships bound for Europe. The little black figures are pygmies who, for a pittance, are willing to spend several weeks on the river, as guardians of the raft. Sometimes the raft comes undone, the pygmies fall into the river, and the logs, adrift, are lost to the ocean until, finally, like Rimbaud's Bateau Ivre, they run aground on a beach where they rot undisturbed.

In short, when everything has been said, we have to admit that in *Heart of Darkness* Conrad demonized Africa, Zaire, the river, the forest and, especially, colonialism. But why this demonization? Why didn't Conrad confine himself to denouncing the evils of colonialism, as Gide was to do later? You might say this was because of an interior conflict that was then translated into an unconscious sense of guilt. On the one hand, as we have said, Conrad was an Anglophile by habit and culture, but on the other hand he was not unaware that colonialism, in its horrors, involved the entire white race, including the English. And so colonialism seemed to him not a historic fact, which after all was not his concern, but rather an indelible stain on that white honor that is the basis of so many events in his novels. It was impossible, in other words, to concede that the crimes of colonialism were part of history, particularly of that white history of which the Europeans, and Conrad himself, were so proud. But what was evil?

Congo on My Mind

Conrad has Kurtz say it, not in the manner of a philosopher or a man of religion, but as the poet: "the horror, the horror."

Another distraction, this one longer than the others: We are landing. The steamer has turned its prow toward the shore; the forest, with its great elegiac trees, is coming closer and closer; the howl of a siren is born and dies in the dazed silence. And to our stunned eyes a little clearing appears, cramped between the river and the forest, with some little huts, and all the inhabitants, probably fishermen and seasonal woodsmen, lined up on the bank in two rows, like the chorus in a Verdi opera. They are wearing holiday dress, with the familiar bright colors; in the first row are those who will come aboard to barter the natural products of the river and forest for the industrial products of the city; in the second are those who want to enjoy the spectacle of the ship's arrival, after days and days of savage solitude. The gangplank goes down, and immediately the vendors of cassava swarm up, the sellers of smoked monkey, fruit, fish and counterfeit fetishes for tourists.

On the decks all the passengers crowd the railings and exchange laughter, calls and gestures with the men who have come alongside the ship in their pirogues. Meanwhile, the river is alive with heads of swimmers, who, out of sheer vanity, perform reckless feats of diving. This display of explosive sociability is not new to me. It occurs at every stop. Are these people happy and thriving? It's hard to say, but there can be no doubt that on this same river, formerly described by Conrad as the place of "horror," life seems to be easier than in the city or in the interior of the forest.

As our stop is prolonged, my mind inevitably returns to Kurtz. What is the significance of Kurtz? Despite his

claims to supermanhood, or, rather, precisely because of them, he symbolizes the maleficent heart of colonialism. Kurtz is in the depths of the forest, two months' navigation from the ocean, and not by chance. The heart, as everyone knows, is a vital organ, but deep and hidden. The heart of the state? But in this use of the metaphor of the heart, there is also an odd motivation, typical of Conrad's perplexity in the face of the grand phenomenon

Congo on My Mind

of European expansion throughout the whole world. According to Conrad, colonialism has not one heart but
two: what we might call the evil heart, personified by
Kurtz, and what we might call the good heart, personified by Lord Jim.

Another interruption. A beautiful gigantic woman arrives, with swelling breasts, solid abdomen, massive
thighs and colossal buttocks, all enwrapped in one of
those multicolored fabrics manufactured especially for
Africa in Holland and England. The giantess advances
regally; she has a huge basket on her head and with one
hand she is dragging along a tiny little girl. On her arm
and around her neck she wears copper circlets. She has
come to occupy an empty cabin on our deck. Her face is
good-humored and yet involuntarily menacing because
of the awesome size of her eyes, nose and lips. She reminds me of something, and all of a sudden I realize
what it is: the giantess who appears in *Heart of Darkness*, in the remote spot where Kurtz seeks refuge. I even
remember the sentence with which Conrad introduces
her: "She was savage and superb, wild eyed and magnificent; there was something ominous and stately in her
deliberate progress. . . ."

Yes, for Conrad colonialism does have two hearts, a
heart of darkness, evil and a heart of light, good. The
heart of darkness harbors Kurtz; the heart of light, Lord
Jim, first mate of the *Patna*, who displayed cowardice
(or perhaps it was unconscious racism; the passengers of
the *Patna* were all Mecca pilgrims, dark-skinned people)
by abandoning the ship entrusted to him. He then re-
deems himself through the rest of his life. And how does
he redeem himself? Ending up in Malaya, in the sultan-
ate of Patusan, instead of exploiting and slaughtering
the natives, as Kurtz does, with analogous authority Jim

tries to protect them, to save them, and in the end he sac-
rifices himself for them. And yet Kurtz and Lord Jim resemble each other in many ways. Both flee Europe to
hide in barbarous places, secret and inaccessible; both
manage to establish absolute dominion over the natives;
both are persecuted by an obscure conscience, which
they try to elude; and finally, both rightfully belong to
the historic moment of pervasive colonialism.

And further there is that identical, Conradian obses-
sion with dark, confined passages, viscera, where refuge
is sought as in the maternal womb. . . .

We are leaving again. The siren shrieks, the vendors
lazily go ashore, the pirogues and the swimmers move
off, the crowd on the bank breaks up. The *Colonel Ebeya*
moves, heading toward the middle of the river. Ah, yes,
Conrad. Colonialism, for him, did indeed have two
hearts, the bad one of Kurtz and the good one of Lord
Jim. Kurtz oppressed the natives; Lord Jim bore on his
back the white man's famous burden. But today Kurtz
and Lord Jim do not exist. Or rather, they may still
exist, but they are no longer symbolic as they were in
Conrad's time. The symbols are dead. As, in fact, Eliot
says in the epigraph of a poem of his, quoting *Heart of
Darkness:* "Mistah Kurtz . . . he dead." We can add
also: "Lord Jim . . . he dead."

I have finished rereading *Heart of Darkness* and put it
in my suitcase. Now I am reading another book on the
Congo of earlier times: *Stanley's Way* by Thomas Ster-
ling. While I am reading this book, I arrive at Kisangani, once known as Stanleyville. From the deck, leaning
over the rail with the other passengers, I see the dock, the
usual cranes, the usual piles of crates and packages, the
usual loafers who look like policemen and customs officers and the usual customs officers and policemen who

Congo on My Mind

look like loafers. The gangplanks are thrown down; all the passengers get off. We get off, too. We have reached the end of our voyage, as in *Heart of Darkness,* as in *Lord Jim.* But we know we will find neither Kurtz nor Lord Jim, neither the bad colonialist nor the good. What will we find then?

Our answer comes the next day when we walk under a fine rain down some of the long avenues flanked by gigantic trees that extend from the center of the city, the nucleus of tropical supermarkets and emporiums, toward the endless brush. Among the trees we glimpse houses, villas, blackened by the dampness. But sometimes the black has another explanation. This is where the former Belgian masters lived, and the houses were set afire in the now distant, murky days of early independence. We walk for a while on broad, grassy pavement; we are looking for police headquarters, where we have been told to collect our passports. Our expedition has a strange background, and it is this:

Last night in the bar of the hotel an African in civilian clothes came over to us and said: "Will you buy me a beer?"

"Happily," we said at once, and ordered it. When the beer came, the African didn't introduce himself, didn't tell us his name but began to inveigh against colonialism and colonialists in a strange fashion, at once violent and insincere, as if he were repeating a familiar part. We pointed out to him that none of us were Belgian; he answered that we're white and that's enough. A tense argument developed, threatening to end badly. My traveling companions were irritated. The African laid it on thicker and thicker. All of a sudden he said to us: "You know who I am? I'm the chief of police in Kisangani. If I want,

I can hold you in Kisangani as long as two weeks. Now give me your passports."

Alarmed at the prospect of a forced stay in Kisangani, we handed over our passports. He took them, stood up and told us we must come to his office tomorrow morning. And that is what we are doing now.

Finally, tired and wet, we arrive at police headquarters, which we find is one of the usual villas, blackened by dampness, at the end of a melancholy tropical garden. A sentry blocks our way with his submachine gun, another directs us toward a hut, which is apparently a kind of waiting room.

We sit down and wait. There is nothing we can do but silently suffer the heat and perhaps look at the few visible objects, which are: (1) two submachine guns propped in a corner; (2) a little table with a ledger bound in black oilcloth and a pad of paper, for announcing visitors; (3) a portrait of Mobutu, wearing the well-known leopard-skin hat; (4) the gray cement floor; (5) the walls, painted green; (6) a little salamander, perfectly motionless in a corner of the ceiling, and a fly, which unaware that the salamander is studying it, adjusts its wings with its legs; (7) some chairs covered with peeling plastic. We wait, we wait a long time, in exhausting heat, boredom and conjecture about the reason for our waiting. How long do we wait? Two hours, let's say. And yet in the garden and all around the villa there is no sign of life. What can the police chief be doing? Why is he making us wait?

And we learn the answer after our two enervating hours. The same armed sentry directs us toward a door of the villa. We enter an ordinary room; the police chief is seated there behind an ordinary desk. He barely glances at us. It all takes a few seconds. He invites us to have a seat, we sit down, he takes out our passports, examines them one after the other, compares the photographs with the originals, hands over the passports. Now we are on our feet again. We take our leave and go out into the fine, hot, silent rain.

What did the police chief want of us? He wanted nothing beyond asserting and making us feel his authority. You have to admit: Since the days of Kurtz and Lord Jim considerable progress has been made!

THE VOYAGE UPRIVER

A trip up the Zaire River is not for the hedonistic and is part of few, if any, standard itineraries. Some agencies specializing in custom travel will, however, put together a trip for those who wish to follow in the wake of Joseph Conrad. In New York, three such agencies are: **Certified Travel Consultants,** 500 Fifth Avenue, Suite 1821, New York, NY 10017 (telephone: 212-354-0007); **Salen-Lindblad Cruising Inc.,** 133 East 55th Street, New York, NY 10022 (212-751-2300); and **Mackey Travel,** 250 West 57th Street, New York, NY 10019 (telephone: 212-757-0722). Another agency is **Abercrombie and Kent,** 1000 Oak Brook Road, Oak Brook, IL 60521 (800-323-7308). The estimated price is about $200 a person a day, exclusive of airfare to Kinshasa.

American citizens who wish to visit Zaire should apply for a visa to the Mission of the Republic of Zaire to the United Nations, 866 Second Avenue, New York, NY 10017 (212-754-1966); a valid passport, three completed application forms (available from the mission), three passport photographs and certificates of inoculation against yellow fever and cholera are required. Applicants should also present a round-trip air ticket

Congo on My Mind

(Kinshasa's N'Djili airport is the only legal point of entry into the country) and a bank statement showing sufficient funds for the stay. The visa can be processed in forty-eight hours, costs about $20 (plus a fee of about $12 for the notarization of signatures) and is good for up to thirty days.

The "Green Land" of the Arab World

DREW MIDDLETON

TWO STORKS NESTED
on the platform below the belfry of the church in Beja
one recent spring. Two storks had been there more than
forty years ago, looking down superciliously at the columns of tanks and trucks winding through the town on
their way to war. The storks' nest was about the only
thing in Tunisia that hadn't changed. Returning to a
land associated in memory with the clamor and smells of
a war and finding it bulging with tourists from every part
of Europe, a land of mile upon mile of hotels beside the
Mediterranean, is a shock to the psyche.

The shock is softened by the nature of the country
and the people. Here are a lovely land with a heritage
of many cultures, and a people who harbor an old-
fashioned courtesy.

Tunisia also is a land of contrasts. Headquartered at a
modern hotel such as the International, the Africa or the

Hilton, for example, the visitor can ponder the vagaries of history while wandering, just outside Tunis, through what remains of Carthage after the Romans destroyed it.

The ruins of **Carthage** are uninspiring. Some mosaics, stunted columns and the vestiges of ancient buildings are about all there are to attract the visitor. The Punic ports, one mercantile and one naval, resemble village yacht basins. But the tourist with an eye to history will remember that from these ports Carthaginian war vessels and merchantmen roved the Mediterranean and ventured westward into the Atlantic and northward to the fog-shrouded British Isles.

Nowhere in these ruins is the savagery of the Carthaginians more evident than at the Tophet. Here stood the temples of Baal Hammon and Tanit, fierce gods who demanded human sacrifice. The Carthaginians were not the only savages. A lion's roar away, their conquerors lolled in the sun and applauded animals killing Christians.

The Carthaginian ruins are dwarfed by the remains of the city the Romans built to replace it. Completed in the reign of Augustus Caesar, it became the second city of the Roman Empire, with baths, an amphitheater, a forum.

The amphitheater, which seated about 36,000, rises stark in stone out of the surrounding greenery, placid in the late afternoon sun. The baths of Antoninus Pius rival the amphitheater. The ruins represent only the basements of the original baths. These held the pipes for hot water and storage for the wood that fed the fires. The actual baths, one for men and one for women, were on an upper floor. The roof was supported by twelve granite columns. One Corinthian capital weighing four tons has been found. All this came crashing through into the basement at an unknown date. But a quick imagination

The "Green Land" of the Arab World

can envisage the glory of the baths when they were in op-
eration.

Some Arabs call Tunisia "the green land," and the
name goes back to the days when the occupiers made the
country the granary of Rome. Wheat, olives and wine,
all introduced by the Phoenicians, now flowed north
across the Mediterranean.

Beyond Carthage is **Sidi-bou-Sa'id,** surely one of the
most attractive towns in the Arab world. All blazing
white and deep blue in the setting sun, it sits on a hill
serenely indifferent to time. The rich, the very rich, from
Europe and the states of the Persian Gulf have villas
there, but anyone can wander the narrow streets and peer
into the tiny shops.

The stores offer the usual variety of souk wares—
brass, toy stuffed camels, copies of water pipes. The fare
in the restaurants is authentically Tunisian and tasty.
The Dar Sa'id and the Dar Zarrouk hotels, the latter with
a wondrous view of the sea, are pleasant oases far from
the bustle and clamor of Tunis.

Tunisia has known its share of conquerors: Romans,
Vandals, the first wave of Islam pressing westward, the
Spanish, the Turks and the French. Outside Carthage
there is a cemetery that holds 2,840 Americans killed in
Tunisia, Algeria and Morocco. The identities of 234
bodies are unknown, and along the wall that fronts the
cemetery are the names of 724 others whose remains
were never recovered.

The American cemetery is a place of quiet greenery.
On one wall a series of maps traces the course of opera-
tions, and the old names come pounding back: El
Alamein, Long Stop Hill, Hill 609, Medjez-el-Bab,
Kasserine.

Only in the mind's eye can the visitor, recalling that

half-forgotten but highly successful campaign, re-create experience. There are no burned-out hulls of tanks. The bomb craters that marked the landscape have long been filled in.

But one can pass Long Stop Hill and remember the bitter battle fought there by the Americans and British on Christmas Eve, 1942; the long, agonizing struggle to take Hill 609; the exultation when, in May 1943, the Allied armies took Tunis and Bizerte and eventually more Axis prisoners than the Russians had taken at Stalingrad.

The weeds have covered the airfields. The hotel where Randolph Churchill and many others "gloried and drank deep" is now a girls' school, and the war is long gone. British cemeteries are dotted around Tunisia with the dead buried near where they fell. In this alien land, these smaller plots somehow have captured the dignity of English country churchyards. In contrast to the ruins at Carthage and the cemeteries is the booming tourist area running along the Gulf of Hammamet eastward to Sousse.

The hotels fronting on the sea range from three- and four-room self-contained suites with television to bring the traveler "Starsky and Hutch" with Arabic subtitles to youth camps where the young can expend their energies on swimming, sailing, volleyball and, for the venturesome, a ride on a camel imported from the far south.

The hotels include pleasant American-style hostelries such as the Sheraton and more ornate places like the Sindabad. In the latter, self-contained suites and double-bed rooms all face the sea, and there is an air of repose unusual in major hotels. The furnishings are somewhat too elaborate for a seaside resort, but the food in the dining rooms, basically French with Tunisian dishes on demand, is admirable and the service fast and unobtrusive.

This, it should be said, is true of every hotel in Tunis and along the coast. Possibly because tourism is such a major earner of foreign exchange, every effort is made to meet the traveler's wishes. And, although Tunisia is an Islamic state, the thirsty visitor, even in the holy month of Ramadan, will get full attention from bartenders.

The majority of the tourists are from Western Europe: the French, who, of course, know the country; Spaniards; Italians; British; and, increasingly, Scandinavians.

Their wants are simple. Most visit Tunis and its bazaar and the ruins of Carthage. Few venture south or southwest into the heart of the country. Most are content to savor the sand and the sea, to drink in the hotels' cafés and, occasionally, in the bars of Hammamet. By day, they lie sun-drunk on the sands or experiment, gingerly, with surf boards. It is a lazy and, probably, healthy life.

The Tunisian economy emphasizes tourism. Much of the country's $2.1 billion in exports last year came from its 1.3 million tourists. Tourism also means 128,000 jobs for Tunisians. Much of the investment comes from the oil-rich states of the Persian Gulf, which are thinking of quick profits rather than the economic future of Tunisia. Critics, for their part, would rather see investment in agriculture and the revival of Tunisia as a major supplier of food for Europe.

A visit to the valley of the **Medjerda River,** scene of some of the Tunisian campaign's bitterest fighting in World War II, gives a glimpse of a land far removed from the gaudy delights of the hotels strung along the Gulf of Hammamet.

Farms once tended by French colons appear only half-cultivated today, and the towns seem down at the heel. The hotel at Beja, which was flourishing in 1968, is now closed. Many shops are empty. Off the highway, the returning visitor sees farms that were productive in the midst of war but are now ill-tended; the roads that lead from the farms to the markets are in poor repair. Gastronomically, the area of the Medjerda valley is a desert. The traveler intent on visiting battlegrounds and

The "Green Land" of the Arab World

cemeteries is well advised to bring his own food and water.

The pity is that in many areas the land is still fertile. Before World War II, wheat yields in the Medjerda valley compared favorably with those in France. But the land is moribund now, and agriculture moves slowly, very slowly.

Even here, though, west of Tunis, the countryside is more European than African. Driving down the tree-lined roads, the visitor can imagine himself in southern France, and the resort areas on the Gulf of Hammamet are strikingly like those of the Côte d'Azur as they were in the '50s.

The old roads are tree-lined like those in Provence. Each tiny village boasts its coffeehouse where the itinerant Westerner can buy a beer, usually at blood heat, or sip coffee in the shade and listen to elderly Tunisians, free from labor, discussing, sometimes in French, the iniquities of the Government and the shabby prices they are offered for wheat. Continuing, the car will emerge from a stand of trees along the road and there on the southern horizon will be the mountains marching to the Sahara. They are not as impressive as the Alps that rise behind the Côte d'Azur, but they have a rugged grandeur of their own. Again, the mind's eye recalls how, in that spring so many years ago, little clumps of blue flowers grew on the slopes, and when the wind blew they looked like small rippling ponds on the mountainsides.

Occasionally there is a touch of the Sahara. Outside Oued-Zarga was a Bedouin encampment. The shelters, however, were not the familiar black tents but old army tents, the peaks protruding strangely from the skins hung on them.

A little girl accosted the car and disclosed that her

mother had just baked some fresh bread and it was for sale. The encampment was alive with camels of all ages, and the girl, running back to her mother, gave one a smart belt on the rump, something not recommended to strangers.

Tunisia is rich in mosques. One of the most striking appears when the visitor emerges from the souk, or market, in Tunis. This is the **Great Mosque,** the largest and oldest in the city. It was completed in 864. Even more impressive is the mosque in **Kairouan,** also known as the Great Mosque, which is even older.

Tunisians are said to believe that the duty of a visit to Mecca can be balanced by seven or nine visits to the mosque at Kairouan. The courtyard leads to the magnificent façade of the prayer room and what has been described as its "forest of columns," some in marble, some in porphyry, Roman, Byzantine, early Christian, Moslem. For those who revel in antiquity, the **National Museum at Le Bardo** outside Tunis contains what is regarded as the world's finest display of mosaics and North Africa's best Roman collection.

The collection at Le Bardo fills three stories. The entrance fee is minimal, but the visitor needs staying power to see all the exhibits. The museum reflects Tunisia's history. The grinning, leering terra-cotta masks from the Tophets, the Phoenician jewelry, the beads and seals recall the might of Carthage and its sinister underpinning. In the Christian Room there are a font, sarcophagus covers and mosaics, and in the Bulla Regia Room statues of emperors and gods. An inner chamber devoted to mosaics is bordered by fifteen more Roman statues.

The life of Roman Carthage is portrayed, often vividly, in the Sousse Room, with its mosaics depicting country scenes and the farms that made the province the granary of Rome. Greece is not forgotten. From a ship sunk in a storm before the Christian Era, divers have recovered bronze bed fittings and miniatures.

Le Bardo, if your legs will take it, is one of the delights of Tunisia.

All these are interesting and, for the visiting expert, vital. But they do not have the flavor of modern Tunisia. That is best experienced in the shaded streets of the capital when the sun has set and the men sit over coffee and soft drinks in sidewalk cafés.

As in any café anywhere in France, the promenaders offer as much entertainment as the coffee. Few Tunisians drink anything stronger, although some bold spirits occasionally order beer. The charm of the cafés is not what you eat or drink, but the opportunity to observe at leisure the flow of life along the pavements. The cafés at the Africa and International hotels are attractive, and when night falls the tourist can walk down the long tree-covered promenade lined with booths selling everything from toys to the latest (three-day-old) Paris and London newspapers.

Food in the cafés and hotels is likely to be standard European hotel variety. Even shashlik, one of the Arab world's finest dishes, has a mail-order taste. Prices are reasonable enough in the regular dining rooms—say, $5 for a light meal. Each hotel has a special dining room with a band and floor show. Their food, one habitué said, is on a par with that in the regular dining rooms but about twice as expensive. Both the Africa and the International have roof-top bars from which the visitor can observe the city at night and enjoy the cool breeze.

Elsewhere in Tunis—along the roads that lead south

and west—such delicacies as cows' heads and freshly killed sheep are strung up to entice the passing Tunisian.

And always there are the mountains, some running in chains, some rising starkly from the plains like Djebel Ichkeul, near Bizerte, where the last of the last Bey of Tunis's buffalo fell under Allied shellfire in 1943.

The majority of Tunisians speak Arabic and French, although English, considered the language of the technological world, is making headway. They are a polite people, eager to show a visitor their city and their country. However, as in most Arab countries, patience is a virtue. Any transaction, even changing an air ticket, takes about three times as long as it would in Europe or the United States. This may be a legacy left by the French, after the Russians the world's premier bureaucrats. Save in the extreme south, where the wastelands lead into the Sahara, Tunisia is not the stereotype desert African country. Rather it is Mediterranean in its affinity for the inland sea and its closeness culturally and politically to southern Europe.

Hannibal and his elephants, the Romans, the Vandals, the Spaniards are long gone. The Germans and the Italians left few traces. Aside from the still cemeteries, the Americans and British are at one with Rome.

INDIA

THE GIFT OF THE DAY
A. M. Rosenthal

IMAGES OF INDIA
Santha Rama Rau

EIGHT HISTORIC CAPITAL CITIES
William K. Stevens

INDIA'S ROYAL GHOST TOWN
Michael T. Kaufman

The Gift of the Day

A. M. ROSENTHAL

WHEN I WAS YOUNG,
and writing from India, I embraced the gift of each day.

Each day was filled with sound and movement, with
thought and action, with a delighted awareness of the
present, hope for the future and the sense of the rolling of
history.

I did not go to India in search of my soul, but just to
be a foreign correspondent. But somehow from the beginning, I understood in India, as never before, that virtue
lies in rushing toward each day with its joys and adventures, and even its pain, and that the only real sin is de-
meaning God's gift of each day by turning away.

How India taught me this I cannot entirely say. But
when I think of my four reporting years there, I see myself surrounded by people and motion and color and joys
and horrors and kindly friends, by heat, rain, the scent

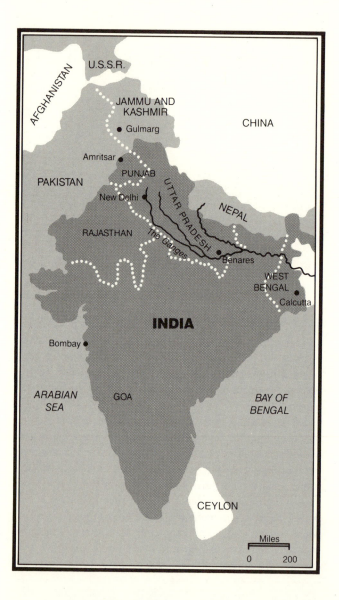

The Gift of the Day

of dung and of the marigold, snow on the mountain, muck in the village, anger, laughter, elegance, decay.

I knew what was happening to me, this acute realiza-tion of the day as gift. And I ran forward and seized what I could.

I thought, well, if I ever come back someday, a long time from now, it will be different, it won't be so full of zest; India and I will be older and drier.

But I did go back, a half-dozen journeys, after I had lost, for long periods, the virtue of joy in the day, and each time I found that India and I were both young again, together.

Now, how can this be? When I tell my friends about my love for India, they say, but how about caste and filth and poverty and stench and disease, riot and death?

Yes, I tell them, of course, of course. But that is not all of India, and it is the rest, I say, the huge infinite va-riety of the rest, that lifted my heart and still does.

It is the sense of color and dash in the dress of every Rajasthani woman brick-carrier. It is the music every-where, the dozen different countries and the races and re-ligions roiling in the one India. It is the warmth of the people you meet who are so kind, so loving, the adven-ture in travel and the still-existing greatest adventure— the Indian adventure in freedom.

So please understand that I really do know all the bad things about India, but you will not find many of them here, for this is a letter of loving thanks for the gift of the day.

All India is an itinerary. Mine always starts in New Delhi simply because it was home for so long—or at least the base from which I kept wandering about the subcon-tinent.

I am, of course, a man of enormous self-control and

concealment of emotion. So it was not until the wheels of the airplane had touched down on my last visit early in 1984 that I pounded my colleague on the back and shouted, "India, India, India!"

This was his first visit to India and he peered out the window at this great country I was presenting to him, saw an airstrip and nodded amiably enough. I assured him that even more wonders lay in store.

There was something I was waiting for, and I rushed out of the airport to find it. There it was, after just a few moments. India at night—the sharp scent of charcoal burning in hundreds of roadside fires of the migrant workers mixed with the aroma, half real, half a memory, of the sweet flower that Indians call Queen of the Night. If you know India at all, you can close your eyes and be home.

Open them in the morning, and there are the great red sandstone government buildings built by the British to celebrate their own sense of power. The British Raj is gone, but the buildings remain—imperial, self-satisfied historic in their Mogul style, very Indian in the memory of history, very Indian in the celebration of national glory and pomp.

What buildings like that need is what India gives them—magnificent mounted lancers on guard every day, the motionless beasts of the camel corps on the bulwarks on national days, huge pipers and drummers whenever there is an excuse for a parade, thousands of oil lamps outlining each balcony and turret at holiday time.

This grand sense of theater and drama is everywhere in India, not simply for tourists, but for India and out of India. Houses are lighted for religious festivals and wed-dings, lighted with oil lamps, with garish electric bulb

The Gift of the Day

strings and with delicate little lights glowing from tree branches—princess lights, they call them.

There is theater in the magnificent military bands at the Gateway to India on Bombay's waterfront, in the bracelets of barefoot women in Calcutta, in cymbals banged and gods paraded ceaselessly in the holy city of Benares, in the starched turbans of Government servants and even in the white homespun caps Indian politicians love to wear at election time to show their undying devotion to Mahatma Gandhi, as they climb into their chauffeured cars.

Sometimes it is cold in India, sometimes terribly hot, often dry, sometimes rainy. It doesn't matter all that much.

Just to go somewhere, anywhere. India is alive all year, and all India is worth visiting one month or another if you don't just look but open your pores.

There is a place called Gulmarg in Kashmir, to which I go often. I ride a pony up a trail to a high meadow and the meadow is full of flowers and above the meadow are more mountains, beyond, touched by snow, always.

It is high and pure and clean and cool, and though I have actually ridden to Gulmarg only twice in my life, I go there often in my dreams and at times of deep pleasure. I know it well, and I never wish to see a photograph or drawing of it, because it is painted in my mind, my own sweet lovely meadow in Gulmarg.

Jawaharlal Nehru, who was Prime Minister of India when I lived there, wrote a book I took everywhere with me in my years of travel in the country. It was called *The Discovery of India*. To me, the title meant that India was a perpetual discovery, too large to be known entirely but always available for one more journey, one more discovery.

Sometimes you discover India for yourself, by your-self, as I discovered Gulmarg. Sometimes another person helps discover it for you.

I had been to Chandni Chowk, the bazaar quarter of the Old City of Delhi, dozens of times. But I really dis-covered it only on my last visit because of my colleague's own eye and interest.

I had not discovered Chandni Chowk in any of my previous visits because I had disliked it so—smelly, dirty streets, beggars, open drains—that I saw it only as a whole—an unpleasant whole, never separately. But on this visit, my friend insisted on going back several times, and I saw it new. I realized that the crowded streets, the hundreds upon hundreds of stalls of cloth sellers and jewelers and spice merchants, were distinct, each one of them, with its salesmen, gofers, hawkers. Suddenly the streets were not a mass but separate, hustling porters and businessmen, running, carrying, moving, buying, selling. Each person, each movement, each noise and sensation was separate but together, quite as real and as powerful as the red sandstone buildings and the mounted lancers.

The discovery lay in the sorting out of individuals and sensations. The sandalwood from the incense, the fried sweets from the spices. The noise was deafening. But there was discovery selecting out of the sounds the whine of motorcycles, the shouting of pedestrians, the clop of horses, the screech of machinery in a second-story fac-tory.

Suddenly, and for the first time, I was comfortable in Chandni Chowk because I was experiencing it as did the people who lived there, separately, face by face, sound by sound.

I discovered Gulmarg in my first year in India; I dis-

covered ancient Varanasi—it is known throughout most
of the world still as Benares—more than a quarter century later.

I wrote to a friend on a postcard: "My God, India at
last! It has taken me almost 30 years of involvement with
this country to get to the heart of India."

Indians call this holy city on the Ganges the navel of
the world, and for all Hinduism it is. They call it the
mother of cities, the mother of us all, the city of light. It
is Jerusalem.

It is Jerusalem with smelly streets, huge crowds, cow
dung everywhere, shrieking horns. It gives you a head-
ache, until you suddenly realize where you are. You are
in the very center of a religious experience, a daylong,
every day religious experience. The city, creature of the
passion of prayer and belief, is the wild and deep inner
heart of Hinduism.

Hundreds of temples—up winding bazaar streets, in
the middle of roads, around corners, huge temples and
small wayside altars. All India is here to worship, to
pray and dance. Small Bengalis, Madrasis plump with
the southern coconut-oil cooking, northwesterners with
faces like mountainsides—each group in its own section,
its own tumbledown hostelries. Separate by night, all
jumbled together by day in Varanasi.

In Varanasi nothing matters but Varanasi. The rest of
the world does not exist. Prayers, singing, chanting, the
gods. What else is there, what else can there possibly be
in Varanasi?

There is a fierceness of devotion, but there is also a
kind of jolliness that I did not expect. The bazaars are
full of children's toys, wooden dolls and bracelets, and
everybody seems to have at least one child for whom to
buy a trinket.

I thought once that Hindus came to Varanasi to die, to be cremated and to have their ashes thrown into the Ganges. But most people come here to pray and see and live and believe. The religion is the reality, the only reality, and they live in it and then they die in it. But mostly they live in it.

Varanasi bounces and shrieks and smells. There are crazy monkeys that jump all over the temples and snatch garlands from around people's necks. It is wild and alive and while you are there, there is no other place.

We saw the sun rise red over the Ganges, and we saw the people wash and pray. At one time I did so want to squat on the steps of the ghats and feel the Ganges, at least just touch it. I restrained myself, which I now regret.

I did not bathe in the Ganges, but will always revisit, rediscover Varanasi, just as I will always, every trip, rediscover Calcutta.

Calcutta is worth the visit, just for the statistics.

All Bengalis seem to love numbers, and we had a guide who was the best Calcutta statistician I've ever met. He had a number for everything. There were 40,500 rickshaw drivers in Calcutta, exactly 180,000 people slept on the streets, 30 tons of spit were spat every day and 18,500 cows roamed the streets, along with no fewer than 72,000 pigs.

Once he told me that 80 percent of India's budget went to national defense. When I mildly questioned that, he shrugged. So it wasn't 80 percent, maybe some other figure, but a figure anyway.

Of course, everybody knows that Calcutta is the worst city in the world, only it isn't. It's bad enough, all right, it's dirty and hungry and diseased. But I would take the action and vitality, the movement and the yearning and the hunger for knowledge and the humor and the wild melee of commerce any day over some of the drab and dreary cities of Eastern Europe and the Soviet Union, or the lifeless creations of the architects like Islamabad in Pakistan and Brasilia in Brazil.

Calcutta is many things, of course—students in coffeehouses, radical mobs and a whole quarter given over to making clay gods, worshiped just one day a year and then thriftily destroyed, so that good fruit and nuts won't have to be fed to them all year round.

There's the municipal government, not quite in collapse, open sewers and moldering buildings.

But mostly it is bazaars. Fruit bazaars, vegetable bazaars, Hindu bazaars and Moslem bazaars, bazaars for cloth and gold and flowers and meat and automobile parts and stolen goods, whole vast cities of bazaars jammed ankle deep in straw and bouncing, bouncing, bouncing all day long. Push, hustle, buy, sell, push, hustle. It isn't neat and it isn't clean, but it surely is alive.

The lovely valley of Kashmir and its streams are India, and so are the sweeps of beaches of the south and the Himalayas of the north. But so is Calcutta and so is Bombay, across the subcontinent. It is to the cities that villagers by the millions come in search of work and a taste of a better life.

About 10 P.M. the day we arrived in Bombay I took a walk around near the hotel with William K. Stevens, the *Times* correspondent in India. There was something on the sidewalk.

"Is that a person?" Stevens asked me. I looked and stared. "Well, I don't know," I said.

Perhaps that says more about Bombay than anything else I can think of—a nice capsule-size symbol. Around the corner from a great hotel that sells silk and gold and jewelry in its shops, a bundle of rags that might or might not be a person, who might or might not be alive.

Calcutta is mostly poor and shabby, middle-class at best, a vast busy tatter of a city. But Bombay is power—Arab princes, skyscrapers, hotels, big business deals, billions of rupees, narcotics, oil, machinery, industry, women with saris slung low about their hips, handsome men, money, money, money.

And everywhere the unending shantytowns, hundreds of thousands of people poured into town looking for work, being born, living, loving, next to those hotels filled with men and women of gold and silk.

Do the people in the hotels and the apartment build-ings along the beaches see the people in the shantytowns they pass every day?

I am not really sure. I will have to return to discover. After all, I never really stopped to find out whether the bundle in the street was a person or not a person, alive or dead.

In India you can discover a lot about yourself, but I suppose that is true everywhere.

It was in a village that I discovered again what meant most to me about India. The colleague with whom I was traveling, Arthur Ochs Sulzberger, publisher of *The Times*, likes villages. He had the notion that he might find out more about India in villages than in garden parties or even politicians' offices. So we saw villages in Rajasthan, in the Punjab, in Bengal, in Goa, in Uttar Pradesh, and we even saw one near New Delhi.

We walked into that village near Delhi, and it looked pretty good to me, compared—compared to the villages I had seen years earlier in the same area.

It was clean, it had some sewers, there was farm machinery to be seen, children had real clothes, not just rags; there were some roads, and the courtyards were swept and neat.

We stopped to talk. We strolled about, and people were open and friendly. There was a handsome farmer of about fifty with a quick wit and a curly gray mustache.

We asked him how crops were, and he said, terrible, awful, ghastly, a misery. I have heard these same words from farmers all over the world, and for all I know crops are always terrible, awful, ghastly. Then we asked him about what he thought of Indira Gandhi, then Prime Minister, and her Government, headquartered just twenty or so miles away. This time, he really got enthusiastic with distaste—terrible, awful, corrupt, inefficient, uncaring, nobody here would ever vote for her. He waited while Stevens got it all down, including his name, and we said good-bye.

A moment later, I stood still outside the village and asked my colleagues where else could that happen—in what few countries in the world could a peasant denounce his own Government and its leaders and spell out his name. In China, in Eastern Europe, in the Soviet Union, the very idea of listening to such questions—let alone answering them—would strike terror.

They could not be asked or answered in most of Asia, in almost all the Middle East or Africa or in many countries of Latin America.

But in a village outside New Delhi, a farmer with bright eyes, a curly mustache and a keen sense of himself said exactly what he thought about his Prime Minister and her Government.

There were a few years when Mrs. Gandhi tried to eliminate the political democracy her father and his generation had created in India, but she failed. She was thrown out by the voters, then brought back by them out of disgust with her successors. She died a victim of India's terrible religious passions. I believe that farmer will go right on talking his heart about any Indian ruler because he has this idea that he lives in a free country.

We used to call that kind of thing—free politics, a free society in a poverty-stricken country struggling upward —the great adventure. It still is. And that is still what means most about India to me, more than all the bazaars, all the great cities, more even than the flowers in the lovely meadow of Gulmarg.

The night we left India, I had a dream that I saw Nehru, whom I had admired. He shook my hand and said, "How are you, Abe," and I thought, now isn't that warm of him to remember my first name after all these years.

Mrs. Gandhi was standing nearby, and I kissed her on the nose. How nice, I thought, to kiss the Prime Minister on her nose.

When I awoke, I realized with a thrill of pleasure that the plane to London did not leave till very late that night. So I had ahead of me one more day in India, one more gift.

SUBCONTINENTAL SAMPLER
HOTELS FIT FOR A MAHARAJAH
The following hotels throughout India are among the most comfortable—even luxurious—in the country. All have good restaurants; exceptional dining rooms are specifically noted.

The Gift of the Day

NEW DELHI
Taj Mahal Hotel, 1 Man Singh Road (telephone: 386162), has double rooms for about $80, suites for about $170 and $250. The Chinese restaurant, the **House of Ming,** has both hot and mild dishes; entrees are about $7 to $9.

Oberoi Inter-Continental, Dr. Zakir Hussain Marg (699571), has doubles for about $85, suites for $180 and $320. The **Mughal Room** restaurant has Indian specialties; entrees are about $4 to $5.

BOMBAY
Taj Mahal Hotel, Bombay Apollo Bunder (243366), is an old, British-style hotel with double rooms for about $80, $110 and $180; be sure to ask for a room overlooking the harbor. There are two good restaurants: **The Golden Dragon** has both hot and mild Chinese dishes, with entrees typically priced at about $8; the **Tanjore** specializes in Indian food, especially *thali* trays, which contain an assortment of curries, breads and other preparations. A vegetarian *thali* is about $5; one with meat is about $5.

Hotel Oberoi Towers, Marine Drive, Nariman Point (234343), has double rooms for about $90 and suites for about $220 to $410. Many rooms overlook the Arabian Sea. The **Mughal Room** restaurant has northern Indian Moslem cuisine; entrees are about $7 to $9.

BENARES
Hotel Taj Ganges, Nadesar Palace Grounds (54385), has double rooms for about $40, suites for about $50.

CALCUTTA
Hotel Oberoi Grand, 15 Jawaharlal Nehru Road (230181), is a comfortable hotel built around a central court; doubles are about $80, suites about $160 and $250.

JAIPUR

Rambagh Palace Hotel, Bhawani Singh Road (75141 or 73796), is a former maharajah's palace that offers double rooms for $50, suites for about $75 and $200.

UDAIPUR

Lake Palace Hotel, Post Office Box 5 (3241), is a former palace set on an island in the middle of Pichola Lake in the Rajasthani highlands. Double rooms are about $45, suites about $70 and $180.

Images of India

SANTHA RAMA RAU

I NDIA, SO OFTEN
described as "the vast subcontinent," is not, in fact, ge-
ographically very big. On a map of the United States, for
instance, it would fit between Chicago and New York
and leave room to spare. But it has a population of
nearly 700 million and its cultural, historical, religious
and linguistic diversity does, indeed, entitle it to the so-
briquet "subcontinent."

Two extremes of this complexity appear in the startling contrast between North and South India, in the look
of the country, the style of living, dress, food, climate,
and, most arrestingly, in the distinctive architecture—a
continuing reminder of the waves of history that have
shaped modern India.

It has been my good fortune to have an intimate access
to both North and South through a mother whose family
home was in North India and a father whose family ties

were on the southwest coast of the Indian peninsula. So it is not surprising that the places I revisit most often and with the greatest enthusiasm are Delhi and the Kerala coast. They serve, besides, to remind me that for all the differences the "subcontinent" displays, India has some inner cohesion that makes it, still, one nation.

DELHI, OLD AND NEW

On the elaborately inlaid marble walls of the Hall of Private Audience in the Red Fort, the walled palace compound of Old Delhi, is inscribed the famous Persian quotation: "If there be a paradise on earth, it is here, oh! it is here, oh! it is here." More than 300 years ago the Peacock Throne stood in this room, under a gilded silver ceiling. It was described by a contemporary French traveler as a solid gold, jewel-encrusted platform, six by four feet, "supported by six massy feet . . . sprinkled over with rubies, emeralds and diamonds." Its back was formed by two peacocks with their tails fanned out, all set with pearls and precious stones to simulate the colors and iridescence of their feathers. Twelve gold pillars held up the pearl-fringed golden canopy, "all richly emblazoned with costly gems." Here the Mogul Emperor reviewed his cavalry and his fighting and ceremonial elephants and received his ministers, his nobles and foreign dignitaries in dazzling grandeur.

Perhaps, for a very short time, the audience hall, opening through scalloped arches onto formal gardens, surrounded by the marble pavilions and arcades of the palace and the enclosure of the Pearl Mosque, may have seemed like a glimpse of paradise—if you were wealthy, influential or lucky enough to be part of the glittering court of Shah Jahan. And even then, only if you weren't troubled by the pervasive intrigue, treachery and sudden, secret murder among the courtiers, entourage and the royal family itself. Only ten years after the "Exalted Fort" was built, the Emperor was deposed by his son Aurangzebe and imprisoned in the fort in Agra where his room gave him a view of the Taj Mahal, the mausoleum he had built for his beloved wife Mumtaz Mahal. Aurangzebe, after destroying his brothers, his own son and his nephew, claimed the Peacock Throne to govern an empire that stretched from Afghanistan through most of India.

Outside the Red Fort was Chandni Chowk, "Silver Street," the bazaar section of the capital, where flower, vegetable and fruit markets were interspersed with open-fronted shops displaying "beautiful and fine cloths, silk and other stuffs striped with gold and silver, turbans embroidered with gold, and brocades." The owners sat, as they still do, cross-legged on white cotton-covered mattresses, inviting customers in and offering them a cold drink while they make their selections. Delhi was, even then, a crossroads of commerce as well as a center of government. In the following three centuries, the Red Fort and whole city of Delhi became the scene of a turbulent series of wars, sieges, captures and victories. Its greatest disaster came in 1739, when the Persian invader, Nadir Shah, sacked and plundered the city, stole the Peacock Throne and gave his soldiers orders for a general massacre. The carnage stopped only when the Emperor Mohammed Shah made a direct appeal for his people and Nadir Shah (surely with some irony) replied, "The Emperor of India must never ask in vain."

Mogul rule never really recovered, and Delhi became the target for various rebellious Hindu and Moslem princes and leaders as well as foreign raiders. By the end of the century, the empire had shrunk to only the small,

unstable "Kingdom of Delhi," a ghostly echo of former
Mogul might. In 1803, even that fragment had to be sur-
rendered when the blind, impoverished, octogenarian
Emperor Shah Alam asked the British Army for protection against the calamitous attacks of his own countrymen. Seated under a shabby canopy in the looted
remains of the Hall of Private Audience, the Emperor received the conquering English Commander-in-Chief as an
ally and deliverer, relinquished all but his title and a few
dignities of rank and quietly accepted his future as the
pensioner of an alien race. In a few years, the whole subcontinent was to come under the dominion of the British.

Half a century later, the British, in turn, found themselves trying to recapture Delhi from the rebel forces in
the Indian Mutiny (which Indians prefer to call the First
War of Independence). After the English sheltering in
the Red Fort had been killed and the Emperor Bahadur
Shah reinstated as ruler, the British Army laid siege to
the city and eventually took it by storm. In the tide of
bitterness and fury that followed, Bahadur Shah was
sent into exile, his sons and a grandson were stripped
and shot, their bodies exhibited to the populace for three
days, and the once-proud Mogul line came to an end.

Since then, Delhi has been the site of great durbars es-
tablishing the power and supremacy of British rule in India. The grandest of these was the Durbar of 1911 when
George V and Queen Mary became the first ruling English monarchs to visit India, and a full panoply of Indian
princes came to pay homage to the King-Emperor.

In 1947, on August 15, far larger numbers of Indians
came to the Red Fort to watch a simple but truly unprecedented ceremony: the first raising of independent India's
national flag by its first Prime Minister, Jawaharlal
Nehru. But four and a half months later, even this mo-

ment of triumph was tempered with tragedy. On January 30, 1948, Mohandas K. Gandhi was assassinated in Delhi. His body was cremated on the bank of the Jumna River, which flows outside the wall of the Red Fort. There, on the same spot, is his memorial, a black marble slab standing in a tree-shaded lawn and inscribed in Hindi with his dying words: *"He Ram"* ("O God").

Delhi has not always been the nation's capital (indeed, throughout its long and complex history, India has not always been a single nation), though for geographic and strategic reasons it has always been an important center. Set on a navigable river, at the site of a useful ford, controlling the fertile lands of the Ganges plain and commanding the routes to central India and to the ports of the west coast, it was the obvious first and best place for invading armies from Central Asia and the Near East to make their headquarters.

My own first memories of New Delhi date from 1939, when it still had a somewhat raw, unsettled look. Its chilly, geometric plan, its neatly matching whitewashed houses each in its plot of white-walled garden, the long severe avenues where half-grown shade trees had not yet softened the lines, all contrasted strangely with the vivid bustle of the old city. The night of my arrival, on the drive from the station in Old Delhi through the bright and noisy bazaars into the residential section of New Delhi, three or four miles away, I felt I was entering a meticulously planned garden suburb on the outskirts of a real city. There seemed to be no pedestrians on the sidewalks and virtually no cars on the streets; the city gave the impression—hard to achieve in India—of being almost frighteningly lifeless.

By daylight, and at the main axis of the city, New Delhi presented an anything but suburban aspect. The imposing processional road, King's Way, led from the War Memorial Arch, past the canopied statue of George V, between spacious lawns and ornamental ponds to the Viceroy's house. Set on Raisina Hill, commanding a view over what Lutyens called "that wilderness of ruined tombs that form the remains of the seven older Delhis," was an extraordinary spread of 340 rooms, huge stairways, domed halls and hundreds of yards of pillared corridors and verandas, set in 330 acres of gardens and parks. The plaza in front of it was flanked by the huge blocks of the Secretariat Buildings, and on one side was the vast wedding cake of the Assembly Building, constructed of red sandstone and encircled by a colonnade of white pillars. In the crystal sunshine of that North Indian winter morning, it did, indeed, look like an acropolis built for a race of giants. But in spite of the architect's careful use of Indian features—the dome of the Viceroy's House shaped to resemble a Buddhist stupa, the Hindu-style sculpture and stonework, the Moslem garden designs—it still looked implacably foreign in that patch of the Jumna plain.

By now, of course, everything has changed. Time, use, political independence and above all the overwhelming growth in population have drastically altered the character of this city that was planned for 30,000 to 57,000 inhabitants and now contains at least 600,000. New Delhi has spread north to merge with the old city, and the Delhi Gate, which used to be the formal entrance to the Mogul capital, is now merely a handsome arch across a busy road in a city of close to 4 million. Yet it still leads past the splendid dome and minarets of India's largest mosque, the Jama Masjid, to the exciting confusion of Chandni Chowk, where the stalls of silversmiths, piled high with bangles, necklaces, anklets, toe-rings,

still glitter like moonlight between the crowds of shoppers. And the scene outside the Red Fort cannot have
changed very much since the seventeenth century; the
fruit and flower markets still flourish and the open-
fronted shops still display fine fabrics or sandals and
Persian-style shoes with pointed, curling toes embellished with gold thread, or stacks of gleaming brass
cooking vessels.

The humming life of the sidewalks, as in all Indian
cities, changes according to the season, the occasion, or
even the time of day. Early in the morning there may be
villagers who have been walking since four or five
o'clock to bring their produce to town. Unable to afford a
regular bazaar stall, they may pile their wares on reed
mats on the ground, spread carpets of scarlet chilies to
dry in the sun. Later their places may be taken by basket
makers or men fashioning children's toys out of colored
paper or a few bamboo leaves. In the heat of the day, the
street will be deserted except for shrouded figures asleep
in the shade. By evening there may be sweet stalls, betel
vendors, a man with a tea urn and little metal cups that
he clinks together to attract your attention, or someone
selling the heavy-scented attars of musk, rose or jasmine
for which Delhi is famous.

Much of this casual Indian use of city streets as places
to conduct business—and even, sometimes, to live—has
cascaded into New Delhi too, with the difference that the
shops and the sidewalks display, quite properly for the
nation's capital, products and handicrafts from all over
India—in itself a brief education in the staggering diversity of the country: Benares brass and brocades, Kashmir carpets and fine wool shawls, luminous Madras
silks, delicate Jaipur enamels, sandalwood boxes and
ornaments from Mysore, curious birds and animals

343

carved in Kerala from buffalo horns, the special weaves and patterns of Orissan saris and, from India's borders, Nepali jewelry of hammered silver set with carnelian, turquoise and spinach jade, Tibetan samovars and furs.

The formal changes that came with independence were only to be expected. Streets that were named for such British dignitaries as Queen Victoria, King Edward or Lord Curzon now honor eminent Indians, among them Rajendra Prasad, Maulana Azad, Kasturba Gandhi. Royal and viceregal statues have given way to those of nationalist leaders. The President of India lives in the Viceroy's House, now called Rashtrapati Bhavan, at the summit of King's Way, translated to Rajpath; the Lok Sabha (parliament) meets in the Assembly Hall of the Viceroy's Council House and Indian ministers occupy the fine residences built for his councilors. But it is Indian living habits that have really transformed the atmosphere. There were no Indian restaurants in the early days, but now there are hundreds, catering to all sorts of regional tastes as well as offering Delhi's own Moglai food, the richest cuisine in India. Genteel English tea-rooms have been replaced by the popular coffeehouses where women meet for a break in the morning's shopping, students make fiery speeches to each other, idlers stop by for a rest, to watch the world go by, to join the uninhibited discussions and gossip. Streets are jammed with cyclists, horse- or ox-drawn carts, tiny taxis converted from motorcycles, jitneys and pushcarts. Laundry dries in backyards, cotton saris and turban lengths are draped over hedges and walls, and garish posters for Indian films contrast giddily with the austere pillared façades of shopping centers. In short, Lutyens's expansive design for a majestic symbol of the British Empire has become an Indian city.

I was most vividly aware of this metamorphosis one year when I was in New Delhi for the Republic Day parade. January 26 is a national holiday, and villagers from miles around had been walking into town or arriving in their bullock carts, with their families, for days before the celebration. The open spaces of the city filled with impromptu camps, carts were unhitched, oxen grazed in the parks or were washed in the ornamental fountains by their owners, the evening air was filled with the haze of open-air cooking fires. Turbaned men and village women in brilliantly colored, ankle-length skirts and tight bodices, often with a baby slung on one hip, strolled unchecked around the sights of their capital. Children ran excitedly about the monuments yelling to each other. Everywhere one felt the bubbling anticipation of an Indian festival.

Indians yield to nobody in their love of pageantry. They can turn the pedestrian business of a local election into a village fair, dressing in their best clothes, decorating their bullocks and carts with garlands of flowers, organizing processions of musicians, dancers and acrobats to enliven the trip to the polling booths. The Republic Day parade is the most spectacular performance of all and the route was packed with spectators from daybreak on. In the course of the morning, the usual food stalls appeared on the edge of the crowd among the tethered donkeys and bullocks, while some families simply sat on the ground where they were and opened white cotton bundles containing their snacks. The procession began with the arrival of the President from Rashtrapati Bhavan at his reviewing stand, surrounded by all the pomp and ceremony of viceregal days—the outriders, the cavalry escort, the great coach drawn by matched horses, shaded by the traditional umbrella-bearer in his scarlet and gold

uniform and guarded by lancers. But out of the coach stepped a small, thin man in a brown *achkan* (the Indian jacket), narrow trousers wrinkled at the ankles, and a Gandhi cap on his head. He smiled shyly at the crowd and responded to their shouts by bringing his hands together in a *namaskar*, the Indian greeting.

The parade itself lived up to all expectations, a dazzling cavalcade of elephants, horsemen, ski troops, the camel corps, the tough Gurkhas, the bearded Sikhs. But at the end of it, the Naga tribesmen in their beads and feathers, who had come to dance in the street in front of the President, were rather late getting started. Their stamping spear-dances coincided with the flypast of the new Indian Army jets. Nobody seemed surprised watching the two performances simultaneously. Both were perfectly natural aspects of India. And anyway, why was a rigid adherence to a time schedule so important in a festival like this?

New Delhi is only the most recent example of India's age-old ability to transmute foreign influences into something peculiarly its own. In its thousands of years of history it has been invaded by Aryans, Persians, Greeks, Bactrians, Scythians, Afghans, Moguls and finally the British. India seldom fought successfully against any of them, but in a way, won the longer, more decisive victory. With the exception of the British, each wave of invaders came as foreign conquerors but remained to become Indian subjects. They lost their allegiance to their homelands, intermarried, settled in India permanently, adopted the customs of the country, modifying some, retaining some of their own, and eventually became another strand in the complicated fabric of Indian life. Even the British, who couldn't be absorbed and had, at last, to retreat, left behind them monuments, institutions, public and private structures. Most notably in New Delhi, and by the same process of assimilation, these have now become entirely Indian.

PASSAGE TO MALABAR

For any traveler, certain journeys hold a remembered en-chantment that bears little relation to the particular mon-uments visited or beauty spots enjoyed. Some other quality seems to inform such voyages, coloring even the most prosaic details of everyday life with its peculiar magic.

I myself have made many journeys to Malabar, in the state of Kerala on the southwest coast of the Indian pen-insula. I have traveled there sometimes by plane, some-times by road and even on one occasion by oxcart. I have always been refreshed by the extraordinary and lovely things that the region holds. But the truly magical jour-ney to Malabar started for me many years ago with an in-vitation from an old friend to stay with her on a farm she owned and managed.

I decided to travel south from Bombay on a small trad-ing steamer largely because it called at ports whose names alone evoked a chapter of romantic and bloody history that had always stirred my fancy. Goa, Manga-lore, Calicut, Cochin, Trivandrum—all centers of the spice trade between India and Europe that began at the end of the fifteenth century, when the West realized its great dream of an ocean route to the riches of the Orient.

We left the superb harbor of Bombay at sundown, passed the scattered islands with their ruined forts, light-houses and ancient Hindu temples, and arrived in Pangim, the Goan capital, at dawn. At that time Goa was still a Portuguese colony, and Pangim (now Panaji) was a charming, somnolent settlement built on the lines of a southern European provincial town, with stuccoed arcades and formal Government buildings, flying the Portuguese flag, surrounding a central plaza. It is set on the bank of the wide Mandavi River, and on the hill behind it the piercing pinks and purples of bougainvillea cascaded over the walls enclosing private villas and compounds.

In the busy harbor traffic, freighters of a dozen nationalities steamed to their moorings, tugs and ferries fussed between the ships and shores. It seemed incredible that Affonso de Albuquerque had navigated precisely this same route up the Mandavi with his fleet of twenty-three ships in 1510, to wrest the tiny, luxuriant state from its Moslem rulers. At the end of desperate hand-to-hand fighting, he rode into the capital bearing the Portuguese standard and a gold cross. Kneeling in the public square, he dedicated the city to St. Catherine, in honor of her feast day, and claimed Goa as a possession of the King of Portugal and of the Catholic Church—which later sparked one of the most brutal and wholesale forced conversions recorded in Asia. All in the search for spices.

I spent my day in Velha Goa, the deserted old Portuguese capital built in the sixteenth century to rival Rome. It was a hushed, mysterious place, about six miles from Pangim. All the original houses, shops, offices and bazaars of an active city had crumbled away, and only the fantastic baroque churches, the Archbishops' Palace, the great ceremonial Arch of the Viceroys, the extraordinarily beautiful convents and their chapels rose out of the encroaching jungle. Nobody stopped me from exploring the vast, empty monuments. The elderly caretakers, when I could find them, seemed, if anything, mildly surprised at any display of interest. Only the Ba-

silica of Bom Jesus was more closely guarded, for the
"incorruptible body" of St. Francis Xavier is enshrined
there and pilgrims were occasionally allowed, on his
feast day, to pass by and kiss his toe. (This practice is
no longer permitted, since a zealot bit the toe off a few
years ago.)

Now, of course, Velha Goa has been expensively
cleaned up for the tourists. Wilderness and scrub trees
have been cleared to make roads and gardens; walls and
façades are newly whitewashed; magnificent ceiling-
high altarpieces have been regilded with each face in the
elaborately carved groups of figures carefully repainted;
chandeliers, sconces, ornaments, ivory statues, lacy
wooden screens and trellises all restored, refurbished
and gleaming. Velha Goa is now very grand and very
impressive, but I still cherish my first sight of the lovely,
fugitive frescoes in the Convent of St. Monica, the
church of St. Francis of Assisi, which had been converted from a mosque, and all those pale, streaky towers
and domes rising with ghostly authority above the palm
trees.

Our next stop was in the emerald harbor of Manga-
lore. Arriving in the evening, we found it crowded with
fishing boats and the brightly painted Arab dhows that
sail across the Arabian Sea to trade dates and gold for Indian cloth and spices. All the way south we had seen the
big, weathered country craft with their huge triangular
sails moving gracefully down the coast on the prevailing
northeast wind that follows the monsoon. As you pass
one of them you catch a quick, intimate glimpse of the
family that lives and works on the boat—a woman in a
bright cotton sari squatting at her brazier, fanning the
charcoal to a glow with a woven palm leaf; her husband,
in a scarlet loincloth and a torn shirt, at the tiller; a son

Images of India

mending a strip of sail or net; another child relaxing in the bow eating an orange, squinting into the sun to wave or shout a greeting.

In the evening, at anchor, the music from the fishing boats calls sweetly across the water, the high, sad trills of a bamboo flute picked up and embellished from one boat to another, perhaps snatches of rowdy singing if some group is drinking arak, the raw, local home brew. Gradually the evening fires are put out, the music trails off as people go to sleep and only the small riding lights rock gently on the water.

Still farther south lies the port of Calicut (now Kozhikode). For me it holds the most pervasive glamour of the spice trade's early years. There, in the pillared audience hall in 1498, after a perilous voyage round the Cape of Good Hope, Vasco da Gama was received by the splendid zamorin (Hindu raja), and thus began one of those extraordinary periods of naval history in which men faced piracy and violent death, made enormous fortunes, negotiated unprecedented trade agreements between European royalty and Asian princes. The first document was inscribed on a palm leaf with an iron stylus, addressed to the King of Portugal by the Zamorin of Calicut: "Vasco da Gama, a gentleman of your household, came to my country, whereat I was pleased. My country is rich in cinnamon, cloves, ginger, pepper and precious stones. That which I ask you in exchange is gold, silver, corals and scarlet cloth."

From that moment on, bitter sea battles raged between the European powers and the Arabs who had for centuries controlled the shipping along the Indian coast. The stakes were enormous, for spices sold in Europe at incredible prices—a pound of ginger, for instance, fetched in England as much as a full-grown sheep. Even now,

"It's as costly as pepper!" remains a common Dutch expression for anything outrageously expensive. And from
the small trading posts established by the British,
Dutch, French and Portuguese eventually grew the vast
and lucrative Asian empires of those distant nations.

Cochin is surely one of the prettiest harbors in the
world, and one of the oldest in India. Spangled with islands, fringed with beaches and coconut palms, brilliant
with tropical flowers, it has been visited, missionized,
traded with and fought over by foreigners for at least
2,000 years, and it hoards the souvenirs of its whole tumultuous history. In the city on the mainland, the Portuguese cathedral and the English churches mingle with
mosques and the Hindu temples. The oldest Indian
Christian community (dating its conversion from Apos-
tolic times) has its home and its churches in Cochin, and
India's small community of Jews built their synagogues
there. Because it was the most important port on the coast
for Arab sailors, it was for a while under Moslem rule,
and Chinese traders of the fifteenth century left their legacy as well: Cochin housewives still store their pickles in
the familiar huge, blue-and-white porcelain jars of the
Ming dynasty, and on the quaysides in the evening men
fish with large, circular "Chinese nets," mounted on
wooden frames with little lights attached to attract the
fish at night. On Bulgatty Island the luxurious eighteenth-century palace of the last of the Dutch governors
is now a tourist hotel.

In recent years Cochin has, inevitably, spread and
sprouted ugly concrete buildings and dreary character-
less suburbs, but old Cochin is virtually a medieval city
with narrow, twisting streets through which even a bullock cart cannot pass, and crooked houses arching over
them. The roads aren't paved but the dark red earth is

packed so hard and swept so clean that it has a surface like tiles.

I left the ship at Cochin to drive some miles northeast to my friend's farm. As I approached she was standing on her veranda—a tiny, commanding figure, white-haired, slender, barefoot, in a rosy cotton sari—giving orders in a rapid rattle of Malayalam to her headman about harvesting the paddy. (She told me she got three rice crops a year.) Then greetings and shouts to the cook for fresh coffee brewed very strong in the South Indian way, with the milk already added, and we settled down to an exchange of news and gossip. Malabar women, famous for their beauty, are famous too for their independence. Inheritors of a long matrilineal tradition (now, alas, decaying as national laws replace the old customs), they lived in their family home and chose their own husbands, who joined them there. Children took their mother's name and inheritance passed through her line; the husband was scarcely more than a visitor (possibly permanent) with no rights over his wife's family. Even now, outside some of the houses you can see the porches that shelter the "husbands' benches"—wooden settles where, according to custom, the returning husband waited out of courtesy until his wife invited him into her house. If he was wise, he looked along the floor of the veranda first, because Malabar women had perhaps the simplest divorce proceedings in the world: The husband's sandals placed outside the door signaled that he had been replaced by another suitor or lover and should, quite literally, go home to mother.

One important Malabar activity is, however, reserved exclusively for men—the great classical dance-drama form, *kathakali*. Boys train from the age of six or seven to become performers in this exacting, flamboyant, rigidly disciplined, immensely exciting form of theater. From the farm one evening we heard the sharp staccato of drums chattering furiously in the distance. This announced that later in the night a *kathakali* performance would be held, and families with their children started walking from their villages toward the sound.

By the time we reached the clearing, the noise was deafening. The drummers, bare-chested, glistening with sweat in the flickering light of the oil lamps, worked in relays, replacing each other without a break in the flow of the rhythms. It was close to midnight before the performance itself began, and by then the audience was half-mesmerized by the drums and the devotional chanting that precedes the appearance of the actors. The effect, then, of the huge figures—in fantastic costumes and glittering haloes, their makeup weird as a mask, hands waving, ankle-bells emphasizing each acrobatic movement—is astonishing, larger than life, a world of gods and demons.

In the sudden bright flares of the erratic lighting, these fabulous creatures acted out the famous stories from the great Indian epics, the *Mahabharata* and the *Ramayana:* the valiant fights, the terrifying dangers, the scenes of requited and unrequited love, the countless adventures of the five noble Pandava brothers and their exploits against their evil cousins, or of the good King Rama and his army of monkeys who recapture his virtuous Queen Sita from the demon king of Lanka.

Halfway through, many of the children had fallen asleep, and some of the adults broke up the intensity of the performance by having a cup of coffee from one of the stalls that had, as usual in India, sprung up on the edge of the clearing. Some bought a single hand-rolled cigarette and stood about sharing it with friends, but

most of us remained seated on the ground until the
kathakali ended as the sun began to rise. Then we all
dispersed sleepily to wander home in the cool dawn
light, our heads still full of battles and sorcery and heroic deeds, adjusting slowly to the familiar sounds of
morning—cocks crowing, waterwheels beginning to
turn—and everywhere the fragrance of wood smoke as
the breakfast fires were lighted. Nowadays the *kathakali*
is presented at the Kerala Kalamandalan in Shoranur, a
little way north of Cochin. It is much more organized—
the performances are shorter and take place at a more
reasonable hour, and they are usually composed of highlights from several narratives.

From Cochin southward for about eighty miles stretch
the Malabar "backwaters," an elegant network of connecting lagoons, canals and rivers winding through the
heart of Kerala. At my friend's suggestion I hired a small
boat to take me down to the river ports of Quilon and
Alleppey, and as it moved slowly along the edge of the
first lagoon, I found myself surrounded with all the improbable and predictable trappings of everybody's
dream tropical paradise. Coconut palms curving over the
water, backed by banana and papaya groves and beyond
them the exuberant green of rice fields. Clusters of
thatched huts were scattered along the banks, and in the
courtyards outside, women were beating out coconut
husks for coir fiber, arms rising and backs arching in
casual grace. Little girls in long, full skirts and tight,
bright bodices walked barefoot in single file on their way
to school, books balanced neatly on their heads, long
glossy braids strung with flowers. Boys scampered along
less sedately, calling the usual questions to the men on
the passing boats: "Where are you coming from?"
"Where are you going?"

The boats are low and narrow, covered with an arched shelter of woven palm leaves, and every morning they turn the canals into floating bazaars as fruits and vegetables, rice and spices are sold and exchanged from boat to boat. In Alleppey the main street is a canal; at market time you can buy cinnamon stick by the yard, fish the color of rubies and jars of delicious pickled green peppercorns. Quilon grows the best ginger in India, so merchants come from all over for the annual ginger auctions.

My last stop in Kerala was at Kovalam beach, outside Trivandrum. Undeveloped at that time as a tourist attraction, it had only a tiny, ascetically simple rest house on a rocky promontory overlooking a very long, perfect crescent of gilt sand between the ocean and the mop-headed palms. Small boys with their loincloths tucked high beckoned me to their primitive catamarans—four or five slender tree trunks lashed together. Skillfully they paddled me out beyond the breakers, where the water is so clear you can't judge its depth, though when you summon the nerve to dive in you find it perfect in temperature and curiously silky in feeling.

But the moment at Kovalam I remember best recurs each day just before sunset, when the fishermen haul their boats onto the sand to the beat of a breathy chant, and the girls from the village go down to the water for their evening bath. They walk into the sea in their saris, duck in and out of the waves for a few minutes, and then in the last golden light of the sun they run up the beach laughing and calling to each other, the wet folds of their clothes sculptured against their bodies, arms raised to wind their hair back into place. They return to the village in an incomparably lovely procession.

I have often been back to Kerala and the Malabar coast since that long-past journey. For all its beauty, it has

never, somehow, given me again that first heady sense of
wonderment.

A trip to Kerala might begin at Bombay. There is
steamer service the length of the Malabar coast; a typical
segment, from Bombay to Panaji, costs about $30 a per-
son for a deluxe cabin. The steamer leaves from New
Ferry Wharf, Mallet Bunder, Bombay, at 10 A.M. and
arrives in Panaji at 8 A.M. the following day. From June
to September, the monsoon season, service is sus-
pended. For schedules and fares, telephone **Moghul
Lines,** Bombay 864-071.

PORTS OF CALL
PANAJI
The Fort Aguada Beach Resort, Sinquerim,
Bardez, Goa (telephone: 3401 and 2184), is built
within the ramparts of a seventeenth-century Portuguese
fort. Double rooms are about $55 to $65 for a room with
a terrace and a private view.

Hotel Oberoi Bogmalo Beach, Bogmalo, Dabo-
lim, Goa (2191, 2192 and 2510), has double rooms for
about $60. Facilities include a swimming pool and
health club.

Velha Goa is easily accessible from Panaji. Guide
service and car rental can be arranged through the major
hotels or through local tourist information offices; the
daily rate for a car and driver is about $25 to $30. Allow most of a day to visit Velha Goa's churches and
other monuments.

COCHIN
Cochin, the chief commercial town of the state of Kerala, is a convenient base for exploring the Malabar

coast. A good way to begin is with a cruise around the harbor and islands that make up Cochin; boats leave the old port at 9 A.M. and 2 P.M. and can also be boarded at Willingdon Island at 9:20 A.M. and 3:20 P.M. The trip takes about three and a half hours and costs about $1.

Recommended hotels are the **Malabar Hotel,** Willingdon Island, Cochin (6811), and the **Sealord,** Shanmugham Road (32682), both of which have double rooms for about $30 and suites for about $55. The Malabar has two swimming pools; both hotels offer boat tours of the quiet backwaters that wind among wooded islands.

ALLEPPEY

The seaport of **Alleppey,** about fifty miles down the coastal road from Cochin to Trivandrum, is a popular side trip from either city. The town has many canals, on which an annual Snake Boat Race takes place. The race, which is part of the harvest festival of Onam, takes place on the second Saturday in August each year.

TRIVANDRUM

A few miles out of the center of town is one of South India's best known resorts, the **Kovalam Ashok Beach Resort** (P.O. Vizhinjam, Kovalam, Trivandrum 695522, Kerala; 303-110), overlooking Kovalam Bay. Double rooms are about $45, suites about $65. Amenities include two swimming pools, a health club, a yoga and massage center and a beachfront restaurant and bar. *Kathakali* performances can be arranged on request.

SPICY FARE

Most hotels serve both Continental and Indian food; a dinner for two averages about $10 to $20. Western fare tends to be predictable, but there are many regional specialties of more than casual interest.

South Indian food is highly spiced. Seafood is widely served, especially succulent king prawns. Goan cuisine includes a number of pork preparations, among them a peppery pork-and-liver sausage called *chourisam*, *sorpotel*, a pickled pork casserole, and *baffat*, a pork (or beef) curry with radishes. The local spirit, *feni*, is distilled from coconuts or cashews; it has been compared to vodka in flavor and effect.

Kerala food emphasizes seafood, hot curries and dishes flavored with coconut. The local drink, toddy, is a sort of coconut beer. Try *appam*—a rice and coconut pancake, fermented with toddy and baked in a clay pot.

Eight Historic Capital Cities

WILLIAM K. STEVENS

OUT IN THE COUNTRY, half an hour's drive southeast of Connaught Place, the center of Delhi, the massive ruin of an old walled city called **Tughlakabad** sprawls across a rocky escarpment, its ramparts and bastions soaring mightily into the sky, dominating everything for miles around.

There are ruins and there are ruins. This one, stark and powerful, dwarfs the medieval forts of Europe that are its contemporaries. The Tower of London could fit into one corner. Here, Tughlakabad seems to say, lived great people doing great things.

But what people and what things? What armies marched from here? What palace intrigues took place? What loves and hates? What cruelties and kindnesses? What did the children look like who played in the streets whose grids are still traceable in the sparse grass that grows where twentieth-century cows graze and only monkeys live?

Many of the answers are lost or hard to find, and few people really take the trouble to look. Yet once, this magnificently silent place was Delhi, all the living Delhi there was, the third in a series of eight separate cities that over the centuries have coalesced into the modern metropolis. Tughlakabad was the first home of a dynasty that lasted nearly a hundred years, of kings and conquerors who ruled this part of the world when it gave rise to empires and cultures whose accomplishments rivaled and sometimes surpassed any in the West at the time. Almost anywhere else it would stand out.

But in Delhi, where a century is not a long time and the sweep of Indian history is traceable in literally thousands of artifacts, ruins, and inhabited neighborhoods dating back 500 years, 1,000 years, 2,500 years, and where greater and more incandescent empires and civilizations than that of the Tughlaks have risen and fallen, and Delhi with them, Tughlakabad is a weaker star—an especially poignant reminder of how transient and perishable are fame, glory and even memory.

It is a good place to begin a tour of Delhi, not only because Tughlakabad provides an immediate sense of humility and perspective, but also because it offers an introductory panorama of a Delhi that is far richer, bigger, more varied and more powerful than any of its past incarnations.

On one of those glowingly fresh, cool days that can occur any time from October to April but especially in the fall and early spring, when the air is like crystal and Delhi seems as pristine as it must have been when civilization first came to India 5,000 years ago, it is well worth the short climb to Tughlakabad's topmost tower.

From there, stretching as far to the north as you can see, is all of Delhi, soft and lush from this vantage point, thickly carpeted by the thousands of trees that make it one of the greenest cities in the world, studded here and there by high-rise buildings, a world metropolis with at least six million inhabitants, twice as many as lived there twenty years ago.

Through the centuries Delhi has grown and contracted, risen and fallen, flourished and nearly disappeared; it has been conquered, sacked, burned, abandoned, rebuilt and repopulated so many times as to mock American urbanologists who foresee permanent disaster in every flutter and fluctuation of their young cities' fortunes.

Every era of Indian history is reflected in some way in the city, although the 5,000-year-old Indus Valley of the Harappans' culture, one of the cradles of human civilization, is represented only in museum exhibits. More strongly represented are the Mauryan empire, which reached a brilliant zenith under the Emperor Ashoka, an early apostle of nonviolence, in the third century B.C.; and the Gupta empire, under which India led the world in art, literature and science, and Indian thinkers invented the decimal system, while Europe slept through the Dark Ages. Later came the Moguls, the great builders who gave the world such buildings as the Taj Mahal, and whose imprint on Delhi is strongest; the British; and finally, Gandhi, Nehru and the independence movement.

Tracing these eras offers a ready-made focus and organizing framework for exploring Delhi. By the time you've finished, you will also have been unavoidably immersed in the dynamic, colorful, sometimes disturbing city as it is today. Some elementary reading of Indian history is helpful. And it is best to tour the city by car. Allow three or four days to avoid rushing too much, but the visit can easily be tailored to individual wishes.

One plan is to begin in the south, where what remains of the first four cities of Delhi, dating from the eleventh to the fourteenth centuries, is situated. These are **Lal Kot,** built about 1060, in the last of the Delhi citadels of the medieval Rajputs; **Siri,** built in the eleventh century by one of the early Moslem sultans of Delhi; **Tughlak-abad,** constructed during the 1320s by Ghiyasuddin Tughlak, founder of the dynasty of Moslem sultans who ruled northern India during most of the fourteenth century, and **Jahanpanah,** built by his son.

None of the eight historic cities of Delhi is inhabited today except the last two. It is not necessary to visit all the earlier ones. Besides Tughlakabad, it is useful to see Lal Kot because nearby is the Qutab Minar, a 237-foot-high, red-fluted victory tower, visible for miles across the flat Delhi landscape. In the courtyard of a nearby mosque stands a celebrated relic of Gupta times, a 22-foot-high iron pillar inscribed with a victory testimonial. Having stood without rusting since the fifth century, it is considered a tribute to the metallurgical skill and, by extension, to the general scientific and technical accomplishments of the Guptas.

All that remains today of the fifth city of Delhi, called **Ferozabad,** built in 1354, is a great pile of rubble, stone and crumbling reddish walls near the banks of the Yamuna River, a little east of present-day Connaught Circle. The Tughlak emperor who built Ferozabad, Feroz Shah, a builder and preserver who ruled over one of Delhi's historic peaks of prosperity, brought to his new city one of the famous Ashoka pillars. The earlier Mauryan emperor had placed stone columns throughout his realm on which were inscribed edicts that set forth his pacifist Buddhist ethical code and a record of his times. It took 8,400 men at a time to drag this particular pillar from its original spot about 120 miles north of Delhi in a wheeled cradle of wet silk and skins. The Ashoka pillar stands there today, gray and smooth, crowning the diminishing ruins of Ferozabad (now called Feroz Shah Kotla), speaking out on behalf of nonviolence, tolerance and the Buddhist ethic across nearly 2,300 years.

Less than fifty years later, Timur, or Tamerlane, swept down from Samarkand across northern India and into Delhi. He put much of the city to the torch and sword, and by the time he left after less than a year's stay, it is said, not a bird moved in the wake of the death, famine and epidemic he left behind. There is no monument in Delhi to that.

For more than two centuries the Moslem Moguls ruled as a conquering minority in a Hindu land, as often as not through force and fear. Roughly during the time of the Tudors and Stuarts in England, the Mogul empire reached a peak in art, literature and particularly architecture. They left northern India, and especially Delhi, strewn with tombs, forts and cities in the distinctive Indian-Islamic style, with its ever-present domes, whose most famous expression is considered to be the Taj Mahal in Agra. (The Mogul capital shifted from Delhi to Agra and back.)

The second of the Mogul emperors, Humayun, built the sixth city of Delhi on the banks of the Yamuna, just south of Ferozabad. Little remains now except the crumbling walls of what is called the Old Fort, a mosque and an octagonal tower of red stone atop a grassy hill. From the top of the tower (care is required; there are no guardrails) is a fine view of New Delhi, as well as an unusual perspective on the first of the Mogul architectural masterpieces, **Humayun's tomb.** A precursor of the Taj, it is done in red and white, and some people consider it even finer and more delicate than the Taj.

But the centerpiece of the Mogul era, and one of the most spectacular and popular places to visit, is the seventh city of Delhi, in the northern part of the metropolitan area.

Built by the Mogul Shah Jahan (Emperor of the World), who also built the Taj, it was called **Shahjahanabad** when completed in the seventeenth century. Today it is called the walled city or simply **Old Delhi.** Indian life, as it was lived both in Shah Jahan's time and now, bubbles constantly along **Chandni Chowk,** an avenue of indescribable clutter whose shops, stalls, crowds and tiny, crooked alleys make it a very model— not pleasant in all ways but certainly juicy—of the Indian bazaar. The best way to appreciate Chandni Chowk and its neighborhood is simply to plunge in on foot (but watch your wallet), by tricycle rickshaw or in the two-wheeled horsecart called a *tonga.*

Two major attractions dominate Old Delhi: the **Jama Masjid,** the largest mosque in India, and the immense **Red Fort.** Shah Jahan had it built of brick-colored sandstone to enclose his inner citadel and palaces. Old Delhi and the Red Fort fairly reek with historical associations. Not to be missed is the evening sound-and-light show inside the Red Fort, tracing the history of Old Delhi with candor and humor. By day the fort crawls with visitors. Levitators, snake charmers and animal acts help entertain them.

After the 1857 rebellion against the British, Delhi again sank into stagnation, not to be fully resuscitated until the British moved their imperial capital here from

Calcutta in 1911. The eighth city of Delhi is, of course, **New Delhi,** the geographical center of the metropolis; the New Delhi of the British and the architect Sir Edwin Lutyens; of elegant flat-roofed bungalows and gardens; of embassies and avenues and concourses; of pink-tinged Government buildings whose imperial majesty differs from, but rivals, that of the Mogul monuments.

While in this area, it is convenient to stop at the **National Museum,** near the corner of Rajpath and Jan-path, to look at Harappan artifacts and Mauryan and Gupta sculpture.

No trip to Delhi is complete without a visit to the site where the Mahatma was cremated, the **Raj Ghat** on the banks of the Yamuna just north of Ferozabad. Or to the **Gandhi National Museum** nearby, where his say-ings, photographs and memorabilia of his life—includ-ing the bloody robe he wore the day he was assassinated and one of the bullets that killed him—are on display. One whole gallery is devoted to a grisly but moving pho-tographic essay on peace and nonviolence. Or, espe-cially, to **Birla House** in New Delhi, once the home of an industrialist where Gandhi spent the last 144 days of his life. It is now a national museum. The room from which Gandhi walked to his death in the garden of Birla House is preserved much as it was, with the Mahatma's sleeping pallet and spinning wheel. Every day, a fresh flower is placed there. Red-painted footprints mark the path to the spot where Gandhi was shot as he was on his way to pray; a modest column marks the spot itself.

Teen Murti House, the residence of Nehru during his years as Prime Minister, has also been preserved as a museum. But the evening sound-and-light show there, while informative, is a little too uncritically adoring of the Pandit for some tastes.

There is a ninth Delhi, of very recent origin, unre-
marked and uncelebrated. But it is important to an understanding of where India has come to today, in its very
short (by Indian standards) life as a modern, independent nation that began in 1947. This is the Trans-Yamuna
area, across the river from the capital, where colony
upon colony of rude brick-hut settlements stretch away
across the flatlands to the east. In block after block of
undrained dirt streets full of children and often fouled by
human waste, where basic urban services and amenities
are few or nonexistent, life in many ways is lived as it is
in the villages of the Indian countryside.

Many who dwell there come from Delhi's hinterland,
one of the poorest and meanest in the world. Migrants in
the classic pattern of seekers after opportunity and freedom the world over, they have been a major factor in the
growth of Delhi over the last two decades.

It is sobering evidence of the great challenges facing
India today. And it provides an essential element of perspective when, back in the hotel, you relax and savor the
extraordinary sense of participation in the endless chain
of human experience that can be the reward for a few
days of communing with India's past.

DEALING WITH DELHI
GETTING AROUND
Although bus tours of Delhi are available under the
auspices of the Indian Tourism Development Corporation, the Delhi Tourism Corporation and private operators, most visitors find that renting a car or hiring a taxi
at one of the better hotels is well worth the expense ($15

to $45 a day, depending on the make of the car) for the speed, privacy and flexibility that it affords. Insist on an English-speaking driver. Maps and guidebooks are readily available (ask in the hotel) and essential. No place in greater Delhi is much more than half an hour by car from Connaught Place or from most hotels, and most are closer than that. Metered taxis are also plentiful.

HOTELS

Delhi has some of India's best hotels. Rates and accommodations range from about $20 a night for a double room at a simple but clean establishment to about $480 a night for the Chandra Gupta Suite in the **Maurya Sheraton** (telephone: 370271), with two bedrooms, a sauna and a terraced garden. Single rooms at five-star luxury hotels generally cost between $45 and $85, doubles are between $55 and $95, and suites begin at about $85 and top out at more than $400. Among the better-known hotels in this range are the rambling old **Ashoka** (370101), with its decor that invokes both the Mogul emperors and the British Raj (and where you can book an elephant ride); **Claridge's** (370211), with its lawns and tennis courts, and the Mogul-style, marble-trimmed **Taj Mahal** (386162), **Taj Palace** (323500) and **Akbar** (370251). Those who wish to stay in the old city will choose **Oberoi Maiden's** (221591). The **Centaur** (391411) is near the Delhi International Airport.

RESTAURANTS

All the five-star hotels have restaurants specializing in Western fare. The **Casa Medici** in the Taj Mahal serves Italian food, for example, while the **Supper Club** at the Ashoka serves French specialties and the **Taksila** in the Maurya Sheraton offers French, Italian and Spanish dishes. A dinner for two, without drinks, should cost between $15 and $30.

But the regional fare should also be sampled. One of Delhi's specialties is *tandoori* food—especially chicken—which is cooked in a *tandoor* or clay oven; the **Bukhara Restaurant** in the Maurya Sheraton serves a good version. Kashmiri food, centered around spicy lamb dishes, is available in the **Mayur Restaurant** of the same hotel. The Taj Mahal Hotel's **Haveli Restaurant** has Peshawari food—which includes lamb and chicken dishes—and Moglai food, again based upon lamb, but dressed with a variety of elaborate and subtle sauces. The **Peacock Restaurant** at the Ashoka has a wide range of similar northern Indian dishes. Dinner for two, without drinks, should cost from $15 to $25 at any of these.

The largely vegetarian food of southern India can be sampled at the **Dasaprakash Restaurant** in the Ambassador Hotel and the **Woodlands Restaurant** in the Lodi Hotel. Try the fried rice-and-lentil pancakes called *dosas*, which can be eaten plain or stuffed with curried potatoes and onions. A stuffed *dosa* costs less than $1. *Thalis*—individual stainless-steel platters— holding portions of *pappadams* (a crisp fried wafer), *puris* (deep-fried puffs of whole-wheat bread), curried vegetables, yogurt, rice, pickles and lentils cost about $3 each.

The outdoor **Moti Mahal** restaurant near the Red Fort is renowned for its *tandoori* chicken. Butter chicken, a rich and messy variant best eaten with the fingers, is the specialty at the smaller **Pindi** and **Have More** restaurants in the Pandara Park Market. Meals at any of these should cost between $8 and $12 for two, again without drinks; none is notable for spanking clean tablecloths.

SHOPPING

The best choice of traditional arts and crafts is to be found just off Connaught Place, on a three-block stretch of **Baba Kharak Singh Marg,** where twenty shops maintained by as many state and territorial governments offer a variety of wares from all over India, including areas few tourists ever visit. A stroll through the state emporia turns up such unusual merchandise as the intricate depictions of tantric symbols and gods and goddesses done by village women in and around the village of Madhubani (**Bihar Emporium;** prices range from about $1 to more than $100, depending on size); brightly colored oil paintings on cloth (**Orissa Emporium,** $1 to $280); ornate and heavily gilded Tanjore paintings on glass from southern India (the **Karnataka, Tamil Nadu** shop; $16 to about $230), and Rajasthani miniatures on old paper (about $22 to $90) or ivory ($28 and up, depending on size and quality).

Fabrics are also abundant, from silk saris (many shops, many prices) to quilted bedspreads from Assam (about $20 for a double-bed size), Gujarati cushions ($1 to $6) and woolen shawls embroidered with a typical Naga spear motif ($16 to $28).

Two blocks away is the three-story **Central Cottage Industry Emporium,** a Government-run craft department store offering carpets, antiques, furs and artwork from all parts of the country. If your Delhi shopping time is limited, the store represents a selection of the goods available at all the state emporia. Prices are fixed both here and in the state shops, and can provide a standard for the goods offered by independent merchants. If you prefer to bargain, try the scores of little shops along Janpath. The better stores in this row are the Tibetan shops that sell chunky jewelry and ornamental bracelets. Another area to visit for jewelry is Chandni Chowk, in the old walled city of Delhi. It is very crowded but has a history of centuries of silverwork. Here, as in other congested areas of the city, Western visitors may be both harassed and disturbed by the beggars who congregate around them. The best practice in such circumstances is to ignore them.

INFORMATION
The **India Tourism Development Corporation**

has offices in most luxury hotels (350331/352336). In New York, information is available from the **Indian Government Tourist Office,** 30 Rockefeller Plaza, 15 North Mezzanine, New York, NY 10112 (212-586-4901).

India's Royal Ghost Town

MICHAEL T. KAUFMAN

A FEW YEARS AGO, while I was in a hospital in New York, my then-eleven-year-old daughter wrote me from our home in India describing her first visit to Agra. In an attempt to cheer me up, she wrote: "When you tell people you've been to Agra, of course, they ask you about the Taj Mahal. It's always the Taj this and the Taj that. Now don't get me wrong, the Taj is really quite nice, it's okey-dokey, but there's a lot of other stuff around Agra and the most fun is this terrific old city called Fatehpur Sikri."

In due course I returned to India and traveled several times to Agra, and learned that my daughter was entirely correct. **Fatehpur Sikri,** a Mogul ghost town twenty-six miles from Agra, is for my money a much more stimulating attraction than the marble Taj.

It is not my purpose to bad-mouth the Taj, though I confess the sheer iconoclasm of such a notion has a certain appeal. But such a stance would be posturing. The Taj is extremely beautiful. It is every bit as beautiful as I thought it would be before I saw it. It is beautiful by moonlight. It is beautiful in morning mist. It is a great place to sigh languorously. One can admire the crafts-manship that went into the construction of the Taj Mahal and applaud the fixation of Shah Jahan, who built it over a period of eighteen years, between 1630 and 1648, as a tomb to commemorate his love for his first and fa-vorite wife, Mumtaz Mahal.

But if the Taj is for sighing languorously, then Fatehpur Sikri is for playing hide-and-seek and having picnics. It is an unpopulated royal city in excellent shape, with secret passageways, courtyards, pools, bridges and palaces. Older than the Taj, it was built more than 400 years ago by Akbar, the most ecumenical and enlightened of the Mogul emperors, and its sand-stone and marble architecture combines elements of Hindu style with the Mogul geometry that itself was mel-lowed by Sufi mysticism.

It is clearly a playful place. On one square a huge par-chesi board was built into the stone to permit courtiers to direct courtesans serving as living pieces. There is a wonderful filigreed building of five open stories that could only have been built as a place of recreation: for feeding pigeons and green parrots, flying kites and watching sunsets. It is still used for such activities. There is one building, the Ankh Michauli, where the Emperor is said to have played hide-and-seek with the women of his harem. But taken separately or viewed as a whole town, the groups of squares, pools and buildings have the majesty of medieval cathedrals while conveying the sense of a Mogul Disneyland.

Part of the charm of the place is in the approach to it

from Agra. You can cover the twenty-six miles by tourist bus, local bus or hired car. In any case the route goes through Agra, a large, dusty, usually hot and noisy city of more than a million people. The road passes narrow bazaar streets and the cantonment quarter, where air force officers occupy high-ceilinged bungalows surrounded by flowering shrubs.

But beyond the city's sprawl, the avenue becomes the quintessential Indian country road. It passes villages where in the warm season people live in front of their homes, chatting from their charpoys, or rope beds. People pray, eat, entertain and work in public view. It is as if the visitor were passing through living rooms and kitchens. Though at times the drive also seems to pass through bathrooms, this green country setting is much cleaner and more organized than the congested cities. Women mill grain. Children drive herds of buffalo to ponds where both beasts and youngsters wallow.

About halfway along the road, past a grove of fruit trees, is a settlement of bear wallahs, families who keep trained Himalayan bears. Wallah simply means person, and along the road, in addition to the bear wallahs, there will be buffalo wallahs, tea wallahs, possibly a camel wallah. The bear wallahs make their animals dance on their hind legs and beg from passersby. Usually there are about ten of the keepers and bears strategically positioned along the road.

A short distance past the bears one gets a first glimpse of Fatehpur Sikri, situated atop a low sandstone ridge that is the only elevation on the expansive plain. Here in 1569 Akbar built his capital. The legend is that the Mogul leader came here to visit a Moslem ascetic, Sheik Salim, who foretold the birth of Akbar's son, Salim. When the son was born, Akbar began to build the royal city near the cave of the ascetic, who is known as the Chishti saint. It is a good legend, but Akbar may also have been influenced by the commanding prospect that his walled city would have over the flat countryside.

Nevertheless, the Emperor lived in Fatehpur Sikri for only sixteen years. He shifted to Lahore to deal with discontent in the northwest and then moved back to Agra. His beautiful royal city, it seemed, had chronic water shortages.

In its glory Fatehpur Sikri must have been a glittering place indeed. In 1574, when Akbar was shifting his court between Agra and Fatehpur Sikri, which was still under construction, William Fitch, a British traveler and one of many foreigners welcomed by Akbar, described the life of the royal community:

"The King hath in Agra and Fatehpur Sikri, 100 elephants, 30,000 horses, 1,400 tame deer, 800 concubines and such other store of leopard, tiger, buffaloes, cocks and hawks that it is very strange to see. Agra and Fatehpur Sikri are very great cities, either of them much greater than London."

Today there remains only a settlement of a few thousand people, whose houses stretch down the hill from the monuments, palaces and the mosque on the crest. It is not a tourist town, and the townsfolk go about their business of selling goods to farmers in the area and caring for goats and buffalo. There is an active market within the old caravansary—a large enclosed square made of soft red sandstone—where the lower ranks dwelt. The shouts of peddlers still evoke the bawdy good humor of the people.

Through the market runs one of the roads to the Grand Mosque or **Jamma Masjid,** with its 176-foot-high victory gate looking out over the main road up to the citadel. The mosque itself is about 70 feet high and is said to be a copy of the Grand Mosque in Mecca, except that the pillars that enclose its three main chambers are carved in an elaborately ornamented Hindu style, with depictions of flower petals and animals, though no deities.

Throughout the city there are echoes of Akbar's tolerance and his attempt to create a state religion combining elements of several beliefs. The Emperor entertained Jesuit priests at his courts and enjoyed their debates. His chief minister, Birbal, was a Hindu, who is celebrated in India today in hundreds of children's stories that emphasize his quick wit and cunning.

At one end of the mosque square is the small marble **tomb of the Chishti saint.** The intricately carved marble screens around the small building have many bits

of thread tied to them. These are left by women who travel from all parts of the subcontinent to pray in hopes that they will conceive. The screens, which measure about four feet by eight feet, have designs in the shape of stars, crescents and curlicues carved into them.

Beyond the mosque area and separate from it on the northeast lip of the hill is the royal city itself, with more than twenty buildings ranging from huge palaces and barracks to jewellike structures whose functions are still being debated by historians. This is the area for aimless meandering or discreet games of hide-and-seek.

There are all sorts of discoveries to be made, such as the frescoes on the walls of the **house of Miriam,** the wife who bore the son Akbar had sought. The frescoes have been defaced over the years, apparently by Moslems who believed that they violated Islamic prohibitions against graven images. One fresco seems to contain the wings of angels and is thought by some scholars to depict the Annunciation.

In a splendid two-story building called the **house of Birbal,** said to have been built by the chief minister for his daughter, there are four rooms decorated with elaborate geometrical carvings. Marble screens, cupolas, pilasters, recesses and arched doorways combine in symmetrical profusion. The craftsmanship is awesome, but unlike the Taj Mahal the building has a lived-in appearance—though the activities there may only be imagined.

On the second floor are carved marble screens behind which the royal harem gathered to view the passing scene outside. There is a half-buried round boulder in the lawn, a large cloister and a conference hall known as the **Diwan-i-Am,** or hall of public audience. It is believed that the Emperor's killer elephant was tethered to the stone and that convicts were hurled into the courtyard and left to the animal's mercy. If they were trampled, it was proof of guilt; if they were ignored by the beast, they were considered innocent.

Such bits of information are hard to glean. At the entrance there are people representing themselves as guides, but their historical knowledge and mastery of English vary greatly.

Myth and fact blur in India. One wonderfully red-whiskered guide pointed to the Panch Mahal, the structure whose name means "Five Building," and said, "Panch Mahal, five stories." He held up his hand with fingers spread apart and counted: "One, two, three, four, five." It did not really add much to his customer's awareness, but the guide's beard alone was worth whatever he charged.

One recommendation, for those who like names and facts and want to know how tall whatever they are looking at is and when it was built, is to buy *A Handbook for Travellers in India, Pakistan, Nepal, Bangladesh and Sri Lanka*, edited by Prof. L. F. Rushbrook Williams and published by John Murray in London. It is fairly expensive at about $27, but the price is worth it, and its section on Fatehpur Sikri, as on all other sites, is far more thorough and intelligible than any local guide. Signs in English at some buildings provide basic data.

But beyond the knowledge that comes with facts there are also the intuitive powers of the traveler, for which no more is needed than open eyes. For me the two most memorable sites at Fatehpur Sikri are the two small buildings that border the parchesi court.

The first is the **Panch Mahal,** the five-story building with its higher tiers diminishing in size like a wedding cake. On the first floor are fifty-six carved pillars holding up the second floor; no two of these are alike. The pillars are about eight feet tall, and their capitals provide a cornucopia of symbols for graphic artists, including leaves, petals and braided cords. The capital of one shows elephants with interlaced tusks; some have human forms, such as that of a man gathering fruit from a tree.

At the top of the building is a cupola to provide shade. It is an excellent place to picnic, and it is recommended that one bring sandwiches and a thermos. Lolling under the cupola, watching the green parrots swoop and hearing them call in the late afternoon is a rare experience, and the pleasures of doing nothing recapture the spirit of the age.

The second delight is the **Diwan-i-Khas** or private audience hall, a square two-story building whose interior is dominated by an ornate, massive octagonal pillar rising from the center and forming a sort of bowl at the upper story. This bowl is reached by marble bridges from the four corners. Its function is as obvious as that of a seesaw. Akbar must have sat on silken cushions in this marble fruit bowl, chatting with his advisers and generals. Perhaps supplicants were led in to cringe on the floor below as the lengthening rays of the sun pierced the marble screens. If one lies in the fruit bowl, it becomes clear that this was a position from which to command.

AGRA AND FATEHPUR SIKRI TOURS

The **Indian Tourism Development Corporation** provides tours of Agra from New Delhi that offer a Fatehpur Sikri visit as an option. Because of its distance from town, Fatehpur Sikri is less frequently visited, and the relative solitude is a benefit for those who go: It is one of the few places in India where you can be virtually alone for several minutes.

WHERE TO STAY

Most travelers will choose to stay in Agra, where the **Mughal Sheraton** is the newest and most luxurious hotel. But there are many other hotels in all price ranges, and the Government guesthouse in Fatehpur Sikri provides clean, sparsely furnished rooms for about $7 a night.

THE COST

A taxi from Agra to Fatehpur Sikri and back costs about $25. The tourism corporation tour from Agra by air-conditioned bus for a two-hour visit to Fatehpur Sikri is less than $4. If one has the time, staying over and walking the alleys and courtyards of the Mogul ghost town in early morning is well worthwhile. —M. T. K.

ASIA AND THE PACIFIC

CHONGQING: THE INDUSTRIAL REVOLUTION COMES TO TOWN
Theodore H. White

TAIWAN'S RICH VARIETY
Fox Butterfield

WHERE EAST MET WEST
John Toland

THROUGH INDONESIA'S ARCADE OF MEMORIES
Bernard Kalb

SOUTH PACIFIC ISLAND HOPPING
Robert Trumbull

Chongqing: The Industrial Revolution Comes to Town

THEODORE H. WHITE

I SAW CHUNGKING for the first time more than forty years ago—a city of hills and mists, of grays and lavenders, two rivers shaping it to a point, and the cliff rising above me like a challenge.

I had landed, in 1939, on a sandbar airstrip in the Yangtze River, been carried up the cliff in a sedan chair borne by chanting coolies, and slept the first night in a Quaker hostel, which was to bombed out by the Japanese a few weeks after my arrival. Then I moved to the Press Hostel at the Ba Xian Middle School, which was to be my home for the next six years. From there I reported the palace politics of this capital of "Free China," our ally.

The sights and sounds enchanted me: the old walls that ringed the city, the peddlers at the gates, the hawkers clacking and yodeling in the streets, the night soil collected in slopping buckets to be shipped upriver to the peasants for fertilizer.

Not long ago I went back.

And it is all gone now, gone forever; the industrial revolution has wiped out the city of my memories. The sleepy river town, already swollen to 250,000 people when I first came, has exploded. The city that is now usually styled Chongqing has become one of the largest metropolitan areas in the world; within its suburban ring live 14 million people. The hills have been leveled, gullies filled, landmarks erased. Nothing remains—not city walls, nor night soil collectors, nor my old home at the Ba Xian Middle School. All cities change with time but to Chongqing the revolution has brought change with the speed of wings. It should be visited—not only because it is still the entryway to the unbelievable gorges of the Yangtze, soon to be reshaped by China's engineers, but because nowhere else can one sense so sharply the sweep and vitality of the Orient's industrial revolution.

Perhaps it was the joining at this point of the two ancient rivers—the Yangtze and the Jialing—that brought the most unsettling of China's revolutions here. Just as the confluence of the Allegheny and the Monongahela rivers made Pittsburgh the first center of American heavy industry, so the joining of the Yangtze and the Jialing makes Chongqing today the industrial center of deep interior China. The two rivers now bring down coal from the Jialing and iron ore from the Yangtze. Natural gas has been discovered nearby to fuel industry, and peasants have come off the fields to supply labor.

We used to divide Chongqing into "north bank,"

Chongqing: The Industrial Revolution Comes to Town

"south bank" and "city." "North bank" across the Jialing was largely scenery—crescent paddies of vivid green rice, where white ducks flecked the fields. "South bank" lay across the Yangtze, too steep to cultivate anything but vegetables. "City" was the walled peasant trading center at the point where the rivers married, shipping rice downriver and importing from downriver cloth, housewares and gadgets. From the "city" one reached either "north bank" or "south bank" by hiring a small sampan.

Today one reaches both banks by broad new bridges. A totally new railway (!) brings trains in punctually from the west, disgorging passengers into the tunnel under the bridges. When you emerge from the tunnel, an entirely new city is spread out before the eyes: unending apartment houses, the skyline spiked with smokestacks, crowned by the flamboyant vermilion and yellow spectacle of the huge Renmin Hotel, so outrageously gaudy, so Chinese, that it is magnificent. And the food there is very good—except for the breakfasts.

You cross the river to find the paddy fields of what was once the "north bank." The iron-and-steel complex there now employs 45,000 people; behind it sprawl the arsenals, for Chongqing is now third only to Shanghai and Manchuria as arms maker to China; behind them stretch the electronic and textile plants of the new city.

Searching for yesterday's past was an exercise in hopeless nostalgia. I drove up and down for two days trying to find the old Press Hostel of my youth. The Peking Foreign Office had tried for three days to find the reporters' capital of wartime "Free China." It could not. Not only have the shacks of "clay and wattles made" been erased, every memory or trace of it is gone.

I could recognize at sight only two spots in all this city

in which I had once made my home. First was the cramped, black-fronted Communist headquarters of Zhou Enlai, where I had so often been a visitor. I used to walk there over cobblestones on mud-slimed lanes. A broad boulevard now leads there and the old building has become a shrine, immaculately preserved, in the sandwich of Kuomintang spy centers that once watched it. I also recognized at sight the last remaining gate of the vanished city wall—the Dong Yuan Men, the "Gate Connecting with Distant Places." That has been left untouched as an archaeological reminder of the near and distant past. It is now a cobblers' passage; cobblers have again been allowed to tap shoes there, fit heels and soles, at bargain prices. Behind the gate is a twisting lane where old men still play cards, and a stall sells Chongqing dumplings that smell delightfully of the cooking of the past. A traveler should visit both.

Apart from these two spots, I recognized nothing. The old town had swollen to one of the world's ten largest cities because industry has its own suction and the suction had drawn in the peasants who could no longer live on the land.

During the war, I once employed such a peasant, just in from the fields, my "boy," Lao Chiang, who was perhaps twenty-eight or thirty years old. Brooks Atkinson (then a foreign correspondent for *The New York Times*) and I had shared his services. Which meant that he was up from seven in the morning (when he brought hot water for our shaving) until eleven at night (when he carried our dispatches to the filing office). Seven days a week. But social conscience had worked on us; we summoned Lao Chiang and told him Americans felt everyone should have one day of rest a week; we would begin by giving him every Wednesday afternoon for himself. He was

Chongqing: The Industrial Revolution Comes to Town

terrified at the news. He felt he was being fired from a good job. What should I do Wednesday afternoon? he asked timidly. We said: Enjoy yourself. He asked: How? I suggested he might go down to the river airstrip and watch the planes come in. The thought had not occurred to him before. He was back the next week: What should I do this afternoon? It was difficult to invent his recreation assignment each Wednesday, but we managed.

Now, of course, it would be different. Airplanes no longer land in the river. But there is a wide-screen movie house just up the road at Liangluko. No less than twenty-three movie theaters serve this population of 14 million, plus amusement parks, cultural museums, gardens; plus the party cell gatherings, or *dan-wei* meetings, which are scarcely amusing but constant. Plus, above all, the new department stores and shops where a Lao Chiang might entertain himself. If he survives, it is certainly better today for Lao Chiang than it was when I knew him. And better yet than it was ten years ago, when the Great Cultural Revolution swept Chongqing with its terrors, its anarchy of factions killing each other.

But the old Chongqing, with its smells of open urine channels, of opium, of oranges and flowers, with its blind and blinking beggars, is gone forever. These millions of uprooted peasants have been frog-jumped from the Middle Ages to the twentieth century. They make oscilloscopes, television monitors, radar. Technology is easily transferred or implanted. Politics are more difficult to enroot. And, since the peasants in their new apartments are still too ignorant to govern themselves, they toil dutifully in the grip of a party which itself is only beginning to learn how to govern an industrial society. These peasants are incomparably better off than when

Chongqing: The Industrial Revolution Comes to Town

first they were crowded off their fields, but their values are incomparably different from our own.

I left Chongqing at dawn on a handsome new tourist boat, after two days trying to recover a lost past. The hooting of boats on the Yangtze was the same; so was the morning fog; so was the swirl of the two rivers as they mingled at the point. But the river traffic control was new; so was the new *téléphérique* cable-car system that hauled people from river to cliff-top level; so were the paved roads by which I had driven to the river point. I had not seen a single rickshaw puller in two days; nor had I been able to order the spicy Sichuan duck for which the city was once famous.

It was futile, I realized, to have hoped to find anything the same; industry and Communism had erased my old home city; I knew I would see no boat-pullers in the clefts of the gorges as we sailed on downstream. This was a new China, with its own hidden turmoil of strivings and sufferings which I would understand only after time had passed.

Taiwan's Rich Variety

FOX BUTTERFIELD

WHEN I FIRST arrived in Taiwan as a graduate student in 1961, a friend suggested a bus trip along the island's precipitous East Coast Highway. For sixty miles the road is cut into the sheer face of marble cliffs 500 to 1,000 feet above the turquoise Pacific Ocean. It is a single lane wide, without protective guardrails. Riding on the outside of the bus, jammed with Taiwanese farmers carrying trussed live chickens and with tattooed aborigines from the mountains above us, I had the sensation of being on the world's most scenic roller coaster. Each turn on the serpentine road seemed to threaten a plunge over the edge. From time to time the track mercifully descended into narrow jungle-covered valleys, where we disembarked for a bowl of fresh pineapple or a drink of guava juice at small roadside stands made of split bamboo and woven straw matting.

Taiwan's Rich Variety

It was a ride I never forgot and I repeated it many times. The road is still there, but seldom taken by American tourists anymore. They are too busy visiting the People's Republic of China, one hundred miles across the Taiwan Strait.

I wouldn't argue against the American fascination with mainland China, forbidden territory for so long. But it's too bad that many tourists now overlook Taiwan. The scenery is among the most spectacular in Asia, with a chain of 10,000-foot-high mountains dominating the island. The food is arguably the best Chinese cuisine available anywhere, and the National Palace Museum in Taipei houses the world's largest and most important collection of Chinese art.

Taiwan lies on the regular flight path between Japan and Hong Kong for a dozen airlines. And thanks to recent relaxation by both the Nationalists and the Communists, you can visit Taiwan and China in a single journey without worrying about visa problems or about being detained as a spy. I have started in Taipei in the morning and ended up in Peking in the evening. Customs inspectors in Taiwan, if they notice stickers from Communist China on your baggage, are apt only to ask what conditions are really like on the mainland.

Passengers disembarking at Chiang Kai-shek International Airport will immediately detect another motive for visiting Taiwan. It is a showcase of the economic development that has made the countries of the Pacific Basin the fastest growing part of the world over the last two decades. When the Nationalists fled to Taiwan in 1949, per capita income was only $45 a year. But with the gross national product growing by an average of about 9 percent annually, income has now risen to nearly $2,500 a person, ten times the level in China. The eight-lane toll

Taiwan's Rich Variety

road from the airport to Taipei would make engineers in the United States proud.

On my most recent trip to Taiwan, I was startled to see long trucks ferrying Mercedes sedans to showrooms in Taipei for local business people made rich by the island's booming electronics industry. When I first lived in Taipei over twenty years ago, to study Chinese, the only cars belonged to American diplomats or a few senior Nationalist officials. The rest of us traveled by bicycle or pedicab, a foot-powered conveyance. On rainy days, I often hailed the pedicab driver stationed on the narrow street near my one-story house. Pedicabs have long since become extinct, and my house has been replaced by a high-rise apartment building.

A good first stop on any tourist's itinerary in Taiwan is the **National Palace Museum,** nestled in a valley a fifteen-minute taxi ride north of Taipei. It houses some 600,000 objects assembled over the centuries by China's emperors. When the Japanese invaded China, in the 1930s, the Nationalist Government packed the collection in 5,000 crates and evacuated it to safety in the interior. In the late 1940s, when the Nationalists lost the civil war to the Communists, they shipped the crates to caves in a remote part of central Taiwan. The crates languished there until 1965, when the Government, accepting the fact that it would not soon recover the mainland, built a small museum near Taipei.

Recently the Government took another important step, opening a new wing that more than doubles the capacity of the yellow-and-green-tiled edifice. It can now show 20,000 pieces of art at a time from its holdings of ancient Shang dynasty bronzes and oracle bones, Tang and Sung landscape paintings, intricate calligraphic scrolls, Ming porcelain and jade carvings. Communist China has the Forbidden City in Peking and the spectacular tomb with an army of 2,000-year-old terra-cotta warriors at Xian. But no museum on the mainland can rival the comprehensive holdings of Taipei's.

Allow at least a morning for a tour of the museum, which is open seven days a week. Taxis are readily available for the drive back into town, but it is a good idea to have someone at your hotel write down the address, in both Chinese and English. Few cab drivers speak English, and differences between Chinese and English nomenclature can cause unexpected problems. For example, the President Hotel, for years one of the best in Taipei, in Chinese is called the Tung-yi, or Unity. Following imperial tradition, it was considered insulting in Chinese to have a hotel named the President when Chiang Kai-shek was President.

When I lived in Taiwan in the 1960s, a Chinese professor with epicurean leanings helped some foreign students set up a small association to sample the best local restaurants. Taipei was unusual, he explained, because unlike cities on the mainland, where restaurants traditionally served only the food of their own region, Taiwan had benefited from the hegira of the Nationalists. Army officers and Government officials from throughout the mainland had brought their cooks with them when they retreated to Taiwan. Even more fortunately, many of these chefs were from Sichuan, the normally isolated province in southwest China that the Nationalists had made their headquarters in World War II. These accidents of history, combined with Taiwan's sudden affluence, have led to an explosion of new restaurants. According to one informal count, Taipei has over three hundred eating establishments serving the peppery cuisine of Sichuan alone.

Taiwan's Rich Variety

Most Chinese and foreigners I know think the restaurants on Taiwan are better than those in China. With its
superior transportation system, Taiwan offers fresher ingredients, and socialist cooks on the mainland have less
economic incentive to delight their customers.

It is no longer possible to sample all the good restaurants in Taipei, as it was twenty years ago, but here are
three personal favorites.

For Sichuan cooking, try the **Chi-yuan,** 512 Tun
Hua South Road (telephone: 708-3111). The restaurant
is in the basement, decorated in modern international
style with mirrors and whitewashed walls. For a spicy
treat, try the fish fragrance eggplant. The name does not
mean fish is used in the recipe, merely that the dish is
prepared as the Sichuanese serve fish—with a blend of
ginger, onions, garlic, vinegar and chilies. Dry-fried
string beans are also excellent, as are the chicken and
shrimp in the _gong bao_ style, stir-fried with dried hot
pepper.

For northern Chinese food, the **Tien Chu** (“Heavenly Chef”), on the third floor of 1 Nanking West Road
(563-2380), is a reliable choice. Among its specialties
are crisp onion rolls, tiny tender peas with slivers of
chicken, salty shrimp balls and Peking duck. If you
must have sweet and sour pork, this is the place to do it,
but don't expect the usual heavy, sweet concoction. Here
the meat is crisp and the sauce subtle.

The **Hunan** restaurant in the basement of the Ritz
Hotel, at 155 Min Chuan East Road (597-1234), proved
a delightful surprise, an elegant combination of Chinese
tradition and modernity. The walls are painted with ink-
wash landscapes of mountains and clouds, the floor carpeted with a thick, red rug and the tables set with
handsome red-and-white porcelain emblazoned with cal-

ligraphy in an archaic script. Each table is decorated with a red candle and a red rose in a thin-stemmed vase. The slender waitresses wear cheongsams, the close-fitting Chinese dress with a high Mandarin collar and slit skirt. At lunch the restaurant provides a demonstration of the old-fashioned art of noodle making, now largely forgotten. A chef tosses a single batch of dough into the air repeatedly, each time pulling the dough and skillfully separating it into more and more strips until—presto!— noodles emerge. At night a musician plays the Chinese form of the zither, a soft, lilting sixteen-stringed instrument.

Especially good is the Viceroy Tso chicken—delicate chunks of boneless chicken fried in vinegar, sugar and pepper. Noble ham—ham marinated in honey—is another Hunan dish. A house specialty is Peng-family bean curd, named after the chef who introduced Hunan cooking to Taiwan and who has since moved to New York. The tender bean curd is cooked with green garlic, leeks, peppers, shredded pork and pungent black beans. Instead of rice, try the silver thread rolls, either steamed or fried.

The **Ritz Hotel** is another sign of the new affluence and sophistication that have swept Taiwan. A small hostelry by current standards, with only 220 rooms, it has chosen to prohibit tour groups and cater instead to individual travelers. Stanley Yan, the hotel's president, who learned both English and the tourist business working for American Express, has been imaginative in creating a sense of intimacy. He has scrapped the usual reception counter, substituting two small, polished wooden desks where arriving guests merely sign their names. The hotel's telephone operators have been carefully trained to use a guest's name each time he or she calls, and all rooms are supplied with not only the usual fruit baskets but also stationery and name cards imprinted with the guest's name. Another thoughtful touch is the double-thick windows, a barrier against the tropical sun and the noise of Taipei's traffic. The decor is French Art Deco. My room had a muted gray carpet, a soft gray plush couch, pink drapes and a gray and pink bedspread.

For travelers tired of Chinese food—if that is possible—the Ritz has a remarkable French restaurant, called **Paris 1930,** with a chef from Paris. The **Brasserie,** another eating place in the hotel, is a good spot to watch Taiwan's leading movie and television stars have a late breakfast or an evening drink.

After a day or two in Taipei for visiting the museum and enjoying Chinese food, it is refreshing to get out of town, for Taipei is ugly, smog-shrouded and snarled with traffic jams.

My favorite trip remains the East Coast Highway, running from **Hualien** to **Suao.** You can fly to Hualien in the morning, make the three-hour bus trip along the cliffs and return to Taipei from Suao by train in the afternoon.

A spectacular and slightly less hair-raising alternative is to start from Hualien but head up the **Taroko Gorge,** a twelve-mile ravine cut through walls of marble. At the western end of the gorge, set in a verdant valley 1,500 feet above sea level, is the **Tien-Hsiang Lodge,** a small hotel and restaurant done in Chinese style. It is a pleasant place to spend the night, with paths for walking and taking in the mountain view.

Another possibility is to continue from Tien-Hsiang on the East-West Cross-Island Highway, which winds up and down mountain peaks that look like scenes out of an old Chinese landscape painting, all green and covered with mist. The road, which took the lives of 450 workers during its construction, climbs up to 10,743 feet before descending back down to the city of Taichung on the flat, western side of the island. The journey from Taichung to Taipei involves either a short plane ride or a lovely trip on Taiwan's efficient railroad. Allow two days to make the cross-island drive, and ask your hotel in Taipei to book you tickets on the Golden Horse bus, which provides air-conditioned, express service.

The less adventuresome or those more pressed for time can make pleasurable day excursions by taxi from Taipei. One drive takes you from the city up to **Yangming Mountain**, the peak overlooking Taipei, and then down the back side, past steeply terraced rice paddies and old brick farmhouses with slanting roofs, to the ocean at Chin-Shan. From there a coastal road curves around the island's northern tip to Tanshui and back to Taipei. The drive should take two to three hours.

Any of these trips will suggest why the Portuguese, who in 1590 were the first Europeans to sight Taiwan, called it Ilha Formosa, the beautiful island.

TAIPEI HOTELS OF EASE AND STYLE

The **Grand Hotel** (telephone: 596-5565), 1 Chungshan North Road, Section 4, an intriguing attempt to use imperial Chinese architecture for a hotel, with giant red columns and a slanting roof, situated on a hill overlooking Taipei. A double room is about $75.

Lai Lai Sheraton (321-5511), 12 Chung Hsiao East Road, Section 1, perhaps Taipei's trendiest hotel. It is a copy of the model originated by the architect and developer John Portman, with glass-walled elevators, waterfalls and rooms arranged around a large central atrium. About $90 for a double.

The **President** (595-1251), 9 Teh Hwei Street, the first of Taipei's good modern hotels, built in the 1960s and long popular with visiting American business travelers. Doubles are about $80.

The **Ritz Hotel** (597-1234), 155 Min Chuan East Road, a smaller, elegant hotel in the European manner with impeccable service. Doubles from about $90.

For further information, contact the **Taiwan Visitors Association** in New York, Suite 8855, 1 World Trade Center, New York, NY 10048 (212-466-0691).

—F.B.

Where East Met West

JOHN TOLAND

T HE REGION WITHIN 50 air miles of the city of Nagasaki—half the size of Connecticut but blessed with more than 700 islands and a shoreline of 2,500 miles—is not only unsurpassed, to my mind, in its varieties of natural beauty, but also rich in a history common to both Japan and the West. As the gateway through which both Chinese culture and Western civilization were introduced into Japan, Nagasaki became the window to the outside world.

Soon after Japan was discovered by European explorers in 1543, a long procession of missionaries and traders appeared from the West, and by the early seventeenth century the Portuguese, Dutch, British and Russians had established trading firms and settlements on the hills overlooking Nagasaki Harbor. The entire area was so marked long ago by alien dress, food, language, archi-

Where East Met West

tecture, religions and customs that today it retains many vestiges of this early contact with foreigners.

Ever since I had read *Silence,* Shusaku Endo's profound novel of Christian martyrdom in this region, I had wanted to explore those historic sites where East and West clashed so dramatically and tragically from the sixteenth century to August 9, 1945. I had interviewed survivors of the second atom bomb for *The Rising Sun,* and later for *Gods of War,* which comes to a climax in Nagasaki in August 1945. And so in late September 1982, my wife, Toshiko, and I set out to do some research and also to follow the trail of the early visitors from the West.

We stayed first at an old traditional inn, the Suwaso, lost in Nagasaki's maze of narrow, hilly streets. Along with other historic structures in the old part of the city, the inn had been providentially protected from the bomb by hills, and we were led into the serene world of the old Japan: Quiet solitude was the hallmark of the Suwaso, a landmark that has unfortunately closed since our visit, and the only thing seen of other guests were slippers outside their doors.

At the Kagetsu restaurant in the Maruyama area, the evening entertainment quarter of Nagasaki for three and a half centuries, the kimono-clad woman who led dinner guests into a huge room proudly pointed out a gash in an ancient wooden post made early in the seventeenth century by a famous swordsman. There were no street noises, only the soothing susurrus of a running brook, as one ate looking out upon a delicately landscaped, hilly garden. It was a scene as Japanese as a Toyokuni woodcut, but that guests sipping tea in an antechamber might enjoy in Western-style comfort—in a chair.

The meal opens with a traditional Nagasaki dish, a soup containing every edible part of a fish, indicating

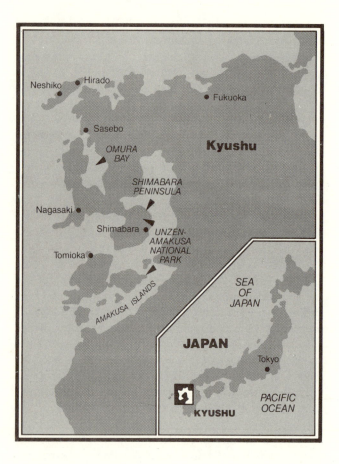

Neshiko
Hirado
Fukuoka
Sasebo
OMURA BAY
Kyushu
SHIMABARA PENINSULA
Nagasaki
Shimabara
UNZEN-AMAKUSA NATIONAL PARK
Tomioka
AMAKUSA ISLANDS

SEA OF JAPAN

JAPAN
Tokyo
KYUSHU
PACIFIC OCEAN

the host has used everything in the kitchen for his guests (the guest is required in reciprocation to eat every bit of the soup before the meal can continue). But the dishes that follow, this being Nagasaki, include, in addition to classically Japanese delicacies, a tasty Dutch stew and fish prepared Portuguese style.

A further exploration of the West's influence on Nagasaki might well begin with the site of Dejima, a fan-shaped artificial island built in 1636 to prevent the propagation of Christianity by restricting first the Portuguese and then the Dutch to the narrow precincts of the island. Today the area has been reclaimed, and the only evidence of the past is a small open-air historical site, featuring a huge, painstakingly accurate model of Dejima, set in a large pool, that manages to bring the former island, and its purpose, vividly to life. A block away, a ramshackle wooden structure haphazardly displays treasures of the past—ship models, charts, globes, records and pictures—and dolls illustrating the costumes and customs of the Dutch inhabitants of Dejima.

Nearby is a former foreign neighborhood much more evocative of the past, the Dutch Slopes. Today the old colonial-style wooden houses, built in the latter part of the last century with blinds and mantels, remain authentic memorials to the Oranda-san (Hollanders), who insisted on bringing along to Japan not only their food but also their architecture. By chance one evening we came upon a much more recent memorial to the Dutch, the creation of a Japanese who, fifty years ago, built a restaurant, the Ginrei, as he imagined the Dutch would have done it. He furnished the place with Dutch antiques and a mass of knickknacks, among them a great wheezy music box, and serves Western food. It looks like a stage setting and, in fact, was once used in a French movie.

On the morning we left Nagasaki to begin investigating the surrounding area, we decided to take a quick look at the city's answer to Williamsburg, the Meiji Village. A re-creation of the graceful late-nineteenth-century era shaped by the man now known as Emperor Meiji, the restoration covers roughly eight acres. Some of the old buildings have been moved from other parts of the city, but they have been replaced with such skill and taste that they appear to have been there always. Even the faithful reconstruction of the Mitsubishi No. 2 Dock House building, originally located at the great shipyards across the harbor, did not seem out of place. Built in 1896 as a dormitory for officers and supervisors of foreign ships brought in for repairs, it houses a large collection of photographs, paintings and models of the ships repaired over the years by what we now know as the Mitsubishi conglomerate.

At the end of the grounds a spacious museum displays all the colorful dragons, stage properties and extravagant floats of the Kunchi Festival, held October 7 to 9 every year at the nearby Suwa shrine. At the museum a half-hour movie of the highlights is shown continuously—the wild dragon dance, the wallowing wale float and a comic Dutch dance among them. This exciting, authentic festival, one of the best in Japan, is so popular that reservations for tickets and accommodations must be made well in advance.

The main attraction of the village, the Glover House, is admired by many tourists (inaccurately) as Madame Butterfly's abode. It was built in 1863 by Thomas Glover, a wealthy Briton nicknamed "the merchant of death" because he sold secondhand weapons used in Europe and the American Civil War to clans opposed to the Meiji regime, such as the Satsuma. Glover's residence,

Where East Met West

the oldest wooden Western-style home in Japan, lost none of its romance when it was recently landscaped, and I found it easy, if unhistorical, to imagine Cio-Cio San, babe in arms, waiting on the veranda for that miserable Pinkerton.

It was so early that we were almost the only tourists at the Meiji Village—except for several hundred Japanese middle-school students in their uniforms. Groups were clustered around, industriously sketching the old buildings for a school drawing contest and adding to our own enjoyment of the scene. My fear that the neighborhood had been turned into a tourist trap was groundless. The spirit of the early Meiji period has not been violated: The entire exhibit remains true to that vital epoch when Japan was energetically emerging from centuries of isolation and selectively acquiring useful elements from Western culture.

Our next goal, near the northwest tip of the island of Kyushu, was the port of Hirado, a thriving gateway to Japan for centuries because of its proximity to the mainland of Asia. Only forty-five air miles from Nagasaki, Hirado turned out to be a five-hour trip by car and ferry. The last leg of the trip by boat from Sasebo was a photographer's delight, as we weaved among a closely clustered group of islets called the Ninety-nine Islands. There are, in fact, some 170, all rising steeply from the water, giving the impression of neat, miniaturized intimacy. It is ineffably Japanese, particularly when seen against the nearby coastal background of terraced vegetable fields and rice paddies. Covered with subtropical evergreen plants and lined with narrow yellow beaches, the islands were a dramatic sight in the afternoon sun against the brilliant blue sea.

With only half a dozen passengers aboard the ferry,

we could scamper from side to side for views of the ever-changing scenery. Some of the islands were tiny and uninhabited; others were large, their inlets dotted with orderly lined buoys marking underwater fields of cultured pearl oysters. Passing through the narrow channels between islands we passed fishing boats. The women, in *mompei* (bloomerlike pants, loose at the hips and tight at the ankles, with slits on both sides of the waist), wore headgear that revealed only their eyes; they seemed to have stepped out of another century.

At our hotel in Hirado, the Ranpu, we donned *yukata,* the cotton informal kimonos provided by the hotel, and headed for the grand baths. There were two pools in the men's section, one of fresh water, the other salt, with a bale of seaweed added. The latter, explained the manager, was full of iodine and therefore medicinal. "Besides," he said, "it's a good gimmick." In the next room was a botanical garden with another freshwater pool for men. On the other side of a high wall was the women's botanical pool. I learned this was on a higher level: "The women can peek over at the men and not be peeked at," said the manager.

Next morning we went to the top of Hirado Castle, built in 1707 and faithfully reconstructed to its original form twenty years ago. Just below was spread the harbor, which had once been filled with the ships of rich and powerful pirates. These marauders had been followed by Portuguese and Spanish adventurers, and not long after by St. Francis Xavier and other Christian missionaries. Then had come the ships of the Dutch and British, bringing prosperity and new customs.

From our vantage point we could see some of the vestiges of the past. There was the Dutch Wall, made of flat stones and mortar composed of powdered shells, still in-

Where East Met West

tact after 338 years. Nearby is the Dutch Bridge, erected in 1702 for the Oranda-san by a Japanese mason. We could also see the steeple of the Catholic church built in memory of St. Francis Xavier, who called the Japanese "the joy of my heart," and just beyond it, ecumenically, a sprawling Buddhist temple hemmed in by lush greenery.

We later found the foreigners' cemetery, with the grave of Will Adams, the prototype of the English captain Blackthorne in James Clavell's *Shogun*. We then drove up the western coast on a mountain road of continuous charm, climbing to Kawachi Pass for an unforgettable view. On a clear day Korea is visible, but far more enjoyable was the pleasing vista of the island itself, with its terraced fields, rolling hills and rocky inlets.

There are scores of fine beaches for swimming. The one at Neshiko, with its white sands extending far into the indigo blue waters with colors subtly changing in the gentle waves, suggests a Turner painting. This beach is revered by local Christians because of the martyrdoms suffered there in the sixteenth and seventeenth centuries: Tens of thousands of Christians were killed all over Japan during that period, as the Bakufu, the central military government, attempted desperately to save the traditional Japanese way of life from creeping Western conversion and colonization.

One legacy of that cruel time can still be found throughout the Nagasaki area: the Hidden Christians, whose ancestors had gone underground by the thousands rather than apostatize. During more than 200 years of secret worship they developed their own form of religion, and many of their descendants still stubbornly cling to the rites passed down from generation to generation. Near the beach at Nashiko we found the recently opened

Hidden Christian Museum. In it there are small wooden images of Kannon, the Buddhist god of mercy (who has no sex), depicted as a woman in kimono holding a baby. Crosses have been carved on the backs of the images. To the Hidden Christians, these statues represented Mary and the Christ Child. Similar statues were placed on an altar located in the most inaccessible room of a home, and there the Hidden Christians covertly worshiped, taking the further precaution of putting a Shinto shrine above the fake Buddhist altar.

We left Hirado over a great red bridge, continuing south along the scenic shore of Omura Bay. After a leisurely four hours we branched off to the east onto the Shimabara peninsula, the scene of a great peasant-Christian rebellion that was crushed in February 1638. This not only ended the peasants' struggle against the landlords but helped bring to a halt the widespread Christian challenge to traditional beliefs and patterns of life in Japan.

After passing the seaside hot-springs spa of Obama, with every hotel along the way emitting clouds of steam, we turned inland onto a zigzag mountain road that brought us up to a famed hot-springs resort, Unzen, which lies atop an active volcano. From our room in the Miyazaki Inn we could see clouds of steam rising from more than thirty holes that spouted air and sulfurous gas.

Unzen had once been a resort almost exclusively for Westerners. In 1912 the second golf course in Japan (the first was in Kobe) was built for the hotel guests. The Japanese who did come here stayed at the Miyazaki, the sole traditional inn. A decade ago it was torn down and replaced by the present structure, which combines Japanese atmosphere with Western comfort. Its autograph

Where East Met West

book reads like a *Who's Who* of Japanese artists, Kabuki and film actors, authors, movie directors, painters, samisen and tea ceremony teachers, poets and singers.

Dinner that evening in our room, Japanese style, began with a collection of hors d'oeuvres, among them steamed dried bean curd and steamed chicken, followed by a delicately delicious soup called *dobin mushi*, served in an earthen teapot with Japanese mushrooms, gingko nuts, white bok choy (a cabbagelike vegetable), a delicate cake made of wheat gluten and sliced red snapper. Then came red snapper boiled with salt and broiled crayfish served with mayonnaise, followed by delectable tempura (prawns, Japanese mushrooms, eggplant and carrot).

Even at that, the best was yet to come—steamed flatfish with white soybean paste and vinegar; chopped pork boiled in soya; jellyfish with seasoned sea-urchin paste; steamed taro garnished with fresh chrysanthemum petals and boiled rice mixed with burdock; an array of pickles, and, as the pièce de résistance, a huge platter holding a whole red snapper (looking alive with head and fins intact) surrounded by slices of raw fish, shellfish and squid. It was by far the best seafood I had ever eaten.

In the morning we toured Unzen National Park, Japan's first national park, which is located on a high plateau dotted with lakes and waterfalls and replete with numerous hiking trails. The entire area is open year round: In spring, the mountains are covered with dazzling azaleas; in summer, with lush greenery; in autumn, with red foliage—except for the large stands of Japanese cedars—and in winter, with silver frost flowers.

A contrast to Hirado and Unzen was Amakusa, the

main island of the Amakusa chain, a place of rugged scenery and panoramic views from the tops of mountain roads. There, near the northern tip of the island, we came upon a genuine Meiji town, Tomioka. Formerly the capital of the Amakusa Islands, Tomioka seems to be forgotten, because of its isolation. But its narrow streets remain a treasury of wooden Meiji-period houses and shops, worn to a soft hue by years of wind and rain from the sea.

We saw no other tourists in Tomioka, and, as we drove to the airport over the five bridges that join the major Amakusa islands to Kyushu, it occurred to me that we hadn't seen a single Westerner once we had left the Nagasaki city limits. An easily accessible, relatively inexpensive area had been enjoyed during that week by few foreign visitors.

Our ten-day tour had made me determined to return to the region, to spend much more time exploring its mysteries and wonders. Just as we were passing through the last town, I had noticed a young girl wearing a sweater with this message in English: "Teenager—American dream." The West was still leaving its mark on this historical area. But the girl had a wistful look that was peculiarly Japanese; the twain had met, but East, fortunately, was still East.

GETTING THERE
From Tokyo, the Nagasaki region is most easily accessible by air. Direct flights are scheduled by All Nippon Airlines (three a day) and Toa Domestic Airways (two a

day). The flight takes about two hours and the fare is about $130 one way, or about $240 round trip.

STAYING THERE
NAGASAKI CITY

Since the Suwaso has closed, the Japan Travel Bureau recommends the **Sakamotoya**, 2-13 Kanaya-Machi (telephone: 26-8211), where room rates range from about $45 to $85 with two meals. The hotel is about a ten-minute walk from Nagasaki station.

The **Kagetsu** restaurant (22-0191) is a landmark of the Maruyama district, and is identifiable by an enormous lantern that hangs in front. Dinner runs about $65 a person, and parties of two to four people are preferred.

Ginrei (21-2073) is at 2-11 Kajiyacho. Dinner is about $30 a person, with two glasses of wine.

HIRADO

The **Ranpu Hotel** (3-2111) has rates of about $110 for a double room with two meals.

UNZEN

The **Miyazaki Inn** (3331) charges approximately $110 to $210 for a double room with two meals.

GETTING AROUND

Nagasaki, Unzen and the Ninety-nine Islands are included in various tours of Japan that depart from Tokyo; these are typically thirteen days long and cost about $1,400, a price that includes transportation, hotels and some meals. The Japan Travel Bureau has a group tour for foreigners to northern Kyushu, including Fukuoka, Beppu, Aso and Nagasaki. A trip of four nights and five days costs $675, including Japan National Railway Fare, hotels and some meals. Information can be obtained at the **Japan Tourist Board's**

foreign tourist section in Tokyo (276-7777). There are
no scheduled English-language tours limited to the
Nagasaki region itself.

The services of a Government-licensed, English-
speaking guide can be arranged through the **Japan
Guide Association** in Tokyo (213-2706), or through
travel agents. Such arrangements should be made before
arrival in Nagasaki; a full day's touring will cost about
$75. A hired car with a driver, which can be booked lo-
cally through hotels, costs about $11 an hour. Renting a
car to drive yourself is not recommended; roads can be
narrow and congested, there are few road signs (almost
none in English), and the Japanese drive on the left.

Most Japanese tourists visit the area's sights by
means of an efficient network of buses. Again, identifying signs are in Japanese, and the traveler will encounter few people who speak English. Hotels and local
offices of the Japan Travel Bureau can be helpful in
writing out destinations in Japanese, and otherwise
making arrangements for visitors to get from place to
place.

Through Indonesia's Arcade of Memories

BERNARD KALB

ALF A WORLD AWAY, a quarter of a century since my address was a side street in Jakarta, I still see, hear, live with an archipelago I never really left. Indonesia is all around me in my house in the suburbs of Washington, D.C. A carved *garuda* bird, discovered in Bali in the late 1950s, threatens to leap off a shelf in the living room. My ears fill with the purring voices of Jakarta every time my daughters call out to each other, using their Indonesian names and nicknames: Tanah, Sarinah, Mina, Siti. I light up one of my few remaining *kreteks*, the distinctive Indonesian cigarettes of tobacco and cloves, and the spicy smoke, wafting through the house like a kind of incense, rekindles memories of evening strolls through village *kampungs* on the islands of Java, Sumatra and Sulawesi.

Right now, a seductive magic pulls me closer to the

largest of the Indonesian paintings in our house. It is the work of the country's most famous artist, Affandi, a painting of Times Square, of all places, vivid, impressionistic, in brilliant colors. I bought it in Jakarta in the early '60s to ease my nostalgia for my own hometown of New York. Affandi had painted it during a visit to the United States. But now the colors, as though responding to my yearnings, seem to swirl mysteriously around the canvas; Broadway and 42nd Street vanish, replaced by a panorama of an Indonesia I once knew.

It is the Indonesia of old, dating back to the years between 1956 and 1961, when I lived there as a foreign correspondent, when the revolutionary President Sukarno kept his newly independent nation in a state of ideological suspense, a country to which I brought a bride, where our first child was born and who, much to the astonishment and joy of our Indonesian friends, was given the Indonesian word for earth—Tanah—as her name.

Over the years I have managed to break loose from less exotic worlds and slip fleetingly into the country, hit-and-run visits that were always unsatisfactory, frustrating, only arousing the appetite. A visit in 1975 came to mind: In before midnight, out the next morning after papaya and thick, dark Javanese coffee, *kopi.* This and other forays were always at the mercy of a work schedule, only heightening my longing for the nourishment of a leisurely stay, a chance to revisit old places, streets, people I knew half a lifetime ago.

Ah, I can hear someone say, all this talk about "revisiting" Indonesia—you know, it has nothing to do with Indonesia, it is only a euphemism, a pretext for wanting to flip backward through calendars in pursuit of youth gone by.

It may be, but that is only part of it.

Through Indonesia's Arcade of Memories

I know. I know that when I recently revisited Indonesia—only a few days but, compared to the 1975 stop, exhilaratingly open-ended—my response was more than one-dimensional. On the superficial level, I felt that I could at last stop jabbering about how nice it would be to get back to Indonesia; that alone, I knew, would be a great relief to a lot of my friends. But on a deeper level, I was on a gallop of excitement, and a stay that should have been exhausting only left me freshened, enriched, a member of a family. *"Selamat pagi!"* I sang my good morning to a teenage bellhop in the lobby of my hotel. He was wearing a black velvet *petji* on his head and a brown-and-white sarong wrapped around his waist. *"Selamat pagi,"* he replied, grinning softly. I felt as though I were involved in a conspiracy of intimacy, Indonesia and I, reunited. My stride quickened as I approached the door to the street, hurrying through an arcade of old memories in search of new ones.

The early morning air is crisp, shining, as if it had been washed before rolling down from the mountains. But I am assaulted by the jumble of Jakarta: crowds, cars, all moving in a nonstop rush hour. Since my day, the capital's population has more than doubled to over 7 million. The island of Java, about the size of New York State, has 91 million people, well over one-third of the population of the United States. Still, I feel very much at home in Jakarta. That Indonesian fellow over there with the thin hair, a folder under his arm. I know him, don't I? The elegant woman in a knee-length batik dress—I know her. It turns out I don't know either of them but I tell myself that it is an excusable case of eagerness and over certainty.

Suddenly I am wealthy with remembrances. I recall a game I used to play in Indonesia, proclaiming to visitors that just one glance at an Indonesian's face and I could immediately tell where the person came from, really, from which one of the main islands scattered over 3,000 miles of the Pacific. I was wrong most of the time but it was great fun, harmless showing off; even more, it was a clue as to how easily mostly Moslem Indonesia, with its assorted cultures, sculptured landscapes and rich history, can intoxicate anyone who stays longer than a week or two.

But Indonesia isn't mistaken, hasn't forgotten. I enter an antique shop on Jalan Kebon Sirih Timus Dalam that I used to visit regularly and ask for the owner, whom I have not seen for more than twenty years. A woman sitting at a small table says she is his wife, that he is at home. She telephones him. I wait, wandering among the Chinese porcelains, wood carvings from Bali, delicate lengths of handwoven cloth from Sumba, an arid island to the east of Bali. The shopkeeper, his hair gray now, enters and studies my face for a moment. Suddenly his eyes gleam with recognition. "Bernard!" he exclaims. It is the most wonderful, reassuring way of being welcomed home. We embrace. His wife takes a few photos of us holding a large sixteenth-century blue-and-white Chinese plate known as a *swatow*.

Out in the street again, my eyes, my senses, my emotions seem to be newly powered, discovering, absorbing, accumulating. A parade of faces, the gongs of a *gamelan*, the aroma of *kreteks*—the kaleidoscope of Indonesia that had dwelled in my mind long distance in Washington—now surrounds me. Inevitably I find myself juggling two Jakartas: my Sukarno Jakarta of almost three decades ago, really a collection of villages barely held together by the slogans of nationalism, and my new Jakarta, practical now, less bombastic, more in-

terested in building the economy than strutting on the
world stage, the main avenues widened, buildings
sprawling in all directions, including up.

"Up!" No accident, this word.

"Up" surfaces from the bedrock of my recollections of
Sukarno's dreams of glory, his cascades of leftist rheto-
ric, his extravagant ambition to make his impoverished
land the tallest nation in Southeast Asia. He is not
around any longer; "the father of his country" died in
1970, by then a figurehead, discarded, suspected of
having had ties to a Communist-backed coup attempted
and quashed five years earlier. But in his time, he had
exulted in the aggrandizement of his country's ego, his
way of shaking off the humiliations of centuries of colonialism. Nineteen hundred sixty: I remember that when
the Hotel Indonesia was being constructed, the first sky-
scraper of a building in the archipelago, the Indonesians
would display a giant numeral on each floor as soon as
the beams were in place, nos. 1 to 14, the top floor. In
New York, fourteen stories can be a cottage; in Jakarta,
it was tall stuff. The hotel dwarfed the ground-hugging
Dutch colonial architecture of the city. The Indonesians
were proud; Sukarno glowed. After all, the hotel was the
grandest structure built by the Indonesians since the
erection, more than a thousand years earlier, of the giant
Buddhist temple of Borobudur in Central Java. The light-
green hulk of Hotel Indonesia now shares the Jakarta
sky with about a dozen luxury hotels—the Hilton, Hyatt
and Inter-Continental, among others—and with an even
greater array of modern office buildings, one thirty-five
stories high, housing national and international corpora-
tions.

Nor does the pleasure of discovery end on the main
thoroughfare of Jalan Thamrin. I stroll through the

417

multistoried uptown branch of Jakarta's main department store that I like to think was named for our young-
est daughter, Sarinah. (Actually the name—at least for
us—derives from the title of a novel about a Javanese
peasant girl; my wife and I gave that name to our Hong
Kong-born baby as one of our links to Indonesia.) Inside the store, I am overwhelmed by the contrast between
now and the early 1960s: the crowds of shoppers, the

Through Indonesia's Arcade of Memories

counter-hopping, the variety of merchandise on display vs. those gloomy *tokos*—small shops—of my day, the shelves bare except for a few tins of cheese, a lonely bolt or two of cotton cloth, some odds and ends. I drive through streets that were once little more than wide trails, now lined with busy stores, cluttered with signs, tangled with traffic. I tour the old downtown *kota* area, the tidied-up harbor district where the Dutch, over three centuries ago, built a warehouse and a fort in a city they called Batavia. From there, they ran their far-flung colonial empire for generations, extracting the wealth of these hot islands and shipping it back to remote, chilly Europe.

Back in my hotel room, I can now instantly phone anywhere in the world via Jakarta's telecommunications satellite. The hotel operator makes it clear that the international hookup was not installed in my honor, but that does not diminish my sense of delight.

Let me pause for a moment to raise a toast to that dial telephone. Have I gone gaga? Well, you had to have been in Indonesia twenty-five years ago. I recall stepping off the plane at Kemayoran Airport—then Jakarta's only airport—for the first time in August 1956. Newly independent Indonesia was only a child then, eleven years old, and the first thing I had to do was to learn eleven words of the national language, Bahasa Indonesia; otherwise I would have been marooned. *Nol, satu, dua, tiga, empat, lima, enam, tudjuh, delapan, sembilan* and *sepuluh*. They were my leap into Indonesia, the numbers 0 to 10, my connection to the outside world. Not only were there no satellites then, there were no dials. You picked up the receiver, listened for the buzz, gave the operator the telephone number you wanted in Bahasa Indonesia—and waited. I mean, waaaaiiiittteeeddddd.

Many times I thought that using semaphore flags would be faster. But you really could not blame the Indonesians; they were busy with more important priorities. In fact, waiting—patience—was portrayed by Indonesia and the nonaligned third world as a cultural asset; impatience was an unmistakable symptom of Western imperialism. I spent my youth waiting, fighting off apoplexy by counting the adhesive-footed geckos scampering across window panes in pursuit of mosquitoes. I became very good at counting those little lizards.

Counting geckos still helps when making local calls, but here I am, dialing a number in Washington, D.C., from my air-conditioned hotel room overlooking the shimmering young skyline of Jakarta and, moments later, I am chatting with a friend across the Pacific.

Satellites. A cluster of baby skyscrapers. The bustle of an Asian city. Altogether, Jakarta's first face, the face a newcomer encounters in the opening hours in Jakarta. Like so many other capitals in the last quarter of a century, the city has changed substantially.

"Surface."

Even now, back in Washington, the word ricochets among the assorted souvenirs of my visit. During my stay in Jakarta, I ran into an Indonesian friend, just as lean as I remembered him all those years ago, and he said to me, *"Salamat datang, bung."* "Welcome, brother, you're back. Good, you've looked around, what do you think?" And I told him of my first impression of a Jakarta reaching for the sky. He nodded, sadly. I could see that my response disappointed him. "Yes," he whispered—we were in a crowded room—and the very whispering troubled me, reminded me of the anxious muttering during the Sukarno era. "But it's mostly *sur-*

Through Indonesia's Arcade of Memories

face." The word hung in midair, separating us, I the out-sider, he the native. "Behind what you see, not all that much has changed, really."

There was more. Other Indonesian friends talked of what they described as trickle-down corruption, the elite taking care of the elite, a few crumbs for the poor, the economic influence of the Chinese minority, the power of the military, the growing authoritarianism of a regime trimmed with a few democratic ribbons. Their talk echoed a thousand conversations of my earlier days, made me feel as though I had never left.

Had I been taken in by architectural cosmetics? A prettied-up Jakarta disguising old blemishes and scars? I had not intended to get bogged down in economics; this was going to be a relaxed homecoming, not a reportorial probe, but it was impossible to keep the two from colliding. I went out into the afternoon heat of the city, walked a couple of blocks off Jalan Thamrin, and there, staring at me, was a sketch of my old Jakarta: ramshac-kle houses, a couple of open-air stalls, kids playing games in the middle of a broken, dusty street. Yes, I knew that the same stagnant scene could turn up any-where. But I did not feel consoled. I had the feeling that I had known these kids' fathers, had seen them twenty-five years ago playing games in the middle of another broken, dusty street.

Yet I must confess that the larger portrait of Indonesia that I picked up here and there, in scattered conversa-tions with other Indonesians and some Westerners, wasn't all bleak, not at all. One Western diplomat said to me, Now wait a minute, let's be fair, there has been progress. There was talk, economist's talk, about an in-frastructure of growth that was now seeping into *kampungs* throughout the archipelago: more industries, more schools, more goods, though even more would be welcome. Indonesian officials handed out booklets noting that the G.N.P. has been climbing, so many percentage points, year after year. But the population continues to grow, too, hungrily biting into that progress: 97 million people in 1961, more than 150 million now, 42 percent under the age of 15. Per capita income, about $500 a year. Statistics show that a laborer earns the equivalent of about $1 a day—about 1,000 *rupiahs.*

Those three zeroes encircle a memory of the economics of Indonesia of my day. Inflation then was runaway, and the Sukarno Government came up with an exotic way of dealing with the problem. One afternoon, I heard a surprise announcement on the radio: The Government had just chopped one zero off the face value of all the *rupiah* notes in circulation. Just like that. A note with "1000" printed on its face was suddenly worth only 100 *rupiahs.* People, the value of their money suddenly slashed, were stunned. Some suicides were reported. After that, I always lived with the fear that, one day, I would be caught in a traffic jam with, say, $2,000 worth of *rupiahs* in my pocket, en route to pay a hefty cable bill at the Government post office, and find out when I got there my $2,000 was worth only $200.

"You know," an Indonesian friend told me over breakfast on this most recent trip, "given the facts, the situation today could not be any better. No, it could not be any better. You understand?" Yes, I understood; it was an invitation to read the cynicism behind his question. The melodious lyrics I had longed to hear, that life was much easier now, that things had really improved, that hope and optimism were as much part of the diet as rice and satay, were never sung. Or at least I never heard them.

Through Indonesia's Arcade of Memories

When, at the end of my assignment in Indonesia, I flew out in 1961, I felt as though I were leaving before the final curtain came down. From my new post in Western Europe, I watched the internal tensions pyramid until the explosion of 1965. It jolted me into realizing that, no matter how much I thought I understood Indonesia, the reality was that I knew so little, so little about its people, its culture, its capacity for violence. In *Background Notes* on Indonesia, 1983 edition, the United States State Department says: "In Java and Bali particularly, where the P.K.I. was strongest, Indonesians retaliated against the Communists in rural areas, killing hundreds of thousands," *Killing hundreds of thousands.* Java with its diverse culture? Bali with all its arts? "The emotions created by this crisis persist today," the State Department adds. Dissent from any extreme, I was told on my visit, whether religious or political, is still not regarded with any particular affection. And so I was not surprised when I read news stories, not long after I left, about an outbreak of political violence in Jakarta, described as the worst in ten years.

A sentimental excursion, inevitably, to look up some of the places where I had lived in Jakarta. It reawakened memories of nights during my first year there when I slept on two chairs in the lobby of what used to be called the "press building."

First, a visit to our small honeymoon house on Jalan Sumbawa, a street that dips from two ends to a V in the middle. We lived in the middle. You can imagine what happened when monsoons hit. On rainy evenings when we had to go out to a diplomatic reception, my wife would slip off her shoes and stockings, hold her skirt high above her knees, and wade uphill to dry land at either end of the street. I would carry my trousers, shoes and socks under my arm. I remember one particular monsoon night when, in my sleep, my arm slipped over the side of the bed and splashed. Sumbawa's waters had invaded our bedroom.

But for the kids in our neighborhood, Sumbawa's floods were great fun. They fished for eels from the small wall in our front yard. Whenever a car half-drowned in the pit of the V, the kids, in their shorts, would strike a deal with the exasperated driver and, for a few *rupiahs,* push the vehicle to terra firma.

When I went back to Jalan Sumbawa, the sun was out. Maybe that was the reason I could not find my old house. I had somewhat better luck when I paid a visit to our second house in the Jakarta suburb of Kebayoran. The house was just where we left it but the insides were undergoing a massive renovation. I picked my way through plaster debris, brick piles and paint buckets, careful not to step on old memories, and found my way to the tiny bedroom just off the living room, where our daughter Tanah spent the first weeks of her life.

Indonesia also treated me to a lovely dessert—a retrospective exhibition of paintings by Affandi. I came across the newspaper announcement quite by accident. Or were the Indonesian gods taking me by the hand? "Now that I am getting old," Affandi, born on Java in 1907, was quoted as saying, "I can finish two or three paintings a month, while formerly I made at least ten paintings." The story listed various international prizes, medals and honors Affandi had been awarded over the years. I went to see the paintings, some eighty of them, painted between 1940 and 1984. His canvases—of faces, flowers, suns, mountains—brimmed with Indonesia. Affandi himself was nowhere in sight. A blurred snapshot of his wife, dating from the time I bought the Times Square painting, came to mind. She had patrolled that particular exhibition carrying a satchel. A satchel? The mystery cleared up when I saw her stuffing the satchel with *rupiahs* every time a painting was sold. *Rupiahs* were not worth very much then, and it took a lot of *rupiahs* to buy an Affandi.

A few weeks after I got back from Jakarta, I found myself sitting next to a young woman on the Washington subway. She was absorbed in a book. I peered over her shoulder. A textbook; some of the lines had been high-lighted with a yellow marker. The section was headed "Dutch East Indies (Indonesia)."

I couldn't resist. "Excuse me," I said. "Are you studying that for school?"

She nodded. A lovely face, long black hair, about nineteen.

"Where?"

"Catholic University."

"Ever been to the . . . Dutch East Indies? Indonesia?"

She was surprised at the question. She shook her head, smiling.

Just then, the train pulled into her station and she got off. There was so much I wanted to tell her.

EXPLORING AN ISLAND NATION
GETTING THERE
Indonesia is about 17,000 miles, an international

dateline and twelve hours away from New York. Eight international airlines link Halim, Jakarta's main airport, and the United States. Since the flight from New York takes about twenty-two hours, not including connections, a layover is recommended.

Singapore Airlines, in conjunction with TWA, offers a round-trip fare of about $1,400 at this writing, with stopovers in London and Singapore; a flight over the Pacific, with stopovers in Los Angeles and Singapore, costs about $1,600.

PASSPORTS AND SHOTS

No visa is required for tourists from the United States planning a visit of less than two months. A passport valid for six months after date of arrival in Indonesia is required, as is proof of onward passage (airline ticket). Inoculations are not required either, but the United States Department of Health and Human Services suggests a booster for tetanus, cholera, typhoid and hepatitis, as well as taking chloroquine and Fansidar pills for malaria.

DRINK

There is a saying that while the British built roads in their colonies, the Dutch built breweries. Many of these still exist. Indonesians have also developed Bali *brem*, a rice wine, and *tuak*, a palm wine that ferments inside the tree and has a kick like white lightning.

CLOTHING

Dress is normally informal in Indonesia. Even in Jakarta, men seldom wear Western-style business suits, opting instead for sports jackets and ties or safari-style jackets with trousers and, in the evening, long-sleeve batik shirts worn over dark pants. Women often wear batik or other cotton dresses or blouses and skirts; shorts and sleeveless tops are, as in many other countries, considered appropriate only for beaches. Clothes are typically inexpensive (about $15 to $40 for a batik dress) and colorful, so many visitors purchase most of their wardrobe in Indonesia.

LANGUAGE

In all, there are some 250 languages and many more dialects spoken in the 13,677 islands of Indonesia. Bahasa Indonesia, a Malay-based language written in Roman script, is the national language; English is spoken and written in most major tourist destinations.

TIME TO VISIT

Indonesia's islands straddle the Equator. Consequently, daylight and night are almost equally divided, and the weather is tropical. The east monsoon, from June to September, brings dry weather; the west monsoon, from December to March, brings rain. Throughout, the temperature ranges from 70 to 90 degrees Fahrenheit, except in the mountains, where the air is considerably cooler. The heaviest rainfall occurs in December and January. Despite the rain, many Australians and Europeans head for Bali from Christmas through January and also in the beginning of April. Consequently, hotel rates often rise during these periods.

GETTING AROUND

Rental cars typically cost about $50 a day, and driving can be hair-raising. Imagine Times Square with cars, trucks, buses, motorcycles, *bemos* and Colts (small vans), *helicaks* (enclosed motorbikes), *becaks* (three-wheeled, peddle-powered rickshaws) and ox carts and you begin to get a sense of what traffic is like in many Indonesian cities. Often it is easier to take a taxi (relatively inexpensive in Jakarta) or, for longer periods, rent a car with driver.

There is rail service (slow but scenic), bus service (typically crowded with would-be Mario Andrettis at the wheel) and excellent air service to many of the islands. Garuda, the national airline, has the most extensive routes.

There are also ships of almost every description. This

is an island nation, and goods and people are still transported, in large part, by sea. Conditions are less than modest and most ships go by what is known as rubber time: The time of departure stretches or contracts depending on the whim of the captain and how full or empty the hold is. The fares, however, are very low.

INFORMATION

Contact the Indonesian Consulate (5 East 68th Street, New York, NY 10021; telephone: 212-879-0600) or the Indonesian Tourist Promotion Office (3457 Wilshire Boulevard, Los Angeles, CA 90010; 213-387-2078).

GETTING AROUND JAKARTA

HOTELS

One of the most attractive hotels, right in the center of Jakarta, is the **Borobudur Inter-Continental** (a double costs about $130 per day). Its grounds include tennis and squash courts, a large pool, and an outdoor café, where a buffet brunch is served every Sunday. Also downtown are the elegant **Jakarta Mandarin** (about $160) and **Hotel Sari Pacific** ($120). Well away from the downtown bustle, in a thirty-two-acre compound, is the **Jakarta Hilton** ($160), its handsome lobby modeled after the sultan's palace in Jogjakarta. Also on the grounds are a theater styled on a Balinese temple, a cluster of shops and restaurants, swimming pools, tennis and squash courts, a jogging path and a fitness club.

Other less expensive hotels are the **Sahid Jaya** (a double costs about $100), **Kartika Chandra** ($110), **Hyatt** ($110), the **Kemang** ($60) and **Garden Hotel** ($60). The rather tired-looking **Hotel Indonesia,** Jakarta's first international-class hotel, continues to be a social hub for the city's elite ($80).

RESTAURANTS

Jakarta, as with many other Indonesian cities, has several good, inexpensive Chinese restaurants. Among these are **Cahaya Kota,** at Jalan Wahid Hasyim 9, or **Hayam Wuruk,** at Jalan Hayam Wuruk 5.

Housed in a Dutch colonial building, the **Oasis Restaurant,** at Jalan Raden Saleh 47, has the feel of an extravagant 1930s Hollywood set, and prices to match. Batak singers from northern Sumatra serenade diners as more than a dozen waitresses dressed in sarongs line up to serve the traditional *rijsttafel.*

For a less extravagant, more authentic sampling of the variety of Indonesian food, try the open-air café that forms every evening in the parking lot of the **Sarinah** department store. Here, many Jakartans and a few foreigners wander from stall to stall, choosing some *ayam goreng* (fried chicken), some *sayur asam* (vegetables), *satay,* a bit of broiled fish and, to finish, *es apocat,* an avocado milkshake with coffee essence, palm sugar and condensed milk; it sounds awful but tastes delicious.

And certainly no trip to Jakarta is complete without going to one of the Padang restaurants—serving spicy food from West Sumatra—such as **Roda,** at Jalan Matraman Raya 65–67. Waiters put down dishes in front of you—*nasi rames* (rice with mixed vegetables), *ayam blado* (hot spicy chicken in coconut milk), beef *rendang, gulai kambing* (curried lamb)—and, at the end of the meal, count up how many dishes are empty to total the check. A cautionary note: Try the food served at street stands and vending carts at your own risk. And no one drinks tap water unless it has been boiled for twenty minutes.

THINGS TO SEE

Stroll to **Taman Fatahillah,** a square in the heart of Old Batavia, where you will find the **Town Hall,** dating back to 1710 and now housing the **Historical Museum;** the **Balai Seni Rupa Jakarta,** the city's art gallery; and the **Wayang Museum,** devoted to the wayang puppets. Nearby, a small Dutch drawbridge crosses over the great canal, **Kali Besar. Pasar Ikan,** the fish market, lies at the mouth of the Ciliwung River. The streets are lined with fishmongers' stalls and small shops, and at the wharf wooden motor-sailors, up to a hundred feet long, unload their cargoes of teak, bananas, indigo and spices. With a little haggling, you can get someone to row you out into the harbor. Not far away, in what were once the warehouses of the old Dutch fort, is the **Maritime Museum,** a rather limited place but good for those interested in the Bugis and Makassar sailing ships.

Back in the center of town, the **National Museum** on Medan Merdeka houses perhaps the world's finest collection of Hindu-Javanese antiquities. It also boasts an impressive collection of Chinese ceramics. On Sundays at the museum there is a *gamelan* concert—music that has captivated Claude Debussy and many other western composers. On Sundays the museum opens its treasure room, which is filled with Javanese gold ornaments, some dating back thousands of years.

In the same area are the **Presidential Palace,** the **Istiqlal Mosque** and the towering **National Monument.** For an afternoon, you could go to **Taman Mini,** the huge park that is something like Disneyland, except that it represents—with buildings, arts and crafts—the culture of all the different islands that make up Indonesia. Or, spend an evening at **Taman Ismail Marzuki Cultural Complex,** Jalan Cikini Raya 13. This is Jakarta's Lincoln Center, and there is always something going on—dances by one of Indonesia's troupes (such as the avant-garde Kyai Semar), a photo or art exhibit, shadow plays, *joget dangdut* (rock) concerts, jazz groups from overseas.

SHOPPING

You can find Chinese porcelains of varying quality, cloth from Sulawesi and Sumba, totems from Irian Jaya at the flea market on **Jalan Surabaya.** Other areas for antiques are **Jalan Agus Salim, Jalan Kebon Sirih**

Through Indonesia's Arcade of Memories

Timur Dalam, Jalam Majapahit. Sarinah, Jakarta's premier department store, seems to have everything from tapes to batik to rattan chairs, rather like an Indonesian Macy's. Prices are set, which, after a day of bargaining, can be a relief.

FARTHER AFIELD

Consider an hour's bus ride to **Bogor,** about thirty miles south of Jakarta. In the highlands, Bogor is the site of the **Presidential Palace,** built in 1870 by the Dutch governor-general of the Dutch East Indies Company. Even more impressive is the **Kebun Raya,** Botanical Gardens, a 250-acre site started by Sir Thomas Stamford Raffles 167 years ago. Here you'll see waterlilies that are large enough to support a baby, paths lined with giant rubber and gum trees, orchids including the *Grammatophyllum speciosum,* bearing up to 3,000 flowers at once; in all, there are more than 15,000 species of trees and plants and 5,000 varieties of orchids.

If you would rather sit on a beach, go to **Pulau Seribu,** coral islands just off Java's north coast. For a day trip, visit **Pulau Onrust; Pulau Putri, Pulau Nirwana** or **Pulau Seribu,** are excellent sites for diving. The islands can be reached by boat from Tanjung Priok or on a Skyvan flight from Kemayoran Airport.

The Visitor Information Center is in the Jakarta Theater Building, Jalan M. H. Thamrin 9.

—Suzanne Charlé

South Pacific Island Hopping

ROBERT TRUMBULL

N ATOLL LIKE
Tarawa, in what was once the British colony of the Gilbert Islands and is now the independent **Republic of
Kiribati,** is a likely place to find the Pacific as it was before resort developers began transforming much of it into
small imitations of Waikiki.

Tarawa's location, just north of the Equator and about
2,500 miles southwest of Hawaii, makes it a handy
starting point for exploring other Pacific islands where
traditional societies have remained more or less intact
amid the spreading Westernization of once unspoiled
tropical islands.

Major island capitals—like Fiji's Suva, among
others—present a thoroughly contemporary façade to
present-day visitors, and some of the squalid settlements
that have sprung up in Micronesia since the United
States began administering those archipelagos after

World War II represent a saddening incursion of urban blight into places that were once described as earthly paradises. However, in many instances one need only go to the outskirts of these Western excrescences to encounter the Pacific that enchanted writers like Robert Louis Stevenson.

Island hopping in the Pacific has always presented a challenge. Stevenson surmounted it by chartering a yacht, but today's traveler may have to reach some remote islands and atolls on local airlines' float planes or by booking passage on small trading vessels with schedules that are extremely variable. Land transportation, unless prearranged with extraordinary good luck, may have to be by pickup truck driven by some friendly islander who happens to be going your way.

Such personal contacts are one of the rewards of travel in the islands. Since English is the common language throughout much of the Pacific, communication is easy. Group encounters are often musical, for young islanders traveling together tend to pass the time singing local airs, whether they be in a jet aircraft, a bus or the back of a truck.

Kiribati is one of the newly independent Pacific island states where cultural obstacles prevent abrupt changes in the way of life. To one returning to Tarawa after a long absence, finding that the brand-new wing of the Otintai Hotel had room telephones was a surprise; discovering that none of them worked was not. Western technology and atoll life have little compatibility. Majuro, in the nearby Marshall Islands, is one atoll that actually has a sidewalk in its one little town, but it is only about a hundred yards long. Because atoll islets are so narrow, seldom more than a mashie shot from one side to the other, developers tend to pass them by.

According to Darwin's theory of atoll construction, now widely accepted, they were formed when volcanoes sank into the sea eons ago, leaving behind the crusts of coral that had gathered around the sides of the mountains. In time these became rings of verdant islets like Tarawa, each ring partly enclosing a lagoon where the mountain used to be.

South Pacific Island Hopping

My first visit to Tarawa more than forty years ago followed by three days the United States Marine invasion of
Betio, one of the atoll's larger islets that is still less than
a square mile in area. The Marines defeated the defending Japanese troops at a frightful cost in lives on
both sides. Aerial bombing and naval gunfire by the
American forces supporting the Marine assault stripped
Betio of almost all vegetation.

Betio (pronounced BAY-show), though green again,
has never recovered its prewar serenity, becoming instead a shipping and commercial center. It teems with
unsuccessful job hunters from other atolls, who fill the
discos at night. For tourists there are relics such as the
battered Japanese command bunker and the rusted and
broken Japanese coastal defense guns still pointing out
to sea.

It is a short ferry ride from Betio to Bairiki, the capital
of the Republic of Kiribati, which sits at the southern
end of a string of tiny islets connected by causeways.
The Parliament meets in a building with a design inspired by the architectural style of the traditional village
meeting house.

Nearby is a real village meetinghouse, with a high
thatched roof and open sides. Inside are spaces allotted
for each family to lay a mat on the earthen floor. On a
festive evening a visitor may be invited to watch young
women in grass skirts perform an ancient dance that ends
with a forward charge that stops just short of the line of
spectators.

The islets of Tarawa are so narrow that there is room
for only one road. It runs along the beach on the lagoon
side, through village after village, past the Otintai Hotel
to the airport a few miles away.

I like to drive along this road in the hour before sunset, when the palm trees make long, thin shadows across the white coral sand, and the lagoon, with its distant fringe of islets on the other side of the atoll, looks like a painted scene. Here and there, on a village shop, are signs advertising Japanese cars and American cola drinks, but the world of Toyotas and Coke seems far away and unreal.

The sunsets on Tarawa are among the most spectacular in the world. They begin with a flare of blazing pink and red that gradually changes to shifting bands of pastel shades that cover nearly half the sky. A few minutes after the great red ball disappears beneath the horizon, it is pitch dark and the stars are out, for there is almost no twilight in the tropical latitudes.

Even farther removed from the world of video games and enclosed shopping malls are outlying atolls like **Abemama,** where Robert Louis Stevenson spent several months, and **Butaritari,** also called **Makin,** which has reverted from a World War II military depot to a collection of villages. One can go to such places on the local airline, which uses the coral airstrips laid down by the Seabees.

Such is the Republic of Kiribati. The name, incidentally, is simply the way the islanders say Gilberts, the old British name of the group, in their own language. It is pronounced KIR-i-bas, since the syllable *ti* is given the sound of *s*. Otintai is thus oh-sin-TIE. This sometimes carries over into English: I once heard a school group singing, "It's a long way to Sipperary."

Elsewhere in the far Pacific many inviting hideaways are to be found among the green hills and lush valleys of the "high islands" of volcanic origin. One is **Yap,** a cluster of four islands in the western Carolines. The group and its outlying atolls form part of the **Federated**

South Pacific Island Hopping

States of Micronesia, one of four largely self-govern-
ing entities in the United Nations Trust Territory of the
Pacific Islands.

The powerful traditional chiefs of Yap, whose word is
law in the many thatched villages, want to keep the distinctive culture of these islands unsullied by foreign
ways. Hence the Yapese way of life outside Colonia, the
shabby, Americanized capital, is pretty much as it has
always been.

Most Yapese women wear dresses or blue jeans and
T-shirts when they venture into the town, but at home
they change to the long grass skirt, worn with only a
necklace. Women from outlying atolls such as Ulithi,
an important United States Navy anchorage during
World War II, often appear in town in grass skirts, however. Yapese men, who frequently come into town in cut-
off denims and brightly printed shirts, at home wear a
kind of G-string, decorated with strands of dried hibis-
cus stem.

In Yap one can eat and sleep Western style in a hotel
and spend the rest of the time exploring scenes that the
twentieth century has affected lightly, if at all. The best
way to do so is to travel by foot and outrigger canoe. The
best view of the islands is from the Roman Catholic mission on top of a hill near the town of Colonia, where the
American staff is hospitable to visitors.

Yap is famous for its stone money, known as rai. The
heavy disks, each with a hole in the middle so it can be
carried on a pole, can be seen everywhere, and they have
a ceremonial value that cannot be translated into dollars.
A piece of rai leaning against a house gives prestige to a
family. Not far from Colonia is a pathway lined with antique specimens, some six feet or more in diameter,
known to foreign residents as the "stone money bank."

Production of rai, from rock quarried on nearby Palau, ceased long ago.

Another island in the trust territory that evokes the past is **Ponape** (now officially spelled **Pohnpei**) in the Senyavin group of the eastern Carolines. The place to stay, though a little remote, is a hotel called **The Village,** built and run by an American couple. The accommodations are in individual cottages resembling Micronesian huts, but with Western plumbing and water beds. The bar and dining room are in a "long house" with a stunning marine view sprinkled with tiny islets.

Many travelers insist that Ponape is the most beautiful island in the Pacific. Its dominant mountain peak, rising nearly 2,600 feet, is one of the highest in the central Pacific. Rushing streams and high waterfalls mark many valleys. An old Spanish wall, the ruins of an elaborate German church and a Buddhist memorial to Japanese war dead are reminders of past colonial regimes in Kolonia (on Ponape the name is spelled with a *K*).

Ponape is renowned among archaeologists, as well as tourists, as the site of the stone ruins of **Nan Madol,** an ancient abandoned city known as the "Venice of the Pacific" because of the network of canals among dozens of imposing buildings. The city, constructed of huge slabs of black basalt by a legendary group of conquerers who were vanquished in turn and who then disappeared, is believed to date to the twelfth century at least. Ponapeans say the place is haunted by the ghosts of these rulers, and they shun it except when guiding tourists through its wonders.

A visitor's first sight of Nan Madol, which must be approached from the sea, is unexpected and breathtaking. On the approach by boat, a featureless vista of mangrove jungle is suddenly breached by the appearance of a

South Pacific Island Hopping

thirty-foot-high rampart of interlaced basalt slabs, each weighing tons. How these enormous blocks were brought there from quarries on a distant part of the island, and maneuvered into place, is one of the many mysteries of Nan Madol. The complex of temples, forts and store-houses covers nearly one hundred islets.

Not far from Ponape, as Pacific distances go, is the magnificent group of Micronesian islands known collec-tively as **Truk.** Partly volcanic and partly atoll and sur-rounded by a tremendous reef dotted with islets, Truk is marvelously scenic and best viewed from a boat in the huge lagoon, which teems with flying fish. The same la-goon sheltered the imperial Japanese fleet during World War II. Many of those ships are on the bottom of the la-goon now, providing an underwater attraction that draws scuba divers from all over the world.

My first view of Truk was from a perch on an upper deck of the battleship *Iowa,* part of the United States Navy task force that sank those ships on a bright day in February 1944. The United States took over the islands after the Japanese surrender aboard the *Missouri* in Tokyo Bay, and the trust territory administration estab-lished its headquarters for that part of the eastern Caro-lines on hilly **Moen Island** (which had also been the headquarters of the United States Navy military govern-ment just after the war). There are several hotels on Moen now, and good beaches, so that is where the scuba divers stay.

It takes only minutes to go by boat from Moen to **Udot,** one of the small, flat islets in the lagoon, but it belongs to a different world. The neat little village on Udot could be a Hollywood set for a South Seas movie.

Since most Pacific islands come in clusters, it is nearly always possible to get away from the ersatz surroundings of relentlessly picturesque resorts that have sprung up in places like Tahiti and Fiji, and find communities that have remained pretty much as they have always been. From Tahiti, head for an island like **Raiatea,** a repository of Polynesian antiquity. Or from Apia, the capital of Western Samoa on Upolu, take the plane or ferry to the sister island of **Savaii,** which some believe to be the cradle of the Polynesian peoples, and drive to the village of **Falealupo** for a close look at the classic Samoan life-style.

The last time I was in Falealupo everyone still lived in the see-through houses of precolonial Samoa, thatched roofs on poles with curtains of woven mats to let down when it rains. Among Samoans, privacy is an alien concept. Nevertheless, to go up close and stare into such a house is considered intolerably rude, and it is equally impolite to take photographs without permission.

There are also places like the lesser islands in the southwest Pacific republic of **Vanuatu,** formerly the French-British New Hebrides and still one of the great sources of primitive art in the Pacific, and the **Marquesas,** scene of stories by Herman Melville, where tourists are rare enough to be curiosities. But even in some of the better-known tourist haunts it is possible to see something of the old Pacific.

On **Viti Levu,** the main island of Fiji, where tourism has displaced sugar as the leading industry, a genuinely indigenous settlement is never far from any of the luxurious hotels along the Coral Coast, Fiji's main resort area. In fact, with communally owned Fijian land being inalienable, under a law inherited from the former British rulers, the villagers may be the hotel's collective landlords.

The sense of common ownership of the land is important to the Pacific islanders. Anthropologists say it identifies them with their ancestors and gives them the strength to withstand the eroding effect of Western influence.

A VISITOR'S GUIDE TO GETTING AROUND THE ISLANDS

HOW TO GET THERE

At present, the quickest route to Tarawa is from Honolulu to Majuro, in the Marshall Islands, by Continental Air Micronesia. At Majuro a connection can be made to Tarawa on the airline called AMI (for Air Marshall Islands). Continental Air Micronesia itself proceeds from Majuro to Ponape and on to other Micronesian points, including Truk and Yap. Its parent, Continental Airlines, operates a direct service from Honolulu to Fiji, which is a hub for air routes leading to numerous destinations in the South and Southwest Pacific. South Pacific Island Airways, based on Pago Pago, American Samoa, flies from Honolulu to several South Pacific islands.

It is wise to ask a travel agent about using local airlines in the Pacific rather than buying a single round-trip ticket between the farthest points of the entire journey; alternative routings can save travelers substantial sums on the total cost of the transportation for a long journey. A resourceful Honolulu travel agency that specializes in offbeat island bookings is **Plaza Unique Travel** (677 Ala Moana Boulevard, Honolulu, HI 96813; telphone: 808-524-5622).

ACCOMMODATIONS

Generally speaking, the smaller the island, the simpler the hotel and the cheaper the rates (which are generally quoted for the room, single or double occupancy). Rooms at the **Otintai** on Tarawa, for instance, run from about $20 to $40. The address is Post Office Box 270, Bikeni Beu, Tarawa, Republic of Kiribati.

A newer and smaller place—only ten rooms—right on one of the Betio invasion beaches is the **Hotel Kiribati,** Post Office Box 504, Betio, Tarawa, Republic of Kiribati.

Spartan is the word for Yap's two hotels, the **ESA** (about $20 to $36) and the **Rai View** ($22 to $33), but Ponape's **Village** ($40 to $60), Post Office Box 339, Kolonia, Ponape, Eastern Caroline Islands 96941, is comfortable and justifiably prides itself on its kitchen (don't miss the mangrove crabs). A favorite on Moen, the main island of the Truk group, is the **Truk Continental** (about $55 to $75).

Any Micronesian hotel can be booked through Continental Air Micronesia.

The most colorful inn of the whole South Pacific without question is **Aggie Grey's Hotel,** Apia, Western Samoa. It is named for the octogenarian proprietor who is said to be one of several South Pacific women whose careers inspired the character Bloody Mary in James Michener's classic *Tales of the South Pacific,* on which the Broadway musical and the movie *South Pacific* were based.

CLIMATE, CLOTHES, SHOPPING

Tarawa and the other islands and atolls along the Equator, or a little north or south of it, have the same warm, sunny climate year-round. Fiji, Samoa and other islands south of the Equator are at their best during their winter—corresponding to summer in the northern latitudes—when it is a little cooler and much drier. Dress is casual everywhere in the Pacific, with brightly printed Hawaiian shirts (also called aloha shirts, or, in Fiji, bula shirts) in proper taste for almost any occasion. Take cotton clothes (and avoid synthetic fabrics, which

South Pacific Island Hopping

are too hot and sticky for the tropics) and sandals or thongs, which everyone wears.

Among attractive, easy-to-pack souvenirs are straw table mats and other woven wear, which come in different designs in each island group. In the major towns throughout the Pacific islands there is usually a Government handicraft shop that offers the best value in locally made goods of all kinds. —R.T.

WORLDLY
PLEASURES

A CHEESE LOVER'S TOUR OF FRANCE
Patricia Wells

PROPERLY SHIRTED
Barbara Gelb

A GRAND HOTEL AS SYMBOL
Lucinda Franks

A WEEK-LONG TASTE OF TUNISIA
Hebe Dorsey

AROUND HONG KONG, CHOPSTICKS IN HAND
Eileen Yin-Fe Lo

IN KYOTO, THE DEFINITIVE JAPANESE INN
Harold C. Schonberg

AN EPICURE IN KYOTO
Craig Claiborne

A Cheese Lover's Tour of France

PATRICIA WELLS

I
F ALL FRANCE HAD
to offer the world of gastronomy was bread, cheese and
wine, that would be enough for me. Of the trinity, it is
cheese that links one to the other. I cannot imagine a
more understated, unified French snack or meal than one
perfectly fresh baguette, a single Camembert, so ripe and
velvety it won't last another hour, and a glass or two of
young, fruity, well-balanced red wine. And I can't imagine a better place to discover French cheese than Paris,
where dozens upon dozens of *fromageries* line the
streets, each shop as different and distinctive as the personality of its owner, each offering selections that vary
according to the seasons.

Just as I frequent certain restaurants out of affection
for a chef's certain talents, I return again and again to
specific cheese shops, according to my mood and the
time of year. Recently, when the shop that serves as my

favorite source of Camembert was about to close for vacation, I chastised the owner, saying, "Now I'll be deprived of your Camembert for weeks."

Her response: "But think of how delicious it will taste in September."

She was right, of course. Nor would I go hungry.

Only the French produce so many varieties of cheese, so graphically reflecting the nation's regional landscape, the ever-changing soil, climate and vegetation. From the milk of cows, goats and sheep, from the green, flat lands of Normandy, the steep mountain Alps, and from the plains of Champagne east of Paris, comes a veritable symphony of aromas, textures, colors and forms. Cheese fresh from minuscule farms and giant cooperatives, cheese to begin the day and end it. The French consume a good deal of cheese—about forty-two pounds per capita a year, compared to the Americans' twenty pounds—and of all the varieties, Camembert is the undisputed favorite.

How many French varieties of cheese are there really? The French are not a people given to simple agreement. The remark that "a country that produces 325 varieties of cheese can't be governed" was, undoubtedly, a bit of cheese hype. The real figure, say the experts, is more like 150 to 200 serious varieties, with perhaps an additional 100 cheeses that are minor variations.

There's an old *New Yorker* cartoon that describes the confusion perfectly: An elderly woman is sitting on the sofa, poring over maps of France. She looks up at her husband and says: "Has it ever occurred to you, dear, that most of the villages and towns in France seem to be named after cheeses?"

The cheese you eat in France and the French cheese you eat outside of France, especially in the United

States, are not exactly the same. A major reason has to
do with United States Department of Agriculture regula-
tions barring the importation of cheese made from unpas-
teurized milk, and that has been aged less than sixty
days. Pasteurization may make cheese "safe," but in the
process the heat kills all the microbes that give the cheese
its character and flavor, that keep it a live, changing or-
ganism. There is no question that pasteurized milk pro-

duces uniformly bland, "dead" cheese. The regulation rules out the importation of France's finest fresh young cheese, including raw milk Camembert and Brie, and the dozens of varieties of lively, delicate goat cheese.

Yet, even in France, cheese made from pasteurized milk is increasingly common. For instance, only 16 percent of the 500,000 pounds of Camembert produced in France each year is made from raw milk. The advantage, of course, is that cheese made with pasteurized milk can be made available year-round, and will have more stable keeping qualities. When in France, take the time to get a true taste of fresh French cheese: Specify raw milk cheese by asking for *fromage fermier* or *au lait cru*. These cheeses are produced in limited quantities, the result of traditional methods of production.

Paris has dozens of *fromageries* that specialize in raw milk cheese, with some shops offering as many as 200 different varieties. Before living in Paris, I thought that cheese merchants did little but buy and sell cheese. Wrong. The best, most serious cheese people actually age with great care the cheese they sell. That is, they buy young cheese from the farmer, then, following a sensitive and tricky aging process, they take the cheese from its young, raw state to full maturity, refining the cheese in cool and humid underground cellars. The process is called *affinage*, and it can last from days to months, depending upon the cheese. As each cheese matures, it takes on its own personality, influenced by the person responsible for its development. Maturing cheese needs daily attention: Some varieties are washed with beer, some with a blend of salt and water, some with *eau-de-vie*. Some are turned every day, moved from one cellar to another, from one temperature or level of humidity to another, as the aging process continues.

A Cheese Lover's Tour of France

The dedicated *fromagers'* love for cheese is totally in-
fectious. In their cellars, they are in heaven as they vig-
orously inhale the heady, pungent aromas that fill the
air, and give the cheese little love taps, the same way
bakers give their unbaked loaves a tender touch before
putting them in the oven. Now, having toured most of the
aging cellars that rest beneath the streets of Paris, I see
what an individual can do to change the course of a
cheese's life, ultimately determining aroma, texture and
taste. Androuët's cheese, for instance, no matter what
the variety, always tastes just a bit richer and creamier
than others. Henry Voy's, from La Ferme Saint-Hubert,
has a lusty, almost over-the-hill quality about it that at
times can be quite appealing. Lillo's cheese is refined
and elegant, always in perfectly presentable shape,
much like the shop's chic, well-bred 16th-arrondisse-
ment clientele.

A few words on selecting cheese: Be sensitive to the
season. For instance, don't expect to find Vacherin or the
best-ever Beaufort in the middle of summer. When in
doubt, ask to know the seasonal specialties in a given
shop. Often the day's specials are posted. In selecting
cheese for a *dégustation* (a cheese tray or sample selection for tasting), either at home or in a restaurant, choose
three or four varieties, generally including a semisoft
cheese, a goat cheese and a blue. Eat the mild cheese
first, then move onto stronger varieties.

Generally, be wary of cheese wrapped in plastic. Like
us, cheese needs to breathe to maintain life and vigor.
Don't be afraid of a bit of mold. Generally the bluish
film is a sign that the cheese is made with raw milk, and
has been properly ripened.

And, be open-minded and adventurous. The first
months I lived in Paris I rarely bought Brie or Camem-

bert, having had so many disappointing pasteurized varieties that I had lost my enthusiasm for these wonderful
cheeses. Then one day I happened to sample a perfect
Camembert and I instantly understood what the fuss was
all about.

In general, cheese in France is quite a bargain, consid-
ering one actually consumes very little at each sitting.
Prices vary from shop to shop, and one will always pay
a bit more for farm-fresh cheese prepared with unpas-
teurized milk purchased at a reputable cheese shop. Most
French supermarkets offer a large selection of cheese,
usually less expensive, and almost always prepared in-
dustrially, with pasteurized milk.

In reputable cheese shops, prices range from as little
as 25 to 30 cents for a very small fresh *chèvre*, to $3 to
$4 for a large goat cheese, such as a Valençay, weighing
about eight ounces. A good Camembert will cost about
$2 each, Roquefort sells for about $5 a pound, Brie
about $3 for an eighth of a wheel, a good Epoisses about
$3.50 each, while hard-pressed cooked cheese, such as
Beaufort, costs about $5 a pound.

A favorite way to discover and enjoy French cheese is
to tour France through a *dégustation*, or tasting of the
country's many varieties. The following shops and restaurants, some of which are also *fromageries*, offer special selections on their menus.

Androuët, 41 rue d'Amsterdam, Paris 8 (telephone: 874-26-93). Metro: Liège. Restaurant open from
noon to 2:30 P.M. and 7 to 9:30 P.M. Closed Sunday. As
this is written the dollar is very strong, so the *menu
dégustation* costs about $15. Reservations advised.

The most elaborate *dégustation* in France is found
here, the mecca for cheese lovers in Paris. The specialty
is a seven-course meal consisting solely of cheese. You

A Cheese Lover's Tour of France

begin with the richest, mildest cheese, move on to the cooked and half-cooked varieties, dip into the goat cheeses and end on a heady finale of blues. As each of the seven trays is presented, the waiter explains a little about each type of cheese, suggesting you try three or four small samples per tray. It pays to set aside an entire afternoon or evening for the experience, so you can savor and compare varieties, spacing them with bits of a crusty baguette and sips of a solid Bordeaux.

La Ferme Sainte-Suzanne, 4 rue des Fossés, Saint Jacques, Paris 5 (354-90-02). Metro: Luxembourg. Restaurant open from noon to 2:30 P.M. Monday through Friday; 7 to 9:30 P.M. Thursday. Closed Saturday, Sunday and the month of August. Light meals at about $8 a person, including wine.

This is a lively, skylighted neighborhood spot, with a simple, cheese-based menu featuring nicely labeled cheese-tasting platters with fabulously crusty baguettes from the nearby Boulangerie Moderne, as well as salads combining a mix of greens, goat cheese and walnuts. The malted Swiss raclette is served with tiny boiled potatoes and slices of delicious smoked ham. There's a small wine list, including an excellent Côtes-du-Rhone.

La Ferme Saint-Hubert, 21 rue Vignon, Paris 8 (742-79-20). Metro: Madeleine. Restaurant open from 11:30 A.M. to 3 P.M. and 6:45 to 10 P.M. Closed Sunday and Monday. About $7 for the *menu dégustation.*

Next door to La Ferme Saint-Hubert *fromagerie* you'll find a tiny, casual lunchroom serving abbreviated tastings suited to cheese enthusiasts with limited time. Their most popular platter is made up of seven varieties, representing the seven major types of French cheese. At La Ferme Saint-Hubert, they are aged to reflect the owner's preference for ripe, full-flavored cheese. Platters of goat cheese and salads are also available. Raclette is served in the evening.

La Maison du Valais, 20 rue Royale, Paris 8 (260-22-72). Metro: Madeleine. Restaurant open from 12:15 to 2:30 P.M. and 7:15 to 10:30 P.M. Closed Sunday. Raclette meal with wine, about $16 a person.

For an unusual cheese experience, reserve a table upstairs at this combination restaurant and Swiss tourist office just off the Place de la Madeleine. You'll feel like putting on your skis once you've finished this meal, for the restaurant is decorated like a rustic Swiss chalet, with waitresses in bright, folkloric costumes. The best fare to order here is raclette, a hearty, filling Swiss dish that includes firm, buttery melted cheese, potatoes boiled in their skins, along with cornichons and a wonderfully spicy condiment of sliced onions mixed with hot mustard. Huge wheels of various Swiss cheeses are split in half, and then the exposed portion is placed under a special raclette broiler. As the cheese melts, it is scraped off—crisp, bubbling brown crust and all—and brought to the table. You will hardly be able to finish the tangy, melted cheese before the waiter is back, ready with another serving on another warm plate. With the raclette, savor the delicate Swiss white wine Fendant, the perfect companion to this filling, comforting and soul-satisfying meal.

A GUIDE TO LEADING SHOPS IN PARIS

Tachon, 38 rue de Richelieu, Paris 1 (telephone: 296-08-66). Metro: Palais-Royal. Open from 9:30 A.M.

to 1:30 P.M. and 4 to 7:30 P.M. Closed Sunday and Monday.

An old-fashioned neighborhood *fromagerie,* near the Louvre and the Palais Royal. Little handwritten signs tell the origin and history of many varieties, and a list notes the ones at their peak. There are some wonderful finds, including many small-production raw-milk farm cheeses: a Burgundian Epoisses, from the Laiterie de la Côte in Gevry-Chambertin; superb Swiss Tête-de-Moine du Bellelay; a better than average farm-fresh Saint-Nectaire, mild, sweet and tangy and aged a full two months on beds of rye straw; and Livarot, from Normandy farms, strong, spicy and elastic, the sort of cheese that sticks agreeably to your teeth. Also try the earthy, air-dried, smoked pork sausages from the French Alps.

Marie-Anne Cantin, 12 rue du Champ-de-Mars, Paris 7 (550-43-94). Metro: Ecole Militaire. Open from 8:30 A.M. to 1 P.M. and 3:30 to 7:30 P.M. and 8:30 A.M. to 1 P.M. Sunday. Closed on Monday and in August.

One of the prettiest cheese boutiques, just off the bustling rue Cler open-air market. Marie-Anne is the daughter of Christian Cantin, whose cheese shop at 2 rue de Lourmel in the 15th arrondissement has long been a Paris landmark. Now, with her husband, Antoine Dias, Madame Cantin is on her own, offering from eighty to a hundred remarkably well-aged varieties from France, Switzerland and the Netherlands. They're both passionate about cheese and their excitement carries over into the neatly organized, appealing little shop.

Their pride and joy are the aging cellars beneath the shop, with one for goat cheese (very dry) and one for cow's milk cheese (very humid). The floor of the cow's milk cellar is lined with rocks, which are watered regularly to provide proper humidity. All cheese is aged on natural straw, and varieties such as Muenster and Maroilles get a daily washing of beer or salt water, to turn mild, little disks into strong, forceful cheese.

A Cheese Lover's Tour of France

The true cheese lover, says Monsieur Dias, is one who invariably selects Camembert, Brie or Livarot as part of his cheese course. The best varieties sampled here include a classic and elegant Camembert; a dusty, creamy Bouton-de-Chèvre (farm-made goat cheese); and perhaps the best Charolais goat cheese in the world: creamy, refined and full-flavored. If you're in the mood for a mercilessly pungent cheese, try the northern Vieux Lille. Strong and rugged, it's a cheese that literally attacks your palate. More soothing is the Cheddar-like Salers, a mild and nutty cooked-milk cheese from the Auvergne.

Androuët, 41 rue d'Amsterdam, Paris 8 (874-26-93). Metro: Liège. Open from 8:30 A.M. to 6:30 P.M. Closed Sunday.

Long one of Paris's most respected cheese shops, Androuët sells some 10,000 pounds of cheese a month, offering two hundred varieties at a given time, including a few rarely seen elsewhere, in or out of France. That's because the Androuët family has been at it longer than just about anyone else. They opened their shop on rue d'Amsterdam in 1909, then twenty years later added a little corner for *dégustation,* or tasting of the many varieties of cheese sold in the shop. An upstairs restaurant was added in 1962.

In the early days, few small-scale farmers transported their cheese to Paris, so the Androuët family went to the farmers, traveling across France in search of honest, regional, raw milk cheese. Today, Androuët employees still go to local cheese fairs seeking new varieties.

Beneath the shop lie five aging cellars, some naturally humid and cool, where cheese may rest from a few days to a few months before it is ready to be sold in the shop. When I first moved to Paris, I went there each Saturday to sample unfamiliar varieties, using the shop as a mini-university of cheese. It is still where I go for a spectacular cheese tray. Androuët, more than any other shop in Paris, understands the play of flavors, colors, textures and shapes of cheese. Each cheese has a little label (ask for the *etiquette*) to identify it when you get it home.

Year-round, Androuët offers superb Brie de Meaux and Brie de Melun. Personal favorites include the triple cream Lucullus; the smooth Soumaintrain, full of flavor as well as character, and the Arome au Gene from the Lyonnais, pungent little disks fermented in *marc de Bourgogne*, an *eau-de-vie* distilled from pressed grape skins and seeds.

Le Ferme Saint-Hubert, 21 rue Vignon, Paris 8 (742-79-20). Metro: Madeleine. Open from 11 A.M. to 7 P.M. Tuesday through Friday, 8:30 A.M. to 7 P.M. Saturday. Closed Sunday and Monday.

Just around the corner from Fauchon, this crowded, compact shop offers extraordinary cheese varieties, including what is probably the best and most carefully selected Roquefort in Paris; a spectacular Beaufort, aged at least two years in special cellars; a vigorous Maroilles, from Flanders, aged for four months and sprinkled daily with beer. They also offer the Swiss Tête-de-Moine—a fruity cylinder of cheese that resembles Gruyère but has more punch, depth and character. It's a good traveling cheese, and will last for weeks refrigerated. Also worth sampling are the delicate, pale goat's milk butter and a rather unusual goat's milk yogurt. Many varieties of cheese are somewhat rough and rustic, like the shop's owner, Henry Voy. For my taste, some cheeses have been aged too long, losing a bit of their charm.

Lillo, 35 rue des Jelles-Feuilles, Paris 16 (727-69-08). Metro: Victor Hugo. Open from 7 A.M. to 1 P.M., 4 to 7:30 P.M. and Sunday 9 A.M. to 1 P.M. Closed Monday.

An elegant, sparkling little shop near the place Victor Hugo. Though few cheeses are aged there, many of the two hundred or so varieties are "finished" for five or six days in the neat cellars beneath the shop. Almost all are raw milk, small-production cheeses. Among the best varieties sampled was a remarkable Pavin d'Auvergne, a flat disk of mildly tangy, soft and supple cow's milk cheese from the Auvergne region. The cheese is similar to but far better than most versions of Saint-Nectaire. Also excellent: raw milk Brie, Muenster and Roquefort. It's no surprise that Monsieur Lillo won a civic award for the most attractive shop window on the street.

Jean Carmès et Fils, 24 rue de Lévis, Paris 17 (763-88-94). Metro: Villiers. Open from 9 A.M. to 1 P.M., 4 to 7 P.M. and Sunday 9 A.M. to 1 P.M. Closed on Monday and in August.

Situated right in the center of the hectic rue de Lévis market, Carmès is a big, open, family-run shop with the father, Jean Carmès, behind the cash register while his son, Patrick, rushes about with a nervous sort of vigor, keeping an eye on incoming deliveries and checking the progress of the two hundred or so varieties of cheese aging in humid rooms below and above the shop. These people are passionate about cheese, taking care to label each variety, happy to help you select a single cheese or an entire platter. Eighty percent of their cheese is bought fresh from the farms. Many varieties spend an average of three to four weeks in the Carmès cellars, aging on fresh, clean straw mats until the cheese is ready to be put on sale. Some specialties: l'Ecume, a triple cream so rich it easily replaces butter; Tantatais goat cheese, much like a Charolais, dry and delicious with a bloomy crust, and a Petit-Suisse *comme autrefois* (like the old days), a fragile cheese that stays fresh just four or five days.

Alain Dubois, 80 rue de Tocqueville, Paris 17 (227-11-38). Metro: Villiers. Open from 7:30 A.M. to 1 P.M. and 4 to 7:30 P.M., Sunday 9 A.M. to 1 P.M. Closed on Monday and in August.

A Cheese Lover's Tour of France

Young Alain Dubois turned the family *crémerie* into a full-fledged *fromagerie* in the early 1970s. The shop is artfully and tastefully arranged, and Monsieur Dubois is proudest of his Epoisses de Bourgogne, washed with *marc de Bourgogne* every day or so and aged according to his own process; his Fribourg, a softer Swiss Gruyère, aged in caves in the Jura region for at least two years, and his Swiss Vacherin Mont d'Or, still made in chalets and available from the end of fall into early spring. Monsieur Dubois offers some seventy varieties of goat cheese, according to the season.

He categorically opposes aging some cheeses, such as Brie, Camembert and Saint-Nectaire, in Paris. "Certain varieties must taste of the soil and the air of the region in which they were made, and they can't be aged in small batches in the city," insisted the outgoing Monsieur Dubois. "For a truly great Brie, you need an enormous amount aged in the same spot." His argument is convincing, for his Camembert—aged in Normandy at the Cooperative d'Isigny—is creamy, refined and delicious. —P.W.

Properly Shirted

BARBARA GELB

TO SOME AMERICANS, the celebratory ritual of ordering custom-made shirts from **Turnbull & Asser** in London is tantamount to investiture, almost like being knighted. After all, Turnbull & Asser, one hundred years old in April of 1986, are shirtmakers by appointment to Charles, Prince of Wales, and many of the establishment's other customers also bear hereditary titles.

I was instantly captivated by the shop's patrician aura when, eight years ago, I accompanied my husband there to order his first bespoke (made-to-measure) shirts. I had watched him evolve from his youthful Wallachs phase (1946—we were childhood sweethearts) through the Brooks Brothers "346" Department (1950—his preppy look) to Paul Stuart's Canadian line (1967—his executive image).

Everything, of course, was purchased ready-made, in-

Properly Shirted

cluding his shirts, although he had, from time to time, flirted with the idea of ordering shirts made-to-measure. Being taller than average and with long arms, he had always had to settle for sleeves that were not quite long enough; he needs them to be 37 inches, and ready-made shirts don't come longer than 36.

So when, in 1976, a friend in London suggested a visit to Turnbull & Asser ("my shirtmaker, the best," he assured us), my husband expressed guarded enthusiasm. Was he ready to take the plunge into made-to-measure?

Our London-based friend, a notorious high-liver, casually mentioned that a Turnbull & Asser bespoke shirt cost between $30 and $50, depending on the fabric (and the fluctuating rate of exchange). My husband was used to paying around $18 for a shirt. As I recall, he flinched. He might even have gasped. But our friend pointed out that not only would my husband's cuffs, at long last, extend elegantly beyond his jacket sleeves, but the shirts would be superbly tailored and the pattern and style would be exactly to his taste. He would, in brief, feel dressed like a prince.

Moreover, said our friend, scornfully glancing at my husband's conventional blue Oxford button-down, anyone who did *not* bespeak his shirtings at Turnbull & Asser was infra dig. He succumbed.

That was the beginning of a long, meaningful and expensive relationship with Turnbull & Asser. Now, every time we are in London, we pay a visit to the shop, and if my husband doesn't really need any new shirts, he has his old ones re-collared and re-cuffed (at about $30 a shirt, but they're as good as new) or he buys a few ties, or (as he did on our last trip) his first Turnbull & Asser "jumper" (in America, a sweater).

On our most recent trip to London we planned our ritual visit to the shop, realizing we'd begun to think of Turnbull & Asser as a kind of club, with its special ceremonies. This sense was confirmed when, on our second day in London we had lunch with David Frost and his wife, Carina. Frost, as always, was late, and when Carina saw my husband she did a charming double-take. He was wearing a four-year-old Turnbull & Asser shirt with alternating wide and narrow stripes of different blues on a cream ground. I had carefully selected a dark blue Turnbull & Asser tie with small red dots for him to wear with it.

"I'm almost sure David is wearing the exact same Turnbull & Asser shirt," Carina said. "Wait till you see! And I picked out his tie." When Frost arrived, we

Properly Shirted

did indeed see that the shirt was identical and the tie very similar.

That customers should often turn to their wives or roommates for assistance in selecting the appropriate tie for a particular shirt is understandable. The patterns of the shirtings can run to the bold: broad stripes of strong color, assertive checks, peremptory plaids. The novelist Joseph Heller, another friend who orders his shirts from Turnbull & Asser, thinks my husband's taste is too timid. Heller himself sometimes wears an assertively checked shirt with an aggressively striped tie—an aesthetic error, in my opinion, and one that I try (in common with Carina Frost) to help my husband avoid.

I have discussed the shirt-ordering process with a number of New York–based members of the Turnbull & Asser club, and they all agree that the first bespoke shirt is the hardest. Not only do you have to bite the bullet as to cost, but you have to learn patience and the enjoyment of small (some might say niggling) detail.

The process begins with a leisurely thumbing through fat books of cloth samples in the shop's "Churchill Room"—named for a cherished customer. Turnbull & Asser, which also has a ready-made shirt department, is situated at 71 and 72 Jermyn Street, St. James's, and its interior spaces are all mellow lighting and gleaming dark wood-paneled walls, peopled by immaculately turned-out and beautifully mannered salesmen. Under the benign and occasionally impish eye of Ken Williams, managing director of the company that owns Turnbull & Asser, the staff takes infinite pains to please, and their time is completely at your disposal.

What shape do you want your collar? How long do you want the points? How full do you want the body? Do you want a pocket? A monogram? (Twenty percent of the customers order hand-embroidered monograms.) Even the shape and color of buttons is open to negotiation.

Most crucial—and Mr. Williams's esteem for you might ultimately rest on this decision—do you want a three-button or a two-button cuff? (A one-button cuff is unthinkable, and not even mentioned.)

"We make what the customer wants," Mr. Williams says. "But of course, three buttons are our hallmark." He says this while shooting his exquisite three-button cuffs (white cuffs attached to a dazzling red-and-white-striped shirt that also has a flawlessly fitted white collar).

There can be endless discussion, with both Mr. Williams and Paul Cuss, the head shirt cutter and pattern maker, before each fateful decision is made.

"There are finicky customers who tell us the number of *stitches* they want in their collars," says Mr. Cuss, who is designated in Turnbull & Asser's mailed circulars as Royal Shirtmaker.

Yet, however carefully you are measured by Mr. Cuss or by Robert Squires, one of his assistants, there are always little adjustments to be made in the finished product. Indeed, it will very likely be six months before the sample shirt is pronounced wearable.

My husband's first shirt was mailed to him in New York about two months after he was measured. He unfolded it reverently. It was a deep, glowing pink with tiny white checks. The cotton was smooth and supple, the cut generously full, the stitching sturdy and almost invisible. When he slipped it on, he instinctively stood taller.

The fit, however, was not perfect. What was acceptable in an $18 shirt became impermissible in one costing over $30. The collar was a bit too high in back; the

Properly Shirted

points were a trifle too long; the cuffs buttoned a mite too snugly.

He dictated some imperious notes to me regarding these minor deficiencies, and I, agreeing with him that we should not overlook the most trifling flaw (nor would Turnbull & Asser wish us to), then mailed back the shirt with written instructions for adjustment. The shirt was returned several weeks later. This time the cuffs buttoned a bit too loosely and the collar was a smidgeon too tight. Once again, I sent the shirt back with instructions.

This kind of back and forth mailing is routine. "Our shirts know their own way across the Atlantic," says Mr. Williams.

The beautiful pink shirt was returned again, after several weeks, with a courteous letter suggesting that my husband wear it, have it laundered, and *then* judge the fit. If it suited, the rest of the shirts would be made exactly the same way. He did as instructed and at last had a perfect fit. Four months later, the remaining shirts arrived, all equally perfect. With new cuffs and collars, my husband is still wearing several from that original batch.

Turnbull & Asser's painstaking methods and courtly atmosphere have been carefully nurtured and cultivated by Mr. Williams, who took over management of the shop ten years ago and began wooing American customers.

"Our business today is, effectively, American," Mr. Williams confesses, adding that while the shop still has a good percentage of English clients, the business could probably not survive without the custom of its American cousins.

Mr. Williams, at forty-six, is president and chairman

of the board, as well as managing director of the company that owns not only Turnbull & Asser but also its sister shop, Hawes & Curtis, whose customers are overwhelmingly English and European. Prince Charles's father, Prince Philip, orders *his* shirts from Hawes & Curtis.

"Each of the shops developed its own personality," Mr. Williams says. "Americans found Turnbull & Asser. Americans' hearts are won by any shop that gives Old World service." He adds that Americans think Turnbull & Asser is typical of British elegance, courtesy and devoted workmanship, and he encourages that image. But, he implies—in truth and to his sorrow—it is atypical and, in fact, artfully contrived.

"Hawes & Curtis is different in style from Turnbull & Asser, quite deliberately," Mr. Williams says. "It's more British and formal. At Hawes & Curtis the salesperson is older, in his fifties. At Turnbull & Asser he's in his thirties. It's a mutual love affair, Americans and Turnbull & Asser."

Mr. Williams describes his efforts to lure and coddle American customers as being "softly commercial."

"It was a lovely old business," he says, "and no one wanted it to become over-commercial."

Reginald Turnbull and Ernest Asser opened their shop in 1885 as hunting-wear outfitters, specializing in the hunting shirt with attached stock. Turnbull was the shirtmaker and Asser the salesman, and it wasn't long before their shop expanded into racing silks and they were appointed shirtmakers to the Quorn Hunt, whose members still ride to the hounds, and whose emblem— three plumes rampant—is embossed on the Turnbull & Asser stationery.

Today Turnbull & Asser sells ready-made suits as

Properly Shirted

well as underwear, pajamas, dressing gowns, socks, scarves, sweaters, ties and braces (suspenders). But, says Mr. Williams, "shirts are our real business."

Mr. Williams's company owns, in addition to the two shops, a group of manufacturers that weaves and dyes the fabrics for the shops' shirtings and knits wools for their sweaters.

"We ourselves make 84 percent of everything we sell," he says with satisfaction. "And we sell only British-made goods."

He delights in naming the celebrated for whom Turnbull & Asser has made shirts (and other items of gentlemanly apparel). Among the shop's British customers are Laurence Olivier, Alec Guiness, John Gielgud and Paul Scofield. Mr. Williams will not name members of the aristocracy who are customers for fear they might close their accounts. "It isn't done," he murmurs.

He sighs over past customers. "We've been losing our good ones lately," he says. "David Niven, for instance, and Richard Burton. And Ralph Richardson—he bought lots of silk dressing gowns from us. I can't imagine what he needed with so many. He wore them all, I know, because he kept bringing them in to be relined and repaired." (Silk dressing gowns cost between £130 and £150.)

Mr. Williams cheers up over his list of very much alive American celebrities, among whom are Woody Allen, Tony Bennett, Mel Brooks, Walter Matthau, Al Pacino, Robert Redford and Tom Selleck.

The silk fabrics that go into dressing gowns can also be made up into shirts, but silk is more difficult to launder and most American customers prefer the cottons. Prices have risen since my husband bought his first bespoke shirt and the least expensive—a standard-weave broadcloth—now costs £50, which, at the current rate of exchange, comes to about $60. (Ready-mades start at $40.)

The most expensive shirts are those woven from Sea Island cotton (imported from the Wayward Islands) and voile (imported from France and Switzerland). They cost £80, but for that price you also get handsewn button-holes and hand-anchored buttons.

"There are only three people left in all of London who can sew buttonholes," says Paul Cuss, who joined the firm twenty-five years ago. "It is practically an extinct craft. In 1950 there were still thirty people who could do it."

Only Prince Charles gets handsewn buttonholes on his everyday broadcloth shirts as well as the fancy ones— and who would begrudge him that extra bit of swank?

With or without handsewn buttonholes, "in excess of twenty thousand" made-to-measure shirts are sold annually by Turnbull & Asser, according to Mr. Williams. The shop employs a workroom force of three hundred, which—deployed in five workrooms throughout London—finishes between forty and fifty dozen shirts a week.

The shirts are cut—on a wood block, with a razor-edged knife—in a basement below the Churchill Room. The basement is also where ties are stored, boxes and boxes of them. Foulards, at £12 each, are the most popular, selling at the rate of about a hundred per day. The fifty-ounce silk ties are a bargain at about $20, compared with the American price for a good silk tie.

Also in the basement is a customers' repair and cleaning service, presided over by Charles Morrow, who is seventy-nine. Mr. Morrow was the manager of the Turnbull & Asser laundry, a service provided to customers until

Properly Shirted

as recently as five years ago, and he remembers the days when shirts were pressed with gas irons.

The second floor of Turnbull & Asser houses Mr. Williams's office, which is modestly appointed and cluttered. "This is a working office," he says apologetically, noting that it is a far cry from the "very posh" executive offices he visits in America. He spends twelve hours a day in the shop when he is in London, much of it on the telephone with his buyers. He entertains a good deal, most of it business-related, and what little home life he has is spent with his wife in a house they own in Dullage, four and a half miles outside of London. His twenty-two-year-old son, Martin, is working at Turnbull & Asser, "learning the business."

To maintain and encourage the American connection, Mr. Williams travels frequently to the United States. Turnbull & Asser ready-made shirts, ties and other articles of clothing are sold at Bergdorf Goodman in New York, where ready-made cotton shirts run from $75 to $120, and at Neiman-Marcus in Los Angeles, San Francisco, Dallas, Houston, Chicago and Boston, and Mr. Williams visits all these shops regularly.

"I do what you might call personal appearances," he says. "I serve tea, chat up the customers, answer questions, give them tourist information about London. It's a total P.R. job. I think I have more friends in New York than I do in London."

And twice a year—in the spring and fall—Turnbull & Asser mounts what Mr. Williams calls a trunk show. The firm culls its file of 16,000 active accounts, worldwide, and sends between 3,000 and 4,000 letters to its American customers, reminding them of the impending visit. (The letterhead of this reminder reads, discreetly, "By Appointment to H.R.H. The Prince of Wales Shirtmakers.")

Four representatives of the firm—fitters, cutters and pattern makers—establish headquarters at a New York hotel (for ten days in the spring, twenty days in the fall), where they make available the same fat sample books of fabric kept in the London shop as well as stock shirts. Anyone can come and buy or be fitted. But it's just not the same as going to the splendid source in Jermyn Street, St. James's.

A Grand Hotel
as Symbol

LUCINDA FRANKS

GRAND OLD HOTEL
is often grand because it has become a metaphor for the
land in which it stands. Ghosts stalk its sculleries,
myths mingle in its lobbies, and the inhabitants are
faithful curators who have collected a thousand stories of
the past.

At the King David in Jerusalem, the bellboy who
carried our bags was just yesterday a soldier in the desert. The impeccably tailored maître d'hôtel spent his
youth in Bergen-Belsen. And downstairs at La Regence
Grill, an aging Zionist freedom fighter sips coffee in the
very spot that in 1946, at the tender age of seventeen, he
blew to smithereens.

The King David is the Middle East's most venerable
hotel, operated in the style of the old spas of Europe, to
which guests return year after year like homecoming
children to the same rooms they have always stayed in. It

is also a bustling oasis of the Levant, to which the mighty and the rich have gravitated from all over the world. Its walls have heard the whispers of kings and the confessions of bishops, the pleas of premiers and the threats of terrorists. Anwar el-Sadat and Menachem Begin made peace here, Liz Taylor and Richard Burton had a public quarrel here, Toscanini waved his baton here. The British occupied it, a future prime minister bombed it, and Mayor Teddy Kollek calls it "a symbol of the existence of Israel itself."

Some Israelis say the hotel is not what is used to be in the days of British colonial rule, when Sudanese waiters in red fezes passed trays of hot cheese puffs in the lobby; garish dripping chandeliers have gone up and instead of King Abdullah of Transjordan riding up with his team of white horses, busloads of tour groups cram the circular driveway. Nevertheless, the setting sun still turns the King David's immense stones as pink as the Judean hills, the lobby's original thronelike chairs still creak with the weight of those who plot peace and war, and from its balconies, the walls of the Old City can be seen winding like a serpent through the valley below.

The revolving doors of the King David loom skyward like the golden gates of heaven. Maître d'hôtel Avraham Weiner watches over them as staunchly as St. Peter. His presence there—to greet VIPs and returning guests—is a mark of the hotel's traditional attitude toward itself and its clients: They are looked upon as larger than life. Some of them think they are, others know they are not, but all are made to feel as if they were. A retired plumber from Elizabeth, N.J.—call him Sam Goldberg—might stand at the check-in desk next to the Queen of the Belgians and both are given the royal treatment.

Both will find cakes and fruit in their rooms and both

A Grand Hotel as Symbol

can put their shoes in the hall in the evening and find them hand-polished when they rise. Mr. Goldberg, you see, probably comes to the King David every few years and therefore he is considered "family." Not that the hotel is insensitive to real VIPs; when it was given forty-eight-hours' notice that Sadat would arrive for his historic visit to Jerusalem, the likes of Mr. Goldberg (and the rest of the guests) were evacuated from the hotel.

The King David was built in the late 1920s by an architect who wanted to "evoke by reminiscence of ancient Semitic styles the glorious period of King David." Square pillars rise up to meet a Nile-blue geometric frieze designed to depict the crenelations in the Old City walls. There is a sweep of floor-length velvet curtain here, a hand-painted ceiling there, a dash of giant sunflowers in an ancient copper urn. In the Banquet Room every morning a table groaning with homemade Danish pastry, fruit, and a medley of cheeses and smoked fish (the famous Israeli breakfast) is laid out; this is the room in which the first "peace meal" between Begin and Sadat was held; a wise chef left out the wine (Moslems are forbidden alcohol) but produced a cake in the form of two pyramids spanned by a bridge labeled PEACE in Hebrew and Arabic. In the main dining room, there are table d'hôte dinners each night reminiscent of an old-fashioned Jewish boardinghouse—noodle pudding, boiled chicken, consommé with kreplach, apple strudel.

The atmosphere is a cross between Grand Central Station, Miami Beach's Fontainebleau and Buckingham Palace. There are so many vignettes in the cavernous lobby that Hieronymus Bosch would be in his glory. Talmudists in yarmulkes stroll arm in arm, their fringes trailing. An American woman in white fur shrieks at the sight of another woman in white fur—they both went to school in Kansas City and this is the first time they've run into each other in twenty-five years. At the reservation desk, there is a commotion. A Frenchman has dropped his suitcase in the middle of the floor, seated his wife upon it and is raising his voice to high heaven.

"I must have my room, now!" "Impossible, *monsieur*," says the desk clerk. Whenever a shot is fired in Israel, the hotel's telex starts clicking with cancellations and therefore it regularly overbooks. Sometimes, newcomers like this Frenchman will arrive to find their reservations have mysteriously disappeared.

"Then I will camp out in the lobby of the King David Hotel!" the Frenchman replies and himself sits down on the suitcase. Ilan Fink, at that time the manager, quickly steps in and a room is found.

Teddy Kollek sashays past. Jerusalem's Mayor is on his way to five o'clock tea, which is served, sometimes to the sounds of a string quartet, as it has been for decades. He likes to bring dignitaries out on the terrace and gaze out over the cypress, date and sabra trees and muse about the three cultures (Arab, Christian, Jew) that live so peaceably inside the Old City's walls. Sometimes artists from the nearby Mishkenot Sha'ananim, a residence for visiting writers and composers, come over to linger also, as do members of the Knesset at the end of the day. Mayor Kollek, who has as large an appetite for good food as he does for the Delicate Balance in politics, sometimes grumbles to Weiner that no, today he does not want some foie gras. Minutes later, however, he is raising his hand: "Oh, well, bring me just a bit of goose liver." A little treat can help soften the fearful intensity with which people in Israel end up talking about the future.

Visiting dignitaries usually stay in one of the presidential or royal suites on the top floor of the hotel, in

A Grand Hotel as Symbol

which, for about five times the cost of what is called a medium room, one can lounge about in two bedrooms, a parlor, a living room, and a balcony and see the Old City, the Mount of Olives, Mount Scopus, the Dead Sea and just about all of East Jerusalem. Lesser mortals can scale downward to a junior suite with a balcony view of the Old City (this is the favored type of room, although before 1967 it was very unpopular since the Jordanians, who controlled the Old City, could take potshots at you), to a standard double-bed room overlooking the new city.

No two rooms in the 260-room hotel are alike, and while the standard rooms are large and comfortable, the suites have large entry halls and are often furnished with antiques. In a flush of modernism, however, the King David has built a new deluxe duplex which looks as if it belongs in Beverly Hills rather than the city of the Old

A Grand Hotel as Symbol

Testament prophets: a spiral staircase leads from the living room down into an enormous bathroom with sauna, chaise longues and a sultan's tub with gilt fixtures. At the same time, the "anniversary" restaurant, installed in 1982, the fiftieth year of the hotel's existence and called The King's Garden, has given a bow to the past by installing high-backed bamboo colonial chairs—made in Tennessee.

This is the kind of thing that the locals love to kvetch about, especially if they remember the hotel when it was a refuge for high society, when the servants were doting Arabs, and the food gourmet rather than kosher. "It's become an establishment geared to the bar mitzvah and the wedding," sniffs one Israeli. "We Jews, I'm afraid, really don't know how to serve."

In spite of the complaints, the King David is booked for months in advance, especially during Jewish holidays. The Hilton and Sheraton hotels that have opened in Jerusalem in recent years have apparently not affected its business.

The last time my husband and I stayed at the King David, our quarters were a modest-sized two-room suite opening onto a balcony just big enough to hold two standing arm in arm to watch the sun set, or one curled up on a bed of blankets watching it rise. Twenty-four-hour room service was fairly prompt, though it would not set any records; both the waiters and maids (many of them seemed to be jolly Slavic mamas with braids wrapped around their heads) were delightfully warm and obliging. The switchboard operators and desk clerks, however, were less familial and more snappish and beleaguered.

In spite of this, and despite the large, noisy big-city hotel atmosphere, there were many personal touches that

A Grand Hotel as Symbol

made us feel like we were visiting friends. When we had to leave to catch an early flight, for instance, the coffee shop opened at 5 A.M. especially for us.

The King David has other little offbeat touches that have been preserved from the past—pages circle the lobby with guests' names emblazoned on a blackboard and a horse and carriage is provided for a tour of the Old City—but none is so cherished as a peripatetic masseur named Steve. He eased the tension from the muscles of Henry Kissinger during the peace process (and rumor has it he was the first to learn of breakthroughs) and when David Rockefeller wrote the King David to request his services on his next visit, Steve personally wrote back that unfortunately he had, like all Israelis young and old, to go into the army to do his yearly reserve duty. He would, however, willingly handpick a replacement.

A Week-Long Taste of Tunisia

HEBE DORSEY

$\mathbb{P}$RECIOUS FEW
Americans know that Tunisia is only two short air-flight
hours from Paris, one hour from Rome, twenty minutes
from Sardinia. Even fewer know where Tunisia actually
is.

"When I told people I was going to Tunisia," Peter
Dubow, president of a New York company that represents major European fashion designers, recalled of his
first visit, "they looked at me as if I was going to China.
I myself had to look it up on the map. I was surprised to
learn it's closer to Paris than Miami is to New York.
Even my tour operator, who is pretty sophisticated,
didn't know where Tunisia was. He kept looking into
'Middle East.' Finally I said: 'Try Africa.' "

The proximity of Europe is one advantage that people
who visit the Continent find attractive for a long weekend. What makes Tunisia even more special is that, in a

A Week-Long Taste of Tunisia

short time, one changes continents, culture and civilization.

It could be an abrupt change. But Tunisia, bathed in
centuries of Phoenician, Roman and Arab civilizations,
Westernized by several decades of French presence, feels
very open to the outside world.

After European resorts, many of which are overpriced
and overcrowded, Tunisia—cheap and relatively empty
—comes as a pleasant relief. But Tunisia is not for people who like their Bloody Mary impeccably butlered by
the side of the pool. It is not for people who have to call
Chicago every hour on the hour. It is not for people who
live for black-tie galas.

It is, rather, for people with a sense of adventure and a
curious mind, people who will enjoy the contrast between Roman ruins and Oriental bazaars. It is for people
who can forget about nouvelle cuisine and appreciate a
relaxed, rustic fare, based on fish, and fruit and vegetables that still taste like fruit and vegetables. It is for people who do not mind going to bed early and reading a
book.

The reason why relatively few people know about Tunisia is that large-scale tourism is fairly new here. There
has been considerable work done on what used to be
plain sand empty beaches. All over Tunisia, but especially in the Sousse region, which is emerging as the Tunisian Riviera, hotels are sprouting up like mushrooms.
Management of these establishments is often in the
hands of foreign hotel groups, such as Sheraton, Hilton
or Trust House Forte. Food and service, and particularly
upkeep, have greatly improved since the early days,
when Tunisian waiters, some of them often straight from
the desert, had a hard time figuring out why people
needed more than one fork.

There are several possible approaches to visiting Tunisia, depending on one's age, sex, intellectual interests and the time of year. The following suggested tour was worked out with a hypothetical American traveler on his first visit in mind. The time was July, when, as throughout the summer, the sun is decidedly and relentlessly African. Tunisia, with 900 miles of beaches, then stands out as a swimmer's paradise. In winter, one might well opt to begin the tour in the Sahara and work north.

Ideally, a first visit need not take more than a week. One should take two days to visit Tunis's most worthwhile sights, including Carthage, the souks, or bazaars, and the museum at Le Bardo. Sidi-bou-Sa'id, an artists' colony in azure and white, is another must.

The next two days should be spent driving south along the coast to Hammamet, some thirty-five miles from Tunis. One could make a slight detour on the way to see an old Roman spa, Korbous, whose hot sulfur springs are supposed to cure everything.

From Hammamet, it is only an hour's drive to Sousse, where the coast unfolds for miles like a dream in Technicolor.

A brand-new complex, called Port El Kantaoui, is the center of it all, with marina, harbor, cafés and restaurants, a fine golf course and the kind of cleanliness that, in these parts, can be very appealing.

Although Tunisia has five international airports, the best way to enter the country is still through Tunis, which is noisy, hot and slow—as indeed are most airports in Mediterranean countries.

Avoid heading for the center of town, which will come as a total disappointment. Instead, rent a car at the airport—making sure it has such basics as a rearview mirror and a spare tire and never mind if it needs a

A Week-Long Taste of Tunisia

wash—and go straight to one of the best beach hotels outside Tunis.

Most of them are located north of the city. **La Baie des Singes,** in Gammarth, some twelve miles out of Tunis, is still the most popular with Europeans, many of whom come from the fashion and show business worlds. It is situated on a hill, overlooking the startlingly blue bay, with bungalows spread out in lavish gardens of laurel, lavender, mimosa, geraniums and pink and white oleanders.

There is a choice between a pool, which these days seems to attract noisy children, or a beach, which is shaped like a shell, shaded with straw parasols and very private. As the sun comes up at around five o'clock, the best time to go to the beach is early in the morning. Then, the sky is a pure azure, the beach silent, the sea without a ripple and hot honeyed smells waft from the gardens.

Arab boys walk along the beach with baskets of sea urchins, caught at dawn over the nearby rocks. One of the most pleasant experiences is to sit by the sea and let them open one, two or three dozen, which you rinse in the surf before dousing them with lemon. At about two dinars ($4) a dozen, the cost of the whole operation, *service compris,* will not add up to the price of a single sea urchin in a Paris restaurant.

Lunch could be a snack around the pool, but a better bet is to drive a short distance to one of many local fish restaurants. **Les Coquillages,** set on a plain but vast and airy terrace overlooking the sea, serves pleasant food at moderate prices. A meal for four, starting with the local *brik*—a tasty egg and pastry combination—came to $34 on a recent visit. The local beer is good and often preferable to wine—although the country also produces unpretentious white and rosé wines, a legacy of the French Catholic missionaries. Tap water should be avoided, although there is a good local bottled water called Safia.

After the sacrosanct siesta, one should spend the first afternoon visiting **Sidi-bou-Sa'id,** the most attractive village near Tunis. It was celebrated by André Gide as "bathing in a fluid, mother-of-pearl, sedative, almost fresh milk."

Walk up and down the narrow, winding streets, admire the jealously guarded houses, closed with hob-nailed, blue Moorish doors and festooned with giant bougainvilleas.

Take a look at the **Hotel Dar Sa'id,** a small old Arab palace, with exquisite inner courtyard and vaulted rooms, as well as **Dar Zarrouk,** a restaurant with a stupendous view over the bay of Tunis. Browse around the various bazaars, which offer everything from silver antiques to brand new djellabas, the loose garments worn in this part of the world; then it is time to sit down at one of the Moorish cafés.

The most famous is the **Café des Nattes,** with straw mats lined up and down its stairs. Inside, in an authentic Moorish decor, people are squatting, playing dominoes and smoking narghiles.

Another favorite is right below, on the main plaza, under three scrawny trees. It appeals to tourists and locals alike. The reason is a delicious mint tea with pignons, which comes so hot that you have to hold the small glass between thumb and first finger. For 200 or 300 millimes (30 cents), you can buy a sweet and musky jasmine bouquet, which Arab men wear tucked over one ear.

For dinner, **Le Typique,** set on a small, cheerful ter-

A Week-Long Taste of Tunisia

race with cypresses and red-and-white checked table-cloths, offers a variety of couscous washed down with *boukha*—the local spirit made out of figs.

The next day should be spent visiting Tunis and its souks early in the morning. Then a swim, lunch and si-esta followed by a visit to Carthage.

Tunis itself is a busy metropolis, whose main ave-nue, the Avenue Habib Bourguiba, shaded with hand-some trees, is worth seeing. After that, head straight for the souks in the old Arab quarters, a labyrinth of crowded alleys lined with shops. The souks are neatly divided according to the different guilds.

Souk el Attarine is devoted to perfumes and soaps, as well as henna, the strong-smelling herb that Arab brides use heavily, both for dyeing their hair and coloring hands and feet. Other souks—often with artisans right outside, carrying on with their work—are devoted to rug dealers, booksellers, drapers, jewelers, leatherworkers and saddlers, coppersmiths and chiselers.

The late afternoon should be devoted to visiting Carthage's Punic and Roman ruins. Despite Cato's somber pronouncement *"Censeo Carthaginem esse delendum"*—"I declare that Carthage must be des-troyed"—Carthage strangely and miraculously comes back to life, especially at sunset.

After such a heady historical beginning, **Hamma-met** is only an hour away by car and something else again. This fishing village, once a favorite of Paul Klee, is widely developed around a splendid beach whose sand feels like flour underfoot. Several miles long and lined with orange groves and jasmine bushes, it is so wide that the local police routinely patrol it on horseback. Tourists can do the same or try a camel ride instead.

The charm of Hammamet lies in the contrast between

gardens and beach. Numerous hotels of various catego-
ries, holiday villages and residential clubs have been
built to harmonize with the surrounding vegetation. The
house of the French aesthete George Sebastian, which
Frank Lloyd Wright called "the most beautiful house I
know," is now an international cultural center.

The drive to **Sousse** is a pleasant hour. On your way,
stop by **Nabeul,** famous for its pottery and only nine
miles away. The vegetation changes from rich and green
land to a drier landscape, dominated by silver-gray olive
trees. Watch how the colorful attire of the peasant
women, who fortunately have not given in to Western
dress, changes as one moves south. Dressed in violent
purple in the region of Hammamet, they change to a
brilliant red near Sousse.

Sousse was built on the Roman Hadrumetum and has
been a busy port since Hannibal used it against Scipio at
the end of the second Punic war. Now a prosperous tourist town, it has a fine beach bordered with hotels.

VISITOR'S GUIDE TO TUNISIA

In general there are no direct flights to Tunisia from
North America. The best bet is to fly to London, Paris,
Rome or Milan and go on from there. A valid passport is
required and a vaccination is not normally necessary.
The national currency is the dinar. Most hotels change
convertible currencies and traveler's checks.

Arabic is the official language, but French is generally used. English, Italian and German are also spoken.

The climate is Mediterranean, warm in summer, mild
in winter with cool nights. The temperature can reach
into the 90s in summer.

A Week-Long Taste of Tunisia

ACCOMMODATIONS

Tunisia has a vast range of accommodations from modest to deluxe. In the latter category, prices are well below Europe's. For instance, the four-star **Hasdrubal,** situated on the sea at **Port el Kantaoui** (a man-made resort that includes a Moorish marina, a port that can take up to 340 yachts and an 18-hole golf course), charges about $45 a day for room and breakfast at the height of the season, from June 15 to September 15.

SHOPPING

Knotted rugs are everywhere, but the *klims,* or coarse and colorful rugs used by nomads in their tents, are far more attractive as well as noticeably cheaper. Leather goods, pottery, lace, silver, djellabas, carved wood and copper articles are also good buys. But remember, in the souks, bargaining is the name of the game. —H.D.

Around Hong Kong, Chopsticks in Hand

EILEEN YIN-FEI LO

I DON'T REMEMBER
it as a huge, ramshackle and temporary building at all,
although my cousins in Hong Kong tell me that is exactly
what it was. My girlhood memory of Chen Cheung Chu
is of a wondrous restaurant in the middle of Sham Sui
Po, once a neighborhood of refugees who had fled revolutionary China. Chen Cheung Chu was a restaurant
quite fitting for its surroundings, for it was a place for
the cooking of China's Hakka people, those nomads who
had trekked through history from above Peking to the
fertile southern basin between Canton and Hong Kong,
bringing with them quite special ways of cooking, among
them such favorites of mine as salt-baked chicken and a
wonderful dish of stewed fresh bacon and mustard
greens that we called *mui choi kau yuk.*

On the first of many trips back to Hong Kong in recent
years, I found much of what had been the Hong Kong of

my teenage years changed. The stucco home behind the high wall in Mongkok, where I had lived for a time with my aunt and my cousins, was gone, replaced by a modern multistory school, and the Sham Sui Po area had become a residential neighborhood of private homes and new high-rises. Nor was Chen Cheung Chu, my restaurant, there.

But such tastes are never lost forever in Hong Kong, for within its borders is the finest, most varied Chinese cookery in the world, as well as a population that never relents in its demands for it. And so I was taken to the **Home Restaurant** at 19 Hanoi Road (telephone: 3-665876), in the Tsinshatsui section of Kowloon, where I had salt-baked chicken that almost erased my old memories.

It was made the way it should be, but almost never is outside of Hong Kong. It is not unusual for most restaurants simply to cook chicken in several boiling salt solutions and then call it "baked." At the Home it was truly baked, in a shell of sea salt so it was tender and juicy and dense with the aromas of the ginger and spring onions with which it had been cooked.

That taste that awakened memories is the sort of thing that happens repeatedly when I go to Hong Kong. I remember different foods, associating them with old memories, unforgotten tastes, legends, stories, and then I seek them out in what I suppose is a recurring effort to renew my culinary past.

I recall that my mother's mother, who was more or less an observant Buddhist, would on the first and fifteenth of every month, and during the first fifteen days of each January, demand that her family prepare a vegetarian meal. She rarely ate meat or fish, and when she would make such a demand we recognized that it was in a sense an affirmation of her beliefs, and so we would prepare

special dishes of fresh vegetables, steamed winter-melon soups in which the melon functioned as a tureen, mock "meats" and "fish" made from bean curd and imaginative dishes using fruits and nuts.

These days, to have an artfully carved winter melon filled with a wonderfully scented broth of ginkgo nuts, snow peas and other vegetables, one might go to the **Man Wah,** an extraordinarily beautiful, lacquered restaurant overlooking Victoria Harbor atop the Mandarin Hotel on Connaught Road Central (5-220111). It may well be Hong Kong's most striking Chinese restaurant, a place for elegant banquets. But if you wish to have a total vegetarian eating experience, a meal that combines tastes and art, then a one-hour ferry ride out to **Lan Tau Island,** followed by a bus ride up to **Po Lin,** a Buddhist monastery and retreat house, would be in order.

The monks cook vegetarian banquets, and on a recent trip there I ate a meal consisting of various stir-fried and steamed vegetables, mushrooms shaped like abalone and called by that name, two different "fish"—one fashioned from mashed taro root, the other made by layering pieces of dried bean curd—mashed squash shaped into "Buddhas" and "goose," also made from wet and dried bean curd.

During the feast of the August Moon, which usually occurs on the fifteenth day of the eighth month—usually during September or October on the Western calendar—we ate moon cakes unceasingly. These were flour cakes filled with a sweet paste of lotus seeds, nuts and whole, cooked, salted egg yolks—the more yolks, the greater the value of the moon cake. In China my mother used to tell me that the sweetness of the cakes would ensure my beauty in my next incarnation, but in Hong Kong we were told that the moon cakes were especially important because in the revolution of Dr. Sun Yat-sen in 1911 important political and strategic messages were baked into their fillings. I used to buy moon cakes in the now long-gone Wing Lung bakery near my Kowloon home, later in the bakery of the Shamrock Hotel and still later at the **International** restaurant, 612 Nathan Road (3-302424), a huge teahouse of many stories that is still as popular on Sunday mornings as it was thirty years ago.

Of course we went to many teahouses in Hong Kong to *yum cha*, or "drink tea," as we say in Cantonese. The first time I had *dim sum* was as a tiny girl when my brother carried me on his shoulders into a teahouse in Sun Tak, the Canton suburb in which I was born, and it was there that I first tasted *char siu bau*, pork-filled baked buns; *har gau*, steamed shrimp dumplings; *siu mai*, basket-shaped dumplings of pork and mushrooms; and *wu gok*, a kind of croquette made of mashed taro root.

In Hong Kong there are more *dim sum* parlors than leaves on an orange tree, but places where I would *yum cha* these days are the lovely old **Luk Yu Teahouse**, 26 Stanley Street (5-235464); the **Luk Kwok**, 67 Gloucester Road (5-280373), where my future husband and I not only had tea for the first time but where we also held our wedding reception; and **Maxim's Palace** in the World Trade Center, Causeway Bay (5-760288), a huge, ornate barn of a restaurant. All three remain as I remembered them, and they still teem with people on Sunday mornings.

Sunday was always shopping day in Hong Kong, for the city's stores are open every day and Sunday is the day off for just about everybody except shopkeepers. It remains so today.

Around Hong Kong, Chopsticks in Hand

I remember that I didn't particularly like being dragged about Mongkok and along Nathan Road by my aunt and older cousins. But I did like the compensations, for after shopping on Sunday afternoons, we almost always found our way into a noodle parlor or stopped for some fresh noodles in chicken broth from the street vendors, who are called *dai pai dong*. Now, as then, Hong Kong abounds in noodle shops where you can get either noodles in broth, topped with pork, chicken, beef or fresh vegetables, fresh pastalike noodles with various sauces, fresh rice noodles with black beans or pan-fried noodles with stir-fried meats, fish or vegetables piled atop them.

Perhaps the best of the *dai pai dong* is on Shanghai Street, a few blocks behind the Peninsula Hotel in Kowloon. It is a collection of booths and carts filled with the smells of freshly cooked vegetables, ducks, geese and soups. For noodles I recommend three shops in particular, all of them situated in that unique Hong Kong gastronomic oddity, **Food Street,** in Causeway Bay, one square block of nothing but various restaurants. They are **Nanking Noodles** (5-772696), **Phoenix Noodles** (5-777973), which also serves a wonderful variety of those thick Cantonese rice porridges called *congee,* and a delightfully named place, **Boil & Boil Wonderful** (5-779788), which also does thick noodle broths in clay pots. The other sort of noodles I loved as a child were so-called Singapore-style noodles, threadlike strands of rice noodles stirred with vegetables, chicken and shrimp in a hot curry sauce. I could eat them any time of the day, and I did.

Those noodles are just one of many Southeast Asian dishes that traveled to Hong Kong and found a home. A wonderful example of that dish can be had at a Malaysian restaurant in Kowloon, **Nam Ah,** 23 Ashley Road (3-667702). The noodles are just right, and the curry is searing. Perhaps a little less incendiary, but quite fine, more Cantonese than Malaysian, are the Singapore noodles at **King Bun,** 158 Queens Road Central (5-431343).

Many preparations such as these are available elsewhere these days, but there are others that can be had only rarely. For example, I remember well the sharp, salty taste of Yunnan ham, somewhat like American Smithfield ham but with a deeper, richer taste. These days it is almost impossible to obtain, but you can taste it at the **Sun Tung Lok Restaurant,** 78 Morrison Hill Road (5-748261), close to the Happy Valley racetrack. Nor is whole roast pig all that common nowadays. I loved the crisp pork skin as a child and would entreat my aunt to take me where I could eat it. There were more restaurants serving it then, but you can have a succulent roast pig at **Yung Kee,** a multistoried restaurant in the middle of Hong Kong Island's business district, 36-40 Wellington Street (5-232343).

For me a rare treat was taking the bus out to **Aberdeen** on Hong Kong Island to go to **Jumbo** (5-53911), the most elaborate of the floating restaurants there. The place where you get on small boats and are ferried out to deep water and those enormous, brightly decorated, multidecked floating restaurants is actually **Shum Wan,** and it is there that the bus let us off.

The brief motorboat ride out was fun, but just as much fun was wandering among the tanks of live fish of every conceivable color, of live shrimp, crabs, lobsters and eels to see just what you would have for a special dinner. Men with nets stood about and when you pointed they would dip their nets and scoop up your chosen fish,

Around Hong Kong, Chopsticks in Hand

weigh it to determine the charge, then write down how you wanted it cooked—steamed with scallions and boiled peanut oil or with black beans, fried crisply or cooked in wine. I loved to go to Jumbo with my cousins because the restaurant had two carved wood thrones with ornate moldings behind them, arranged so children like us could sit on them and pretend we were empresses, or that we were getting married to rich men.

Jumbo was where we ate tiny clams from Shanghai, so small the shell was tinier than the nail of my smallest finger; it was where we had rare yellow fish and giant crabs. And when I went there again recently it was exactly as I remembered it.

Perhaps what I remember most vividly, however, are the New Year banquets we had over the years. The New Year banquets—because it comes on the first day of the first month of the Chinese calendar, because it symbolizes newness, rebirth, regeneration, because there are elements of religion in it—is perhaps the most important occasion of the year for all Chinese. It also happens that during this period, on January 7, it is everybody's birthday, no matter on which day you happened to have been born, so it becomes a birthday party as well. The Chinese rarely celebrate birthdays, but they do celebrate birth.

Every year we used to go out to the New Territories, to Sha Tin, for New Year, first to pray in the Buddhist temple there, then to eat a banquet in the temple. When I was quite young the tunnel connecting Hong Kong Island with Kowloon had not been built yet and cars had to be taken over on the Jordan Road ferry. At least four hours of waiting was required to get one's auto ferried across because so many people wanted to drive to see relatives that day. So my cousin's older son would take the car across the night before New Year's Day, and park it near the ferry slip. Then we would simply take a ferry ride over the next day and have our car waiting for us.

All of this careful planning is not required these days because Hong Kong not only has its tunnel, but also an under-the-harbor Metro. As for the New Year banquets, those that I remember are the ones that I helped my aunt prepare in the house behind the wall in Mongkok. I have had perfectly marvelous, varied banquets in the **Bun Kai** restaurant in Canton and recently in one of Hong Kong's newer and finer Cantonese restaurants, **Flower Lounge**, 3 Peace Avenue (3-7156763), and in **Man Wah** atop the Mandarin, but as fine as they've been, I remember those of my girlhood in Mongkok best.

DIM SUM TO BANQUETS

Prices for the special dishes mentioned throughout the above article vary, of course, from restaurant to restaurant, but in general these are about the prices, in United States dollars, you might expect to pay in Hong Kong's restaurants.

Salt-baked chicken, usually $10 for a whole chicken, $5 for the half; *mui choi kau yuk,* about $4. A steamed winter melon, cored and filled with an elaborate soup, will cost about $25, but one elaborately etched and carved can cost as much as $70. A meal at the **Po Lin Monastery** will cost about $4 to $5 a dish. Moon cakes are anywhere from $1 to $2 each, depending upon the filling, and the various *dim sum* selections usually range from 50 cents to slightly more than $1. Dishes of noodles run from $3.50 to $4; those in soups or broths are less, costing about $2 to $3 a bowl, and Singapore noodles will cost about $4 a dish.

Yunnan ham, usually cooked in combination with seafood, chicken or other meats, can cost as much as $8 a dish. An entire roast pig would be sold by the pound. A suckling pig will cost about $50 to $60, and a portion serving six to eight people will cost slightly under $10. A fish selected in Aberdeen will range from $20 to as much as $50 for a rare, fat grouper; Shanghai clams will cost about $10 a dish; yellow fish about $10 and platters of giant crabs as much as $25 each.

Banquets in Hong Kong can be simple or extravagant. A traditional banquet is usually ten dishes for ten people. A simple kind, with perhaps several stir-fried dishes, a steamed fish, a whole chicken and roast duck, would cost about $300, or $30 a person. An elaborate variety, such as I have had at **Man Wah,** for example, will include steamed melon, shark fin, rare abalone, perhaps exotic game, expensive fish, huge spiny local lobsters and live shrimp and can cost as much as $100 a person. —E.Y-F.L.

In Kyoto, the Definitive Japanese Inn

HAROLD C. SCHONBERG

IN JAPAN THE traditional inns are called ryokan, and every visitor is urged to try one, if only to experience an older, different way of life. So my wife and I, on a recent visit to Japan, did exactly that—but with a slight difference. Ryokans run about $30 a person to infinity. We took dead aim at infinity, at $380 a night for the two of us at the **Hiira-giya Ryokan** in Kyoto.

Was it worth it for the two nights our bankroll held out? Yes, very much so, and we are still trying to put to-gether our impressions. It was a subtle yet overwhelming experience. The best ryokan exemplify the way Japan used to be, not the way contemporary civilization has made it. As such they represent a kind of tradition alien to Western thought and manners—perhaps only a native Japanese can fully appreciate their nuances, symbolism and folkways. Yet there is a quality, an aristocracy, that

In Kyoto, the Definitive Japanese Inn

even the alien sensibilities of a Westerner could grasp and vaguely understand.

The Hiiragiya was established in 1818 and has always had a distinguished clientele. When we told a friend where we would be staying in Kyoto, he looked at us with sudden respect. "The Hiiragiya!" he exclaimed. "My God! Nobody gets in there except prime ministers, movie stars and millionaires. The Hiiragiya! Take notes! Tell me all about it! Don't forget a thing!"

We arrived around 5 P.M. The ryokan is on a quiet, narrow side street, full of small shops and bicycles. We were met in the vestibule, a stone entrance on the street level. Among those to greet us was a canary in a cage hanging just inside the gateway. (At night it was taken inside.) Shoes off, and up two steps into the hotel proper. Into slippers. We were escorted to our room. Slippers off in the foyer of the room. Only stockings or bare feet are permitted within the living quarters. There was a knock on the door, our housekeeper arrived bearing a tray of tea, and our adventure got underway. Suddenly we found ourselves transplanted in time from twentieth-century hysteria to nineteenth-century serenity.

Our attendant was a middle-aged woman. Later we learned that her name was Miyuki Akiyama. She spoke no English. With smiles, she motioned for my wife and took her into the anteroom, helped her out of her clothes and assisted her into a double kimono and *haori*, a sort of overcoat (it was chilly). My wife came back looking like Madame Butterfly. Then I was summoned. Mrs. Akiyama pointed to my jacket and shirt. Off they came. She pointed to my pants. Off they came. What would happen next? I paled. My wife, vastly interested, peeking around the corner, giggled. But my shorts re-

In Kyoto, the Definitive Japanese Inn

mained on. Mrs. Akiyama helped me into a cotton kimono, put a wool-lined silk kimono over the cotton one,
tied the sash (knot at the back, which is regulation for
men), put a blue silk *haori* over everything and led me
back into the living room. She sat us down and poured
tea. There were no chairs in our room; instead, there
were floor cushions and two backrests around the low
table.

We had two varieties of tea—first a bowl of the traditional bitter green brew and then a delicate jasmine-
flavored tea. With the tea came ginger cookies. While we
were sipping, Mrs. Akiyama explained a control unit on
the floor. One button took care of room lights, two others
drew window drapes to ensure privacy. Then she retired,
and we were able to explore our surroundings.

In Kyoto, the Definitive Japanese Inn

They were luxurious. The suite was, as expected, spotless—the Japanese must be the cleanest people on earth. The front door was the only one in the apartment; everything else worked with sliding panels. Off the foyer was the private bath—the toilet and the hot tub, each in a separate compartment. In the toilet were a small wash-basin and two commodes: one Western, the other Japanese and lower to the floor. The Western toilet seat had an electrical attachment to warm it and protect sensitive buttocks.

The hot tub, already filled with what appeared to be boiling water, was made of heavy, aromatic slabs of pine and had wooden covers to keep the heat in. Next to the tub was a shower attachment. In a ryokan one washes thoroughly before entering the bath—and you don't know what hot water is until you slip, gasping, into a ryokan tub.

The anteroom consisted of four walls of sliding doors, one of which opened to reveal closet and storage space. Off the anteroom was a sink with a small vase of flowers. Equipment included soap, toothbrushes, bottles containing hair conditioner, hair lotion, skin conditioner and after-shave lotion, all labeled in English. There was a disposable razor and a can of shaving cream. Adjoining the washroom was a tiny antique dressing table with a pier mirror at floor level and a cushion in front of it. In the center of the anteroom was a *tagasode*—a kimono stand—decorated with open obis.

Traditional Japanese rooms are measured even today by the number of tatami mats on the floor. Each mat measures roughly 6½ by 3½ feet. Our living room was a ten-tatami affair. Our eyes wandered over the room. A big piece of calligraphy, obviously old, over the entrance panels. A folding screen with a painted landscape in a corner. On two sides of the room, sliding panels with windows that looked into an L-shaped porch-balcony and a garden. The *tokonoma,* or traditional alcove, had a scroll and flower arrangement. Adjacent to it was a shelf with a digital clock and writing materials. At the other end of the wall, an antique chest and small television set. Everything breathed quiet, tasteful luxury. And every-thing looked expensive. The kimonos we were wearing, for instance, must have cost a small fortune.

We had ordered a Japanese dinner for seven-thirty. Promptly at seven-thirty Mrs. Akiyama arrived with a large tray. First, of course, there were the hot towels to clean hands and face. On the tray was an assortment of lacquered dishes with a raw and a smoked fish, vegeta-bles and condiments. That was only the first tray. Sev-eral more were to come.

Japanese food is prepared not only for taste. If some-thing appeals to one sense, it must appeal to all of the senses. There must be not only a variety of tastes, there must also be a harmonious variety of colors, textures, ar-rangements. Aesthetic appearance is of immense impor-tance. Even the humblest fast-food place off the Ginza takes pride in arranging a plate so that it is beautiful.

There is also a seasonal factor. It has to do partly with what is available at certain times of the year. But more: It has to do with the harmony of nature, and certain foods belonging to certain seasons. Even serving dishes and the dress of the server enter into it. All top ryokan will have separate sets of dishes and serving utensils for each season, and the server's kimono and obi are changed accordingly.

Much of this was over our heads, and we were not ex-perienced enough to respond to the nuances. But every dish was an aesthetic as well as culinary delight. Here was a bowl in which reposed a sweetened smoked sardine, its spine curved to represent a fish in the water. It was carefully placed against two slices of raw white fish set off by a delicately preserved peeled plum and two berrylike ovals (we never did discover what they were), one of which was crisp and one soft, both dipped in a chartreuse coating. Another bowl held a paper-thin slice of raw white fish, cut to catch the silver stripe down its back, underpinned by a sliver of seaweed to empha- size the stripe, all resting on molded rice. A small half lobster was garnished with sweet preserved chestnuts. Onions were thin-sliced and curled, cucumber ends cut into rosettes. A red pickled onion heart was wrapped in a red cabbage leaf. A variety of sauces lent all kinds of pi- quant tastes to the meal. Color arrangements were differ- ent for each dish.

After dinner, around nine-thirty, Mrs. Akiyama cleaned up, moved the table and set out our futons (sleeping mats). Orthodox pillows were used instead of the wooden blocks of yore. The sheets were of pure cot- ton and the blankets were top-quality Western style. We slept well; the futons were as comfortable as the beds in any home or hotel. Mrs. Akiyama woke us at eight- thirty, and at nine served the Western breakfast we had requested. On the way out we were asked what time we wanted to have dinner and what kind of food. This time we chose to try a Western dinner with beef.

Japanese inns do not encourage guests to be on the premises during the day. The whole idea of an inn is to take in and feed a weary traveler at night, feed him breakfast and speed him on his way in the morning. The Hiiragiya has a sort of common room near the front desk, but we never saw anybody use it. As a matter of fact, we saw very few people. Nor did we ever hear anything; the place operated at an absolute hush. On the way out and in, we did see Japanese and Westerners at the front desk, all speaking in murmurs. Nobody raises his voice at the Hiiragiya.

Yet it is not a small establishment. The Hiiragiya has thirty-three rooms and employs a staff of forty, including eighteen women for room service. Each woman is responsible for two rooms. From the beginning, the Hiiragiya has been family-owned; the current owner, Genichi Nishimura, is the fifth in his line.

Hiiragiya means "holly," the sacred tree that drives away evil spirits. The building's architecture is in the *sukiya-ukuri* style, stemming from homes built for the tea ceremony. The tiles in all apartments are of Kiyomizu ceramic, and all meals are served on Kiyomizu porcelain. This predominantly white-and-blue irregularly patterned ware was originally made in the seventeenth century for the Buddhist tea ceremony (which had started in Kyoto and Nara); it is the most famous and representative example of Kyoto porcelain. We were later told that some of the dishes from which we had been eating were probably priceless.

We spent the day sightseeing and returned to the Hiiragiya in the late afternoon. We took our bath, got into kimonos, ordered hot sake, watched sumo wrestling on television and waited for dinner. Promptly at seven Mrs. Akiyama appeared, bearing a tray with an American salad (lettuce, tomatoes, white asparagus), and bowls containing chopped meats and roots of some kind. A third appetizer contained a slice of fish roe mousse, a big mushroom and two slices of cold boiled potato.

The main course was a sizzling club steak, served on an equally sizzling iron plate. Accompaniments were three French fries, three green asparagus spears and two slices of carrot. We put everything away and should have known better, because after the steak came a plate of tempura with side dishes of pickled cabbage, chopped spinach and pickled white radish. A bowl of clear soup followed. Finally came fresh strawberries with an egg-white sauce. Strawberries were just coming into season in Japan. In Tokyo they were selling at about $5 a pint.

When we checked out of the Hiiragiya we were given a present—two sets of lacquered chopsticks. The entire front desk and Mrs. Akiyama came out to see us into the taxi, with Mrs. Akiyama helping us into our shoes and dusting them off with a polisher. She beamed, we beamed, everybody beamed. The canary chirped a sweet good-bye.

GOING TO THE MATS

If you want to try it for yourself, the address of the Hiiragiya Ryokan is Fuyacho-Anegakoji-agaru, Nakagyo-ku, Kyoto (telephone: 075-221-1136). Average price per person is about $150 per day, but charges vary from about $125 to over $400 a person, depending on the room.

Apart from Hiiragiya, Kyoto's most exquisite ryokan may well be the nineteen-room **Tawaraya**, a slightly newer inn—the building dates back 120 years, compared with its rival's 150—just across the street (same address as Hiiragiya; 075-211-5566). Rates are from about $130 to $250 a person; the inn does not accept single guests.

A smaller ryokan in the quiet western suburbs of Kyoto is the eight-room **Rantei** (12 Saga-Tenryuji,

In Kyoto, the Definitive Japanese Inn

Susukino-Banbacho, Ukyo-ku, Kyoto; 075-871-0019). Rates are about $125 a person.

Yachiyo Ryokan is in a lovely spot near Nanzenji Temple. The area is famous for a hot tofu dish called *yudofu*, in which tofu is dipped into soy sauce (34 Nanzenji Fukuchi-cho, Sakyo-ku, Kyoto; 075-771-4148; about $100).

For those who would like the comforts of a Western-style hotel but want to sleep on tatami mats in a Japanese-style room, both the **Miyako Hotel** (Sanjo Keage, Higashiyama-ku, Kyoto; 075-771-7111) and the **Kyoto Grand** (Shiokoji Horikawa, Shimogyo-ku, Kyoto; 075-341-2311) have a few Japanese-style accommodations. Rates for each are about $125 a night for the room itself; meals are not included.

An Epicure
in Kyoto

CRAIG CLAIBORNE

T IS INCONTESTABLY
a partisan point of view, of course, but there are some
restaurants that are living monuments. These are establishments of such legend and august import that I might
very well skip a visit to some local and highly acclaimed
museum, some historic temple or storied statue, to
sample the glories of their kitchens.

This notion occurred to me when I was about to em-
bark recently on a two-week visit to the Orient. I have
visited Asia many times and in many seasons, and I
have come to look forward most to explorations that take
place outside the hot and humid summer months. On this
voyage I was destined for Japan, and there, especially,
each season has its own flavor and ritual: the autumn
flame of the maple, the plum blossom of spring and the
winter snow blanketing the roofs of ancient temples on
the hills above Kyoto.

It is Kyoto that I think of when I think of Japan, and there is one celebrated landmark that comes to mind reflexively, before even the great temples and palaces: **Kitcho,** to my mind the greatest Japanese restaurant in the land.

It has long been my opinion that dining in Japan is a theatrical event. The kinds of eating establishments open to the public are numerous beyond estimate and include sushi bars galore, as well as a five-seat restaurant that specializes in beef dishes; a small dining room that serves only teriyaki and rice; another that specializes in noodles, and another that will serve you six or more courses made of one part of the chicken or another.

But if your purse can afford it, the Kitcho in Kyoto is to my mind the quintessential Japanese dining experience. When you arrive at the large, wood-frame building set in a landscape of woods and water, bamboo trees and rock gardens, you are ushered into your own private dining room, furnished with a low lacquered table, tatami mats and pillowed backrests. There is in each room a recessed *tokonoma,* a wall niche with fresh flower arrangements that signal the season. The various dishes are served in meticulously chosen vessels that may range from a simple black-and-red lacquered bowl to a painted bamboo stalk to individual scallop shells placed over individual braziers for cooking or reheating small pieces of food, a practice that is most inviting to the senses.

I would like to admit in some haste that a reservation at the Kitcho, as in many of the most luxurious establishments in Japan, requires patience and much advance planning. The restaurant has a steady and loyal clientele to whom it caters primarily, so it is impossible to decide willy-nilly to dine there. Also, since the staff does not speak English, the management suggests that you bring

An Epicure in Kyoto

along an interpreter to aid you, although one is not strictly necessary.

In the company of Jacques Pepin and a British food critic, I took the bullet train (an hour's ride) from Tokyo to Kyoto. When the three of us were seated at the table, a waitress in full regalia—kimono, obi and all—arrived with what would be the first of a ten- or twelve-course meal, a clear soup with delicately pickled rose petals. There followed a dramatic display of seafood—conch and clams—in their shells; vegetables in a sesame paste; a bit of curried jellyfish; chopped clams in a mustard-horseradish sauce. After this we were served another hot clear broth, this one with a snow-white fish fillet sculptured to resemble a scallop shell. The courses that followed, one at a time, included a bit of shrimp to be cooked on fiery-hot rocks placed before each guest and assorted skewered foods, including sea urchin roe.

At this point individual braziers, filled with burning charcoal, were brought out and placed before each guest. A glistening scallop shell was placed on each brazier; each shell contained medallions of scallops to be cooked with a bit of orange juice. When the shells were removed they were replaced by tiny grills for heating the partially cooked, minnow-shaped fish that were dipped, when hot, into a green vinegar sauce.

The waitress then brought a magnificent platter of curved bamboo, covered with an arrangement of bundles of sushi, small bundles of rice topped with rosy raw tuna, white thinly sliced sea bream and red caviar—sumptuous to the eye and irresistible to the palate.

Two more soups were served, each with a different flavor and texture. The penultimate course was the juiciest, sweetest melon that has ever passed my lips. It was followed by a sweet bean curd dessert and foamy green tea. For those who desired them, there were copious servings of hot sake or Japanese beer.

Kitcho's menu changes with the calendar, since Japanese aesthetics demand foods served in their proper season. Even the serving utensils and the serving dishes and the kimono and obi of the waitress are appropriate to the time of year. But whenever the repast is taken, it is one of the culinary experiences of a lifetime.

———

A meal at Kitcho takes planning. Budget about $150 to $200 a person; American Express cards are accepted. The front desk of any major hotel can help you make a reservation. A guide/interpreter, should you wish one, can be hired from the Japan Guide Association (in Tokyo, telephone: 213-2706) for about $100 a day.

Afterword:
The Way It Was,
and Is

M. F. K. FISHER

WHY IS IT THAT
people refuse, or are unwilling, to go back to a place
where once they have been happy? If you ask them, they
will say that they do not want to spoil a beautiful memory, or that nothing can ever be the same (a wonderful
thing can only happen once!).

Perhaps they believe they are being kind and compli-
mentary, thus to imply a perfection that must remain
unflawed. Actually I think they may feel afraid that they
will be disillusioned, if indeed they have had to convince
themselves that a privately dull or ugly event was indeed
a glamorous one. Or they may suspect that they are less
attractive than they wanted to be, or that the other people
are.

This has puzzled me since I was twenty-one years old
and first married.

My husband and I went from Dijon in Burgundy,

where we were students, down to the fishing village of
Cassis, for Christmas. I lived in a mist of clumsy passion and ignorant naïve wonderment, and although I
cannot remember a single word we spoke, almost everything else rings like crystal in my memory: midnight
mass, with fishermen playing wild, sad songs on oddly
shaped hautbois and windy flutes, over the bleating of
two sheep by the altar glittering with candles; a new human baby wailing in its modern cradle trimmed with
blue satin bows and filled with Christmas straw; all the
short square women dressed in black, with shawls over
their heads. We felt shy and bedazzled later, in the
bright hall of the Hotel Liautaud, when the villagers
gave us thick glasses of a sweet brownish *vin cuit* and
everyone talked a very fast dialect as if we understood it
well, and finally kissed us and cheered as we went up to
bed. And ten thousand other happenings: They are yesterday and tomorrow for me.

Of course, I never thought of anything but a long full
life with my love, but a heavy foreboding hit me about
two years into this planned bliss, when he said firmly
that we must never go back to the fishing village where
we had spent our first Christmas. And a cruel mixture of
disbelief and sadness filled me as I came to understand
how thoroughly and firmly he stood by his conviction,
that if people know real happiness anywhere, they must
never expect to find it there again.

I did not like to argue, then or ever, but I did want to
find out why, and his basic answer was that it was fool-
ish to try to recapture happiness. When I told him that I
honestly did not have the faintest wish to be the ninny of
two Christmases ago (to ''recapture'' anything), he was
deeply hurt, feeling that I had considered him a fitting
partner in our ingenuous love, a fellow fool. Plainly I

The Way It Was, and Is

was out of my depth: I fumbled along about how beautiful the wild hills were, back of Cassis, and how good the
wine was, and how much I had learned since then. It
would be wonderful to see it with older eyes, I said. Impossible, he said in a pitying way, as if I could never understand the pain of being a truly sensitive poet driven
forever from his former paradises by crass realism.

So that year I think we went to Nuremberg, and the
next year Strasbourg and and and, but we never returned
to any place we had been before, because once, according
to his private calendar, we had been there. And in a few
more years we parted. You might say that we ran out of
places.

I remain astonished, and very puzzled. It was obviously impossible to find out why he felt as he did, and to
understand it, because I did not, and I still don't. When
I tried to tell him that I did not want to "go back," it hurt
him that I had not recognized the bliss he had tried to
give me. And when I said that of course we were not the
same as we had been, he thought I was telling him that
he was older, which indeed we both were, and that I was
unhappy that we were, which I certainly was not. And so
on. Yes, impossible!

Fear may be a reason for refusing to admit change.
And why would anyone be afraid of that? It is as inevitable as death, or "the ever-returning roses of the dawn,"
or curdled milk. And what reasonable human being
would want to see always with the eyes of a bewildered
lovesick timid child, which I was in 1929?

Many years after I was told by my young lover that we
must never go back, my sister Norah and her three young
boys, and my two little girls and I, walked over the high
white stone hills above the little fishing port of Cassis,
and I cried out, "There it is, exactly as it was! Nothing

has changed!" And we ran down toward its quays feeling delighted and happy.

True enough, wisteria hung richly from the trellises
above the fishermen's doorways, and newly washed jer-
seys hung bright against the blue and green and white
walls. Tough bleached old boats moved up and down
gently on the flat indigo water, and down the quay there
was a sound of a pianola I remembered from some thirty
years before. My heart pounded with delight, and I
grabbed the hands of Johnnie and Anne. "It's all the
same! It's exactly as I knew it would be," I babbled, and
I gave a big happy whack to one of the old familiar
rusted bollards that still stood like sturdy mushrooms
along the quay.

And it was made of papier-mâché! It tipped over like a
matchbox and rolled off into the dirty bay, and my sister
and the other children watched while, as I was told often
and gleefully for several more decades, my jaw dropped
like a startled puppy's and I seemed to stop breathing,
stop being. And then we all began to laugh, which we
still do whenever we think of that wonderful return to the
real-fake-phony-true place.

Maurice Chevalier was remaking one of Pagnol's
movies there—*Fanny*—and the whole village was a set,
as much like Marseilles of many years before as it could
be made, and everyone was in a high giddy fever of participation, with the Mayor and the priest talking together
in the striped sunlight of the main café terrace with some
of the stars and grips, and people laughing as much as
we were, if for different reasons.

My sister knew about my lasting puzzlement at my
first love's firm refusal to go anywhere that had been
happy for him, and we talked about it as we watched our
five kids melt into the little gangs of actors' and fisher-

The Way It Was, and Is

men's children. We sat under the paper wisteria in front of a fake café at the edge of the main set and watched one of the actors get out of a very ancient limousine countless times, for the cameras. Every take looked perfect to us, and every time the old actor creaked pompously from the backseat and stepped out, we smiled at his skill and then waited for him to do it again.

And I doubt that either of us had ever felt much more contented, serene, reassured. Quite aside from being well and with our children and filled with various kinds of love, we were in Cassis, exactly as we should be at that moment in history and time. And Cassis was there as it had been for more than 2,000 years, and as it would be as long as there was a fjord-filled coastline between Marseilles and Toulon on the north shore of the Mediterranean.

I think I was the first of our family to be there, between the world wars, when my love and I went there in 1929. A young fisherman rowed us far into some of the coves to show us where the homesick German sailors from the submarines lurking there in 1917 or so had climbed up the stony sides and painted their sweethearts' names on the highest rocks: HANS & ANNA . . . ICH LIEBE HULDI, K. v. G. We ate the yolklike meat of sea urchins that he reached down for in the still dark waters. It was so still that we could hear a fish jump. We did not talk much, but the three of us liked each other, and for several more days we would call and wave and smile, along the three short quays of the village.

He might have been any of the older fishermen who stood about now for the cameras, so long later. They wore their grandfathers' baggy pants and stocking caps instead of Levi's and beat-up visored baseball gear, and the children of Cassis were blissfully arrogant as they strutted among the real movie kids and our envious five, in some designer's idea of how Marseilles street brats dressed when Panisse ran his pub. One or two little boys had tried some makeup in their adventure as potential stars, and marked freckles over the bridges of their noses, like some blond, blue-eyed urchin they had once seen in a Hollywood movie. They looked touchingly improbable; dark-eyed descendants of the Greeks and Saracens never freckle.

But they were part of our private return. They had been there forever. And so had I. And I realized that the dear man who had first gone there with me had never really been there at all.

Where had he been, then? We'd eaten and drunk and made love, listened to the wild sad rejoicings of the Christmas midnight mass together. Why did he fear to do it again?

Norah and I moved on down past the cameras and the serious village extras and the old actor getting in and out of his ancient car, and sat under the bamboo slats at the big café, talking and wondering. Lots of children came and went, and Mr. Chevalier came in alone and smiled tentatively at us, wondering why I looked almost like somebody from the Paramount lot in Hollywood a long time before—as indeed I was. The white wine was cool and like delicate flint, as it had been even further years back. (Why had my love not wanted to taste it ever again, at least there and with me?)

Norah and I decided without words to stay by ourselves, and not smile back at the charming old actor, who looked suddenly lonely and wandered away. The children came along the quay with two American kids traveling with their movie parents and several locals, still exhilarated by their professional debuts as extras. They

The Way It Was, and Is

were incredibly rich at three dollars a day, even if their pay would go directly to their parents, but temporarily they were as broke as any proper thespian and consented graciously to drink a lemonade or two with us. The whole gaggle sat at the far end of the striped shade, like a scene from a child's version of *La Dolce Vita*. Norah and I looked remotely at them, and out into the afternoon shadows along the broad quays and the darkening water, and wondered how we could be anywhere but there, then.

I still think that first fine young man was mistaken. Perhaps his stubbornness was admirable, but his refusal to change his idée fixe was plain stupid, to my older, wiser mind. Who wants always to look at a café or an altar or an oak tree with the first innocence and the limited understanding of a naïve lovesick girl, or a born-again Byron?

Five minutes or five centuries from now, we will see changeless realities with new eyes, and the sounds of sheep bleating and a new child's wail will be the same but heard through new ears. How can we pretend to be changeless, then? Why be afraid to recognize the baby in the straw, just because it is not as it once was, innocent, but is now tied about with nylon ribbon? Is it wrong to see the phony painted mushroom-bollard on the quay and accept it, as part of the whole strong song that keeps on singing there, in spite of wars and movies and the turtling-on of time?

(There are other places to go back to, even after wars both inward and outward, and new eyes keep on being opened. Nuremberg, anybody? Cassis?)

Notes on the Contributors

R. W. APPLE, JR., is chief of the London bureau of *The New York Times*.

GEOFFREY BIBBY, director of oriental antiquities at the Prehistoric Museum of Aarhus, Denmark, is the author of *Looking for Dilmun*.

RACHEL BILLINGTON's most recent novel is *Occasion of Sin*.

ANTHONY BURGESS is the author of *Enderby's Dark Lady: Or, No End to Enderby*.

FOX BUTTERFIELD, a national correspondent for *The New York Times*, has been the paper's bureau chief in Hong Kong and Peking. He is the author of *China: Alive in the Bitter Sea*.

SUZANNE M. CHARLÉ is a New York writer and editor with a long-standing interest in Asia.

CRAIG CLAIBORNE is food editor of *The New York Times*.

HEBE DORSEY, the fashion columnist for *The International Herald Tribune* in Paris, was born and raised in Tunisia.

M. F. K. FISHER's most recent book is *Sister Age*.

LUCINDA FRANKS, winner of a Pulitzer Prize for national reporting, lives in New York.

NICHOLAS GAGE is the author of *Eleni*.

BARBARA GELB's most recent book is *Varnished Brass: The Decade After Serpico*. She is the co-author, with her husband, Arthur, of *O'Neill*, a biography of the play-wright.

RUMER GODDEN, who lives in Scotland, is the author of several novels and children's books.

P. D. JAMES is the author of *Innocent Blood* and *Death of an Expert Witness*, among other novels.

BERNARD KALB was chief of *The New York Times* bureau in Jakarta in the late 1950s. He wrote the article in this book before his nomination to be Assistant Secretary of State for Public Affairs.

MICHAEL T. KAUFMAN has been a *New York Times* correspondent in Africa, India and Canada. He is now based in Warsaw.

PAUL LEWIS is a correspondent in the Paris bureau of *The New York Times*.

EILEEN YIN-FEI LO is the author of *The Dim Sum Book: Classic Recipes From the Chinese Teahouse* and *The Chinese Banquet Cookbook*.

MALACHI MARTIN's recent books include *The Final Conclave*, *There Is Still Love* and *Rich Church, Poor Church*.

DREW MIDDLETON, the retired military correspondent of *The New York Times*, reported from London in 1940 and 1941.

ALBERTO MORAVIA's most recent novel is *1934*. The translation of the article in this volume from the Italian is by William Weaver.

JAN MORRIS's works include *The Venetian Empire, Conundrum* and *The Matter of Wales*.

BENEDICT NIGHTINGALE, who reports regularly for *The New York Times* on the theater in London, is the author of *A Reader's Guide to Fifty Modern British Plays*.

SARI NUSEIBEH, who lives in the Old City of Jerusalem, is a professor of philosophy at Bir Zeit University on the West Bank.

V. S. PRITCHETT has published several collections of his short stories, in addition to biographies and criticism.

SANTHA RAMA RAU is an Indian playwright and writer.

FREDERIC RAPHAEL is the author of novels and film scripts as well as a biography of the poet Byron. *Oxbridge Blues*, a collection of his short stories, has recently been published by Arkansas University Press.

A. M. ROSENTHAL, executive editor of *The New York Times*, has served as chief of the *Times* bureau in India.

A. L. ROWSE is emeritus fellow of All Souls College, Oxford, and the author of many books on Shakespeare.

JOHN RUSSELL is chief art critic for *The New York Times;* his most recent book is *Paris*.

HAROLD C. SCHONBERG is cultural correspondent and former chief music critic of *The New York Times*.

ALAN SILLITOE, who was born in Nottingham, is the author of many works of fiction, including *Saturday Night and Sunday Morning* and *The Loneliness of the Long Distance Runner*. His most recent book is *The Last Flying Boat*.

TERENCE SMITH, formerly an editor in the Washington

bureau of *The New York Times*, has served as the *Times* bureau chief in Jerusalem.

MURIEL SPARK, the British novelist and poet who has lived in Italy for seventeen years, is the author of *The Prime of Miss Jean Brodie*, *Territorial Rights* and, most recently, *The Only Problem*.

FRANCIS STEEGMULLER is the author of many books, including several on Flaubert, among them *Flaubert and Madame Bovary*, *Flaubert in Egypt* and two volumes of Flaubert's letters in English translation.

WILLIAM K. STEVENS, a national correspondent of *The New York Times*, was formerly chief of its New Delhi bureau.

JOHN TOLAND has written extensively on Japan, most recently in *Gods of War*, a novel of two families—one American and one Japanese—bound in friendship but made enemies in 1941 by a war they neither wanted nor made.

ROBERT TRUMBULL covered the islands of the Pacific for many years as a correspondent of *The New York Times*. He now lives in Honolulu.

JOHN VINOCUR is the Paris bureau chief of *The New York Times*.

WILLIAM WEAVER is the author of several books on Italian opera and the recent biography *Duse*. He lives in Tuscany.

PATRICIA WELLS, restaurant critic of *The International Herald Tribune*, is the author of *The Food Lover's Guide to Paris*.

PAUL WEST's most recent book is *Out of My Depths: A*

Swimmer in the Universe; he is now working on his tenth novel.

THEODORE H. WHITE first went to China in 1938. He is the author of *Thunder Out of China,* written with Annalee Jacoby, and *In Search of History.*

ELIE WIESEL, Andrew Mellon Professor of Humanities at Boston University, is the author of more than twenty books, including *A Beggar in Jerusalem.* This piece was translated from the French by Iver Peterson.

EMLYN WILLIAMS, actor, autobiographer and play-wright, is the author of *Night Must Fall* and *The Corn Is Green.*

Index

About the Editors

A. M. ROSENTHAL is the executive editor of *The New York Times* and has been in charge of its news operations for the past fifteen years. He is the recipient of a Pulitzer Prize for his work as a foreign correspondent for *The New York Times*. Mr. Rosenthal is the author of *38 Witnesses* and co-author with Arthur Gelb of *One More Victim*.

ARTHUR GELB is deputy managing editor of *The New York Times* and supervisory editor of the new *Sophisticated Traveler* magazine. He was formerly chief cultural correspondent of *The Times*. He is co-author with his wife, Barbara, of the Eugene O'Neill biography, *O'Neill*.

MICHAEL J. LEAHY is the editor of *The New York Times* Travel section. He has been a *Times* editor since attending Columbia University's Graduate School of Journalism, where he won a Pulitzer Traveling Fellowship that took him around the world. NORA KERR, deputy editor of the Travel section, was formerly an assistant metropolitan editor of *The Times*.